Imagination, Emblems and Expressions

Imagination, Emblems and Expressions:

Essays on Latin American, Caribbean, and Continental Culture and Identity

Edited by

Helen Ryan-Ranson

Bowling Green State University Popular Press
Bowling Green, OH 43403

Acknowledgments

With deep appreciation, I wish to acknowledge and thank the following people of The University of Akron who have the publication of *Emblems and Expressions of Identity: Essays on Latin American, Caribbean, and Continental Culture* possible: first to Stanley W. Akers, Director of Audio Visual Services, and Roger Durbin, Associate Dean of University Libraries and Associate Professor of Bibliography, for spending numerous hours referring the many manuscripts submitted for consideration, and to Claibourne E. Griffin, Dean of The Buchtel College of Arts and Sciences, and Hugo Lijerón, Professor of Modern Languages, for their generous support of this and many other academic projects that I have undertaken. Thanks also to Ariana Ranson for carefully proofreading and correcting the final copy. I especially wish to acknowledge Pate Browne, Coordinator, The Popular Culture Association, and Editor, Bowling Green State University Popular Press, for her patience and support of my work from the inception of this project in March 1988 to its completion in December 1992.

Most of all I would like to express my gratitude and appreciation to my wonderful husband Nicholas Ranson, who has spent countless hours proofreading, formatting, and printing the camera-ready copy of this manuscript. His cheerful good humor, patience, love, and kind words of encouragement have not only reassured me, but also have enabled me to persevere and to complete this book.

Library of Congress Catalogue Card No.: 93-70305

ISBN: 0-87972-580-x clothbound
0-87972-581-8 paperback

Cover design by Laura Darnell-Dumm
Drawing by Gary Dumm

To my parents Helen Maxwell Ryan and the late Charles B. Ryan, Jr., who encouraged me to have confidence in my own abilities and to strive for excellence.

Contents

HELEN RYAN-RANSON

INTRODUCTION

> . . . What's past is prologue, what to come
> In yours and my discharge.
> *(The Tempest,* II, i, 253-54)

When I became Area Chair of Continental, Caribbean, and Latin American Culture and Literature for The Popular Culture Association in 1986, I began to gather a group of serious, responsible, and energetic scholars, who faithfully have presented worthwhile papers every year at the annual joint meeting of The Popular Culture Association and The American Culture Association. By 1988, a number of dedicated participants in our sessions approached me at the Popular Culture Association conference in New Orleans and indicated their desire to publish a volume of scholarly essays that would not merely be a collection of papers presented at the meetings, but a unique book focusing on the theme of culture and identity in Latin America, the Caribbean, and on the Continent. They were interested in writing about the theme of identity, because the search for rootedness or the quest for identity has become of paramount importance to those of us in the Western Hemisphere.

After the devastation of the two world wars, the breakup of the old colonial empires, and the reconfiguration of the political structure of Europe, some Europeans increasingly became engrossed in the search for self and in clarifying their own personal value system, while others such as the Basques and Catalans in Spain struggled to keep their regional identities and languages alive. In Latin America and the Caribbean, where the inhabitants are an amalgamation of Asian, European, Amerindian, and African ancestry and culture, many have struggled to define and to recognize a set of markers that distinguishes them from others. At this moment, the question of identity is crucial in Latin America and the Caribbean because of the continuing cultural hegemony of the former and present colonial powers and the increasing rapprochement between North America and its

Southern neighbors. The peoples of Latin America and the Caribbean need to have a clear sense of their uniqueness so that they will not slavishly imitate European models nor succumb to the preeminence of the United States, dubbed the "Colossus of the North" by José Martí.

I presented my idea for the theme of the book to Pat Browne, Coordinator of the Popular Culture Association and Editor of Bowling Green State University Popular Press. She enthusiastically supported it and agreed to publish our collection of essays, if it met the standards set by Bowling Green State University. In June 1988, I issued a nationwide call for papers to the members of The Popular Culture Association, The Modern Language Association, and The American Associations of Teachers of French, German, and Spanish and Portuguese, respectively. The theme of culture and identity was defined in a very broad sense. Culture included its expression in literature, cinema, art, or mass media; identity encompassed self, regional, or national identity. Any approach to the topic (semiotic, thematic, feminist, historicist, cultural materialist, etc.) also was acceptable. By the deadline for submission on March 1, 1989, I had received more than seventy essays for consideration; by January 1990, the referees had selected twenty-four for inclusion in this volume. Over the past three years, I have worked with the author of each essay making suggestions for revisions and additions in order to prepare a coherent and unified manuscript.

Imagination, Emblems and Expressions: Essays on Latin American, Caribbean, and Continental Culture and Identity is divided into three sections. Latin American Culture and Identity contains five essays; Caribbean Culture and Identity, ten essays, including two on the works of Derek Walcott, who was the 1992 Nobel laureate for literature; and Continental Culture and Identity, nine essays.

In the lead essay of the section devoted to Latin American culture and identity, "Popular Culture: The Roots of Literary Tradition," David William Foster analyzes the symbiosis between popular culture and high art. After defining the term popular culture and discussing the problems associated with its definition, Foster presents an historical overview of such elements of Latin American popular culture as the tango, comic strips, and the *fotonovela* and examines the techniques used by the well-known writers Luis Rafael Sánchez, Elena Poniatowska, and Daniel Kon to incorporate popular cultural material into the contemporary

Latin American narrative. Next, in his study, Frederic Murray examines the influence of utopian ideas in the origin and formation of Spanish-American culture. He cites many historical examples of Spanish-American endeavors to establish a good and just society. He maintains that to this day the utopian model drives the attitudes and belief system of Spanish Americans and that, on the concrete level, the utopian intent is seen in specific acts, laws, and institutions.

Raymond J. Lewis assesses the changing perceptions of British and North American travelers of Argentine and Mexican identity during the nineteenth and early twentieth centuries. Lewis compares and contrasts the commentaries of five travelers who went to Mexico between 1800-1850 with those of four travelers who went to Argentina between 1860-1910. He notes the tendency of these foreign commentators to stereotype their impressions of, and reactions (whether positive or negative) to the Mexican and Argentine people, customs, and culture.

Reynaldo Ruiz examines the Mexican and Chicano *corrido* (popular ballad) as a medium through which many needs, deeds, incidents, desires, aspirations, and concerns are communicated to the people. Ruiz makes it clear that the *corrido* is a primary source for developing cultural identity at the personal, local, and national level and concludes that the individuals who hear these ballads reaffirm their ties to their Chicano and/or Mexican communal heritage. In the last essay in this section, David Jordan analyzes José Lins do Rêgo's novel *Foggo Morto* as part of a regionalist movement to promote genuine Brazilian culture. The novel portrays the conflict in values and attitudes between the traditional independent small plantation owners of Northeastern Brazil and the outsiders who come to the region to take control of the land in order to modernize the ancient agrarian patriarchy by turning the small farms into conglomerates. Lins do Rêgo incorporated regional language, customs, and themes into the novel in his quest to preserve what he perceived to be authentic Brazilian values and traditions.

In the second part of the book, devoted to Caribbean culture and identity, three essays focus on the writings of Cubans and Cuban exiles, one on the Guadeloupean novelist Daniel Maximin, and six on the West Indian writers Roger Mais, Alfred Mendes, Edgar Mittelholzer, Jean Rhys, Jean Breeze, Derek Walcott, and Earl Lovelace.

In his essay on *Reasons of State*, a novel written by the Cuban Alejo Carpentier, Matthew Stewart investigates the reasons that the protagonist, who is constantly referred to as the Prime Minister or Head of State, rejects his own identity. Carpentier's central character, an enlightened Latin American despot, incorporates a false identity, due to feelings of inadequacy and insecurity. At first the Head of State decides to take on a French persona, because, for him, Paris is emblematic of the height of European culture, elegance, and civility. After being rejected by French society, the Head of State briefly flirts with taking on a German identity. Ironically, at the end of the novel, after the Prime Minister has been forced into exile, he is reintegrated with the authentic aspects of his culture when he no longer can return to his native land.

Rafael Ocasio's essay focuses on the attempts in Castro's Cuba to develop the so-called socialist man as the prototype of Cuban identity. Ocasio traces the ideological development of Cuban children's literature and explains the writers' efforts to reinforce a socialist identity among impressionable children and young people. He also presents an historical and bibliographical survey of an often ignored form of revolutionary writing by listing key authors of Cuban children's literature and their contributions to this genre.

In his study, Jorge Febles draws our attention to the cultural hybridity of the language of *Raining Backwards,* a novel by the Cuban-American Roberto G. Fernández. The novel is written in a combination of English and Spanish that elucidates an interbreeding directly related to the bicultural and bilingual society of many Cubans who are living in the United States. Ambiguous cultural signifiers show both integration and rejection, conformity and non-conformity; they emblematize a past rapidly mixing with a present that augurs an undefined future.

Lauren Yoder studies the quest to know oneself and one's culture in two novels by the contemporary Guadeloupean author Daniel Maximin. In his novels, Maximin stresses the interdependence between history and literature, since history provides a source of inspiration, and literature gives new life to events of the past. Both novels depart from a specific and real historical event and make numerous references to literature and to other forms of art such as painting and music. Maximin's characters, like Maximin himself, are preoccupied with the interplay of literature and history, and with the goal of using that interplay to help them understand themselves, their community, their culture, and their place in the twentieth century.

The first essay dealing with Western Indian literature, by Margaret K. Bass, underscores the fact that race, class, and gender have traditionally been the only markers of identity in the West Indies. Bass studies four novels *Pitch Lake, Corentyne Thunder, The Hills Were Joyful Together, and Wide Sargasso Sea.* The characters in these works never define themselves as Jamaican or Trinidadian because their identity is based on external features, not on internal qualities. The inability of the characters to define themselves creates feelings of rootlessness and fragmentation; they are caught in a net of non-being. Next, in her study, Elizabeth Wheeler discusses female and national identity in "Riddym Ravings," a poem by sister Jean Breeze. In this poem, Breeze uses rhythmic Creole English to represent her opposition to the British-style English of Jamaica's white and light-skinned rulers, and embraces a vision of Caribbean brothers and sisters united against foreign imperialism. Breeze employs a rich variety of women's voices to overturn the macho and male conventions of Jamaican dub poetry, thereby giving a feminine rendering of traditional themes.

Tejumola Olaniyan and Ashton Nichols analyze two works written by the recent Nobel laureate Derek Walcott — *Dream on Monkey Mountain* and *Another Life.* Olaniyan considers *Dream on Monkey Mountain* a poignant dramatization of the construction of identity and formation of subjectivity by those who are subjected to imperial dominance. The central character, Makak (monkey) begins as the exemplary victim of the colonial hegemonic discourse and gradually negotiates his way towards self-definition. The play is more than the story of Makak, or Walcott; it is the epic of the construction of cultural identity for the Caribbean. Ashton Nichols compares and contrasts Walcott's *Another Life* and Wordworth's *The Prelude* suggesting how much Walcott owes to the Wordsworthian tradition of verse autobiography and showing how our understanding of Wordworth's poem deepens when seen in the light of its Caribbean counterpart. Both poets struggle to forge their own identity. Walcott is torn between the conflicting worlds of his ancestral and hereditary past — the white world of the colonizing British and the black world of St. Lucian slaves. As an adult, he recreates his past to incorporate his dual racial and cultural sides and to form an identity. Walcott's conflict is similar to Wordsworth's; Wordsworth was torn between the conflicting worlds of the rural and bucolic Lake District in which he spent his childhood and the urban and cosmopolitan Cambridge and London of his adult years. Wordsworth, like Walcott, reflected upon his past to comprehend his roots and to understand who he was.

In their respective essays, Renu Juneja and Chezia Thompson-Cager study Earl Lovelace's works *The Wine of Astonishment, The Dragon Can't Dance.* and *The Schoolmaster.* Juneja explains that *The Wine of Astonishment,* Lovelace's fictional account of the Spiritual Baptists of Bonasse, closely follows the historical circumstances of the Spiritual Baptists, or Shouters, as they are called in Trinidad, during the period of ban against their religious practices from 1917 to 1951 (The Shouter's Prohibition). The novel systematically presents the Spiritual Baptists as a counterculture within colonial Trinidad; the syncretist religious practices of these descendants of ex-slaves are legitimate tools both of resistance, and, of a collective reconstruction and expression of their identity that was dislodged by colonialism. They not only repudiate the hegemony of the existing colonial order, but also use their rituals, dance, and music as a vehicle for self-representation and self-realization. In her study, Chezia-Thompson Cager describes three recurring types in Lovelace's novels — The Bad John, The Street Prince, and The Masters of Schools. After describing and characterizing each of these types as either figures of resistance or non-resistance to the mainstream culture and/or politics, Thompson-Cager analyses their role in the Trinidadian black community's hierarchy of power. She concludes that by understanding these common Trinidadian personalities, one can have a clearer sense of how they can be managed in more effective ways to strengthen the black community's potential for united action and resistance against forces that oppress its growth and enlightenment.

The third part of the book is devoted to Continental culture and identity; it contains one essay on the Czech writer Milan Kundera, three on German culture and identity, and five on Spanish culture and identity. In her study, Vicki Adams explores Milan Kundera's search for self in a post-modern world and describes Kundera's resistance to aligning himself either with Eastern orthodoxy or Western nihilism. Adams concentrates on two works, *The Book of Laughter and Forgetting* and *The Unbearable Likeness of Being,* and shows the importance of Kundera's folk heritage in his formation of a world view and in his search for identity. Adams infers that Kundera's folk heritage offers not a collision with the post-modern forces of hopelessness, absurdity, and lack of connection, but an accommodation to them.

In the first essay about Germany, Renate Gerulaitis discusses Christine

Brückner's Quin(d)t trilogy whose plot follows the fortunes and misfortunes of a Pomeranian noble family. The von Quindts will do anything to preserve their estate; their values and world view are patriarchal, hierarchical, anti-materialist, anti-modern, anti-technological, and anti-urban. Gerulaitis explains the popularity of Brückner's novels by proposing that they reaffirm the values and convictions held dear by millions of Germans, but frowned upon by the guardians of high culture.

Max Noordhoorn analyses Wilhelm Busch's *Max und Moritz* in which Busch criticizes German society by discovering the sympathetic and alluring in what middle class society deems malicious behavior. Max and Moritz execute their pranks, striking out at the great weaknesses of adults: their property, comfort, and self-satisfaction. Noordhoorn makes clear that the apparent innocence and straightforwardness of Busch's cautionary tale reveal an irony of expression and intent that indicates an attitude critical of the petit bourgeois values it professes to uphold. Thus, this tale of seeming innocence — where crime is punished and good triumphs over evil — may be read simultaneously as a tale of disillusionment, of mundane experience. The sanctity of property, the respect for adults, and above all the observance of social custom, law and order that the work seems to affirm are called into question when this society has to resort to extreme means of suppression to cope with its mischief makers. In the third essay, Ursula Beitter criticizes the bowdlerizing of the traditional Grimm fairy tales by the rewriting of them in accordance with the tenets of currently fashionable ideas, and by making them into situation comedies. The work of the Grimm brothers, in particular their collecting and rewriting material from the oral tradition, has had a decisive influence on the German language and culture; their tales also serve to transmit something of Germany's cultural identity to other peoples. Beitter concludes that the made-for-television video tales produced by Shelley duVal and others not only deprive the tales of whatever intrinsic value they had, but also destroy the value they had as a transmitter of German culture and identity.

Antonio Olliz-Boyd and Gabriel Asoanab Abudu use a semiotic approach to establish an Afro Iberian identity in the early literature of Spain. They discuss positive and negative images of blacks in the poems "The Black Swimmer," "The Raven and the Lily," *El Cavallero Cifrar*, and the *Poema de Fernán González*, and in the picaresque work *Lazarillo de Tormes*. They prove that there is a verifiable Afro Iberian identity in Spanish literature from the time of the Arab and Moorish invasions that began in the eighth century up to the point of recognizable racial and cultural assimilation in the sixteenth and seventeenth centuries.

Patricia Hart and Jaume Martí-Olivella's essays concentrate on the efforts of Catalan writers to preserve the Catalan language and culture from destruction. Pat Hart explains the collaborative efforts of the Ofèlia Dracs group (a pseudonym for ten Catalan writers who have published four collective works to date) in *Negra i consentida*, a detective novel. The writers from Barcelona depict the society of Barcelona from top to bottom, collect colorful Catalan sayings, comment on local foibles, and even provide linguistic insight. The Mallorcan members of the group show the uniqueness of Mallorcan culture. Hart believes that the primary function of the tales in *Negra i consentida* is that they encourage reading by the Catalan consumer and that they preserve and define Catalan culture and identity. Jaume Martí-Olivella uses Bachelardian myth as a framework for his analysis of Mercè Rodoreda's *La plaça del Diamant*. Because of her political views, Rodoreda was forced into exile at the end of the Spanish Civil War. In *La plaça del Diamant*, Rodoreda endeavors to recapture her Catalan identity. Martí-Olivella examines the ways in which Rodoreda's tremendous identity loss was transformed into a subtle literary myth: the myth of language as preserver. *La plaça del Diamant* is a mythical story of the death and rebirth of the protagonist Natàlia. Natàlia's journey of self-discovery, death, and rebirth becomes emblematic of that of the author herself and of the whole Catalan nation.

Nancy López-Aranguren discusses Pío Baroja's *Vidas sombrías*, a collection of thirty-five stories. In *Vidas sombrías*, Baroja's description of local customs, institutions, and types particularly the *golfo* (scoundrel) and the *vago* (bum) serves as a background for him to express his own utopian ideals. Baroja's *golfo* devotes his whole existence to catering to the demands of selfish desire; his characteristics have no redeeming social value. On the other hand, his *vago* belongs to a higher class of people who are capable of withdrawing from society's rat race and ignoring the demands of their vital desires. In his ideas about happiness and the ethical life, Baroja was deeply influenced by Schopenhauer and his *vago* is an emblem of the Schopenhauerian virtues of intelligence, ironic detachment, lack of ambition, and indifference to worldly things. Baroja melds conventional Spanish types and cross currents of modern mysticism, pessimism, and humanitarian anarchism that were surging through Europe at the turn of the century.

Eduardo López-Aranguren attempts to identify and analyze the image that Americans have of Basque people, of Basque culture, of Basque political, cultural, economic, and social institutions, and of Basque contemporary problems. López-Aranguren studies the images of Basques presented by the American press in newspaper and magazine articles from 1953 to 1989. The general impression of the Basques among Americans has changed from the 1950s to the 1980s. In the fifties, the Basques were thought to be a rural, unsophisticated, and rather primitive people. In the eighties, they were considered as a modern, urban, and industrial people who, nevertheless, had some idiosyncrasies such as their non-functional (impossible to learn) language. They are also seen as a politically violent people who support acts of terrorism, daredevils who risk running in front of the bulls, and expert *jai-alai* players.

To my contributors, I would like to express my appreciation for the many hours that you spent in preparing essays for this volume and for presenting a multiplicity of points of view. I hope that our readers will enjoy this collection, and, after reading these essays, that they have a deeper understanding and greater appreciation for the coherence, primacy and importance of the search for identity in such vastly divergent areas as Latin America, the Caribbean, and the Continent.

I

Latin American Culture and Identity

DAVID WILLIAM FOSTER

Popular Culture: The Roots of Literary Tradition

I

Were the Western cultural tradition not so fragmented in its conception of the hierarchical relations between the vast and diverse phenomena that arise from a reasonable definition of culture, this essay would not be necessary. To be sure, there are interesting historical factors that have contributed to such a fragmentary hierarchy and the complex play of exclusions and inclusions, but this is not the place to rehearse them. The very fact that our approach to culture is dominated by categories based on high, academic, institutionalized phenomena poses from the very outset the question of how to deal with all of those other cultural manifestations that do not comfortably assimilate to the accepted canon. It is true that one of the lasting projections of the countercultural movement of the 1960s (in reality, an echo of similar rethinkings of the canon throughout the history of modern culture) was the imperative, often uneasily fulfilled, to expand the scope of our humanities programs to include many topics previously considered outside the margins of their purview. So-called "popular culture" is one such phenomenon. The majority of research in the field continues to be conducted in departments or schools of communications or interdisciplinary programs like American Studies, Twentieth Century Studies, History of Consciousness, and the like. Nevertheless, some topics like film have achieved a status of recognition in English and the various foreign language departments and their forums, like scholarly journals and professional meetings. But this is because one may speak of an "art film," as opposed to commercial cinematography, and the former seems to lend itself without too much embarrassment to the forms of critical discourse prevalent among humanists, while soap operas and sitcoms do not. The dichotomy survives when one realizes that there are mass comics that are unattractive to critical analysis and there are art comics that are: that there is a large area of fiction that is widely read but rarely investigated; and that there is a fiction that often seems to be read only by graduate students and their professors.

It does not take an iconoclastic spirit thundering against the pretentiousness of academic criticism and militating for graduate seminars on Beetle Bailey and the Harlequin Romances to accept the fact that these continuities are profound and that, except for the most reactionary humanist, they present some serious problems in charting the boundaries of academic scholarship. Moreover, the fact that the most salient feature of what is called "postmodernist culture" is the mixing or blending of categories, the decentering and "anarchicalization" of cardinal points of reference, and simply the flouting of all definitions that attempt repressively to hold the line on the game of exclusions and inclusions. We may see, therefore, that keeping popular culture out of academia may be difficult, but fitting it in is going to be a hellish task. Finally, to all of this must be added the eloquent fact that Latin American writers, faced with the greater cultural repressiveness of their official institutions and irked by the institutionalized need to adhere to first continental and now American definitions of the arts and the humanities, have been quite aggressive in engaging in postmodernist conduct, which is one of the bases of the newfound interest in Latin American writing in the West.

The problems associated with the definition of the term "popular culture" are both a consequence of how such a category is used as a dumping ground for everything academic criticism has rejected or been slow to recognize as a legitimate object of analysis and a reflection of the definitional limitations imposed by the parameters of elite culture only able to accomodate what official cultural arbiters consider beneficial

In both English and Spanish, there is no agreement as to what "popular" really means. Certainly, it means what is most preferred, which is the poor-taste definition that underlies the scholarly repudiation of most mass media phenomena. In the U.S., a cultural authoritarianism might reject such culture as failing to meet standards of merit or substance. In Latin America, the rejection is associated with a nationalistic, pan-Latin American, or international left that repudiates the multinational capitalism that imposes a homogenizing mass culture. It is for this reason that so much research on mass media culture in Latin America, whether imitations of dominant Western modes (e.g., soap operas) or essentially autochthonous products (e.g., *fotonovelas*) that have appropriated multinational techniques of distribution, is colored to varying degrees by Marxist perspectives.

At the other end of the spectrum, "popular" is also taken in its root sense of having to do with the populus, the *pueblo*. It is unclear how *pueblo* can be kept different from the growing masses of urban citizens whose daily people's culture is what they buy at the newsstands and see on television — that is, mostly what the tycoons of the multinational and capitalistic culture industry have educated them to prefer. However, the idea of a popular culture in the root sense of a culture by and for the *pueblo* is foremostly associated with folk traditions that, in a Romantic conception of culture, embody the specific identity of people viewed in localistic and regionalistic terms as the incarnation of the national genius or spirit. Such a popular or folk culture, whether purely indigenous or a postconquest mestizo amalgam, has continued to survive in Latin America, steadily eroded by the tumultuous demographic shift to urban megalopolises and by the incursion of the transistor radio into previously remote areas. And, too, Latin American folk culture has been relentlessly commercialized, both at home and abroad (e.g., the Argentine tango or Mexico's *Ballet Folklórico* derivations).

The Creolist tradition of Latin American writing sought renovation in the assimilation of folk motifs, but it is questionable whether that led to anything more than the expropriative vulgarization of the folkloric by a writing intended to please and reassure the elite. Furthermore, so much of what is called today the preservation of folk culture by those who honestly oppose the dominance of a Western aesthetic means essentially its accommodation to the mass media structures the counterculture sees itself appropriating.

If this in itself were not enough of a contradiction, addressing folkloric motifs to a dispossessed populace manipulated by the dynamic of modern Latin America's megacity, which some have argued is truly more monstrous than its Western models, is not without some dimension of the ludicrous. Since it is unlikely that cities like Mexico City, São Paulo, Buenos Aires, or Lima will shrink with the return of the populace to the countryside, the equation of non-elite culture with these folk traditions may not be especially productive. This is not to say that folk traditions do not survive in the big city: Brazil's rural *literatura de cordel,* ballads on timely topics sung in the marketplace and offered for sale arranged on a line of string appears to have made the transition to the city. But much of what one finds of folk culture in Latin American cities today is a commercial adaptation, a mass media translation, rather than preserved traditions: the political expropriation of the *guayabera* in Mexico might serve as an illustration of this point.

But certainly a revolutionary culture in Latin America is not interested primarily in keeping alive a rural folk culture that may not survive the trip to the megalopolis. Such folk culture may need to be preserved as a point of reference for individuals' discovery of their roots and as part of a political-cultural program of national identity: the *canción ranchera* may serve more the latter function than be a surviving folk tradition in today's Mexico. But the emphasis falls understandably on the need to create a popular culture that responds to the actual social, political, historical, and economic realities of life in Latin America. Thus, the term "popular culture" refers less to specific formats and strategies of distribution (as it does in the first sense of the term above) or to particular cultural forms and their sources (as in the second sense) than it does to a project for the elaboration of cultural phenomena that will serve a specific programmatic goal from either a purpose that is institutional (as in the case of the few socialized cultures of Latin America) or para-institutional (as in the case of those areas where such practices are countercultural vis-à-vis dominant manifestations). It is in this sense that a constellation of popular cultural writings in Latin America today is continuous with what Western academics call a postmodernist aesthetic and what the practitioners of the former may insist is, finally, the acquisition by Latin American culture of its own voice — or range of voices, from the point of view of those who are uncomfortable with a monolithic and non-disruptional view of Latin American society.

This essay uses the term popular in all three senses, to the extent that the cultural manifestations of all three belong to any comprehensive survey of the culture available to Latin Americans. However, it is precisely the first two definitions that are most taken into account by extant research, the first by sociologically-based research on the mass media and the second by a humanistic scholarship concerned with Latin American folklore and sensitive to the Creolist mandate among certain practitioners of institutionalized (if not always elite) writing. But it is the latter sense of "popular culture" where the greatest amount of creative originality may be found and where there is, with the possible exception of narrative manifestations, the least critical recognition. One might insist that, to whatever degree this writing meets standards of creativity (whatever they might be), it becomes a form of high culture and does not merit any separate categorization. Leaving aside one's suspicion that this "openness" may be territorial expansionism or cooption on the part of high culture gatekeepers, a statement dictated by the need to globalize all cultural phenomena and to eschew the temptation to stake out new islands of humanistic discipline is reasonable. The problem of definition and the question of territoriality will not be (re)solved by this; rather they will remain as an underlying tension that bespeaks a vast question that will eventually have to be tackled from the perspective of postmodernist criteria.

Nor will this essay engage in any comprehensive review of the staggering amount of material that could be identified from any one of the definitions proposed: indeed, the problem of Latin American cultural scholarship continues to be the large amount of material encompassed by even a tightly restrictive definition of high culture, an inventory that popular culture studies serve to make even larger. Rather, the goal here will be to identify a few casebook examples of Latin American cultural manifestations that may serve as major points of reference for research on the issues posed.

II

Argentina has long been one of the leaders in Latin American culture, a circumstance related to the relative size and prosperity of the country, the enormous variety of international influences (which swiftly accelerated with massive immigration in the late nineteenth century) that have passed through its port capital, Buenos Aires, and the very aggressive stance taken during the early years of independence by leaders anxious to overcome the area's legacy as a backwater of the Spanish colonial empire.

In the inventory of important Argentine cultural contributions, perhaps none enjoys more international stature than the tango. Although the tango is pretty much an archeological phenomenon in Argentina, in the sense that it is associated with a bygone era and, like virtually all national forms of popular music in Latin America, it has been replaced by multinational products of Anglo-American inspiration, it has acquired a romantic aura, like the rumba and the samba, that is part of its international identification as characteristically Latin. The fact that it is probably associated in most non-Latin American minds with an image of Latin America as the passionate tropics says more about foreign perceptions of Latin America or the ways in which Latin American cultural empresarios have appealed to foreign conceptions than it does about the sociocultural roots of the tango in the

River Plate region. Indeed, one might want to argue that the Argentine tango is one thing, and American and European (mis)interpretations of it are quite another, although foreign understandings of the tango now filter back into Argentine perceptions.

As it emerged in its definitive form during the dramatic modernization of Buenos Aires in the early part of the century, the tango is a constellation of art forms, bringing together instrumental music and song, dance, and poetry in the form of lyrics. Although the tango may be referred to by any one of these three forms singly (or four, if we separate song and instrumental interpretation), it is generally understood as a fluid combination of all of them. (There is a related art form, graphic interpretation, which has also contributed an impressive array of paintings, drawings, sketches, and the like, complemented by photographic archives on the tango and its settings.)

We may identify four periods or moments in the development of the tango, depending partially on whether song, instrumental music, dance, lyrics, or combinations of them have received most attention. This complex history points to the interpenetration between the tango and Argentine social and cultural history.

The first period covers the obscure origins of the tango in the river front brothels and other "low-life" settings of Buenos Aires and Montevideo. The word itself appears to be of black African origin, related to a drum dance. There is no question that, like so many important cultural phenomena, the tango's origins are countercultural, and the problems associated with recovering all of the details of that origin are a consequence of a society's determination to ignore or destroy even oblique challenges to its conventions (and such challenges are more oblique or circumstantial than overtly disruptional). If the origin of the word tango derives from the black slaves of the River Plate shore, as a Creole cultural manifestation it is first associated with highly colloquial verses of a ribald and scatological nature that circulated among European and Middle Eastern immigrants, mestizos, mulattos, and other social outcasts on the fringes of two cities that were officially attempting to become very respectable and European. The merging of spoken verses and the dance appears to have occurred in the brothels, where risqué rhyming was a traditional pastime among waiting customers. It is reasonable to suppose that clients and employees danced together some sort of erotic step related to the complicated minuet that would become the final version of the tango.

But much has been made of the fact that the tango was foremost something men danced together in these houses. No social historian has explored whether this may be taken as one of the homosexual motifs of Argentine culture that are still shrouded with almost impenetrable taboo — the male bonding of gaucho culture and some military traditions are other potential topics of interest here. Perhaps the dance was a form of rivalry, perhaps it served to release tensions, or perhaps it served as a form of sexual arousal to be satisfied subsequently in the arms of the prostitute. Whatever one's interpretation may be, all of these factors contributed to the categoric rejection by polite society of anything associated with the tango. At this same time, brothel musicians most certainly must have contributed instrumental accompaniment for words and dance.

When the tango, because of its unique nature and its undeniably erotic primitivism, began to attract attention beyond the confines of the brothels and life in general along the river front, it emerged as principally a conjunction of dance and music. Quite understandably at this time, the turn of the century and a period of acute Victorian decorum in Buenos Aires, the original inventory of tango lyrics would be unsuitable for higher social classes of the city. While it remained taboo among the most respectable, the tango began to acquire at this time considerable acceptance. It should be noted that, although during the post World War I period there was to be a fad for tango contests and marathons, the tango was never a ballroom dance until well into the 1940s. Rather, it is something people dance in small family and social gatherings, and it is rarely a display dance in the sense of the ballet. There are, however, two reservations here: it is certainly likely that some of the original lyrics were retained with the tango as a social dance, and even new ones of a piquant nature were undoubtedly coined; and the tango did get some form of public display as an element in theatrical works dealing with popular themes — the Creole circus and the *sainete,* the Creole melodrama.

The third period of the tango is the emergence of a body of lyrics that could circulate without violating decorum. Beginning in the second decade of this century, there was an explosion of lyricists, and, increasingly, their texts reflect the profound poetic innovations going on in high literature. The tango now becomes a song, a showcase for lyrics that reveal an impressive array of themes and a notable stylistic and linguistic complexity. Concomitantly, these lyrics are accompanied by complex forms of instrumentation, centering on the *bandoneón,* a direct descendent of the concertina but with the symphonic subtlety of the violin or the piano. Groups consisting of musicians and song artists emerge, and it is their subsequent foreign tours that contribute to the internationalization of the tango. Of these artists, none is more famous than Carlos Gardel, a singer born in France but raised in one of Buenos Aires's humbler quarters. It has been argued that Gardel couldn't sing very well by art-song standards, but precisely his defects as polished interpreter seemed to contribute to his enormous success. Gardel composed much of the music of his songs, and Alfredo Le Pera wrote many of the lyrics. The combination of the two enjoyed immense success, and Gardel saw the tango finally accepted in both Argentina and abroad as a *nec plus ultra* of Argentine culture. Gardel's public performances and the nine movies he made with Paramount (when that studio had a whole program of production for Spanish-language distribution before World War II) did not accord the tango as dance any particular prominence. But the rhythms of the tango become translated on the foreign scene (usually in softer registers) as a combination of dance and music: it would have made little sense to import the lyrics in English or French translation, less so because of their colloquial texture. Gardel died in a plane crash in Medellín, Colombia in June 1935, and the subsequent war severed the romantic attachment with Latin America (Argentina remained neutral but, in effect, abetted the Axis powers). Although the tango continued to survive in the person of the many artists who arose with Gardel's popularity, it quickly lost the vitality of a dynamically original art form.

Thus began the fourth phase, that of the tango as museum piece. To be sure, there continue to be tango stars, and tango lyrics and accompaniments continue to be written. But the tango simply no longer exists as an area for sustained innovation in Argentina, and those places where one goes to see the tango in Buenos Aires satisfy the curiosity of foreign businessmen and infrequent tourists. Claudio Segovia's show "Tango argentino," such a hit during the 1985-86 season in New York, may be irreproachably authentic in its display of the art forms of the tango, but general reaction in Argentina to its success was bemusement over foreign interest in a cultural phenomenon of the past. One reservation: the composer Astor Piazzolla has incorporated the tango brilliantly in his symphonic works, but diehard tango purists in Argentina disdain what others might see as one legitimate attempt to restore dynamic creativity to the tango.

It is questionable whether one can continue to speak of the tango as countercultural while recognizing the enormous commercial success of Gardel and those who followed his lead. But certainly the tango never lost its countercultural origins, and the lyrics, although they may have been scatological only by virtue of certain modes of reading but no longer overtly so, focused insistently on girls who went wrong, prostitutes, kept women, pimps, assorted criminals, and the like. Moreover, the very language of the tango lyrics, with a colloquiality that is alternately sociolinguistically authentic and poetically innovative, defies in numerous ways the respectable language conventions of polite Argentine society. Finally, the heavy beat of the music, the machismo of the male persona of the tango, and dance steps that suggest unmistakably clitoral and anal stimulation of the woman, through greatly stylized movements, all serve to remind the alert spectator that the nuns of yore were right in warning their innocent charges of the dangers lurking in the tango.

III

Numerous contemporary writers in Latin America, primarily novelists, are concerned with question of providing an adequate image of what they consider to be the detritus of their contemporary social and cultural life, whether with a focus that is Latin American in general or specifically national. This image identifies an essentially degrading and degraded nature of cultural life for the majority of the populace, with or without specific reference to social issues, although certainly one would, from a Marxist point of view see popular forms as determined by the ruling class's need to promote a cultural hegemony to serve its historical interests.

In general terms, Latin American culture is viewed as having been fatally corrupted by the artifacts of a multinational imperialism that is said to exploit Latin American society. Such corruption is foremostly identified with the U.S., as a consequence of the aggressive penetration of the Latin American market during U.S. expansionism after World War II. However, French and British economic and cultural imperialism intensifies in the nineteenth century, and Japanese commercial incursions into Latin America are very evident. Finally, it must be noted that countries like Argentina, Mexico, and Brazil exercise an imperialistic influence over their client states in the Latin American marketplace. The concepts of dependency theory, which attempt to explain the disastrous nature of the Latin

American economies as vassals of First World financial lords, have been logically extended to cover the configurations of Latin American culture as the result of similar historical relationships: folk music has been replaced by attention to and slavish imitations of foreign rock bands, Coca Cola and Pepsi have gained ascendancy over regional drinks, foreign bestsellers (often in sloppy translations) are preferred to Latin American literature, and all of the cultural images of TV, advertising, and the movies look like Madison Avenue in Spanish or Portuguese. Even if this summary simplifies concepts of dependency — as do, indeed, popularized forms of this current in Latin American social thought — the important point is that a significant segment of Latin American writers thematize the hypotheses of cultural (and behind them, economic and political) dependency.

Nationalistic sentiment in the majority of the Latin American republics continues to be strong enough to provide some sort of resistance to this cultural expropriation, although many artists and ideologues feel that there is considerable reason to maintain a state of alarm. For example, in Argentina since the 1983 return to democracy, there has been an impressive amount of national cinematographic production as a challenge to the virtual dominance of the marketplace by foreign films permitted under the military. Yet, as of this writing, six years after the restoration of democratic culture as an official goal, the theatergoing public overwhelmingly prefers American movies. The administration of channel 7, the state-owned television station, is understandably proud of the fact virtually all of its programming is national, and it is hoping to sell programs to other Latin American countries (Argentine cultural imperialism, some could say). Yet, there is considerable pressure for the channel (along with state-owned radio stations devoted to so-called "public" programming) to be privatized, which would surely mean U.S. and U.S.-style programming. Nevertheless, the intensity of cultural debate in Argentina, no matter how "Americanized" so much of that country's culture may now appear to be, is an encouraging sign of resistance to multinational homogenization.

But there is the case of those Latin American republics that do not have as powerful a block of cultural resistance as does a country like Argentina. (One might, however, say that smaller countries are more "protected" to the degree that they do not have an internal market large enough to make cultural invasion profitable.) And, at the bottom of this hierarchy of cultural lines of defense, is a thoroughly dependent entity like Puerto Rico, neither state nor republic, neither completely colonized (Puerto Rican Spanish still maintains a proud Creole identity — more or less) nor independent in any meaningful way.

Puerto Ricans have had to struggle to maintain their cultural identity against the inevitable domination of its "protectors" of the past hundred years, but, ironically, one of the ways it has done this is by asserting cultural relations with Spain, precisely the colonial power from which U.S. occupation putatively liberated them. Without going into a facile synthesis of the profound contradictions of Puerto Rico's divided cultural allegiances, suffice it to say that it has become for many a symbol of a dependent Latin American people.

In terms of one set of cultural points of reference, Puerto Rican culture is a flotsam and jetsam of fragments of a cultural imperialism that are non-biodegradable: they refuse to go away and they are impossible to assimilate into a healthy life cycle. This constellation of degrading, dependent images are in rhetorical juxtaposition to two official postures, which just happen also to be in conflict with each other: the assertion by one strand of political power that Puerto Rico must prize its ties to the U.S. as potentially the fifty-first state (the advertising campaign of the recent Romero Barceló administration) and the insistence by another posture that Puerto Rico recover its four hundred years of Hispanic heritage (the campaign of the current Hernández Colón government). In all of this debate, it is difficult to lose sight of the simple fact that, objectively, Puerto Rico is dependent on the United States, to the extent that it is presently unable to survive economically without that tie.

As a countercultural proposal defended perhaps by a coherent ideology but perhaps appealing in vain for acceptance by those in Puerto Rico who get around to reading Puerto Rican literature, Luis Rafael Sánchez's *La guaracha del Macho Camacho* (1976) is a carnivalized interpretation of a trash-bin culture. It is significant to note that Sánchez's novel was originally published in Buenos Aires. There is a fine 1980 English translation by Gregory Rabassa, but the novel has yet to be published in Puerto Rico (it should be noted that Puerto Rican authors customarily publish abroad). Censorship may not exist officially in a society governed by American law, but there are many ways of repressing those who insist on speaking unpleasant truths. One of these ways is by appealing to a conventional morality that works to repudiate any incursions into the distasteful, and the

Puerto Rican establishment has worked very hard to maintain a patina of Victorian decorum.

By contrast, Sánchez has promoted what he calls a "poética de lo soez" (poetics of vulgarity), a set of principles that encourage the artist to examine the clash of juxtapositions between the Palmolive Soap version of refined social models (Sánchez begins by referring to a popular radio program of yesteryear sponsored by that product) and the "unwashed" masses of real people whose daily social reality has virtually nothing to do with the icons of the imported cultural products. Puerto Rico has little to do with such American images because it is Puerto Rico and not the U.S., of course, but also because of the economic and social realities that derive inevitably from Puerto Rico's relationship of dependency. Sánchez's poetics is divided, a consequence of the contradictions that beleaguer all discussions of Puerto Rican reality, between a revindication of the soez and a denunciation of the circumstances that, according to Sánchez, maintain his national culture on the margin of what is considered decent.

In the first place, for something to be considered dirty (if we may refer to anthropological relativisms like Claude Lévi-Strauss's cooked vs. crude dichotomy) is only possible within a fabricated or socially-conditioned ideology of what is considered clean vs. dirty. Since an exaggerated Anglo, WASP mentality considers anything Latin dirty by definition (both in the sense of unwashed and in the sense of morally reprehensible), Puerto Rican society is assigned a fixed relationship to its new political masters. But this binary relationship between clean U.S. culture and dirty Puerto Rican culture can be inverted, with the "natural ways" of Puerto Rican life (or mores argued as being natural) prized over the corrupting pieties and hypocrisies of an allegedly superior social model. In this way, what is rejected by the dominant cultural model is revindicated as legitimately and authentically popular, and therefore to be accorded the dignity of the ironization of the term "soez" (vile), which is precisely what Sánchez does in his essay.

But alternatively, or perhaps coextensively, what is dirty is a correlative of the perpetual margination of Puerto Rican society by the dominant culture, a margination that results inevitably in the degradation of the quality of life of a people. The obligation, both naive and disingenuous, that Puerto Rican society mold itself willy-nilly to the images of its protectors has contributed to the disruption of the social and cultural codes of Puerto Rican society.

It is this latter tack that Sánchez pursues in *La guaracha del Macho Camacho,* a novel in which nothing really happens because there is nothing of interest that can really happen in a Puerto Rican society so thoroughly trashed by the social models offered to it. It is a discordant novel in which a number of topics move in and out of narrative focus. These motifs concern a representative sample of members of Puerto Rican society from the powerful to the social outcast, from the bored and disaffected to the hip playboy. The controlling motif of the novel is "Macho Camacho's Beat," a vacuous song that is meant to capture the lusty beats of the tropical paradise but only underscores with ironic eloquence its essential meaninglessness. Significantly, the colloquialism of the lyrics and the references to local cultural phenomena only serve to reinforce the texture of the song as nonce:

> LA VIDA ES UNA COSA FENOMENAL.
>
> La vida es una cosa fenomenal
> lo mismo pal de alante que pal de atrás.
> Pero la vida también es una calle cheverona,
> arrecuérdate que desayunas café con pan.
> Ay sí, la vida es una nena bien guasona
> que se mima en un fabuloso Cadillac.
> La trompeta a romper su guasimilla,
> las maracas que no cejen pa trás,
> y los cueros que suenen a la milla,
> que la cosa no puede reposar,
> que la negra quiere sudar,
> que la negra se va a alborotar.[1]

La guaracha del Macho Camacho was considered distasteful if not downright pornographic by those Puerto Ricans who objected to its strident assault on cherished social myths, principally that of the island as "a nice place to live." The novel as a mosaic, built around the popular song played on the radio in the background, fragments a conventionally coherent image of Puerto Rican society, which is reduced to a series of hapless San Juan residents arduously making it through a typical late afternoon, confronted by the tedium and emptiness of their

---

[1]LIFE IS A PHENOMENAL THING. / Life is a phenomenal thing, / frontwards or backwards, however you swing / But life is also a groovy street, / it's coffee for breakfast and bread that you eat / Oh, yes, life is a nice chubby chick / spoiling herself in a Cadillac trick. / The trumpet breaking up the ball, / don't let the maracas back down, / the drums heard way across town, / the thing can't have any stop, / black women want sweat to mop, / black women are getting hot.

lives. The nonsensical song, synecdoche of the worst detritus of a decidedly non-alluring tropical popular culture, negates with inadvertent eloquence in the twelve lines of verbal commonplaces the upbeat assertion of its title: "Life is a Phenomenal Thing."

Written in "Puerto Rican," Sánchez's novel deftly and boldly captures the sociolinguistic texture of Puerto Rican life on various class levels. Alternating narrative focuses and significant transitions and juxtapositions contribute to a unified text that homologizes varying social and cultural commonplaces in one mordant denunciation of the delusion of tropical-beat gaiety by which, to use the term coined by the island's major modern writer, René Marqués, the "docile Puerto Rican" distracts himself.

Sánchez's novel is, therefore, an outstanding example of the use of popular cultural material in the contemporary Latin American narrative. This material points to an immediately sociological level to the degradation of a people by extraneous but powerful images that, for numerous and complex reasons, they cannot assimilate and that only serve to distract them from material poverty and to confuse and alienate them from the possibilities of a meaningful social life as a coherent culture. But as a narrative text that is meant to contribute to productive cultural discourse, a novel like *La guaracha del Macho Camacho* is a striking example of the recontextualization of those motifs in a powerful countercultural document.

IV

One of the abiding paraliterary phenomena of Latin American culture is graphic narrative, either in the form of the ubiquitous *fotonovela,* in which still photographs of actors are accompanied by balloons of text, or the more venerable comic book. A large number of comic books are little more than repetitions of repetitions in terms of style of illustration, basic plot formulas, and narrative devices, and many Latin American comics imitate U.S. ones in format and cast (i.e., the Mexican *El Payo* is an autochthonous version of the Lone Ranger, and the Chilean *El Condorito* is an indigenous Woody the Woodpecker) with Spanish-language translations of American products. Comic books and *fotonovelas* are so much a form of popular reading material that, throughout Latin America, one finds people of all ages (but not of all social classes), men and women, reading them in public transports, in waiting rooms and plazas, and seated in chairs tilted against the doorjambs of their houses. Any one issue passes through dozens of hands, and neighborhood entrepreneurs administer lending libraries and used copy exchanges. Popular print fiction also circulates widely in Latin America in cheap formats, but the true alternative to serious, creative fiction is these illustrated narratives.

This is so much so that several attempts by high-art writers to adapt the format of these two forms of popular fiction have resulted in some interesting materials, like the Argentine Julio Cortázar's *Fantomas,* a quasicomic book or the expropriation by socialist governments of the comic book and the *fotonovela* as vehicles of massive information campaigns, a technique also used by U.S. public interest and public service groups. The materials produced in Chile during the *Unidad Popular* government of Salvador Allende (1970-73) have especially attracted attention in this regard.

However, a number of creative artists throughout Latin America, particularly among leaders in the genre like Argentina, Brazil, and Mexico, have sought to blend the highly commercialized product that is typically available at "kioscos" (newsstands that are also minibookstores) with a creative impulse that defies the features of apparent naturalness and expectability that characterize routine popular culture materials. That is, if popular culture materials strive for a criterion of apparent naturalness, such that there is nothing to disturb, upset, or challenge the conventions of the reader (the exaggerated, almost ludicrous, photographic realism of *fotonovelas* is instructive here), the work of experimental artists is often openly disruptional: this is the case of the Peruvian Juan Acevedo's *¡Ola, Cuy!,* a Third-World Mickey Mouse, like the prairie dog, that engages in consciousness-raising discourse by defying the conventions of the Walt Disney formulas: for example, his animal characters sport unmistakable genitalia. In tandem with the criterion of apparent naturalness is that of expectability, whereby plot configurations follow a handful of schematic developments, and denouements are expected and predictable: just as the Lone Ranger and Superman always triumph against malefactors, El Payo and Kalimán (another Mexican comic) always win the contest with evil.

To be sure, one can raise interesting questions about just how natural these representations are or the function of expectability in plot schemata and development. All art functions within certain boundaries of these two criteria, so they cannot serve independently to distinguish between routine popular culture and high art. But where the latter is more characteristically disruptional in the many ways in which it functions to challenge readers and to ask them to reconsider ideological conventions, mass-consumption popular culture is confirmational to the degree that it confirms in readers the sanctity of conventionalized ideologies and excuses them by implication from any discomforting questioning. Thus, as critical students of mass culture have repeatedly noted, the Walt Disney comic books, even when read in translation in the Third World, confirm a constellation of American imperialist values and trivialize any challenge to them, or the Superman genre of narratives legitimize authoritarian, paternalistic, essentially fascist varieties of force and violence in the name of some sort of ethereal concept of Good.

One of the primary aspects of creative artists who use the comic book as a format of countercultural popular culture (I know of no examples in the field of the *fotonovela*) is the strategy of recontextualization. This involves the deployment of the conventions of the comic book, but in such ways as to go beyond the criteria of apparent naturalness and expectability in order to promote a degree of disruptional interpretation of the part of the reader. This recontextualization is accomplished precisely by violating the two dominant criteria of routine material and by linking the referents of graphic narrative to social issues that challenge conventionalized beliefs.

We can see how this strategy works by examining a highly popular but mildly disruptional example like the material created originally by Rius (Eduardo del Río), one of Mexico's most important graphic artists. Rius has turned his attention to a wide range of social and political issues and no longer draws the series *Los supermachos*, and it is now the product of an anonymous consortium. Nevertheless, it is one of the many vehicles he established to poke fun at the self-serving seriousness of the Mexican bureaucratic establishment and to suggest to his readers ways of viewing the dynamics of their society other than those touted by the institutionalized revolution. Rius has drawn a number of series that are very markedly disruptional, like his many manuals on political topics (e.g., "Marx para principiantes," "Cuba para principiantes"), but products like *Los supermachos* or *Los agachados* (a series Rius founded after he left Los supermachos but no longer draws either) are not as aggressive as Acevedo's ¡Ola, Cuy! or the material coming out of Argentina associated with the humor magazines Humor registrado and Superhumor.

Los supermachos involves graphic details that fluctuate between the markedly local-colorist and the markedly expressionistic or antirealistic, the latter constituting moves toward ignoring the criterion of apparent naturalness. For example, we can easily spot in the comic thoroughly local-color features like the use of a certain kind of clothing, details about professions and occupations and the social class of the characters (the pharmacist's tie and vest, the beata's black and formless garb, and so on), as well as the gestures and the typical behavior patterns of a gallery of immediately identifiable Mexicans who are, to be sure, presented as no more than convenient caricature types. All of these elements function to present — to confirm — a specifically rural Mexican setting, the Mexico of the fictitious village of San Garabato. *Los supermachos* is constructed around the element of caricature projected by the characters and by the unambiguous contexts in the process of referring to a familiar social scene. With no pretense at profundity or semantic density as human types, it is enough for them to be transparent indexes of Mexican local color, and the element of caricature gives weight to the expressionistic features, which are one of the techniques of recontextualization that makes *Los supermachos* of interest to this discussion.

Los supermachos is not particularly subtle nor is it characterized by any degree of semantic density, qualities that we like to attribute to non-commercial, innovative art. However, as a form of popular narrative that reaches millions of readers in Mexico, the Southwestern United States, and other parts of Latin America, *Los supermachos,* by going beyond the routine conventions of the bulk of comic book art, demonstrates the possibilities for that symbiosis between popular culture and high art that concerns us in this essay.

V

The bibliography has grown to be quite extensive on the so-called new journalism and non-fiction novel. However, despite the presence of names like Truman Capote, Tom Wolfe, and Norman Mailer, this blurring between journalism and the modernist or high-art conventions of modern fiction seems to have made little profound impact on the American novel. Novelists like Robert Coover and E. L. Doctorow, who have striven for a continuity between historical writing and fictional narrative, are not in the mainstream of what academic critics prefer to study, and the American novel continues, despite the acknowledgment of a postmodernist aesthetic, to refine the high-art conventions of modernism.

The contrast with Latin American narrative writing is instructive, especially if one refers to authors whose works have been recently translated into English: Isabel Allende, Manuel Puig, Augusto Roa Bastos, Jorge Ibargüengoitia, Elena Poniatowska, Enrique Medina, Darcy Ribeiro, Autran Dourado, Mario Vargas Llosa, and so on. Some of these writers can be identified with the experimental criteria of modernist writing. Nevertheless, the abiding criterion has been the questioning of the limits between documentary or sociohistorical reality and the cultural writing about it. This project is frought with problematical issues (like the ideological mediatization that all text production involves) and perhaps not an insignificant amount of naiveté: Is literature an appropriate vehicle in the first place to appeal to the populace at large? — a question that creative artists who are dedicated to the cultural role of the comic book, another form of narrative, have already answered in the negative. Whatever assessment one renders these efforts, the emphasis has been on smudging the distinctions between artistic (specifically, fiction) and social-science discourse (specifically, history, but also sociology and anthropology) in favor of a postulate whereby all text production represents under-differentiated forms of mediated and ideologically-conditioned interpretation. What this has meant are writings by individuals identified as literary figures that often look a lot like social-science texts, a renewed status for literary journalism, and an inventory of documentary writing that antedates Capote's trumpeted nonfiction novel and goes far beyond it in scope and techniques. Concomitantly, this emphasis has also meant the enlisting in the ranks of literature writers who, in a classification predicated on the primacy of *poesis,* might not even be accorded literary status.

The history of journalism, as is well known, is that of an elite cultural phenomenon. It arose to serve the needs of a emerging mercantile bourgeoisie and went on to support and confirm the ideologies of the ruling classes. Early in the twentieth century, more popular forms of journalism emerge in conjunction with the rise of anarchism, socialism, and assorted local antiestablishment political efforts.

In both sectors, but more especially in that of the upper and professional middle-class papers, norms of U.S. and European-style professional journalism emerge. Whereas many of the founding figures of Latin American literary culture had been associated with journalism in the nineteenth century and, indeed, many of the founding texts of Latin American literature had appeared in newspapers on either their editorial pages (e.g., the sociopolitical writings of a Domingo Faustino Sarmiento) or in their literary supplements (e.g., texts of Spanish American Modernist poetry or the many serialized novels of the period), the professionalism of journalism with few exceptions relegated literature strictly to the literary supplements and promoted a sense of differing missions for literature and journalism.

However, hypotheses to the effect that Latin American sociohistorical experience exemplifies the magically real, that Latin American reality outstrips even the most fevered fictional imagination, and that it is hopeless to attempt to interpret official histories with the techniques of rational investigation touted by professional journalism (and, in other quarters, the social-science professions) have led Latin American writers to pursue ways of interpreting collective experience that a strict critical constructionism would call non-literary and a professional journalism blatantly fiction. One of the goals of such a criterion for writing is to demonstrate that a "rational explanation" for events and phenomena cannot be contained by the well-disciplined discourses of mutually exclusive categories of text production (by extension, it is also suggested that the compartmentalization of writing is a power strategy to forestall deeper interpretations than those sanctioned by categorically-defined disciplines). Another goal is to give full play to the ambiguities and contradictions of the social, historical, and political text, in opposition to the traditional goal of social-science research to account unambiguously and non-contradictorily for matters empirically determined to be the case. This does not mean a privileging of a conception of history as irrational and ultimately uninterpretable, a conclusion that would clash with the essentially Marxist commitment, in one form or another, of the majority of Latin American intellectuals and artists who attract critical attention, although it may mean prizing the ways in which phenomena cannot be circumscribed by the facile political formulas of vulgar Marxism. (An issue that we cannot go into here but which is related to any comprehensive analysis of Latin American culture is the extent to which, from an authentic point of view, one can legitimately speak of a Third World at all: there are those who would insist that it is only a matter of a pseudocapitalist and/or feudal world that has yet to be reorganized in conformance with socialism, but, then, the U.S. State Department by constrast sees it as a world threatened by socialism/communism that has yet to be fully democratized and capitalized.)

What all of this has to do with the intersection of Latin American literature and popular culture is that documentary writing serves historically to confirm the tenuousness of the separation between high literature and other forms of cultural production: this is so if it is true that categorical definitions of literature are the rather limited but dominant adherence to European classifications. This line of thought also underscores how in contemporary Latin America there is an enormously productive quest after new varieties of writing that both conform to the Latin American experience and reveal it in all its complexity.

One of the most outstanding representatives of a writing that blurs the categories between journalistic reporting and narrative fiction is Elena Poniatowska's *La noche de Tlatelolco* (1971), an enormously successful book that is a mosaic of texts built around interviews with participants in and bystanders of the massacre of student protestors in Mexico's Plaza de las Tres Culturas or Tlatelolco on the night of October 2, 1968. This event was a Mexican loss of innocence. The government, anxious to squelch any semblance of social disorder during the national apotheosis surrounding hosting the Summer Olympics, overreacted to student protests. This demonstrated, to the horror of many and the grim satisfaction of some, that Mexico was not exempt from the Latin American practice of using the armed forces to make war on the national citizenry. Poniatowska interviewed a large number of individuals, and their own words make up the text of her book. *La noche de Tlatelolco* has had an extensive influence in Mexican culture as the most famous document to report on the Tlatelolco massacre. Thus, it serves as the centerpiece of what is recognized as a subgenre of contemporary Mexican writing that goes beyond the bounds of journalism vs. novel and fiction vs. reporting.

Of course, Poniatowska's text is not unmediated expression. The author is very much present in the choice of individuals to interview, in the fragmentary distribution of their words throughout the book, and in the juxtaposition of the words of one individual with another and the conjunction of individual declarations with official proclamations and other non-personalized texts (e.g., political banners and slogans). Poniatowska describes her goal in the forthright explanatory terms that are a hallmark of this sort of documentary text:

> En su mayoría estos testimonios fueron recogidos en octubre y noviembre de 1968. Los estudiantes presos dieron los suyos en el curso de los dos años siguientes. Este relato les pertenece. Está hecho con sus palabras, sus luchas, sus errores, su dolor y su asombro. Aparecen también sus, "aceleradas," su ingenuidad, su confianza. Sobre todo les agradezco a las madres, a los que perdieron al hijo, al hermano, el haber accedido a hablar. El dolor es un acto absolutamente solitario. Hablar de él resulta casi intolerable; indagar, horadar, tiene sabor de insolencia.
>
> Este relato recuerda a una madre que durante días permaneció quieta, endurecida bajo el golpe y, de repente, como animal herido — un animal a quien le extraen las entrañas — dejó salir del centro de su vida, de la vida misma que ella había dado, un ronco, un desgarrado grito. Un grito que daba miedo, miedo por el mal absoluto que se le puede hacer a un ser humano; ese grito distorsionado que todo lo rompe, el ay de la herida definitiva, la que no podrá cicatrizar jamás, la de la muerte del hijo.
>
> Aquí está todo el eco del grito de los que murieron y el grito de los que quedaron. Aquí está su indagación y su protesta. Es el grito mudo que se atoró en miles de gargantas, en miles de ojos desorbitados por el espanto el 2 de octubre de 1968, en la noche de Tlatelolco. (164)[2]

The documentary, journalistic purpose of Poniatowska's text is amply demonstrated by this fragment, but so too is a mode of discourse that, whether it is called "novelistic" or (non-journalistically) "subjective," has a communicational appeal that explains the reception *La noche de Tlatelolco* has had among Mexican readers.

As dramatic as the Tlatelolco writings has been the role of sociopolitical commentary in Argentina since the mid-1982 Malvinas (Falklands) conflict and the return to constitutional democracy and institutional normality in late 1983.

---

[2]The majority of the following interviews were recorded in October and November 1968. The students who have been imprisoned offered their testimony during the two years following Tlatelolco. This is their story, woven out of their words, their struggles, their mistakes, their pain, and their bewilderment at the turn events took. Their impatience, their ingenuousness, their confidence also play a part in it. I am especially grateful to mothers who lost their sons and daughters, to brothers and sisters of the dead who were kind enough to allow me to record their words. Grief is a very personal thing. Putting it into words is almost unbearable; hence asking questions, digging for facts, borders on an invasion of people's privacy.

This story is also that of a mother so stunned that for days and days she uttered scarcely a word, and then suddenly, like a wounded animal — an animal whose belly is being ripped apart — she let out a hoarse, heart-rendering cry, from the very center of systemher life, from the very life that had been taken from her. A terrible cry, a cry of terror at the utter evil that can befall a human being; the sort of wild keening that is the end of everything, the wail of ultimate pain from the wound that will never heal, the death of a son.

Here is the echo of the cries of those who died, and those who lived. Here is their rage and their protest. It is the muted shout stifled in thousands of throats, the look in thousands of eyes that started from their sockets from the terror of October 2, 1968, on the night of Tlatelolco. (199)

While there continues to be the enormous literary productivity that marks Argentine culture, which includes major examples of documentary narrative, sociopolitical commentary has emerged as a dominant form of cultural expression with the abolishment of the military censorship that forbids "calling things by their right name" (I should note that although literature and other forms of artistic expression suffered from censorship, the "allegorical" modes the latter may employ meant that the censorship of art was often less comprehensive than it was in journalism or social-science writings). These commentaries may be seen as a revindication of the modes of interpretation of the professional social sciences, which have enjoyed extensive development in Argentina. However, few of them are academic documents, with rigorous methodologies, protocols of exposition, and scrupulously punctuated footnotes. Rather, those that have circulated most widely are more in the nature of Poniatowska's book, and the one that has enjoyed the greatest success is also built on narratives.

Daniel Kon's *Los chicos de la guerra* (1982) focuses on the young conscripts who made up the bulk of the fighting men in the Malvinas conflict. Kon's subtext is the assertion that all of the political cynicism surrounding the decision by the military to engage Britain in armed conflict over the Malvinas is synthesized in the way in which untrained and naively patriotic boys were sent to the South Atlantic. For many, the conflict was a means of distracting the attention of the Argentine populace from the disintegration of an ever more obviously corrupt political process. The way in which they took stock of their experiences and perceive, no matter how partially and inchoately, the cynicism and ineptitude of their superiors is what guaranteed the popular success of the book and its 1984 film version, in the filming of which several of the men interviewed by Kon served as technical advisors.

Although *Los chicos de la guerra* may be read as a series of direct statements by a group of representative young men about their combat experiences, there can be little escaping the fact that their comments have considerable resonance for a collective Argentine experience that extends far beyond their self-absorbed point of reference. It is understandable that these eight men were obsessed by their individual feelings and actions. Kon interviewed them, virtually clandestinely, within weeks of their return and his questions dwelt on the details of their personal stories. This explains why they are under-identified in the text, which was published before censorship was officially lifted. Moreover, the defeat of the war, the discovery that food and clothing had been incompetently distributed and that some superiors had actually hoarded provisions for their own comfort, and their excellent but condescending treatment at the hands of the British during their repatriation naturally contributed to a less than sanguine point of view.

Thus, although the subtitle of Kon's book stresses the question of personal testimonial — "Hablan los soldados que estuvieron en las Malvinas" (The soldiers who fought in the Malvinas are speaking) — the natural and spontaneous speech of the soldiers is considerably mediated by the contextualizing operations of Kon's reportage like his own comments, the organization of responses, and the juxtaposition of the words of the various informants. It is not so much a question of the material used by the writer to frame the book as a whole and to introduce the individual interviews as it is the matter of his questions, which are hardly a model of probing journalism. Rather, *Los chicos de la guerra* must be read inescapably against the backdrop of both the so-called *guerra sucia* (dirty war) prior to the invasion of the Malvinas and the information about military incompetence during the conflict that had begun to emerge the minute the hostilities were officially over. In this sense, the repeated references to the lack of adequate clothing or food, to the sense of having been abandoned by superiors, and to information provided to them by their British captors become less a litany of grievances about the ill-prepared Argentine war effort than a series of very telling allusions to the cynicism of a military apparatus that made the entire country an instrument of its ambitions. And nobody overlooked the fact that the Argentine armed forces, which have so often been called on to make war against Argentines, were ridiculously inept in "real" war.

There are two consequences that derive from the foregoing circumstances of contextualization. The first is that *Los chicos de la guerra* allegedly represents the truth about the Malvinas conflict as told by those at the bottom of the military hierarchy. The second is that the truth inherent in their stories must be read as a counterpoint to the official and self-serving reports of military propaganda, which was meant to deceive both the soldiers in the trenches and the civilians back home as to the true course of the war. The result of these factors has served to make Kon's book the most popular documentary narrative of the body of works on recent Argentine social and political history.

VII

The four examples of texts that can be examined as a challenge to the separation of high literature and popular culture can only allude to the range of the subject. There has been no room in this exposition for film or for the relations between film and the novel, and all students of contemporary Argentine literature are familiar, of course, with the question as it relates to Manuel Puig's writing, for the televized soap opera and its intersections with narrative (Argentine *telenovelas* are particularly inviting), or for the complex issue of popular, colloquial speech as it relates to the linguistic standards of high literature. Almost all postmodernist writing in Latin America would be pertinent to the latter topic, as well as the late nineteenth-century *poesía gauchesca* (gaucho poetry) or the early twentieth-century Mexican *novela de la Revolución* (novels about the Mexican Revolution). Yet, the close treatment of a few casebook examples of the subject is meant to suggest how the latter and other analyses might be approached.

In the personal note by "El autor" that supplements, complements, or closes the Argentine Tomás Eloy Martínez's excellent documentary novel *La novela de Perón* (1985), we read "[En] La novela de Perón, el autor defiende la idea de que la frontera entre los géneros es imprecisa, y que sus textos deben ser leídos como una puesta en escena de la realidad o de la historia, no como meros documentos o ficciones" (431).[3] The sort of "amorphization" and jumbling to be seen in the many varieties of writing this essay has referred to is indeed the source of so much that is vital and fascinating about contemporary Latin America cultural texts.

WORKS CITED

Foster, David William. *Alternate Voices in the Contemporary Latin American narrative*. Columbia: University of Missouri Press, 1985.

——. "Argentine Sociopolitical Commentary, the Malvinas Conflict, and Beyond: Rhetoricizing a National Experience." *Latin American Research Review* 22.1 (1987): 7-34.

——. *From Mafalda to Los supermachos: Latin American Graphic Humor*. Boulder: Lynne Rienner, 1989.

[3]In this novel about Peron, the author defends the idea that the boundaries among the genres are imprecise and that his texts should be read as if they were a staging of reality or history, not as mere documents or fictions.

——. "Latin American Documentary Narrative." *PMLA; publications of the Modern Language Association of America* 99 (1984): 41-55.

Poniatowska, Elena. *La noche de Tlatelolco*. México, D. F.: Ediciones Era, 1971. Trans. into English by Helen R. Lane as *Massacre in Mexico*. New York: The Viking Press, 1975.

Sánchez, Luis Rafael. *La guaracha del Macho Camacho*. Buenos Aires: Ediciones de la Flor, 1976. Trans. into English by Gregory Rabassa as *Macho Camacho's Beat*. New York: Pantheon, 1980.

FREDERIC W. MURRAY

The Image of Utopia as a Conceptual Determinant in the Structural Development of Spanish American Culture

In spite of the conspicuous lack of utopian communities in Latin America historically, utopia as a theme in Latin American culture and literature is a topic that has attracted periodically the attention of the scholarly community both inside and outside of Spanish America.[1] Carlos Fuentes for example, in a cogent essay on Mexican culture, has stated that utopia is the most hidden and profound of features that was involved in the origin and foundation of Spanish American culture and that in the course of Western history Topia represents the Old World while Utopia stands for the New World (*Tiempo Mexicano*, "Mexican Time" 28). Indeed the view of the interaction between the Old World and the New as having coalesced from the beginning around the concept and image of utopia has attracted the attention not only of the novelist Fuentes but also of many Latin Americanists. Stelio Cro, in a seminal work, has traced in detail the empirical nature of Spanish utopian thought as it relates to the conquest and colonization of the New World beginning with Columbus's 1492 expedition and ending in 1692, a date generally accepted as closing the first phase of conquest and active colonization. More than one writer has noted the significance of Sir Thomas More's *Utopia* having been published in 1516 shortly after the discovery of the New World and so possibly reflecting the first discoverers' idyllic descriptions of the New World Indian communities. Moreover, at this same time Spain was in the beginning stages of establishing the European community in the new found lands, and many of those involved in the enterprise, whether directly as missionary or colonizer or as administrative planner based in the Royal Court of the Spanish monarchy, were conversant with More's work. Thus, it would appear that from its inception the New World/Old World dichotomy was based upon an abstract con-

---

[1]Preliminary versions of the present study were presented to the Society for Iberian and Latin American Thought Conference on "Philosophy, Culture, and History," University of Puerto Rico Mayaguez, February 18, 1985 and to The International Conference on Utopia and the American Continent, McMaster University, Canada, March 31, 1978.

cept involving the possibilities for reordering a more just society, at least in the New World, along idealized lines. It could be done. The proof was to be found in the descriptions of seemingly ideal indigenous communities in the New World. Sir Thomas More's work provided a name for the enterprise and a suggested social structure: in effect, More's *Utopia* offered a conceptual model that was based along European lines but that had its origins fundamentally in the idealized descriptions of the New World indigenous communities. The Inca empire, as one example, proved to be one of the major examples, rightly or wrongly, of the possibilities of a utopian society that extends beyond the merely community level. Carlos Cox has profiled the utopian strain of thought in the major early interpreter of the Inca Empire who was, as well, a descendent of Incan nobility — The Inca Garcilaso de la Vega. Alberto Flores Galindo, in turn, has traced the idea of an Andean Incan utopia and its influence of the intellectual community in the Andean area through the centuries and down to the present. Even such out of the way Indian communities as the Patagonians have received their share of utopianistic musings, as can be found in Gabriel François Coyer's work published in the eighteenth century and recently translated into Spanish.

Although Carlos Fuentes does not elaborate upon his thesis in any great detail, it is apparent that he obtained the Topia/Utopia dichotomy from the work of the Spanish philosopher Eugenio Imaz who, in *Topía y Utopía (Topia and Utopia)* published in Mexico in 1946, considered the utopian theme as applied to the New World/Old World schema in terms of neo-Hegelian dialectics. The Mexican philosopher Leopoldo Zea adopted a similar viewpoint in a much later study in which he considered utopia as part of a failed dialectical process that has inhibited the development of Hispanic America. That is, the search for an ideal and just ordering of society has been continually caught up in a series of antagonistic juxtapositions: civilization versus barbarism, liberalism versus tyranny, liberal republicanism versus conservatism to name a few. Trapped within this dialectic "the future never became the present, the past never became the past (the past is never synthesized into the present as it is always rejected) and utopia instead of becoming an actuality, receded farther and farther everyday" (Zea 13).

Carlos Fuentes' first major novel, *La región más transparente (Where the Air is Clear)* is a striking aesthetic exposition of Zea's view of the failure of social/cultural cohesion at the stage of synthesis. Not only do the various social classes in the novel, representing an ethnic and cultural diversity that extends from the lowest Indian and mestizo urban proletariat to the highly Europeanized "jet set," fail to form a cohesive social structure, but even the several past epochs of the Mexican historical process have failed to coalesce. Each historical period has rejected the previous period and has been rejected, in its turn, by the generation that succeeds it so that each new generation finds itself rootless so to speak and suspended, as it were, over a cultural abyss: sustained over nothingness, or better yet, sustained temporally in limbo, or "nowhere" only by its own efforts.

In terms of Fuentes' Topian-Utopian dichotomy, each Topian social philosophy, from the sixteenth-century Spanish colonial culture to the twentieth-century North American capitalist cultural traits adopted into Mexico, has failed to form a coalescence with its historical predecessor. Hence the utopian goal of establishing a justly ordered society is continually being frustrated. And the specific object of Fuentes' and Zea's criticism is the inability of the Mexican Revolution to have achieved a just ordering of the social structure. This failure on the part of the most significant social movement in the history of Mexico, and of the historically first social revolution of the twentieth century has lead Zea, in the view of Michael Weinstein to elaborate a social philosophy that "is the most utopian and perhaps the most mystical of all Mexican finalist philosophers" (86). It is for reasons, then, of a particular historical circumstance that the Mexican intellectual, artist as well as philosopher, is driven to a utopian view of social destiny.

The concept and image of utopia is a theme that appears with a great deal of consistency from the Spanish colonial period down to the present in the thought of the Latin American intellectual not only in Mexico but also throughout the rest of the region. Indeed, such is the hold of the utopian ideal upon Latin American culture that it apparently forms one of the basic concepts regarding the area's historical destiny. Harold E. Davis addresses this attitude upon stating that "utopianism was a major element in the New World optimism, in the form of an assumption that America was destined to be the scene of a society free from the evils of the old world" (14). A major example of New World optimism is José Vasconcelos who, in his masterpiece essay, *La raza cósmica (The Cosmic Race)* presents the New World as the crucible in which there is being forged a new race and a new culture that, being free of the defects of the world's past societies, will form the future destiny of the human race: Latin America as cradle of the future of mankind. Alfonso Reyes in *Ultima Tule (Furthest Thule)* states explicitly that "America is Utopía" (93) and offers as one element of demonstrable proof the example of the Latin American constitutional codices.

Ultimately Ezequiel Martínez Estrada, in an essay published in 1963, sees the utopian destiny of Spanish American culture as in the process of being actualized quite literally in the Cuba of Fidel Castro. As such, Martínez Estrada considers More's *Utopia* as a remarkably intuitive prediction of a future historical event.

It is problematic that Castro, upon instituting the new social order in Cuba, had Sir Thomas More in mind. But that is not to say that during other historical periods and in other areas of Latin America the direct influence of More's *Utopia* had not been felt. Carlos Fuentes, for example, bases his statements concerning the importance of utopia in the origins of Spanish American culture not only upon the theories advanced by Eugenio Imaz but more concretely upon the deeds of Vasco de Quiroga, the sixteenth-century Bishop of Mexico, who established a network of Indian communities in the province of Michoacan that were modeled directly upon More's *Utopia*. With regard to the colonial period, Silvio Zavala has noted several substantial citations from *Utopia* in Solórzano's *Política indiana (Policies Governing the Indies)*. The references are significant since, as Zavala points out, Solórzano knew at first hand the administrative problems involved in governing the Spanish Indies, and it is precisely with reference to these problems of administration that Solórzano cites Sir Thomas More. Finally, and as an example of some significance to the interrelationship of the concept of utopia to the origins of Latin American culture, the acknowledged founder of Spanish American culture, Bartolomé de Las Casas, has been categorized as a utopianist with regard to his views as to the structure of society possible for the New World (Maravall).

Not only has utopia appeared as a conceptual social model and as a goal of historical destiny, but the very landscape of the New World, at times, has taken on a utopian hue in the minds of foreign observers as well as in the works of the region's major thinkers and artists. John Mander, for example, states that "the landscape of America is also the landscape of Utopia." Nor only that, but he further states rather sweepingly that:

> it is the Utopian element in the Latin American that has produced Brasilia. It has also produced Neruda's panorama of the continent in his *Canto gen-*

> *eral* (General Song): or that ideal of an 'Indoamerica,' once dreampt (sic) of by Haya de la Torre in Peru; or the indigenista vision of Rivera, Orozco and Siquieros in Mexico, or, for that matter, the universalist, messianic idealism of Fidel Castro. (25)

The utopian theme has been noted by other investigators not only in the work of Pablo Neruda but also in those of numerous other writers of Spanish America throughout its history. Juan Durán has analyzed the utopian theme in ten major literary works from each of the principal Latin American historical periods, beginning with Columbus' *Journal* and ending with Julio Cortazar's novel *Los premios (The Winners),* published in 1960. Finally, Martin S. Stabb, in a seminal article on utopia as a theme in the essayistic literature of Spanish America, reaches the conclusion that the image of utopia is a major unifying trope in the historical development of Latin American literature.

Given the prevalence of the image, one is led to the conclusion that utopia represents something more than a merely spurious image and that, apparently, it is fundamentally involved in the very framework of Hispanic American culture as such. In point of fact, utopia as a cultural determinator has been acknowledged by F. S. C. Northrop in his study of the meaning of Western civilization. Rather than concentrating upon any one epoch, Northrop traces briefly the idea of utopia as it appears in each succeeding period of Latin American history. In passing, Northrop also distinguishes the utopian thrust of Latin American culture from that of the North American variety by observing that while the former is derived from "the traditional Latin hierarchic political and religious forms and the novel utopian ideals of a Las Casas or a Sir Thomas More, obtained by way of St. Thomas, St. Augustine, Aristotle, and Plato," the latter springs from "the different religious and political utopia of John Locke, derived from the scientific investigations of Galilei and Newton" (291).

It is only upon turning to the idea of utopia as a model for small communal experiments that one finds a noticeable lack of application in Spanish America. Indeed, this lack has led Joseph Love to conclude that utopia is a negligible feature of the history of Spanish America. It must be noted, however, that Love's definition of utopia is restricted to the phenomenon of isolated communal experiment and that few utopian communities (other than the great experiments of the colonial period) have been attempted in Latin America, especially during the nineteenth and early twentieth centuries, the period of major concern to Love.

This fact only underscores Michael Weinstein's view that utopia functions as a conceptual principle operant in Spanish American civilization and that "the function of these utopias in human existence is not to provide a blueprint for a small communal experiment or for a set of postrevolutionary institutions, but to provide encouragement for human beings who seek to oppose the demands of their present circumstances" (74).

Although Weinstein is addressing the specific topic of the topian strain evident in the finalist philosophers of postrevolutionary Mexico, his assertion is in accord with Martin Plattel's statement in *Utopian and Critical Thinking* to the effect that utopia is "the portrayal of a social ideal which is not dogmatically fixed but varies according to the historical time and culture. This portrayal functions as a guideline for social thinking and acting, and it makes us more aware of the imperfections of the existing social order" (81).

Given the weight of evidence, it becomes clear that the concept of utopia is central to the cultural dynamics of Latin America. That is, Latin America has taken the image of a just society as its ideal and changes in the course of time, as historical exigencies demand, the methods used in the attempt to force social reality to conform to this overriding ideal.

The basic question to be confronted is that of defining the cultural mechanism by which the concept of utopia functions within Spanish American civilization. The basic premise that seems to be operative is that at the heart of any given culture or civilization there exists a matrix of governing ideas and concepts that determines the configuration of the culture and acts as a guide to its historical development. Thus any given culture is motivated and energized by a nucleus of governing ideas that, implanted during the formulative period of the culture under question, determine the overall tenor and tone of the social structure; furthermore, the nucleus of ideas manifests its existence in the major facets and ethos of the culture as it develops through time.

With Spanish America the time, the place, and the circumstance of the founding of its culture can be fixed with a great deal of precision. The nucleus of governing ideas is elaborated upon the concept of utopia, a situation that came about not by happenstance but rather by a fortuitous coalescence of historical circumstances; for the discovery, and in particular, the colonization of the Spanish New World came at a time when Western civilization was undergoing a process of re-evaluation in the guise of the Renaissance and as such was open to innovation. The early missionaries, and in particular the Franciscans in Mexico (and later the Jesuits in Paraguay), seizing upon the ideals of the Renaissance, saw in the New World an opportunity to recreate a new and better European Christian civilization in a new land unencumbered by an ingrained centuries' old degenerating social/cultural structure. Not only the religious but also the political arm of colonization became involved in the utopian process, an understandable development given the entwined relationship of Church and State at this period of Spain's history. The Castilian monarchy's rigid control over the movement of men, material, and even of ideas from Europe to the New World, its attempt to regulate every facet of the conquest and colonization, down to the specific rules for the laying out of new cities and towns, illustrates a desire to establish in the New World a culture based upon what was perceived as the best elements of European civilization while assuring that the baser elements were not transferred to the new found lands to corrupt the inhabitants thereof. The accepted explanation of the Crown's almost obsessive preoccupation with how things were to be in the New World is that the Spanish monarchy was fearful of losing political control over the vast new empire that was coming into being across the ocean. While such an attitude was certainly true enough, of perhaps equal importance was the Crown's attempt to keep this vast new social experiment from becoming contaminated by outside and unwanted factors as well as to keep it from developing major deviations from the abstract master plan. It is no accident, therefore, that Solórzano, the Crown administrator and historian, in considering the serious administrative problems involved in setting up a new society in the New World, had recourse to More's Utopia.

Thus the seed of the idea of an ideal society, a utopian society was planted in the culture of sixteenth-century Spanish America. Each successive period of Spanish American history can be seen basically as an attempt to establish a good and just society by utilizing a variety of different social postulates that depend upon the prevailing sociocultural theories of each epoch. In this view the New World Hispanic culture can be seen not so much as emerging organically or spontaneously out of conflicting tensions of widely diverse cultural tendencies but rather as the product of a certain degree of attempted planning following certain principles. Each historical period of Latin America offers its particular method for achieving the utopian goal. It is as though a new method were advanced as each in its turn failed or was defeated in its confrontation with the prevailing or contending ideologies: in other words, Zea's dialectic in operation.

During the Independence phase of Spanish American history the utopian nucleus of ideas changes from what was basically a religious to a secular orientation. The influence of utopian socialism as well as romantic socialism dominates the thinking of the leaders of political and cultural independence from Spain. A utopian strain of thought runs through the actions and writing not only of Simón Bolívar but also in the writings of the *Asociación de Mayo* (The Association of May) in Argentina and in Estéban Echeverría, whose ideas served to found the Argentine historical school and to the proclamation of a utopian socialist program in 1837 (Ainsa 29).

In Mexico a utopian theme has been traced in Spanish America's first novel, *El periquillo sarniento (The Mangy Parakeet)* written by Fernández de Lizardi at the close of the colonial epoch and published in 1816 (Joset). The novel tenders not only a biting criticism of society as the colonial period was coming to an end but also offers a running commentary of how a society should and could be ideally organized. At the end of the novel the protagonist is shipwrecked on an isle off the coast of China and finds there an ideal utopian social system (the western movement of the image of utopia having gone about as far as it could go). This last incident has the effect of bringing together the criticism of the social system that runs through the novel with an offer of a solution: a utopian one.

Once independence is achieved the diverse impulses of early nineteenth-century thought lead to the founding throughout Spanish America of utopian republics, to the creation of "repúblicas aéreas" (aerial republics) — in the words of Simón Bolívar — based upon abstract sociopolitical concepts rather than upon the social and historical reality of the particular areas of the region. During the late nineteenth century the growing influence of positivism led to attempts to establish the just and ideal society based upon the scientific ideals coming out of the France of Auguste Comte, Saint Simon and Charles Fourier, and influencing most notably the social theorists of Mexico and Brazil.

The twentieth century bears witness to the search for the utopian ideal being developed along several lines. One major tendency is that of economic and state planning, thus the efforts at implementing planned societies, from Castro's Cuba to Peru's failed 1970s experiment in leftist military government. In this light H. B. Hawthorn's statement that while literary utopias have gone out of style, the "creation of new national societies, with utopian features, is more common than it has ever been" seems quite applicable to many areas of Latin America (50). The result, however, often has been a marked heightening of the Topian-Utopian tension. On this same basis Joseph Gusfield speaks of state economic development and planning as a modern utopia.

One curious development in the phenomenon of utopian intent in Latin American civilization is that, in one respect, the concept appears to have come full circle. That is, utopia began in the New World as a religious enterprise, as an opening of the political possibilities of Christianity (as Carlos Fuentes called it). In the mid-twentieth century one notable aspect of the political possibilities of Christianity is the appearance of liberation theology and "comunidades de base" (foundation communities), representing, in the main, a welding together of Catholic social concern with (in-part) Marxist economic theory with the goal in mind of restructuring the social order and the social structure, from within: the implanting of a nucleus of ideas of utopian intent at the nodal points of the social structure in the hope that through time this nucleus will gradually reform the social and economic system and bring the overall structure of society into conformance with utopian and humanistic principles.

In general Latin America demonstrates a certain propensity toward assuming an abstract and humanistic stance concerning the resolution of the ills that bedevil the social order. This inclination is underlined, for example, by the Latin American contribution to the "Preferred Worlds for the 1990's project of the World Order Models Project." The authors, Gustavo Lagos and Horacio Godoy speak of establishing a humanist society on a world-wide scale that calls for the emergence of a "new individual" based upon five basic principles institutionalized into a World Commonwealth of Peoples that is to act as the principal governing body. The entire structure of the "preferred world" (as the authors call it) assumes the tone of a utopian ideal, particularly when contrasted with the present world situation which the authors qualify as dystopian.

In conclusion, the idea and image of utopia may be utilized as a conceptual model to explore the basic structural pattern of Latin American culture and civilization. This structural pattern has as its organizing nucleus what Alfred North

Whitehead has called a complex eternal object. A complex eternal object is "any entity whose conceptual recognition does not involve a necessary reference to any definite actual entities of the temporal world. As such, eternal objects are pure potentials of the specific determination of fact or forms of definition" (Hall 73). In this light, utopia is a potentiality at the heart of Latin American culture, it is energized through intent and is manifested in the culture on two levels; one, on an abstract plane that is expressed through the ethos component and illustrated by the humanistic principles that seem to determine the attitudes and belief system of the members of the culture; and secondly on a more concrete level, the utopian intent is seen in the specific acts, laws, customs, institutions of the culture. In this way the internal order of the civilization is expressed as it develops through time.

WORKS CITED

Ainsa, Fernando. "La función de la utopía en la historia del pensamiento América Latina." *Memoria del XX Congreso de Literatura Iberoamericana*. Budapest: Departmento de Español de la Universidad Eötvös Lorand, 1982: 23-31.

Cro, Stelio. *Realidad y utopía en el descubrimento y conquista de la América Hispana (1492-1682)*. Troy, MI: International Book Publishers and Madrid: Fundación Universitaria Española, 1983.

Cox, Carlos Manuel. *Utopía y realidad en el Inca Garcilaso*. Lima: Universidad Nacional Mayor de San Marcos, 1965.

Coyer, Gabriel François. *Sobre los gigantes patagones: carta del Abate François-Gabriel Coyer al doctor Matay*. Trans. and prol. by Alamiro de Avila Martel. Santiago: Universidad de Chile, 1984.

Davis, Harold E. *Latin American Thought*. Baton Rouge: Louisiana State University, 1972.

Durán, Juan G. "Literatura y Utopía en Hispanoamérica," Diss. Cornell University, 1972.

Flores Galindo, Alberto. *Europa y el país de los inca; la utopía andina*. Lima: Instituto de Apoyo Agrario, 1986.

Fuentes, Carlos. *La región más transparente*. Mexico: Fondo de Cultura Económica, 1958.

——. *Tiempo mexicano*. Mexico: Mortiz, 1972.

Gusfield, Joseph. "Economic Development as a Modern Utopia." *Aware of Utopia*. Ed. D. W. Plath. Urbana: U of Illinois P, 1971: 75-85.

Hall, David L. *The Civilization of Experience: A Whiteheadian Theory of Culture*. New York: Fordham UP, 1973.

Hawthorn, H. B. "Utopias and Durability in Literature and Reality." *International Journal of Comparative Sociology* 4 (1963): 50-56.

Imaz, Eugenio. *Topía y Utopía*. Mexico: Tezontle, 1946.

Joset, Jacque. "La utopía degradada de J. J. Fernández de Lizardi," *Memoria del XX Congreso de Literatura Iberoamericana*. Budapest: Departmento de Español de la Universidad Eötvös Lorand, 1982: 353-368.

Lagos, Gustavo, and H. H. Godoy. *Revolution in Being: A Latin American View of the Future*. New York: The Free Press, 1977.
Love, Joseph. "Utopianism in Latin American Culture." in *Aware of Utopia*. Ed. D. W. Plath. Urbana: U of Illinois P, 1971: 117-134.
Mander, John. *The Unrevolutionary Society*. New York: Alfred A. Knopf, 1968.
Maravall, José Antonio. "Utopía y primitivismo en el pensamiento de Las Casas." *Revista de Occidente* 47 (diciembre, 1974): 311-388.
Martínez Estrada, Ezequiel. "El nuevo mundo, la isla de Utopía y la isla de Cuba." *Cuadernos Americanos* (marzo-abril, 1963): 89-122.
Northrop, F. S. C. *The Meeting of East and West*. New York: MacMillan, 1946.
Plattel, Martin. *Utopian and Critical Thinking*. Dusquene Studies: Philosophical Series 29. Pittsburgh: Dusquene UP, 1972.
Reyes, Alfonso. *Ultima Tule*. Mexico: Imprenta Universitaria, 1942.
Solórzano Pereira, Juan de. *Política indiana*. Madrid: BAE, 1972. Vol. 5.
Stabb, Martin S. "Utopia and anti utopia: the theme in selected essayistic writings of Spanish America." *Revista de Estudios Hispánicos* 15 (Oct. 1981): 377-393.
Weinstein, Michael. *Latin American Thought*. University Park: Penn. State UP, 1976.
Zavala, Silvio. "Algo más sobre Tomás Moro en lengua española." *Cuadernos Americanos* (julio-agosto, 1975): 134-138.
Zea, Leopoldo. *The Latin American Mind*. Trans. by J. H. Abbot and Lowell Dunham. Norman: U of Oklahoma P, 1976.

RAYMOND J. LEWIS

Changing Perceptions of Nineteenth-Century Mexican and Argentinian Identity

The nineteenth century was a time when North Americans indulged their curiosity about Latin America. Because Mexico and Argentina were among the most accessible, they attracted a number of travelers willing to comment on the lifestyle, religion and other cultural aspects of Mexico and Argentina. The differences that appear among the visitors between 1800-1850 and those from 1860-1910 are revealing. A major shift in the things emphasized by the writers had taken place by 1870 and are especially obvious in the descriptions of Argentina written by English visitors. Works such as these are storehouses of social commentary, and they reflect the cultural values of the writers, often highlighting the ethnocentrism of the writer and even the lack of knowledge of their own country. Mexico's proximity to the United States is an excellent starting point, because there is a wealth of literature. The major problem is selection.

Mexico

Several appealing works relating to Mexico cover the first half of the nineteenth century. These are *Fanny Calderon de la Barca, Life in Mexico: The Letters of Fanny Calderon de la Barca*, edited and annotated by Howard T. Fisher and Marion Hall Fisher in 1966 from the work originally published in 1843. A second work was William W. Carpenter, *Travels and Adventures in Mexico*. Maturin M. Ballou wrote *Aztec Land* and is countered by the work of Mary E. Blake and Margaret F. Sullivan's *Mexico*. All of these travelers had differing backgrounds and perspectives on Mexico.

Fanny Inglis was born and educated in Scotland, but she migrated to the United States for financial reasons. There she met and married Angel Calderon de la Barca, who was Spain's representative in the United States. After their marriage Señor Calderon was appointed the first Spanish Minister to the Republic of Mexico since the War of Independence. They traveled by sea to Vera Cruz in 1839 and overland from there to Mexico City.

Mr. Carpenter was a well educated New Englander, who enlisted in the Kentucky Volunteers at the outbreak of the Mexican-American War of 1848. He went to Mexico of his own free will, but was detained far longer than he anticipated. Carpenter was taken prisoner by the Mexican Army during his first combat engagement and marched on foot to San Juan del Río where he was detained during the war and for some time after it ended.

Maturin M. Ballou was a Boston businessman who visited Mexico for a reason he never explained, but his view of the country was entirely negative. Margaret F. Sullivan was another New Englander who visited Mexico about the same time as Ballou, but her perception of Mexico and the Mexicans contrasts sharply with that of Mr. Ballou.

Señora Calderon and Mr. Carpenter are in agreement that travel in Mexico was difficult and dangerous. The former traveled from Vera Cruz to Mexico City by diligence. She emphasized the physical discomfort caused by the bad roads, but she had a military escort to discourage bandits. Mr. Carpenter, on the other hand, was captured by the Mexican army at Ramos, which is not far from Monterey, and marched to San Juan del Río far to the South. His trip was made on foot with an armed escort as a Prisoner of War. The trip was physically demanding and the soldiers often had to protect their prisoners from hostile Mexicans civilians. Carpenter did mention individual acts of kindness, when Mexican women with Christian charity provided food and water to the unfortunate prisoners. Later he talked of the kind acts of an unnamed doctor and a priest, Julian Miranda. They often discussed religion, which was a topic of mutual interest, coming as both did from agrarian societies.

Fanny Calderon de la Barca, a convert to Catholicism, was intensely interested in religion also. She made it her business to visit the major churches in Mexico City and participated in the Catholic religious festivals and the Mass. Her attitude was a mixture of admiration and criticism. She enjoyed the Mass and the festivals, but disapproved of some individual clergymen and some Church practices. The Church's wealth, which did nothing for the poor or the friars preying on the piety of the gullible, met with her disapproval and her attitude was mirrored by Mr. Carpenter's.

Carpenter experienced Catholic charity to a far greater extent than Señora Fanny. Carpenter was a well educated man and the Mexican government was reluctant to have him leave the country. He was offered land, position, and a beautiful wife if he would stay. He preferred to return home and secured false papers presenting himself as a member of the Irish Catholic San Patricio Battalion which had deserted the American cause to fight with their co-religionists. With those papers he solicited and received Church charity while on route to a west coast port. The clergy had been directed to give aid to any member of the battalion, and on his journey to the port of Blas, Carpenter received, by order of President Santa Anna, food and lodgings. Rarely was aid denied or given grudgingly. In fact, priests often gave him a little extra money to make his travel more comfortable.

Maturin M. Ballou, an American businessman, wrote *Aztec Land*. In addition to his search for commercial opportunities, he visited many cathedrals, venturing out from the comfort of his private rail car. His assessment of the Church was negative. The clergy he perceived as immoral but cited no evidence. To him they were an immoral brotherhood dedicated to the subjugation and exploitation of the flock. All his contacts with Mexicans he interpreted negatively. He concluded that Mexico should borrow its culture from North America. Ballou's ethnocentric attitudes kept him isolated from the people he scorned. All their great works he attributed to prior cultural contact with ancient Egypt. In this respect he followed the extreme cultural diffusionist version shared by some early anthropologists, who argued that all culture began in Egypt. On the other hand *Mexico* written by Mary E. Blake and Margaret F. Sullivan, who also were touring Mexico from Boston, presented other ideas about Mexican culture. They commented on the basic kindness, honesty, and courtesy of the average Mexican. Certainly, these two ladies saw no need for the Mexicans to adopt North American culture. In fact, they argued the Americans could learn from the Mexicans. Here were two well educated Americans, who did not perceive Mexican culture in negative terms. It might be argued that their ideas bordered on the Polyanna complex, but their assessment is far closer to Señora Fanny's and Mr. Carpenter's than to Mr. Ballou's.

Mr. Carpenter and Fanny de la Barca had intimate, extensive social contacts with Mexicans of all classes. The former was briefly hired as a tutor for the son of a wealthy rancher near Guadalajara. As a family member, speaking Spanish, which he had learned in captivity, he participated in the social activities at his employers home. The music and dancing he enjoyed, and he observed that this was a time for the ladies to wear their best jewelry. All classes seemed passionately fond of personal ornaments, but only the jewels of the upper class were real. Carpenter and Señora de la Barca agreed that the Spanish ladies were graceful and beautiful, but were divided on the beauty of the Indians. Carpenter, also, found Indian women to be lovely.

Both authors commented on the unsanitary conditions surrounding food preparation. Mr. Carpenter observed the ladies picking lice from each others heads, wiping their hands on a cloth and turning to fix the meal without washing, but one must note that water was a scarce commodity and had to be conserved in many areas. Moreover North American personal hygiene was not much ahead of Mexico. Nevertheless, both enjoyed Mexican food. As for Mexican honesty, neither Carpenter or Señora Fanny were as trusting as Blake and Sullivan. Carpenter on one occasion while on his escape journey was robbed of all he owned, including his clothing. The latter vividly described her travels with armed guards to the well armed ranches, and discussed the constant fear of robbery. Carpenter noted that a stranger entering a town was always asked if he had seen any bandits. Robbery and murder, while common events and of concern to Mexicans and foreigners, were not the sum total of Mexican culture.

Argentina

John A. King wrote *Twenty-four Years in the Argentine Republic* and his work covered the formative years of the Republic. This young man had many interesting observations, which were quite different from the Mexican materials. Edwin W. Clark was the author of *A Visit to South America: With Notes and Observations on the Physical Features of the Country, and Incidents of the Voyage.* This engineer's perceptions of Argentina focused on the possibilities for economic development. W. H. Koebel was responsible for *Modern Argentina: The el Dorado of Today.* He was interested in convincing English investors to invest their money in the Santa Fe Land Company of Argentina. Campbell P. Ogilvie wrote *Argentina from a British Point of View.* As a representative of the Santa Fe Land Co., Ltd., his book was a report to the company stockholders.

A seventeen year old North American landed in Buenos Aires in 1817 without money, employment, friends or knowledge of the language. John Anthony King's *Twenty-four Years in the Argentine Republic* was reconstructed from memory because his original papers had been destroyed to protect him from the brutal dictator Juan Manuel Rosas.

King learned to speak Spanish working in a perfume shop owned by a kindly French couple. Once acclimated he took a commission with a General Ramírez, whose mission was to invade the Banda Oriental, a southern Uruguayan province, and destroy General José Artigas, who was an Uruguayan hero. The campaign was a fiasco as were most of his military adventures. Imprisoned for a time, he gained freedom and a Major's commission in the federalist army to participate in a campaign to free Bolivia from Spain.

Even in Bolivia or upper Peru his military career did not prosper and at one time he was forced to live with the Chirivone Indians for a while. He was constantly depressed by the government's inability or unwillingness to compensate him and his men for their services. King's popularity with his troops suffered because he refused them permission to loot the captured towns as the other commanders did. At last, he decided to retire from the military and that decision was based partly on the rise of Juan Manuel de Rosas. This brutal gaucho or cowboy took control of Argentina and initiated a reign of terror comparable to that of the French Revolution.

King did not appear to be much interested in religion, although he did have one incident with the religious authorities in Jujoy. He was arrested for failure to observe proper respect for the Holy Eucharist as it was passing in a street procession. Once released, King turned his attention to the civilian life and the possibility of marriage and family.

King's return to Buenos Aires was slow and pleasant as he visited with friends, staying sometimes for months. Finally he met and married a wealthy heiress, and went into an unspecified business. Much of the rest of his story concerned his feeling toward the dictator, Rosas. The stories he told were ugly. Any person suspected of unreliability by Rosas was as good a dead. King claimed the firing squads were stopped because the constant shooting made people nervous, so the condemned were slaughtered like sheep by having their throats quietly slit. Citing an 1843 pamphlet by Don Jose Rivera Indarte, he gave the death count as follows:

Poisoned	4
Throats cut	3,765
Shot	1,393
TOTAL	5,884

Even allowing for political partisanship, the total killed must have been substantial.

King's situation must have been dangerous because as soon as his wife and youngest son died, he took the opportunity to sell out and return to the United States with his oldest son. There he reconstructed his twenty-four years from memory. Those who came to Argentina later did not share the Colonel's dark political views. Rosas was gone and the new visitors were more interested in economics than politics.

Edwin W. Clark in *A Visit to South America*, which was published in 1878 represented the interests of the new group of Latin American visitors. As an engineer his perceptions of the country were technical rather than cultural. He was disturbed by the quarantine imposed prior to landing, but he admitted it biased his judgment in some areas. He described Buenos Aires as a city of straight streets intersecting at right angles, which disturbed him for some reason. The low homes with a single entrance, which enclosed a patio and garden intrigued him, but as an engineer he felt compelled to comment on the cistern in the homes. He believed this was the result of the recent turbulent political past, when each home had to be defended, and have an independent water supply. Comfort and the fact that in the recent past there had been no central water supply did not seem to occur to him. The public buildings he observed were constructed on a grand scale by Italian laborers, whom he praised for their industry, but the administration of the public projects he regarded more critically. The federal system, in his opinion, was government by mini nations each with a private army and president, creating excessive duplication and cost to the taxpayers. Public employees he charged with neglect, rudeness and incompetence, although the basis for these assertions were not clarified nor was evidence given. On the plains he saw little beyond the hospitality extended by the managers on the great ranches. The things on the ranches that interested Mr. Clark were the bridge building techniques, railroads, barns and haystacks. He was definitely interested in technical not cultural topics.

The next technical writer to visit Argentina had a more balanced view of the technical and cultural aspects of the country. W. H. Koebel wrote *Modern Argentina*. His book covered the urban and rural life in Argentine in 1907 rather sympathetically. Koebel enjoyed Buenos Aires and was impressed by the grand public buildings, the public transportation network, including the double decker trams, and the cabs. The one way streets inconvenienced him at first. He found numbers of Englishmen residing in Argentina. They had come to participate in the business opportunities there. He reported the English permanent residents were on the whole well adjusted to the life style there. The children were automatically dual citizens and Koebel urged the parents to send them to Argentine schools and universities to become good Argentines as well as good Englishmen, and to become acquainted with the nation's future leaders. He noted the rising influence of other national groups such as the Germans, North Americans and the Italians with regret.

Argentines, regardless of ethnic origin, enjoyed sports. Koebel indicated that the national passion at that time was football, a form of soccer. Baseball had dropped in popularity, because in their passion to have the best athletes, the Argentines imported Spanish professionals, who promptly fleeced the locals, returning to Spain with improved personal finances. A little polo was played, but horse racing was far more popular. Fine horses, in fact, were one of the nation's profitable exports.

The horse was an important part of life on the Argentine plains or *pampas*. Except for the railroad it was the most important means of transportation outside the city. The cowboys or gauchos evaluated people on their ability to ride and understand horses. Koebel told a number of amusing stories of Argentine horse dealers selling second rate horses to the British and American military buyers, who came hoping to get first rate animals at low prices. In each case, the astuteness of the Argentines sent the second string steeds to participate in the South African and North American military campaigns at high prices. The horse held a place of special affection for all Argentines. Many different breeds were seen, including the Clydesdale used in agriculture.

The agricultural potential for wealth had been discovered by the time Mr. Koebel wrote his book. The land nearest the urban centers had already been fenced and was producing large quantities of wheat and maize. The soil was so productive some Italian laborers were able to accumulate enough money to retire to Italy in their old age after leading a Spartan life in Argentina over a span of years.

The ranch managers were often North American or British. They were responsible for the agriculture, cattle and horse production on the estates. Koebel discovered a keen rivalry for the sale of agricultural implements. One English manager complained that the North Americans were winning the market. British machines, he explained, were superior to the American ones, but spare parts were almost impossible to get from Britain, while the owners of North American machinery had no spare parts problem.

Nature was the Argentine agriculturists' worst enemy. The Argentine soil was fertile and normally if a drought occurred the next crop made up the deficit. Spectacular storms sometimes raged across the plains doing damage to building and the stacks of alfalfa, if they were not properly built. The locust was the worst of the natural enemies. Wheat usually was free of total destruction because it was almost mature by the time the locust swarmed, but maize, a more profitable crop, was devastated because the ears were still immature and tender when the insect pests arrived for their feast.

The Europeans had introduced the rabbit to the plains and Koebel feared the destructive nature of the creature as a result of its rapid breeding potential. He claimed a party of eight shooters could bag no less than forty of the little rodents in one day's hunting. After reading this book I discovered a clever satirical novel based on the rabbit menace. *Los relatos porteños* ("Stories of Buenos Aires") satirized the growth of bureaucracy, using the lowly rabbit as the focal point of the novel.

Europeans had introduced also the grape vine in the region northwest of Buenos Aires, launching Argentina's wine industry. In the early state the quality of the local vintage was poor, and the market confined to the less affluent locals. Those who could afford to do so imported the best European wines regardless of cost. Koebel claimed that each year the wines improved in quality, and he expected them to equal the European wines quickly. A similar process occurred in Chile and more recently in California.

Campbell P. Ogilvie wrote of his experiences in Argentina in *Argentina From a British Point of View* in 1910, and he reinforced most of Mr. Koebel's earlier observations. The author was connected with the Santa Fe Land Co., Ltd, and his book was in the nature of a report to present and prospective investors. Ogilvie also discussed the significance of the railroads to Argentine life and how they could assist the investor.

The railroads began with a shipwrecked North American sailor, William

Wheelwright, who convinced English investors of the potential in Buenos Aires. In 1863, they built a sixteen mile section between Buenos Aires and the suburb of Quilmes. By 1909, Argentina had almost 16,000 miles of track to exploit the agricultural potential of the nation. The railroad had made it possible for Argentina to export more than she imported by 1909 by £19,000,000.

Free access to the land had been lost to the cowboys by 1890. Fences to separate cattle, horses and sheep from the wheat and maize had taken freedom of the range from them. Britain was the major buyer of Argentine agricultural products and Ogilvie was concerned that his country would lose its market to the United States. Given the nature of our protective tariff structure, which prevented Argentine agricultural products from freely entering the United States, he should not have been overly concerned.

New breeds of cattle had enabled Argentina to develop a dairy industry. Ogilvie claimed that in 1890 the country was importing tinned milk from Switzerland, but ten years later Buenos Aires was receiving an adequate supply of fresh milk and butter from local sources. Koebel earlier had claimed the dairy industry was a Basque monopoly. They produced milk, butter and cheese. Great Britain bought most of the butter exported, but all the cheese produced was consumed at home. Milking was done by hand, although there were experiments with milking machines. The milk was then processed into cheese by machines and eaten as fast as it could be made. The manufacturers were driven to keep pace with local demand.

Conclusions

One of the striking features in the travel books coming from Mexico and Argentina was the marked change in emphasis between 1850 and 1910. Those who visited prior to 1870 described an agrarian economy, where religion was still of paramount importance. As Gerhard Lenski in *Human Societies* explained, an agricultural world with its limited control over the environment claims to know and uses the supernatural to explain and overcome nature. It was natural for Mr. Carpenter and Doña Fanny to be so interested in religion. Robert Redfield in *The Primitive World and Its Transformation* discusses what he refers to as the "Little Tradition," making the point that in non-industrial civilizations, which is to say in a peasant society, religious matters not economics and technology are dominant cultural themes. Religion was important in industrial societies, but we must not lose sight of the fact that its influence varied from region to region in Latin America. Argentina experienced nothing like the Cristero Rebellion in Mexico where rural peasants revolted when the government attempted to suppress religious practices. A different degree of religious intensity was suggested between Mexico and Argentina. Mr. Carpenter experienced the rural areas, while Doña Fanny concentrated on the urban religious life. Colonel King's single encounter occurred in an isolated rural part of northern Argentina not in Buenos Aires. Variation in religious intensity was suggested by many of the writers. Herbert J. Muller in *The Uses of the Past* argued that urban centers, even in agrarian societies, tended to breed religious indifference or at least less intense religiosity.

English travelers in South America after 1870 came from industrialized or almost industrialized nations, and they were interested in economic development. More specifically, they were reacting to the second phase of the Industrial Revolution and devoted themselves to exploiting the economic opportunities in less industrial nations especially for the raw materials and food needed at home (e.g. Great Britain, the United States, France and Germany). Economic concern replaced religion as a focus of concern for the travelers. Also, the progress of religious toleration at home and in Latin America made the writers less critical of the local faith. In most instances the visitors socialized with members of the upper class, who were oriented to European culture, and that fact colored their narratives.

North American travelers in Mexico remarked how difficult and dangerous travel was, implying that conditions were different from those in the United States. Travel was difficult and dangerous in the United States as well. Stagecoaches were robbed in this country just as in Latin America. Beyond the railroads were poor secondary roads even in the industrialized nations, which were no better than their Latin American counterparts. Bandits, Indians and other dangers plagued North American travelers until the late nineteenth century. While reading travel adventures, it is important to consider reality. An individual, who has lived for a few days or weeks or even twenty years does not comprehend the totality of the culture, but those with more lengthy stays and closer cultural contacts tend to be more accurate. Some of the writers judged the Latin American by their own cultural yardsticks. In contact with the elites of Mexico or Argentina they were on familiar cultural ground, but, when meeting with the rest of the population, they were in a cultural matrix with which they were not familiar.

WORKS CITED

Ballou, Maturin. *Aztec Land.* Boston: Houghton, Mifflin & Co., 1890.

de la Barca, Fanny Calderon. *Life in Mexico: The letters of Fanny Calderon de la Barca.* n. d.

Blake, Mary E. and Margaret F. Sullivan. *Mexico: Picturesque, Political, Progressive.* Boston: Lee & Shepard, 1988.

Carpenter, William W. *Travels and Adventures in Mexico: In the Course of Journeys Upward of 2500 Miles Performed on Foot.* New York: Harper & Bros., 1851.

Clark, Edwin W. *A visit to South America: With Notes and Observations on the Physical Features of the Country, and Incidents of the Voyage.* London: Dean and Son, 1878.

King, John A. *Twenty-four Years in the Argentine Republic.* London: Longman, Brown, Green and Longmans, 1846.

Koebel, W. H. *Modern Argentina: The el Dorado of Today.* London: F. Griffiths, 1907.

Lenski, Gerhart. *Human Societies: A Macrolevel Introduction to Sociology.* New York: McGraw-Hill, Inc., 1970. [Although other editions of this book have been forthcoming, I believe the first edition is far stronger than the others.]

Muller, Herbert J. *The Uses of the Past: Profiles of Former Societies.* New York: The New American Library, 1952.

Ogilvie, Campbell P. *Argentina From a British Point of View.* London: Wertheimer, Lea & Co., 1910.

Redfield, Robert. *The Primitive World and Its Transformation.* Ithaca: Cornell UP, 1953.

REYNALDO RUIZ

The *Corrido* as a Medium for Cultural Identification

The Mexican and Chicano (Mexican American) *corrido* ("popular ballad") has been a popular vehicle through which the two groups have expressed many of their sentiments. The origin and evolution of the *corrido*, has been traced back to early oral tradition in the Iberian Peninsula. Today, six hundred years later, the *corrido*, as composed and sung by Chicanos and Mexicans, essentially has retained the same basic characteristics as the earlier manifestations of the romance of the thirteenth century. It is a lyric narrative through which *el pueblo* ("the common folk") has expressed its sentiments and points of view regarding its social reality. Dickey writes that the *corrido* in the Southwest "in its most usual form is defined as a ballad of octosyllabic quatrains, narrating a story, and sung to a simple tune in ternary rhythm whether it be 3/4 or 1 6/8 meter" (7). The *corrido*, by its very nature (which is the oral tradition) lends itself to the creativity of the common folk. It, therefore, will manifest itself with variants in structure, content, and function. Some *corridos* are narrative in nature and yet, others are not. Others will be epic-like, and others will deal with more mundane incidents or circumstances encountered and experienced by the people. There are *corridos* that document historical events; natural disasters such as earthquakes, and floods; accidents such as shootings and train derailments; deaths of local and national leaders such as Gregorio Cortés, Tiburcio Vásquez, Elfego Baca, Pancho Villa, John F. Kennedy, etc.; ethical and moral questions such as family and father and son relationships; respect and discipline in the family; *corridos* in praise of a town, region, state; *corridos* of social protest, and of miscellaneous interest. Although there are several views regarding the simplicity and complexity of the *corrido*, it is imperative that the *corrido* be taken for what it is — an expression of the community. The well known Mexican composer Carlos Chávez considers "the *corrido* a low, 'primitive' musical form. The many four-line versus are all sung with the same monotonous melody, accompanied by tonic-dominant cords on the guitar" (Af Keijerstam 55). On the other hand, there are others who do not share

Chávez's view. Regardless of the differences in assessing the value and the extent of the contribution of the *corridos*, it must be clearly understood and accepted that these folk manifestations are an expression of the common people who have something to state and contribute. The *corridos* propagate a message. And the message serves a function in the community. It is within this restricted function that the *corrido* becomes a medium through which many needs, deeds, incidents, values, desires, aspirations, and concerns are going to be not only communicated, but also used as primary sources for developing cultural identity at the personal, local, and national level.

The *corrido*, then, due to its intrinsic and extrinsic characteristics, and its function, becomes a most effective vehicle for developing cultural identification in its listeners. The second part of this essay will attempt to show how the *corrido* serves this purpose. The primary elements that make the *corrido* an excellent medium for cultural identification and transmission are its highly elaborated structure and its content.

The Structure of the *Corrido*

Merle Simmons in his book states that:

> The *corrido* is an integral part of Mexican life. Of, by, and for the *pueblo;* it is one of the most typical expressions of the Mexican masses. But what is the nature of the *corrido*? What are its characteristics? It all but defies precise description.
>
> It may be a simple narrative ballad which relates an event of interest to only a small region; it may be a song with a love theme and lyric overtones, although these are characteristically subordinated to the narrative element as the minstrel sings of his amorous adventures; or it may become a narrative with strong epic flavor if the singer chooses to report an incident which concerns some heroic figure, be he bandit, general, or president. (7)

Although Simmons only refers to the Mexican community, it is safe to state that the *corrido* for many Chicanos in the United States, be it along the border, Colorado, Nevada, Northern California, New Mexico, Michigan, Illinois, Ohio, etc., essentially holds the same function and serves as a means to strengthen group and cultural identification. Furthermore, a strong case could be made that the *corrido* exerts a greater and more significant role as a medium for cultural identification among Chicanos, who have for the most part, lived in a country that is highly insensitive to Chicano issues, concerns and culture.

The popular views expressed in the *corridos* are encapsulated into a standard formula which contains a fairly well elaborated format. Although there will be variants in the structure, most *corridos* will have a least five components. According to Vicente T. Mendoza, the *corrido* will have the following basic elements (17):

1. An opening by the singer in which an attempt is made to engage the audience in the narrative. The information that is given in the first strophe usually deals with the date of the incident:

> El veintidós de noviembre
> del año sesenta y tres.
> (Dickey, "Corrido de Adiós Señor Presidente"
> by C. García: 77)[1]

In the second strophe there is an attempt by the singer to ask for the audience's indulgence:

> Señores, con el permiso,
> prestándome su atención,
> voy a cantar el corrido
> de la tal Revolución.
> (Mendoza; "Corrido De Agripina" 120)[2]

2. The place, date, and name of the principal character:

> Año de mil ochocientos
> ochenta y dos al contado,
> en el Real de Piedras Largas
> falleció Juan Alvarado.
> (Mendoza, "Corrido de Juan Alvarado" 235)[3]

3. The circumstances of the event or episodes:

> Los Piñeda con los Nava
> siempre han sido enemigos,
> han llevado sus cuestiones
> por causa de los partidos.
> (Mendoza, "Corrido de Los Piñeda y Los Nava" 139)[4]

4. The message and/or lesson to be learned:

> Vuela, vuela, palomita
> párate en aquella higuera;

---

[1]On the twenty second of November / in the year seventy three.

[2]Gentlemen, with your permission, / by giving me your attention, / I am going to sing a ballad / of the Revolution.

[3]In the year eighteen hundred / and eighty two, / in the town of Piedras Largas / Juan Alvarado died.

[4]The Piñedas and the Navas / have always been enemies, / they have always had differences / because of their parties.

que consejos de una madre
debe atenderlos cualquiera.
(Mendoza, "Corrido de Reyes Ruiz" 263)[5]

5. Farewell of the singer and at times from the character:

Antes de subir al cerro
Valentín quiso llorar
— ¡Madre mía de Guadalupe,
por tu religión me van a matar!

Vuela, vuela, palomita;
párate en aquel fortín
estas son las mañanitas
de un hombre valiente que fue Valentín.
(Mendoza, "Corrido de Valentín de la Sierra" 199)[6]

Content and Function of the *Corrido*

To attempt to present an historical and logical rationale for the existence of the *corrido* would not be appropriate for this essay. Nevertheless, certain premises should be established to ensure that the intent, use, and role of the *corrido* is kept in focus. *Corridos* have always had a communal function. Although the initial inspiration and impetus emanates from a personal view, its immediate concern is to express imaginatively the people's reactions to their circumstances and experiences. In expressing a response to the reality at hand, the *corrido* provides not only a personal interpretation and perception of reality, but also an emotional response, which indicates the degree of sensitivity to the incident or circumstances. The uniqueness of the *corrido* does not rest with the intrinsic characteristics of the form, but with the collective acceptance of the spirit and emotion transmitted. The truer the *corrido* reflects the sentiments and emotion of the people, the more impact and acceptance it will have. The content, then, is multifaceted in that *corridos* will respond to the social realities that cause deep emotional concern on the citizenry. As Castañeda states, the *corrido*:

> entrega la nota informativa popular, es un estupendo noticiero, que cuenta con la colaboración de un ejército de poetas anónimos que llevan versificados, los relatos de los asuntos públicos. (13)[7]

---

[5]Fly, fly little dove / stop on that prickly pear / advice from a mother / should be understood by everyone.

[6]Before reaching the peak / Valentín wanted to cry / Oh Virgin of Guadalupe / I have faith in you and I am going to die. // Fly, fly, little dove / stop at that fort / these are the verses / of a man named Valentín.

[7]The corrido delivers an informed popular message; it is an excellent newscast, that narrates in verse form, with the collaboration of an army of anonymous poets, the concerns of the public.

In short, as has been stated elsewhere, the *corrido* deals with a wide spectrum of themes, topics, values, points of view, and emotions.

In studying the *corrido*, one must consider the recurring polemic regarding form and content in the arts. Inextricably, the form and content of the *corrido* come into play with the function. This combination results in a unique verse and music structure that is accepted by the community. The *corrido*, then, is multi-functional. The primary intent of most *corridos* is to document, and narrate experiences of incidents and episodes that have stirred the emotions of the community. The intent will also vary from *corrido* to *corrido*. In general, there are over twenty types of *corridos*. Vicente T. Mendoza, in his *Lírica narrativa de México: el corrido*, documents twenty-two types of *corridos*. Among the most popular are those that deal with historical events, the agrarian movement in Mexico, political actions, assassinations, bravery, bandits, prisoners, rapes, rivalries, fatal accidents, personal tragedies, natural disasters, famous horses, famous people, bullfighters, etc. Within this broad array of *corridos* lies our point of departure: *Corridos* have been and are a medium for cultural identification among the listeners. *Corridos* contain a variety of information with which *el pueblo* identifies. Again, the intent and content will serve as a medium for cultural identification. Below are five ways in which cultural identification takes place.

1. *For Local, State and National Identification.*

The easiest type of *corrido* in this category is one that for the most part is used to praise a city. The *corrido* below refers to San Diego de la Unión in Guanajuato. The first stanza immediately tells the listener of the beauty of the town which, of course, is compared to a beautiful and sincere woman:

> ¡Qué rechulo es mi San Diego, mi San Diego de la Unión!
> Donde hay mujeres muy lindas que se entregan con amor,
> con amor, con amor.
>
> (Mendoza 362)[8]

In the second stanza, the singer proceeds to praise the workers who not only work for the improvement of the town but also for the benefit of the nation:

> Sus labradores trabajan con empeño y fervor para servir
> a San Diego y también a la Nación, a la Nación, a la Nación.
>
> (Mendoza 362)[9]

---

[8]Oh, how beautiful is my San Diego, my San Diego of the Union. / Where there are many beautiful women that give of themselves to love, / to love, to love.

[9]Its laborers work with interest and passion to serve / San Diego and also the Nation, the

Cuernavaca, a city in southern Mexico, is described by presenting its most cherished characteristics: landscapes, mountains, bougainvilleas, eternal spring-like weather, and imposing cathedral:

> Desde las altas montañas Cuernavaca luce ufana
> sus moradas bugambilias, y a su hermoso panorama.

The singer goes on to underline his sentiments and his love for the city:

> Patria chica de este bardo que te escribe esta ovación,
> Te llevo siempre grabada dentro de mi corazón.
> (Mendoza 364-65)[10]

The *corridos* that sing about the qualities of cities also elaborate on the characteristics of its brave men, beautiful women, products, rivers, and cathedrals. As a result, any listener hearing these positive attributes will naturally identify with the city and feel proud. The idea of being from the particular village, town, or city, will automatically raise pride in its residents and a bond will be established.

2. *A Call to Support a Political or Social Cause.*

It is no secret that the Revolution in Mexico caused an impact at all levels of the social order. John A. Crow in his *Panorama de las Américas* writes: "México explotó como un volcán y las masas rurales, con grito 'Tierra y Libertad' destrozaron las grandes haciendas y ocuparon sus tierras" (Crow 77).[11]

The attempt by the *pueblo* to seek political reform was based on philosophical and ideological principles of democracy, freedom, individual rights, religion, and other values. The numerous revolutionary leaders — Madero, Zapata, Alvaro Obregón, Carranza, Villa, etc. — embodied the political and philosophical views of many factions that, for the most part, were propagators of a point of view. The *pueblo* aligned itself with the most compatible political groups and accepted the ideology and supported its leader. The different factions effectively used the *corrido* to document their ideology and values, instill pride, and develop a sense of identification with a political group. For example, "De las esperanzas de la patria por la rendición de Villa" contains the aspirations and desires of Obregón's followers :

Nation, the Nation.

[10]From its high mountains Cuernavaca shows proudly / its purple bougainvilleas, and its beautiful landscape. / My beloved country from this bard who writes this ovation. / You will always be with me in my heart.

[11]Mexico erupted like a volcano, and the rural masses with their cry of 'Land and Liberty' destroyed the big *haciendas* (ranches) and occupied the land.

El pueblo y la fuerza armada son de la misma opinión,
quieren que suba a la silla el general Obregón.
(Mendoza 102)[12]

The qualities, characteristics and values that Obregón exemplifies are:

Y es quien dará bienestar al pueblo, que no es tan necio
(Mendoza 102)[13]

It is the hope of the *pueblo* that the country achieves a high degree of integrity:

A la honradez y energía junta también la prudencia,
es lo que México quiere y espera con impaciencia.
(Mendoza 103)[14]

A close analysis of social and revolutionary *corridos* will reveal the ideals, values, aspirations, and political views of the different factions. Nonetheless, this folk expression provides a mechanism which the followers will use to synthesize, identify, and demonstrate their personal, regional, and national concern. As a result, the followers, and to some extent, the listeners will identify with the ideology and cultural values. Two other major social actions that caused much political turmoil in Mexico were the Cristero and Agrarian movements. These two, as revolutionary movements, produced a good number of *corridos* that presented their ideology and point of view.

3. *Focus on a Social Issue which Requires Attention.*

A common topic for many Mexicans is the idea of having to emigrate to the United States. There are numerous *corridos* that detail the hardships, adversities, injustices and discrimination that the people experience. Generally there are two types of *corridos* in this category — those that admonish the prospective emigrant and those that detail the adversities encountered in the United States. Maciel's essay, "Visions of the Other Mexico," presents a popular *corrido* that reflects not only the attitudes of the Mexicans vis à vis the United States but also attempts to instill pride in being a loyal and patriotic Mexican:

No vayas al gringo
no traspases la frontera
buscando el honrado pan,
que si trabajo te dan,

[12]The citizens and its armed citizens are in agreement / that General Obregón assume the presidency.

[13]He is the one to provide for the country's well being, since he is no fool.

[14]Honesty and vigor together with prudence, / is what Mexico wants and waits with impatience.

te aventarán un centavo,
te golpearán como esclavo
y a tu patria humillarán.
México tiene a montones
todo lo que has menester,
y trabajo para hacer
felices a las naciones.
Deja a los gringos Nerones
que te engañan y te halagan
labora, y si mal te pagan
aunque en razón les repliques.

(Maciel 71)[15]

In another popular *corrido* that deals with a group of musicians planning a trip to California, the singer assures everyone that his performance in the United States will underline Mexico's beauty and riches:

Yo se los digo y es la verdad,
que México es muy hermoso y es tierra de libertad.

(Mendoza 396)[16]

The *corrido* ends by reassuring the group that if it encounters adversity and bad luck, it should return and appreciate a free country:

Si lejos de nuestra tierra, la suerte, los trata mal.
¡Vénganse, pues camaradas a México a trabajar!

¡No sufran, más, jalen pa' allá!
Pa' que sepan lo que vale tener Patria y Libertad.

(Mendoza 396) [17]

A very popular *corrido* that details the misfortunes of the Mexican and Chicano while in the United States is the "*Lavaplatos*" ("Dishwasher"). It deals with a Mexican who deceives himself into thinking that once he is in the United States he will experience instant economic and social success in the land of plenty. To his disillusion and dismay, things do not work out as nicely as he anticipated. He first states that during his youth he dreamed of becoming a movie star:

Soñé yo en mi juventud ser una estrella de cine

---

[15]Don't go to the *gringo* / don't cross the border / looking for a living / if you get a job / they'll pay you a penny / and treat you like a slave / and insult your country. / Mexico has in abundance / everything you need, / and lots of work to do / to make the country happy. / Let the cruel *gringos* / deceive and flatter you / work, and get paid poorly, / even though you object / with reason.

[16]I will tell them and it is the truth, / that Mexico is beautiful and a land of liberty. (Del viaje de la típica de policía a California.)

[17]If far from your country, you encounter bad luck / Friends, come back to Mexico to work! / Don't suffer anymore, go over there / So that you can know what it is to have a country and liberty.

y un día de tantos me vine a visitar a Jolibud.
(Mendoza 376)[18]

After crossing the border without being detected he is invited to work on the railroad:

Al llegar a la Estación me tropecé con un cuate
y me hizo la invitación de trabajar en "El Traque."
(Mendoza 376)[19]

And after getting tired of working on the tracks, he goes on to work in the fields, which turns out to be a worse job:

Cuando me enfadé "Del Traque" me volvió a invitar aquel
a la pizca del tomate y a desahijar betabel.
(Mendoza 376)[20]

Working in the fields is extremely hard work which few can endure for a long period of time. He goes on to describe it in the following manner:

Allí gané indulgencias caminando de rodillas,
haciéndoles reverencias tres, o cuatro y cinco millas
O, que trabajo tan mal pagado
por andar arrodillado.
(Mendoza 377)[21]

The *corrido* goes on to elaborate on the other jobs that the immigrant had. Eventually he ended up being a lowly dishwasher. Although this *corrido* is very funny, it presents reality as experienced by many immigrants. The poor worker thinks that once in the States, life will be easier, and prosperity will be just around the corner.

4. *Articulation of Conflicts and Adversities Experienced by Mexicans and Chicanos in the United States.*

There are many *corridos* written and sung by Chicanos that not only describe the injustices, antipathy, and ill-feelings towards the Mexican and Chicano, but, also attempt to arouse an emotional spark in the listener by pointing out the feeling of "We the Chicanos and Mexicans" vis-á-vis the White Middle Class. The following ballad by Joaquín Murrieta presents some injustices suffered at the hands of Anglo-Americans:

---

[18]I dreamed in my youth of becoming a movie star / and one day I came to visit Hollywood.

[19]Upon reaching the station I ran into a friend / who invited me to work on the railroad.

[20]When I got tired of the railroads, my friend invited me / to work the fields picking tomatoes and beets.

[21]In the fields I earned indulgences walking on my knees, / showing reverence for three, or four and five miles. / Oh, what a poor paying job / for being on your knees.

Cuando apenas era niño
huérfano a mí me dejaron
Nadie me hizo un cariño
y a mi hermano lo mataron
y a mi esposa Carmelia
cobardes la asesinaron.
(Joaquín Murrieta; Author's private collection
of recordings; hereafter PCR)[22]

Another popular *corrido* that was written in the 1970s, during a protest of the Vietnam War by Chicanos, describes a Chicano journalist who was killed by the police:

El 29 de agosto
fecha tan particular
la policia asesinó
a Don Rubén Salazar.
("Corrido de Don Rubén Salazar" PCR)[23]

The emigrant and Chicano are the victims of insensitive people and an impersonal system. They are also at the mercy of agribusiness and other employers:

Porque los americanos
no nos tienen compasión
a hombres, niños y mujeres
los llevan a la prisión.
(Los Emigrantes PCR)[24]

5. *Transmission of Values such as Honesty, Sincerity, Loyalty, Family Relationships, Disobedience, etc.*

There are many *corridos* in this category that play upon some tragic or fatalistic event. The intent of this type of *corrido* is not to present the misfortune of someone, but to concretize values that transcend the personal level. "Rosita Alvírez" is a very popular *corrido* that offers a lesson regarding several values. It deals with a young daughter who insists on going out to the dance in spite of her mother's request to stay home. Inevitably, Rosita goes to the dance and refuses to dance with Hipólito who becomes incensed and shoots her because she had rejected and shamed him:

Rosita, no me desaires, la gente lo va a notar.
A mí no me importa nada, contigo no he de bailar.

---

[22]When I was just a boy / I was left an orphan / No one ever caressed me / and my brother was killed / and my wife Carmelia / was also assassinated by cowards.

[23]On the 29 of August / on this special day / the police assassinated / Mr. Ruben Salazar.

[24]Because the Americans / don't have any compassion / men, children and women / are taken to prison.

Echó mano a la cintura y una pistola sacó
Y a la pobre de Rosita no más tres tiros le dio.
(PCR)[25]

The *corrido* ends by presenting many other problems, other than those of disobedience — for example, the idea of being subservient to a man, the idea of ridiculing a man in public, the notion of risking your life, the idea of confessing your sins, and the idea of being punished for not using common sense:

Su mamá se lo decía: Por andar de pizpireta
Se te ha de llegar el día en que toca la fiesta.
Rosita le dice a Irene: No te olvides de mi nombre,
Cuando vayas a los bailes no desaires a los hombres.
Rosita está en el cielo dándole cuenta al Criador,
Hipólito esta en la cárcel dando su declaración.
(Mendoza 308)[26]

Other *corridos* in this category deal with incidents that attempt to show the tragic ending of people who do not abide by and follow the value system of the culture. For example, disobedience, dishonesty, sincerity, cruelty, illicit love affairs, and other cultural values are presented in the *corridos* to show that transgressions against these traditional values will be punished by God or will have some tragic repercussion on the transgressor. In short, the intent of this type of *corrido* is to show that people must lead a life that conforms to the norms of the community.

Although the *corrido* continues to be a popular expression of the Chicano and Mexican communities, it has not flourished and dominated the music business. The *corrido* in many ways serves as a gauge for measuring the social consciousness of its people. Often, when the community is faced with adversities, pressing social ills, and conflict, a new *corrido* surfaces. In this regard the *corrido* is a vehicle to elicit and arouse favorable sentiments regarding an incident or situation. As these sentiments are carried throughout the community, the populace hears, assesses, sympathizes, judges, and integrates them. Neatly encapsulated in the *corrido* is a personal and communal view of reality. The content might deal with values, ideology, pride, social injustices, discrimination, abuse, and death. In ad-

---

[25]Rosita don't reject me, the people will notice. / I don't care, one bit, I won't dance with you. / He went for his gun and pulled it out / and shot poor Rosita three times.

[26]Her mother advised her: being daring and willing / will eventually catch up to you. / Rosita told Irene: Don't forget my name / When you go to dances don't reject or shame men. / Rosita is now in heaven, confessing to God / Hipolito is now in jail making his statement.

dition the content can also include praise of leaders, cities, heroes, or causes. The *corrido* leads to the identification with a value system and an acceptance of oneself as a member who is caught in the underpinnings of the culture. Because of these reasons the *corrido* is most effective as a medium for cultural identification and transmission.

WORKS CITED

Af Keijerstam, Claes. *Popular Music in Mexico.* Albuquerque: U of New Mexico P, 1976.

Castañeda, Daniel. *El corrido mexicano.* México: Editorial Surco, 1943.

Crow, John A. and G. D. Crow. *Panorama de las Américas.* New York: Holt, Rinehart and Winston, 1985.

Dickey, Dan William. *The Kennedy "Corridos": A Study of the Ballads of a Mexican American Hero.* Austin: Center for Mexican American Studies, 1978.

Maciel, David R. "Visions of the Other Mexico." *Chicano Cinema.* Binghamton: Bilingual Review P, 1985.

Mendoza, Vicente T. *Lírica narrativa de México: el corrido.* México: UNAM, 1964.

Simmons, Merle E. *The Mexican "Corrido" as a Source for Interpretive Study of Modern Mexico (1870-1950).* Bloomington: Indiana UP, 1957.

DAVID M. JORDAN

Regionalism, Nationalism, and Modernism: José Lins do Rêgo's *Fogo Morto*

In post-colonial countries of the Americas, regionalist literature has always been linked to cultural identity. In the late eighteenth and early nineteenth centuries, regionalism was seen as a means of severing dependance on Old World culture; romantic poets turned to local settings as symbolic representations of New World purity. Throughout the nineteenth century, authors saw regionalism as a necessary step in the evolution of distinct New World cultures; realist authors catalogued local details in the belief that only through detailed knowledge of its parts could a country attain an autonomous national identity. As traditional notions of cultural unity came under question in the early twentieth century, distinct regional cultures were no longer seen as parts of a larger whole, but instead regionalist authors promoted autonomous local identity as an end in itself.

Brazil has a rich history of regionalist literature, and the Northeast figures prominently in Brazilian regionalism. The distinct folk culture that arose in the arid backlands of the Northeast provided material for nineteenth-century authors, most of whom portrayed Northeasterners as ignorant backlanders. Such early-nineteenth-century romantic authors as José de Alencar portrayed Northeasterners as simple folk linked to nature by their ignorance of corrupt civilization. Later in the nineteenth century, such realist and naturalist authors as Franklin Távora and Euclides da Cunha portrayed Northeasterners as a missing link in Brazil's social evolution by describing Northeasterners as rustics who would add a distinct Brazilian flavor to the national culture once their crude natures were tempered by civilization's influence.[1]

---

[1] José de Alencar wrote a series of Northeastern novels including *O Tronco do Ipê* (1871), *Sonhos d'Ouro* (1872), *Til* (1872), and *O Sertanejo* (1875). Távora's best-known Northeastern novel is *O Cabeleira* (1876). Euclides da Cunha rewrote his journalistic coverage of the Canudos uprising as *Os Sertões* (1902; translated into English as *Rebellion in the Backlands*), which the author describes as an anthropological study of "significant present-day characteristics of the subraces to be found in the backlands of Brazil" (*Rebellion* xxxi).

Northeasterners themselves had very little say in the subservient role imposed upon them by southern urbanites seeking a unified national identity, and toward the turn of the century a simmering confrontation pitted local advocates of regional autonomy against external advocates of national unity. The cultural conflict spilled over into a political confrontation, and in 1896 erupted in an armed conflict when federal troops were sent to the Northeast to disband a colony of religious fanatics led by an itinerant backwoods mystic. Resenting the intrusion of national troops on their native soil, inhabitants of the religious colony at Canudos rallied local support and the conflict soon came to be seen as a battle to preserve regional autonomy in the face of oppressive national forces. The rebellion was not quelled until two years later, after more than five thousand federal troops had been sent to the region, over a thousand of whom had been killed.

Tension between Northeasterners and political authorities in the South was exacerbated following World War I, when the South prospered due to soaring coffee prices and rapid industrialization, while the Northeast sank into increasing poverty due to the collapse of the plantation system upon which its economy was based. Northeasterners blamed the South for their poverty: the collapse of the plantation system had begun with the abolition of slavery in 1888 (by decree from the emperor), and continued unchecked in the twentieth century as the federal government promoted industrial development in the South while ignoring the Northeast.

The rivalry between Northeasterners and Southern urbanites expanded from politics to aesthetics when in 1922 a group of São Paulo artists introduced European modernism to Brazil with a series of expositions that has since come to be known as the Week of Modern Art. São Paulo artists shocked their audiences with samples of cubist painting, expressionist dance, and futurist poetry. These artists claimed that by infusing Brazilian themes with art forms borrowed from the European avant-garde, they would establish Brazil's place in the international art community. The Week of Modern Art focused national attention on these southern artists, and their international perspective overshadowed regionalism in the Northeast and elsewhere.

A group of Northeast writers, galvanized under the influence of the sociologist Gilberto Freyre, protested that São Paulo modernism was nothing more than an eclectic grab bag of Brazilian themes, defaced by abstract aesthetic values borrowed from Europe, and that the São Paulo artists did nothing to promote a distinct Brazilian cultural identity. With the aim of promoting a genuine Brazilian culture, Gilberto Freyre organized the First Brazilian Conference on Regionalism (*Primeiro Congreso Brasileiro de Regionalismo*) in 1926, held in the Northeastern city of Recife. This conference, devoted to the preservation of distinct Northeastern customs, language, and folklore, spawned a regionalist movement that influenced some of Brazil's best known twentieth-century authors, including Jorge Amado, Rachel Queiroz, Graciliano Ramos, and José Lins do Rêgo.

Among these authors, José Lins do Rêgo was Freyre's most devoted follower. Prompted by Freyre, Lins do Rêgo inaugurated his literary career by publishing three realistic novels chronicling plantation life in the Northeast. Following another series of novels devoted to regional themes such as mysticism and banditry, in 1943 Lins do Rêgo returned to the plantation theme with his novel *Fogo Morto*.[2] The Santa Fe plantation on which *Fogo Morto* is set is a self-contained agrarian patriarchy of the kind described by Freyre in such sociological studies as *Casa-Grande e Senezala* ("*The Big House and the Shack*") and *Sobrados e Mucambos* ("*Mansions and Shanties*"). The Santa Fe of Lins do Rêgo's novel was founded by Captain Tomás, a fiercely independent pioneer, and was handed down to Luís de Holanda (nicknamed Lula by local residents), who became the sole male descendant by marrying Tomás's daughter.

Typically, the founding fathers of such plantations faced formidable challenges: the region's periodic droughts and barren soil demanded a tenacious resilience in the face of adversity. The values embodied by these settlers — their resilience, and an accompanying sense of individualism — are prized by Northeasterners and are revered to the present day in the region's folklore. The demise of the Northeast's plantation society in the early twentieth century stems from a conflict between these traditional regional values and threatening external forces of modernization. In *Fogo Morto*, this clash is played out in two central confrontations, one political and the other sociological.

The novel's political conflict stems from a local election pitting Rêgo Barros, a native Northeasterner and supporter of the traditional agrarian society, against José Paulino. Paulino advocates dismantling the small, independent plantations to

[2]The "dead fire" of the novel's title refers to the extinguished furnace of the plantation's sugar-cane refinery, symbolically the heart of the typical Northeastern plantation.

form one modern, efficiently run conglomerate. *Fogo Morto* portrays this political conflict through a single character, Captain Vitorino, who supports Rêgo Barros and wages a quixotic battle against the massive political machinery of Paulino and his backers from the South. Vitorino takes his political battle to the streets of Pilar, the neighboring town, where he is ridiculed by townspeople and beaten up by a gang of thugs hired by Paulino.

Fogo Morto portrays the sociological consequences of the conflict between tradition and modernization by focusing on the plight of José Amaro, a Santa Fe tenant who is evicted by Lula de Holanda, the owner of the "big house" at the center of the plantation. Lula typifies a phenomenon described by Freyre in *Sobrados e Mucambos*: an outsider marries into land ownership and aspires to the accompanying luxuries, but lacks the resilience and dedication necessary to sustain a plantation. Lula surrounds himself with luxuries absurdly incongruous with the local environment — most notably, a grand piano for his daughters and an ostentatious carriage for himself — and sits by idly while his Santa Fe plantation falls to ruin. As the victim of Lula's decadence, Amaro typifies traditional Northeast values: he admires the individualism and determination of Captain Vitorino, and dreams of taking revenge on Lula by aiding Silvino, leader of a local band of outlaws. (The *cangaceiro*, a kind of roving bandit, is a traditional Northeastern folk hero, embodying such Northeastern values as individualism, resilience, and disrespect for social convention.) Amaro's dream is realized when Silvino and his gang plunder the mansion; however the bandits only flee, leaving the mansion in ruin and offering no salvation for Amaro.

Stylistically, *Fogo Morto* is more than a realistic illustration of Freyre's sociological treatises. Rather than mimic the sociologist's authoritative perspective through the traditional device of an omniscient narrator, Lins do Rêgo employs innovative modernist poetics to portray the collapse of the plantation from within. Through a cyclical plot structure, and exaggerated internal focalization, *Fogo Morto* portrays the claustrophobic effect of encroaching external forces that threaten both the cultural identity of the region and the individual identities of its inhabitants. The novel is divided into three seemingly independent sections: Sections One and Three describe events covering approximately one month in 1911, and Section Two goes back a generation to describe the founding of the plantation by Captain Tomás. By focalizing the narration of the first section entirely through

José Amaro, a character whose paranoid delusions border on psychosis, Lins do Rêgo creates a surreal fictional world distinctly at odds with the well ordered universe of his earlier realistic fiction. The repeated narration of events in 1911 (the death of the plantation fire is narrated twice, once at the end of Section Two, and again at the novel's conclusion) has led to criticism that the novel is haphazard and uncohesive; one critic, for example, describes *Fogo Morto* as a collection of "three successive sections that do not really complete or unify one another" (Martins, lx).

Fogo Morto's first section (approximately one-third of the novel) portrays a claustrophobic world defined by the severely limited perception of José Amaro. The novel opens with Amaro in his leather shop; before him is a window overlooking the street, through which he is conversing with Laurentino, and behind him, in the dark recesses of his house's interior, are Amaro's wife and daughter. Throughout Section One, the walls of Amaro's room define a strictly circumscribed fictional world: Amaro's wife and daughter remain for the most part an indistinct murmur in the background; the neighboring land is described only as Amaro perceives it through his window or in the obscure light of his nocturnal wanderings; and the world beyond the Santa Fe plantation is only vaguely sketched in through second-hand accounts related to José Amaro by passing travelers.

The few passages that describe the natural environment beyond the walls of Amaro's house in the first section only serve to emphasize conflict between the character's internal world and the threatening world outside. We repeatedly get glimpses of sunlight, flowers and songbirds as perceived through Amaro's window or doorway, but these glimpses are immediately contrasted with the dark, tormented world of Amaro's interior world. A typical description begins with what would appear to be the voice of a traditional omniscient narrator, who explains that "outside it was a beautiful May afternoon" (16).[3] After a brief description of some local flora, Amaro's wife passes in front of Amaro's window, and it becomes clear that the description is focalized from within the leather shop. The narration turns inward to describe Amaro's thoughts; we are told that "he could not hide his hatred for her" (16), and he vents his frustration by pounding furi-

[3]All translations in this essay are my own.

ously on the leather before him. Similarly, references to a songbird outside Amaro's shack only serve to heighten his inner torment. Following an idyllic description of a bird singing in the sunshine, for example, the narration switches abruptly to the contrasting fury of Amaro's own heartbeat, which "pounded with the violence of a burst dam" (47).

Alienated from the world around him, Amaro retreats to a mythical world defined by local folklore. In Amaro's imagination, Silvino, the leader of the *cangaceiros*, takes on the stature of a local folk hero, and becomes the "saviour" who would deliver Amaro from this "world of perdition" (49). At one point Amaro himself is even compared to the wandering saint of the Northeast backlands, a popular figure in Northeast folklore (106). However, Amaro's dreams are not realized; when he finally gets up the courage to leave his hut under cover of darkness and attempts to join Silvino's men, he is overcome by an epileptic fit, and has to be carried back to his shack. The *cangaceiros* finally do come to Amaro's aid by over-running the plantation house, but by then it is not only too late to save the plantation, but the nomadic *cangaceiros* cannot offer any viable alternative to Lula's despotic rule: they plunder the mansion and leave it in a shambles before deserting the region.

Section One establishes a conflict between the personal, interior world of a character, and the exterior world of his environment, as well as a conflict between traditional regional values and a contradictory modern world. Amaro is alienated from those around him; his wife fears him, his daughter is insane, and his neighbors believe he is a werewolf. Condemned to a solitary subsistence as the plantation saddle-maker, Amaro loses even that consolation when Lula evicts him from the plantation. As the only world he knows collapses around him, Amaro seeks refuge in a plot borrowed from local folklore, but there he finds no relief from the encroaching forces that threaten his world.

At the opening of Section Two the narrative focus "zooms out" to tell the history of Santa Fe from a distance, with the significant dates and names provided in the impersonal voice of an external observer. The focalization varies throughout the rest of the novel, from external to multiple internal focalizations, but the isolation that separates individuals from the world around them that was established in Section One remains constant. Husbands are ostracized from family and community (Lula, Vitorino, and Tomás), and wives are alienated from cruel husbands and insane daughters (Amélia, Adriana, Mariquina). The internally focalized narrations are fragmentary, but the effect in each instance is the same as that of the continuous internal focalization of Section One: brief passages focalized through each of these characters create fictional worlds in conflict with the exterior world. While Amaro represents the sociological consequences of a cultural conflict between regional tradition and the modern world — individual alienation, the dissolution of traditional family values — Vitorino illustrates the broader political consequences of the same conflict. Vitorino is alienated from the community by the taunting of local boys with their cries of "Papa Rabo"[4] much the same way as Amaro is driven inside by cries of "werewolf," but Vitorino's response is the opposite of José Amaro's: rather than seclude himself inside his house, he turns outward and takes his battle against the encroaching forces of the outside world to the streets. Vitorino's courageous fight against overwhelming odds typifies the individualism glorified in Northeast folklore. His ultimate defeat, however, suggests that the pride and determination of the community's founders belong to a bygone era, that they are no match for the political and economic forces of the modern world.

Fogo Morto incorporates all the regional themes that had become institutionalized by previous generations of Northeast literature, including bandits, mysticism, drought, and the heroic resilience of the backlanders. But by portraying the world of his novel from the perceptions of the region's native inhabitants, Lins do Rêgo offers an alternative to the romantic glorification of the region that had been established by observers from the outside, from Alencar's romantic primitivism and Tavora's realism to Euclides da Cunha's journalistic chronicle of the Canudos uprising. *Fogo Morto* contests traditional perceptions of regional culture by drawing a parallel between the universal confrontation between individual and world with a similar confrontation between region and world. The death of Amaro and the concurrent death of the fires of the Santa Fe plantation signify the final defeat of individualism, and the victory of the federalist forces to the South over regional values of the Northeast.

While introducing formal innovations that break from realist tradition, *Fogo Morto* also succeeds in portraying a national identity crisis that transcends the re-

[4]Translated literally *rabo* means "tail"; *Papa Rabo* cannot be translated literally, but here it is meant as a term of derision.

gional concerns of the Northeast: the Week of Modern Art in 1922 had shaken the cultural community with its futurism, cubism, and other borrowings from the European avant garde; following the revolution of 1930, and successive rewritings of the constitution that gave increasingly centralized power to a military dictator, the country's political identity was unstable; and rapid industrialization and the disappearance of the agrarian economy on which the country was founded resulted in further social upheaval. Having long since lost its secure identity as a colonial possession, Brazil was finally forced to face its selfhood. José Amaro's struggle to maintain his own identity in the face a world closing in around him reflects the broader struggle of a nation to establish and preserve its own autonomous identity in the face of a changing world.

WORKS CITED

Alencar, José de. *Sonhos d'Ouro*, 1872. Rpt. in *Obra Completa de José de Alencar*. Vol. I. Rio de Janeiro: José Aguilar, 1960.

——. *O Sertanejo*, 1875. Rpt. in *Obra Completa de José de Alencar*. Vol. III. Rio de Janeiro: José Aguilar, 1960.

——. *Til*. 1872; Rpt. in *Obra Completa de José de Alencar*. Vol. III. Rio de Janeiro: José Aguilar, 1960.

——. *O Tronco do Ipê*, 1871. Rpt. in *Obra Completa de José de Alencar*. Vol. III. Rio de Janeiro: José Aguilar, 1960.

Cunha, Euclides da. *Os Sertões*, 1902. Trans. Samuel Putnam. *Rebellion in the Backlands*. Chicago: U of Chicago P, 1944.

Freyre, Gilberto. *Casa-Grande e Senezala*. 11th ed. Rio de Janeiro: José Olympio, 1964. 2 vols.

——. *Sobrados e Mucambos*. 2nd ed. Rio de Janeiro: José Olympio, 1968. 3 vols.

Lins do Rêgo, José. *Fogo Morto*, 1943. Rpt. Rio de Janeiro: José Olympio Editôra, 1968.

Martins, Wilson. "A Língua Simbólica de José Lins do Rêgo." In *Usina* by José Lins do Rêgo. Rio de Janeiro: José Olympio Editôra, 1967: xvii-lxiv.

Távora, Franklin. *O cabeleira*. 1876. Rpt. Rio de Janeiro: Edicões Melhoramentos, 1963.

II
Caribbean Culture and Identity

MATTHEW C. STEWART

Identity and Authenticity in Alejo Carpentier's *Reasons of State*

Ostensibly Alejo Carpentier's 1974 novel, *Reasons of State*, concerns itself with the political and military problems and actions of a mythical Latin American dictator who chooses to live in Paris as much as possible. The Head of State, as we know him, embodies nearly absolute power, as near as might be supposed possible in one man. Unsurprisingly political and military activities comprise the assertion of power and authority in this novel and also provide the series of events which propels the narrative forward. Nonetheless, these activities do not define and shape the novel's primary theme of identity; rather, they provide the background against which this topic is shown. Despite the implications of his title, Carpentier has not written a novel whose main enterprise is to examine the effects of power upon the autocrat who is its protagonist; nor has he examined at any length the consequences for the state, polity or population affected by the concentration of power in this one man. Nor yet does the novel concentrate on the mechanics or dynamics of political power in action. Indeed, except at the very basic level of event and fictional context *Reasons of State* can hardly be said to be an overtly political novel.

If Carpentier's main interest is not in political explorations, then in what is it? Simply put, it is in the Head of State as a *letrado* [enlightened head] and more importantly, as a Latin American who incorporates a false identity because he rejects his own indigenous identity. Beyond the simply intuitive apprehension that Carpentier's preoccupations (whether or not he is aware of them) are not politically oriented, textual analysis brings us to the same conclusion. Overtly political and military sections of the text pass quickly in that relatively large periods of time are devoted relatively few pages; thus such sections, because they do not demand extended attention and because they are not replete with detail or elaboration of theme, must be relegated to secondary status. Indeed, the most overtly and concentratedly political section of the novel — the section wherein the dictator crushes his erstwhile compatriot Hoffman's rebellion, reconsolidates power and tries to hold on to it in spite of increasingly active opposition — comprises 158 pages (107-265) yet represents "several years," as we learn from his daughter, Ofelia (273).[1] On the other hand, ten pages alone are devoted to a visit by the Distinguished Academician, which could not be thought to take more than an hour of the Head of State's time. Such dense sections as this all have as their central significance the question of identity and authentication, and it is upon such scenes that critical enquiry should focus if it wishes to penetrate the heart of the text's meaning. It should also be remarked that even the term used in the above paragraph, *concentratedly* political, must be taken as relative because even in that middle section, the novel's most overtly political, the theme of identity recurs many times, usually in the form of a "slow" scene or a motif appearing within the texture of the fast-moving political section.

Very early in the novel it becomes clear that the Head of State's chief pleasures are not brought about by the mundane duties of governing: "Happiness due to an empty agenda-tray, on the night-table beside the hammock, instead of a whole timetable of interviews, official visits, presentation of credentials, or ostentatious entry of soldiers . . ." (11). In fact the Head of State rarely seems to be a man who takes pleasure in the wielding or working of political power, who defines himself by the political and military power he embodies, who desires to exercise that power above all else. To be sure, his violent outbursts upon hearing of each of the rebellions with which he is confronted are based in part upon the betrayal and ingratitude he feels in the rebels. Yet an even larger element of his outrage comes from the fact that he is far from eager to return to his homeland, or, more properly put, to leave Paris. This regret is especially keen at Hoffman's rebellion: "He longed to stay here [in Paris], to get out of the magic circle, but just as if it really enclosed him he could not" (117). The "magic circle" which he so wants to escape here is the Head of State's own conception of his country's history, with which, of course, he is inescapably involved.

What is this Paris which has or represents more attraction to the despot than his own country? The previous quotation seems to suggest that Paris's function in the text is symbolic, but it is so only in a very direct and emblematic way. Paris

[1]Roberto Gonzalez Echevarria has delineated the novel's time frame convincingly. Using his work, one can judge this section to account for between ten and twelve years (Echevarria 263-4).

epitomizes the height of European culture, elegance and civility, but it is conceived differently in the minds of the reader and the dictator. For the Head of State, Paris is all that is marvelous in *La Belle Epoque,* but it is even more; it is the principal mediator of his desire, the means by which he defines himself. I am using *mediator* here in the sense put forth by Rene Girard in his model of triangular desire as elaborated in *Deceit, Desire and the Novel:* "The disciple pursues objects which are determined for him, or at least seem to be determined for him, by [a] model. . . . We shall call this model the mediator of desire" (2). To discuss an authoritarian dictator as a disciple perhaps presses hard on the reader's credulity or expectations. Certainly the terms and orientation of discussion are far removed from those which are commonly associated with a dictator. Yet this is precisely how the novel asks to be read.

In a salubrious model of desire, no mediator is interposed between the subject and his object of desire so that the desiring subject wishes for the desired object without the "help" of any model he wishes to imitate or impress. The interposition of a mediator necessarily indicates a lack of ability to generate or find autonomous desire, that is, a lack of self-determination and authenticity. As the subject of triangular desire, the Head of State reveals and perpetuates his lack of self-definition and his misguided notions of identity.[2] And, as we shall see, the dictator's lack of identity is also present in the country he governs. What precisely does the dictator desire? Not power, for he has power. Those parts of the text (and they are undeniably important) which treat the Head of State's relationship to power portray him trying to maintain the status quo, not to increase his power. Indeed, there are certain boundaries to and infringements upon his power to which he is content to resign himself, such as the towering presence of the United States as hemispheric giant. Yet no reader can fail to note the authentic, "homegrown" vitality which courses through the dictator prior to his return to quell the uprising of General Ataulfo Galvan:

[2]If Girard's argument has a weakness, it is in his too infrequent recognition of the fact that because human beings are in great measure the products of social learning and because they live as social beings, there can be no such thing as completely autonomous desire except at a theoretical level. Desire cannot spontaneously generate themselves within human beings without reference to society. Nevertheless, on both theoretical and actual levels, degrees of autonomy do exist, and some desires are more, even much more, self-generated than others. That Girard ignores these actualities does not negate the usefulness of his model, and the validity of his observations remains once the above proviso is realized.

> The Head of State . . . was pouring himself great swigs of Santa Ines rum — a rum that no longer seemed merely the nostalgic breath of patriotic feelings in *laissez-faire* Paris, but the rum of battle, hot and strong, foretelling hard rough marches and counter-marches in the near future, the smell of horses, soldier's armpits and gunpowder. And all at once, blotting out Jean-Paul Laurens' blessed Radegonde, Elistir's seascape and Gerome's gladiators, they were in the middle of a Council of War. Forgotten was the adolescent hero of the Arc de Triomphe. . . . (29)

Epitomized here is the sort of exercise of authority which does truly pleasure the dictator. Only in his military endeavors and in his bombastic speech-making do we see him "lose himself" to the moment — a paradoxical, yet true, metaphor in that at such infrequent moments the dictator is most truly himself and hence most genuinely happy.

If the dictator does not try to accumulate power, his desires must lie in another direction. This direction is apparent in the above quotation in the form of the works of art "blotted out" by the dictator's vision of the Council of War. But the works of art do not represent the object of desire; instead they epitomize the mediator of desire which in the fuller and more general form it takes throughout the text might best be called French culture. The real object of the dictator's desire is a sense of meaning, identity and legitimation for his life and activities. To fulfill his desires he repeatedly turns to models of European (particularly French) high culture and away from any models which his own Latin America might provide. In other words, he shuns desires which seem most nearly to arise spontaneously within him, such as those exemplified by the rum in the above quotation. Despite the fact that he had become more his true self during his return home to crush Galvan, upon his subsequent return to Paris, the dictator immediately and happily reimmerses himself in Parisian life, saying to his secretary Peralta: "We're better off here than in the Mummies' Cave," a statement which belies authentic desire and identity (82). Apparently the symbolic import of these native mummies, accidentally discovered by the Head of State while he briefly camped in their midst, is lost on him. He fails to see them as relics of an indigenous Latin American past. Shortly after this statement, the narrator remarks that the Head of State " [feels] something approaching an organic need to re-establish relations with the city" (83). The language of this assertion at once conveys the depth ("organic") and the inauthenticity ("approaching") of the dictator's mediated desires.

To best understand the Head of State, it must be recalled that he is the leader of a nation which uses European models in its efforts to achieve beauty, culture, respectability or any sort of "improvements": "To make the resort more attractive, the municipality had constructed a cement pier with a casino at the end supported on piles, the whole affair copied from Nice . . ." (125); "Surveying instruments transformed flooded regions, waste land and goat pastures, dividing them into a number of marked-out squares, which having been since remote times 'The Lazar's small-holding,' 'Mexican farm' or 'Misia Petra's ranch,' suddenly *adopted* the names of 'Bagatelle,' 'West Side' or 'Armenonville' . . . (132 my italics). Apparently, "sophisticated" citizens share their dictator's desire to replace indigenous ways by importing styles and names, however ludicrous their (mis) application The lamentable irony of this sort of imitation is that the nation has its own particular, often strange (from a European perspective) but rich, beauty and culture, as the novel makes abundantly clear.

Clearly not all the dictator's pretension and lack of self-knowledge can be blamed on him. Nor is this sort of mediated desire peculiar to him, though he exceeds the degree to which desire is mediated in his fellow countrymen because his powerful position enables him to do so. The dictator's own education was dominated by "text's in which more space was occupied — naturally enough — by the Soissons Vase than the battle of Ayacucho, and by Cardinal Balue's cage than the conquest of Peru, and which necessarily laid more stress on Saint Louis of the Crusades than on Simon Bolivar of Carabobo . . ." (61). As Girard has said, desires may be defined or generated according to "the Other in a movement which is so fundamental and primitive that [characters] completely confuse it with the will to be Oneself" (4). This statement explains why the Head of State's school texts may have appeared "natural enough," but from a less Eurocentric posture, the domination of French history to the detriment of indigenous history could hardly appear more unnatural. As a native citizen of his country, the dictator is naturally in part a product of its self-perceived inferiority; as Head of State, he is in part responsible for the perpetuation of this mind-set.

The Head of State values culture above all else, though not always for mature or disinterested reasons. The relationship between the dictator and culture is impossible to summarize with terse quotations because it is complex and contradictory. On the one hand his pleasure in being asked to attend the Parisian sophisticate Madame Verdurin's musical evenings is surely not entirely grounded in savoring the evening's artistic endeavors. No small measure of his satisfaction stems from the sense of prestige and inclusion in influential European circles which the Head of State desires. The connection between high culture and high places in Paris is a happy one for the dictator. On the other hand, he *does* make sincere pronouncements about his attitudes toward culture. He is a ruthless tyrant only in the political arena: "Bullets and machetes for bastards. But complete liberty of criticism, polemics, discussion and controversy concerning art, literature, schools of poetry, classical philosophy . . . the concept of Beauty, and everything else in that line . . . that's culture" (139).

The depth, and from his own perspective no doubt, the sincerity, of his attachment to French culture as mediator becomes apparent shortly after the dictator learns of the rebellion of Walter Hoffmann and the necessity of once again leaving Paris to reconsolidate his power. At this point, the Head of State conflates his present situation with that of Christ. He takes on several important Christ-like aspects and subsequently remembers the words declared by the Christ in a passion play he had once seen in his own country: "And if you take this from me, what shall I be? What will remain of me?" (118). These words — originally spoken by the passion-play Christ to a distraught spectator who had come out to aid him on his trip to Golgotha — resound in the dictator's memory because he feels deprived of that which he supposes to be his rightful destiny, that is, to live his version of the life of a cultured Parisian. Clearly the dictator sees his own identity as defined not by the functions of state he performs, not by the tremendous power he can yield, nor by his martial abilities, and least of all by the fact of his Latin American heritage and origin, but rather by this interaction with objects and persons who represent French culture and Parisian high society.

Peralta, sensing the thoughts of his *patrón,* suggests to him that he ought to abandon his duties and remain in his beloved Paris. "And suppose I get rid of *all that,*" the dictator replies, "what should I be? What would remain of me?" (119). We should not suppose that this question reveals the dictator's awareness of, or any sudden awakening to, his genuine (or at least more authentic) identity. Indeed, quite the opposite is happening, as is revealed by the Head of State's next words: "Yes, I remember . . . thinking about the people who had turned against me because of that business at Nueva Cordoba, so that my personality had dwindled and become too small and helpless to play a part in this Apocalyptic world. I was taking on the Crusade for Latinity in order to reinstate my image" (119). Here the dictator reveals that his feelings of self-worth are not generated from any desire to please his fellow countrymen or other Latinos, let alone from within himself. He hopes to recoup power only in order to regain his status in Paris, in order to become the *image* of Latinity he feels is required by the mediator, Paris. At this point the dictator has moved as far away from any desire for authentic identity as he will go in the novel. At this moment of potential crisis, he most explicitly states the falseness of his desires.

Later, when all is lost by the dictator in the United-States-backed coup and he is without power, he endures all sorts of ignominy within his own country, bears up under all manner of loss until he is made to think of the fact that he is not included in the *Petit Larousse:* "And that afternoon I wept. I wept because a dictionary — *Je seme a tout vent* — was unaware of my existence" (265). Betrayal, utter powerlessness, disrespect for his authority, the hatred of his former polity, none of these break the dictator. Book six ends with him weeping because he will never be validated by French society in the way he has desired all his life.

The fact that the dictator blindly defines himself by European terms is further demonstrated after his first return to Paris when all his former "friends" (that is, his sources of legitimation) except the Academician spurn him. After the publication of the photographs of "that business at Nueva Cordoba" have changed his supposed image from that of the enlightened and encultured autocrat to that of the bloody tyrant, the dictator becomes depressed and angry. Yet instead of examining himself and searching for appropriate means of legitimation, the Head of State cynically turns toward Germanic models which function as no more than replacements for the equally false French models. His notable lack of concern about being a tyrant is, of course, hypocritical and despicable, but what is perhaps more noteworthy is the immediacy with which the dictator turns to another Old World model as a mediator of his desire for identity. The dictator, even here, refuses or is unable to return to his own origins for models of behavior. If he cannot define himself according to Frenchness, he will adopt a Germanic nature — just like that! — and in his eagerness to become Germanic we see too his sudden childish dislike and ill-will for things French. But this should not surprise us, for, as Girard has said, any:

> hostility [from the mediator] does not diminish his prestige but instead augments it. The subject is convinced that the model considers himself too

> superior to accept him as a disciple. The subject is torn between two opposite feelings for his model — the most submissive reverence and the most intense malice. This is the passion we call *hatred.* Only someone who prevents us from satisfying a desire which he himself has inspired in us is truly an object of hatred. (10-11)

The events of *Reasons of State* clearly fit this pattern. As we have seen, Paris is the model of inspiration for the dictator, and Paris clearly rejects the bloody manifestations of his true self as exhibited at Nueva Cordoba. We have seen elsewhere the dictator's "submissive reverence" in his cynical Crusade for Latinity, and his "intense malice" displays itself as, among other things, the hopeful predictions that France will fare poorly in the war.

The dictator's flirtation with a Germanic identity does not last long, just long enough for the reader to assess the profundity of his lack of autonomous identity. This flirtation does not in fact seriously undercut the role of Paris as mediator. Nonetheless, part of *Reasons of State's* brilliance lies in its desire to undercut or reverse its own structures. Such undercutting, or the willingness to depict and reveal paradox, however, does not mean that the text eventually fails to assert any consistent meanings. One of the prime examples of such self-undercutting is germane to our discussion, and that is the ability of the Head of State to take his friend the Academician with a grain of salt. As we have seen, the dictator desires identity and authentication and seeks it through the mediator epitomized in the word *Paris*. The Academician, by virtue of his position and status, ought to serve as an ideal representation of the mediator, but he does not. Just as the dictator is a false image of a Head of State — false because tyrannical, cruel, uninterested in his own people and nation — so is the Academician a spurious image of Old World reason and culture — self-important, chauvinistic, racist, opinionated.

The section wherein the Academician is introduced is the principal one concerning him, and this section is narrated by the dictator. Oddly it is through the Head of State, who is otherwise so blind to his devotion to French models, that the Academician's failures and shortcomings are revealed. He is both the central consciousness and the voice through which the Academician is at once presented and deflated. The dictator is knowing and indulgent. Only the reader, never the Academician, is privy to the dictator's parenthetical criticisms. Often the Head of State keeps his peace rather than contradict the Academician or defend his own people: "I remain silent rather than tell him how . . ." (19); "At this point I decide to remain silent . . ." (20). Later, when all of his other Parisian acquaintances have thrown him over because of the bloody debacle at Nueva Cordoba, only the Academician remains loyal to the dictator. However, the dictator receives little long-term comfort from this fact, although he is temporarily bucked up. At this point the Head of State feels the need for authentication by Paris so strongly that he feels "his strength of mind restored, and his mood made more aggressive by the conversation" (88), but Peralta soon exposes the ignorance and chauvinism of the Academician in a justifiable outburst which restores the dictator's perspective concerning the Academician. Thus the narrator comments near the end of the scene: "And in the sole place in the Universe where other people's opinion had some importance to him, everyone was giving him the cold shoulder" (91). Here, through the use of the word *everyone*, we see that the Academician is not truly regarded as important by the dictator. They use one another in times of crisis: the Head of State can supply money; the Academician can wield influence in the press.

At the height of the verbal confrontation between Peralta and the Academician, "the President silenced his secretary with an expression of fatigue" (90). Once again the Head of State refuses to truly confront the Academician. These refusals to let that false embodiment of reason be deflated are partly due to the dictator's pragmatic streak, which allows him to recognize a useful ally. The refusal to defend his native land and people from the Academician's ignorant and racist onslaughts does little to endear the dictator to the reader. But more interesting is the fact that the Academician, even so potentially damaging a representative of the idealized, faultless culture of Paris as he, does nothing to dislodge or reshape Paris as the dictator's mediator. The Academician actually undercuts Old World culture: if his position of eminence marks him as a paragon and spokesman within that culture, then surely that culture has some serious flaws. The dictator would appear to ignore these flaws. He cannot afford to do otherwise since serious reflection on the mediator would necessarily involve the dictator in troubling questions about his own identity and about the worthiness and origins of his desire, and these sorts of questions the dictator never confronts. As Girard has said, "The obsessed man astounds us with his clear understanding of those like himself . . . and in his complete inability to see himself" (74).

If this were a novel primarily concerned with exploring political power or systems, it would be unlikely to devote several pages to the preparation of lunch undertaken by the exiled dictator's live-in, the Mayorala Elmira, in book seven. It would certainly not have as its primary concern, as does *Reasons of State,* the dictator's movement toward (re) discovery of his authentic self. This last book begins with the epigram, "And deciding not to seek more knowledge than what I could find in myself . . ." and this is precisely the decision that the dictator makes, whether consciously or not, after his final disillusionment with France (267).

The adage, "you can't go home again" applies in every way to the overthrown dictator. Obviously he cannot return to his own country — he never even entertains hopes or illusions of doing so — nor is he at home in Paris, the false model through which he has striven to fulfill his desires his entire adult life. The Paris that the dictator returns to after his ouster is not the Paris fixed in his mind before his arrival, and he reacts with astonishment and dismay to the modernist works of art which have replaced the pieces that he had held so dear. His former friends and acquaintances, even his faithful *homme,* Sylvestre, are either dead or somehow so changed in circumstances (as is he) as to be socially unavailable to him: "I was afraid a princess — or someone with the presumptions of one — would scorn a man who was, after all, only a Latin-American president thrown out of his palace" (278). This particular parenthetical aside concerning Madame Verdurin's possible presumption could never have been made by the Head of State in his previous Paris years because he was so blinded by his desire and self-deceit that he could not see the possibility of falseness in himself nor dare to admit its presence in the mediator. Logically the dynamics of mediated desire suggest that any devalorization of the mediator by the desiring subject would consequently necessitate a devalorization in the object of desire (and the inverse is also true). With an object of desire as vitally important as his very identity and worth, the dictator could not have afforded to ponder his chosen model too carefully, for the ramifications of unworthiness would have been unbearable.

But in his final return to Paris, the deposed tyrant's eyes are opened, and it would be a serious mistake not to recognize the depth of his change. Ironically, the dictator's epiphanic moment occurs in the brothel named *Aux glaces,* a name which suggests, of course, illusion and distortion, and which is full of prostitutes assuming false identities. But it is here that the dictator, or the *Ex* as he now prefers to be called, sees a true reflection of himself which he is ready to voice:

> Here, looking at what I am looking at, I feel I am witnessing the Arrest of Time. . . . I am . . . less of an exiled ruler, or actor in decline, and more

> identified with my own *ego,* still possessing eyes for looking, and impulses arising from the depths of vitality that is deliciously stimulated by something worth looking at — riches definitely preferable (I *feel* therefore I am) to those of a fictitious existence in the stupid ubiquity of a hundred statues in municipal parks, patios and town halls. (279-80)

"Actor in decline," "fictitious existence," "stupid ubiquity" — the Head of State could never have made these remarks. The *Ex* Head of State can.

When the Ex speaks of "the Arrest of Time," he is saying more than he realizes. Inside the brothel, the Ex feels a timelessness, and the reader hearkens back to the previously quoted passage wherein the dictator professed his desire to escape time: "He longed to stay here, to get out of the magic circle, but just as if it really enclosed him he could not" (117). As I have said, the magic circle from which the dictator wished to escape was his country's history, his involvement with his own origins. Ironically for him, the Ex does achieve this "timelessness," but he does so precisely when he is actually beginning to embrace his own origins and reject the model of Paris. Of course in one sense he has escaped his country's history in that he no longer wields power or influence there, but in the central sense of the novel, that of identity, he is reintegrated with the authentic aspects of his country's culture.

The word *sense* is a fortunate word here since it includes the concept of reason (the text's Cartesian component which is rejected finally by the *Ex*) as well as the signification found in the words *sensory* and *sensual,* which best characterize the experiences that lead the Ex back toward his origins ("I *feel* therefore I am"). The prime example of the *Ex's* unification with the authentic through the sensual is the Mayorala's meal — which even the ultimate fake and snob, Ofelia, cannot resist partaking in — that occurs shortly after the *Ex's* epiphanic moment in the brothel. By this time we recognize that food is a sign whereby cultural identity is displayed. Earlier during the campaign to crush Galvan's rebellion, the Head of State and his cronies dine on a medley of foods from Europe and their home country: "sardines, corned beef, baked bananas, *dulce de leche* and Rhine wine" (52). This ethnic potpourri is matched to the dictator's level of authenticity at that time, and it marks the point when the dictator is most nearly his authentic self until his ultimate exile in Paris. Yet even on this campaign the staples are European, as is the wine with which the meal is washed down. Only the dessert and side-dish are native. This propensity of the dictator's for the food of others, like all his matters of identity, is mirrored by his fellow countrymen's habits during the boom-time coincident with World War I: "while only in Chinese eating houses could one eat the national dishes, now scorned as something connected with rope-soled shoes and ballads sung by the blind" (175-76). However the Mayorala, whose unpretentiousness has been evident throughout the novel, had already pronounced her opinion of French food in a piece of foreshadowing which occurs long before her accompaniment of the dictator into Parisian exile: "She found a derogatory name for [it] all; the Burgundian snails were 'slugs'; the caviar, 'buckshot in oil'; the truffles, 'chips of charcoal'; the halva, 'nougat trying to be like turron from Jijona' " (156). Thus, long before the meal in exile, it is clear that in this text man is known by the food he eats, and the significance of the dictator feasting on his native cuisine is clear. Finally, ill in exile, the *Ex* convalesces on what he calls " a meal of our own sort — pancake, tamale . . . the only things that seem to me to taste of anything" (304). The *Ex's* movement toward authentic desire is clearly demonstrated by the foods he chooses to eat.

Girard has said that "the great novel does not succeed in shattering" ["the lie of spontaneous desire"] although it never ceases to denounce it" (16). The dictator's slavish pretension toward Old World culture is clear enough, and while the objects of his desire (identity and feelings of self-worth) are not overt, they can be discovered through inference and textual analysis. Indeed, one of the lessons of the text is that the ostensibly enlightened despot is in fact quite in the dark in the most fundamental way; he is ignorant of himself. More than ignorant, he deceives himself with a mediated desire that at once reveals self-hatred, as well as stimulates and perpetuates his country's own lack of identity.[3] To know all is most assuredly not to forgive very much in the present case, for no amount of explanation can excuse the sort of cruel, ruthless exploitation and tyranny which the dictator subjects his country to, and which is there for every reader to see.

I have said that *Reasons of State* is not primarily a political novel, and indeed the novel's major weakness is in its awkward and belated attempt in the final chapter to move the overtly political strand (represented in this chapter by the Student and other, newly introduced, revolutionary figures in Paris), which has been of a secondary nature up to this point, into the foreground with the primary

[3]"The wish to be absorbed into the substance of the Other implies an insuperable revulsion for one's own substance" (Girard 54).

material concerning the *Ex's* identity. The belated appearance of this material is an intrusion which makes it seem as though Carpentier felt compelled to write a political novel, or at least to end his novel on an overtly political note, in spite of his own desires for his text.

To point out that the novel's main theme is identity is not to say, however, that the text has no political ramifications. The dictator and his countrymen clearly reflect an archetypal and actual problem of peoples from underdeveloped Latin-American countries, that is, the necessity of searching for a means by which their identity may be created or known, standards by which it may be measured and means by which it may be reinforced. A people that do not know who they are can hardly expect to know where they wish to go or how they intend to get there. It is from this level that the text's most important actual/historical lessons emerge from its largely mythical treatment of Latin-American particulars. To recognize and understand the ramifications of a lack of authentic identity in a figure of political power and the feelings of inherent inferiority in his polity is surely an important first step toward understanding a regrettable facet of Latin-American history and of Third World sociopolitical dynamics.

WORKS CITED

Carpentier, Alejo. *Reasons of State*. Trans. Francis Partridge. London: Writers and Readers Publishing Cooperative, 1977.

Echevarria, Roberto Gonzalez. *Alejo Carpentier: The Pilgrim at Home*. Ithaca, NY: Cornell UP, 1977.

Girard, Rene. *Deceit, Desire, and the Novel: Self and Other in Literary Structure*. Trans. Yvonne Freccero. Baltimore: Johns Hopkins UP, 1965.

RAFAEL OCASIO

In Search of a Socialist Identity in Revolutionary Cuban Children's Literature[1]

> The impulse behind socialism is to help mankind achieve its greatest potential and to raise to its highest degree the freedom to create, not only with respect to form but also with respect to content. *(Fidel Castro, IV Congress of Cuban Authors and Artists, 1988)*

Although the Cuban Revolution was purely political in origin, it quickly developed into a socialist movement supported by its own literary and artistic productions. Revolutionary doctrine moved efficiently to develop the so-called socialist man, devised by Marxist theorist Ernesto Che Guevara in his *Socialismo y el hombre en Cuba* (*Socialism and the Cuban Man*), as the prototype of Cuban identity and as a central concern of revolutionary ideology. The basic thrust behind the Revolution was the creation of an essentially Cuban identity by pulling together diverse social sectors into a shared political-historical paragon of social equality. One way to promote that purpose was a re-definition of the island's artistic life with the specific aim of instituting Fidel Castro's form of socialism among all power structure groups, such as peasants, workers, blacks, women or children.

In Cuba, Marxist didacticism appears in its most visible expression in children's literature. First, this paper focuses on the ideological development of Cuban children's literature specifically intended to shape children's popular culture and, therefore, to reinforce a socialist identity among easily impressionable children and young people. Second, this essay presents a historical-bibliographical survey of an often ignored form of revolutionary writing by listing key authors of Cuban children's literature and their contributions to this genre. More than any other revolutionary program, children's literature responds directly to political themes, which, in turn, deal directly with the issue of post-colonialism and the Cuban national identity. An essential part of a highly complicated

[1]I should like to express my gratitude for the Children's Literature Association's research fellowship, awarded during the summer of 1991. I would also like to thank Professor Emerita Eloise Herbert for her helpful comments on an earlier version of this paper.

educational process, revolutionary children's literature provides the necessary ideological training intended for incorporation of young people into the proposed, and abstractly theoretical socialist Cuban identity.

As Cuba set the goal of creating civic awareness rooted in revolutionary doctrines, simultaneously a strong political theory, begun in early January, 1959, outlined a program of politically correct revolutionary behavior. After much vacillation, Fidel Castro in 1961 delineated the field of action for the socialist citizen: "Everything within the Revolution, nothing against it" (*Palabras* 11).[2] The controversy and dissent which followed statement of this proposition brought the need for intellectual leadership to educate the proletariat in revolutionary theory. The transition from a pre- to a post-revolutionary society was not to be an easy task; difficulties were reflected in the educational campaigns organized to incorporate the working class into socialist postulates. The expectation was that eventually the re-educated members would become spokespeople, themselves, as expressed by Cuban artist Gerardo Mosquera:

> Some time ago I said that formerly the "artist" used to paint "peasants," "blacks" and "workers"; whereas nowadays, the "peasant," "blacks" and "workers" have begun to be "artists." (68).

Under the aegis of the Cuban government, intellectuals were charged with the responsibility for disseminating socialism. The close relationship between ideology and creative work produced art of a strong underlying allegorical nature common to third-world literary productions, in a schematic sociopolitical process described by Marxist critic Fredric Jameson (69). Cuban literature addressed specifically revolutionary ideals and abstractions, implementing them in more concrete form easily understood by masses. Reaching a highly diverse and mixed population was difficult. The problem was resolved by individualization so that each social group received ideological training specific to its background and needs. As the indoctrination process gained strength, it was predicted that these social groups would play an essential role in the cementing of social and political power.

In the making of native popular culture, Cuba's revolutionary leadership directed particular attention to their youth. The inclusion of youth issues in the po-

---

[2] The translation is mine. "¿Cuáles son los derechos de los escritores y los artistas revolucionarios? Dentro de la Revolución todo; contra la Revolución, ningún derecho."

litical platform set the tone for the very rhythm of the Revolution in securing political ordinances intended to create social changes. As women began working in greater numbers, more children became dependent on governmental care and instruction. Housed in day-care centers, state-of-the-art schools and field camps, Cuban youth received constant political instruction about the responsibility they faced within their society. The following statement by Fidel Castro illustrates this kind of socialist indoctrination:

> We have great confidence in our young people, and we know that they will go forward. They will always get inspiration from the ideas and the examples of Marx, Engels, Lenin, Martí, Maceo, Mella, Abel Santamaría, José Antonio Echeverría, Frank País, Camilio and Che; they will get inspiration from this vast and admirable legion of pure and true revolutionaries, of so many great men that the world and our country have produced. May our youth be the builders of communism and the forgers of a new world!
> (*Discursos* 139)[3]

The names quoted above are national heroes who actively opposed foreign intervention during various periods of the island's colonial history. Thus, the call for political action was passed on to the younger generation, encouraging them to participate in the process of re-construction that was about to take place.

On the other hand, Ernesto Che Guevara, aware of the obstacles to future political transformations, constantly pointed out the difficulties of ideological change and of the maintenance of a fighting spirit. For example, in 1960 he spoke of the widespread dissatisfaction about the availability of some consumer goods:

> . . . a moment ago someone gave me a piece of gum. This is representative of a whole line of consumer goods, many of which, if you stop to think about it, the imperialists taught us to use. And now that these things are no longer available, people protest and begin to wonder if this government is really going to raise the standard of living or if it is going to deprive them of such important things as chewing gum.[4]

---

[3]The translation is mine. "Tenemos gran confianza, y sabemos que nuestra juventud marchará adelante. Se inspirará siempre en las ideas y el ejemplo de Marx, de Engels, de Lenín, de Martí, de Maceo, de Mella, de Abel Santamaría, de José Antonio Echeverría, de Frank País, de Camilo, del Che; en las ideas de esa legión inmensa y admirable de revolucionarios puros y verdaderos, de hombres maravillosos, de tantos hombres maravillosos como los que ha producido el mundo y nuestra patria. ¡Qué nuestra juventud será la constructora del comunismo y forjadora de un mundo nuevo!"

[4]Ernesto Che Guevara in an interview for the television program "Cuba Avanza" on June 18, 1960. The translation is mine. ". . . hace un momento me acaban de regalar un chicle, por ejemplo. Esas son toda una serie de artículos de consumo, que incluso si ustedes se ponen analizar, muchos de ellos, la colonia nos lo ha enseñado a usar. Y entonces, cuando hoy faltan, se protesta; entonces se empieza a pensar si este gobierno de verdad va a elevar el nivel de vida del pueblo, o va a

Among the visible symbols representing political change, chewing gum (especially Adams Chiclets) came to be associated dramatically with international capitalism and, more concretely, with American imperialism. Cuban socialists agreed that use of native materials should replace consumption of foreign products. One of the rejected American commodities was Coca-Cola, replaced successfully by a locally produced drink called "Tropi Cola." Cubans re-discovered abundant tropical fruits that took the place of imported beverages and candies. International goods from new foreign markets, such as the Soviet cinema, received official preference over the popular Hollywood movies. On the other hand, other customs like baseball games and boxing, brought to Cuba by American troops after the Spanish American War in 1898, were kept and developed into national sports by teams that today boast of superiority over their American counterparts.

Revolutionary education controlled natural popular resistance to socialist change. For children and young people, the state began a program of socialization designed to bring Cuban youth into the revolutionary manifesto.[5] The plan had a two-fold purpose. First, political indoctrination created a strong populist culture for children and youngsters in order to promote a reformed national identity. Second, the educational programs supported a rich literary production created specifically for teaching the new socialist youth. For the sake of clarity, I shall indicate four distinctive stages in the creation of a formal revolutionary children's literature (Ocasio).

Interest in the child in revolutionary Cuba goes back to José Martí (1853-1895), pre-modernist poet and ideological mentor of the Cuban Revolution. Martí, a revolutionary who died fighting in the Cuban War for Independence, was also a didactic moralist. Centering on the improvement of human relations, his philosophy called for an end to the prejudices that limited relationships between

---

quitar cosas tan importantes como el chicle o algunas cosas."

[5]Perhaps because of its openly Marxist aegis, this movement has not been fully explored by international scholars. In contrast, other children's literature in Europe, most specifically the West German student movement during the late 1960s, has been fully recognized for its socialist content in children's texts. See Jack Zipes, "Down with Heidi, Down with Struwwelpeter, Three Cheers for the Revolution: Toward a New Socialist Children's Literature in West Germany," *Children's Literature* 5 (1976): 162-180; "Educating, Miseducating, and Re-educating Children: Attempts to Desocialize the Capitalist Socialization Process," *New German Critique* (Winter 1973): 142-159.

individuals of different social classes. Indicative of his predilection for children's literature are the numerous images of the child in his poetry and in his short stories. That interest culminated in a children's magazine, "La Edad de Oro," ("The Golden Age"), published in New York City between July and October, 1889. Within those pages, Martí addressed children at their own level and discussed their favorite topics. Martí's rejection of his patron's demands that he publish religious material resulted in discontinuation of "La Edad de Oro."

Clearly, the Cuban Revolution took its cue from José Martí's intellectual defiance of oppressive foreign rulers. The first formative stage in the making of a revolutionary children's literature began in 1961 with a series of literacy campaigns in which children were both teachers and students. This movement affected specifically peasants who had traditionally received either a minimal education or no education at all. The goal was ambitious: the eradication of illiteracy, which in 1961 amounted to 1,032,849 adults (Kozol 5), or 23.6% of the national population, according to the 1953 census, the last census before the Revolution (*Report* 15). About 100,000 youngsters responded as *brigadistas* (volunteers) in the campaigns and went into the countryside as teachers (Kozol 6). Confrontations with counterrevolutionary groups led to the brutal murder of some volunteers of only fourteen or fifteen years of age. Nonetheless, the *brigadistas'* efforts paid off. The official reports recorded 588,000 people who had learned to read and write by December, 1961 (Seers et al. 194).

During this early stage, distinguished pedagogues began writing socialist publications for children of specific ages. In 1962, Herminio Almendros became the first director of Editora Juvenil, a publishing house devoted exclusively to instructional material for children and adolescents. His prolific works are impressive: grammar and secondary-level readers, literary works of his own, adaptations from local and international folklores, critical analyses of José Martí's "La Edad de Oro," and studies on various pedagogical subjects.[6] To complement these critical works, well-known writers composed new readers for the literacy campaign: Renée Potts,[7] Adelaida Clemente, Dora Alonso,[8] and Mirta Aguirre.[9] Others, like

[6]Herminio Almendros, *Nuestro Martí* (Editora Juvenil, 1965). *Pueblos y leyendas* (Teide, 1967). *Lecturas ejemplares: aventuras, realidades y fantasías* (Cultural Centroamericana, 1966). *Estudios sobre la literatura infantil* (Ediciones Oasis, 1971). *Cuentos de animales* (Gente Nueva, 1973). *Narraciones interesantes* (Gente Nueva, 1978). *Blanca Nieve* (Gente Nueva, 1980).

[7]Renée Potts, *Las babuchas de Abú Casim*, 1963.

novelist and poet Eliseo Diego, translated fairy tales by Hans Christian Andersen, the Brothers Grimm, Charles Perrault, and Madame Leprince de Beaumont. Diego also translated most of the poems in an anthology of Russian poetry for children.[10]

In this development of a national educational program, a second stage promoted activities compatible with the newly-created social consciousness, opposed to the consumer practices typified by American popular culture. In the literary domain Excilia Saldaña, a children's writer and current president of the Children's Section at the Union of the Cuban Writer and Artist (UNEAC), summarized the popular North American youth culture which the revolutionary leadership was rejecting:

> The Revolution rejects the world of American baseball cards and the comics full of anticommunism, superstition, sadism, or castration, as is the case of Donald Duck, the Big, Bad Wolf, Agatha the Witch, protagonists in a world of uncles and aunts, nephews and nieces where sex is repressed and where the family and sexual relations between couples are replaced by a world of spontaneous reproduction: a strange prudery which in turn engenders an aberrant system of asexuality. (Saldaña 18)[11]

As a direct result of this policy, cards featuring revolutionary fighters replaced North American baseball cards. Walt Disney comic books disappeared in favor of cartoons featuring native heroes like Elpidio Valdés y Valdés, a personage from the War for Independence.[12] Another revolutionary creation was the *fotonovela* ("photographic novel"), similar in structure to the comic book but with photographs instead of drawings or animated cartoons. Both the *fotonovela* and the reformed comic book dealt with various national projects (e.g., the agrarian reforms or the incorporation of ethnic minorities) or just politically correct fictional

---

[8]Dora Alonso, *Aventuras de Guille en busca de la gaviota negra* (Editora Juvenil, 1966). *Espantajo y los pájaros* (Editora del Consejo Nacional de Cultura, 1966). *Ponolani* (Granma, 1966).

[9]Mirta Aguirre, *Juegos y otros poemas* (Gente Nueva, 1974). *Doña Iguana* (Gente Nueva, 1982).

[10]Eliseo Diego, *Muestrario del mundo o libro de las maravillas de Boloña* (Gente Nueva, 1967); *Fogata roja* (Gente Nueva, 1985).

[11]The translation is mine. "La Revolución rechaza el mundo de las "postalitas" de los peloteros norteamericanos y los "muñequitos" llenos de anticomunismo, superstición, sadismo o castración sexual, tal es el caso del Pato Donald, el Lobo Feroz o la Bruja Agata, protagonistas de un mundo de tíos y sobrinos, donde el sexo repelía la compañía doméstica del otro, y donde la familia y las relaciones amorosas de la pareja estaban sustituídas por un reino de partenogénesis espóntanea: extraña mojigatería que engendraba a su vez un aberrado sistema de asexualidad."

[12]Juan Padro, *Aventuras de Elpidio Valdés* (Gente Nueva, 1979).

subjects. This is the case of *Los mundos que amo ("The Worlds that I Love,"* 1980) by young science fiction writer Daína Chaviano (1957), whose characters are highly intelligent space aliens from a sophisticated society.[13] Incidentally, children and young people resisted these changes by creating a black market for U.S. comic books that they had always favored. The market also catered to teenaged girls by supplying the *novela rosa,* or romantic novel, (specially that of Spanish novelist Corín Tellado), much in the tradition of the U.S. "Harlequin" series.

Despite young people's opposition, the government insisted upon changes. One radical change was the creation of the Day of the Child, celebrated on the third Sunday in July (replacing the Christmas-related celebrations of Epiphany). The school year also became longer, and children spent part of the summer vacation in voluntary work in the fields. The indoctrination process continued in the countryside, as children and youngsters, organized in large working groups, had the opportunity to experience hard, physical agricultural work while witnessing the implementation of socialist principles.

One might view the third stage of re-education as incorporating Cuban youth into the ranks of the revolution through officially promoted organizations. One such group, *La Organización de Pioneros José Martí* (*The José Martí Young Pioneers*), founded in 1961 as the Cuban version of the Boy Scouts, instilled in its members a spirit of revolutionary cooperation and military discipline. A next step produced literary journals for Cuban youth. Outstanding examples include *Mella,* the official magazine of the political group *Juventud Socialista* (*Socialist Youth*), which on April 4, 1962, became *La Unión de Jóvenes Comunistas* (*The Union of Young Communists*), and *Pioneros,* the official organ of the Young Pioneers. The importance of these publications is significant. For *Pioneros,* well-established intellectuals, such as short-story writer Jorge Onelio Cardoso,[14] worked side by side with such up-and-coming young talents as Ivette Vián,[15] David Chericián,[16] and

---

[13]Daína Chaviano, *Los mundos que amo* (Unión Nacional de Autores y Artistas Cubanos, 1980).

[14]Jorge Onelio Cardoso, *Abrir y cerrar los ojos* (UNEAC, 1969). *Tres cuentos para niños* (Instituto del Libro, 1968).

[15]Ivette Vián, *Como te iba diciendo* (Universidad de la Habana, 1977).

[16]David Chericián, *ABC* (Gente Nueva, 1987).

Froilán Escobar,[17] all of whom would later develop triumphant careers in children's literature. Other young future writers acquired their literary training as *brigadistas,* such as Rafael Hernández[18] and Reynaldo González,[19] of the Conrado Benítez Brigade.

To cater to the young readership, the government provided new meeting places. The José Martí National Library, Havana's main study center, created a youth division and a Department of Children's Literature, directed by novelist Eliseo Diego. Among various activities appealing to children's taste, this literary section created the Children's Hour, when writers would read traditional and their own children's stories to their young audience. One writer, Reinaldo Arenas, a notable short-story writer and novelist, started his career as a children's literature writer. Later he became one of the most outspoken counterrevolutionary writers.[20]

The fourth and final stage involved the re-organization of the publishing world, which was nationalized and structured according to subject divisions. The Youth Publishing House in 1967 became Editorial Gente Nueva (Young People's Publishing House), for readers ages one to fifteen years old, it was divided into four specialized departments: Redacción Infantil (Children's Works), Redacción Juvenil Literario-Social (Juvenile Literary-Social Works), Redacción Juvenil Histórico-Patriótica (Juvenile Historic-Patriotic Works), and Redacción Enciclopedia Juvenil (Encyclopedias for Young People). At this point, most of the creative fiction in the field of children's literature began to emerge. By 1966, the wide acceptance of this genre led to the creation of the Premio David, a literary prize sponsored by the UNEAC exclusively for young unpublished writers of poetry, drama, and the short-story. Science fiction and the literature of the fantastic also found recognition as revolutionary expressions. For the writers of children's

---

[17]Froilán Escobar, *Erase una vez un hombre* (Gente Nueva, 1985).

[18]Rafael Hernández was a *brigadista* in 1961 and graduated with a Bachelor's degree in Humanities in 1965. He received an "Honorary Mention" in the literary competition sponsored by the UNEAC for his poetry collection, *Pañuelo de cuadros rojo (Red Plaid Handkerchief)* in 1967. His *Versos de un soldado (Poems by a Soldier,* Instituto del Libro, 1974) was first prize in poetry the year of its publication.

[19]Reynaldo González, *Siempre la muerte, su paso breve (Death Always, its Slow Pace,* Casa de las Américas, 1968).

[20]Reinaldo Arenas, exiled in New York City, committed suicide in December, 1990. His name is often associated with the Revolution's success in turning nearly illiterate peasants into intellectuals of national reputation.

literature, the Ministry of Culture and Education in 1972 created a prize for their genre called *La Edad de Oro,* in obvious homage to revolutionary hero, José Martí.

In addition, the Cuban government established a number of groups to propagate Cuban children's literature, including the National Puppet Theater, founded in 1963. After a Congress on Culture in 1971, the Escambray Theater and the Brigades Hermanos Saíz and Brigades Raúl Gómez García were also established. More opportunities for formal literary instruction and training were promoted by seminars at the Organization Young Pioneers, organized by the Union of Young Communists and the National Council for Culture and Education. In 1966 there appeared the internationally renowned journal *El Caimán Barbudo, (The Bearded Alligator)* originally a monthly cultural supplement to the newspaper *Juventud Rebelde (Rebel Youth). El Caimán Barbudo* was run by up-and-coming writers, many of whom had developed literary skills while serving in brigades or in *cursillos* (workshops) organized by juvenile organizations.

Through these four stages, it appears that Cuban children's literature has become a highly structured and well organized sociopolitical and literary endeavor. Works for children appear in truly amazing numbers: between 1968-1983 some 1,120 titles with 80,310,600 copies were distributed at low prices (Elizagaray 21) and 365 joint editions with such socialist countries as Bulgaria, Poland, Czechoslovakia, Rumania, and the Soviet Union (Editorial Gente Nueva). This impressive literary production resulted from incorporation of young writers into cultural institutions. The revolutionary goal had been achieved: "Young people are the bearers of a popular culture and at the same time they are 'cultured' artists" (Mosquera 68).

Today the making of a national identity continues with the exploration of national folklore (Western and non-Western, particularly the rich African substratum). Mosquera describes the process:

> Cultural roots are not displayed — they are put to work. Identity becomes action from deep within oneself, and not an identity card. A deepening Latin Americanist spirit is forming, which is very significant for art in a country that for a long time ignored its continent to a large degree. (67)

A striking illustration is the fact that the Afro-Cuban religious belief system called *santería* is the central theme of Excilia Saldaña's *Kele Kele* (1987), a collection of short-stories for children.[21]

Future studies would do well to point out how Cuban authors accommodated their work to the rapid changes which the dynamics of the Revolution made necessary. Fidel Castro has stated repeatedly that the hallmark of Cuban society has been its total commitment to the progress of underdeveloped societies. Cuban children's literature may be studied as an ideal medium for an evaluation of revolutionary praxis and for an analysis of the use of language, form and content for didactic purpose.

WORKS CITED

Castro, Fidel. *Discursos en tres congresos*. Havana: Editora Pública, 1982.

——. *Palabras a los intelectuales*. Havana: Ediciones Consejo Nacional de Cultura, 1961.

Editorial Gente Nueva. *Catálogo General 1968-1984*. Havana: Gente Nueva, 1986.

Elizagaray, Alga Marina. "El libro y la literatura infantil-juvenil." *Panorama de la literatura cubana (1959-1984)*. Havana: Letras Cubanas, 1985. 20-28.

Guevara, Ernesto. *El socialismo y el hombre en Cuba*. Barcelona: Editorial Anagrama, 1975.

Jameson, Fredric. "Third-World Literature in the Era of Multinational Capitalism." *Social Text* 15 (Fall 1986): 65-88.

Kozol, Jonathan. *Children of the Revolution: A Yanqui Teacher in the Cuban Schools*. New York: Delacorte Press, 1978.

Mosquero, Gerardo. "Plastic Art in Cuba." *Being América: Essays on Art, Literature and Identity from Latin America*. Eds. Rachel Weiss & Alan West. New York: White Pine Press, 1991. 61-70.

Ocasio, Rafael. "La Revolución cubana y su literatura infantil: Estudio histórico-bibliográfico." *Confluencia* 6:1 (Fall 1990): 55-64.

Report on the Method and Means Utilized in Cuba to Eliminate Illiteracy. Havana: Cuban National Commission for UNESCO, 1965.

Saldaña, Excilia. "Sólo hay una literatura infantil: ¡La buena!" *Caimán Barbudo* 18 (1984): 16-18.

Seers, Dudley, Andrés Bianchi, Richard Jolly, Max Nolff. *The Economic and Social Revolution*. Chapel Hill: U of North Carolina P, 1964.

---

[21] Excilia Saldaña, *Kele Kele* (Letras Cubanas, 1987).

JORGE FEBLES

English and Spanish Pop Songs as Part of Character Speech: Cultural Hybridity in Roberto G. Fernández's *Raining Backwards*

When Cuban-American novelist Roberto G. Fernández was asked in 1988 by a *Time* magazine interviewer why, after having produced four books of fiction in Spanish, he chose to write his latest work, *Raining Backwards*, in what his questioner naively perceived as a borrowed language, he responded with a humorous allusion to the pop music scene which is so alluring to him. "I did it for the same reason that Miami Sound Machine sings in English," he said. "I wanted to reach a wider audience" (47). However, Fernández's attempt at penetrating mainstream, non-Hispanic literary tradition, his *Crossover Dreams*[1] as it were, cannot be viewed simplistically as the standard dilemma of an immigrant writer who is forced by circumstances to assume the dominant language of his adopted environment. Unlike Nabokov's or Conrad's, his fiction is as alien in English as it is in Spanish, for he appears intent on representing an arbitrary microcosm, a bizarre poetic ghetto dynamically inserted within a culture that, although denaturing it radically, does not manage to bring about its disintegration. In fact, as *Raining Backwards* implies, they may devour themselves mutually to constitute a hybrid entity whose roots would be effaced from the collective memory.

Both narrative language and character speech elucidate to a greater or lesser degree an interbreeding directly related to the bicultural society they attempt to demythologize. As in Fernández's other novels (*La vida es un special* and *La montaña rusa*), in *Raining Backwards* the impersonal narrator's voice often partakes of the community's linguistic blemishes or peculiarities. Transcending par-

---

[1] I refer, of course, to the 1986 motion picture that was produced and directed by León Ichaso. In it, Rudy Veloz, the main character portrayed by Rubén Blades, forsakes temporarily his Latin *salsa* roots to make a failed incursion into the North American rock scene. *Crossover Dreams*, therefore, denounces the opportunistic substitution of a minority language and cultural code by the dominant English system. I employ the expression ironically to denote the humorous self-deprecation inherent in Fernández's comment.

ody, his discourse affirms heterogeneity much in the same manner as The Miami Sound Machine intone in their classic hit "Comunicación," where they proclaim the virtues of an ambiguous bilingual code, of a youthful and protean group language.[2]

This significant role of the narrator notwithstanding, Fernández's texts are dialogic constructs in which character speech acts are both confrontational and revealing. The reader encounters what Bakhtin has termed, in reference to Dostoevsky's works, "a polyphony of battling and internally divided voices" (*Problems* 250). Proceeding directly from Miami's Cuban-American community, these often incoherent voices gain vitality because of their linguistic diversity. In Spanish, of course, Fernández was able to suggest conflicting levels of speech by means of vocabulary, phonetic transcription and the representation of various bilingual strata. Unable to pursue this self-same pattern in *Raining Backwards* for obvious reasons, he opted for an original solution based upon a contemporary controversy: whether English should be recognized as the official language of the United States. In Fernández's novel, the Tongue Brigade, a fanatical organization unmistakably conceived after the English-Only Movement, succeeds in imposing English upon the entire population of Miami through threats and violent activities. Indeed, the Supreme Court is forced to adjudicate in a five to four decision "that it is unconstitutional to prohibit the use of languages in the United States and that the persecution of Spanish-speakers by the Tongue Brigade is equivalent to a violation of the civil rights of the handicapped." For, as the Chief Justice argues, "speaking in any other tongue, and especially in Spanish, is a form of disglosia, a degenerative disease of speech centered in the brain" (158). Therefore, the Tongue Brigade's terroristic victory provides Fernández with the fictional excuse to introduce into his book different levels of English because the speakers' command of the language varies according to age, education, and social reality. In addition, since the aggression encompasses all forms of verbal culture, songs, poems, titles must all be translated, producing the comic distortion which the author attempts in all his Spanish works.

---

[2]The Miami Sound Machine's text promulgates code-switching as an unavoidable means of communication within a Hispanic community in the United States by humorously applying to song this linguistic phenomenon. While Gloria Estefan proclaims that, as long as one is understood, it is acceptable to use two languages at once, voices interrupt to utter phrases like: "Oye, Quique, ¿quieres ir shopping con nosotros este weekend?" To some degree, Fernández's novels evidence the same creative technique.

Hence, Fernández's most recent parodic construct posits a flexible narrator ambivalently distant and near to characters who periodically questions his degrading authority. Regardless of their debased nature, these voices are prone to express pathetic truths in almost lyrical fashion. They are powerful antagonists to the omniscient dictator. Witness the case of Manny, blind comic hero, grotesque clown, who nonetheless — and as if to counteract his narrative portrayal — implies the agonizing reality of any transplanted population. Walking on the beach with his granddaughter, he asks: "Tatiana, which way is Cuba?" "Cuba?" she answers bewildered. "Yes, which way is Cuba from this beach? I want you to turn me in that direction. I want to breathe that air." Tatiana's response confirms an immigrant's greatest fear: the unavoidable eradication of his past from the hybrid collective memory. She states: "But why, Grandpa? Cuba is a restaurant and the air there stinks. It smells like onions and garlic and grease. It's just fattening" (213). Such bittersweet whimsical dialogue humanizes debunked characters like the one in question, transforming them at times into conveyors of meaning, into rhetorical opponents of the controlling consciousness.

Evidently a carnivalesque text in which character voice is essential to accomplish parodic objectives and to integrate a truly dialogic structure, *Raining Backwards* evinces as well an exorbitant intertextuality in which sublime and ludicrous antecedents coalesce to supplement discrediting mechanisms. If, as Kristeva suggests, "any text is constructed as a mosaic of quotations; any text is the absorption or transformation of another" (66), in this particular book the mosaic becomes a kaleidoscope, an arbitrary collection of borrowed signifiers frequently leading absolutely nowhere. Like an onanistic act, they provoke a burst of pleasure, of laughter in this case, and then die unto themselves leaving only the image that everything is ridiculous when taken out of context or when placed in a degrading context. It is within this framework that the critic must perceive Fernández's constant use of allusions to pop artists, pop song titles, and selected pop song words. Yet, by focusing on this marginal component of his narrative technique, one realizes the importance of hybridity, of the author's poetic interest in the emergence of what he perceives as a bicephallic culture, a culture in flux which loses its roots while affirming them. References to pop icons and pop music are temporal emblems. Entangled as they are within the falsely monolingual ambience *Raining Backwards* puts forward, these citations insinuate cultural mixture, psychological ambiguity, even miscegenation. There are three essential manners in which the pop music world manifests itself in Fernández's novel. The first one entails the mere naming within character speech of notable pop singers or celebrated compositions. They operate as societal signifiers, and may be perceived as trivial or exotic depending upon the degree of information available to the reader. Although these allusions sometimes trigger responses from internal addressees, their role is confined and momentary. Secondly, selected words from English or Spanish popular songs are incorporated in extemporaneous fashion within character speech or narrative discourse to debase the verbal act itself, to increment its parodic virtue. At the same time, the pre-text appears defiled as signifier of culture and attitudes. Its frivolity underlined by context, the entire song seems grotesque. Finally, references to pop songs may provoke events within the plot. Thus, societal contradictions are clarified and demythologized.

In what may be termed the novel's overture, a chapter symbolically entitled "Retrieving Varadero," nostalgia manifests itself as theme in the voice of Mirta Vergara. A paradoxically virginal erotomaniac, her life is devoted to a particular memory: her romantic encounter at age fifteen with a young man who, with the passage of time, has achieved mythical stature. Although she is over sixty years old, Mirta awaits the arrival of her teenage beau in an artificial environment created to simulate metonymycally the tropical paradise which, to her, was that Varadero beach where she met her "one and only love" (59). At the text's beginning, Mirta's limited world view is assaulted by a radio announcer, who urges listeners to vacation in resort areas located in Mexico and Florida. His hyperbolic description of their beauty motivates this character speech:

> Why do you go on with your lies? Everyone knows that Varadero was the most beautiful beach, not only in the world but in the whole universe! The waters were forever changing colors, the sand had the texture of baby powder, the breezes were always warm but never hot. So how dare you say that Cancún or Sanibel are better and more beautiful. Liar! Communist! And there you go again. Isn't it enough just to say it once? You're getting me mad. I'd love to turn your program off, but you know I'm waiting for Julio's latest hit with Germán García. But I'm losing my patience! (11)

Mirta's grotesque response to the radio announcer incorporates a double-edged allusion to the pop world. The act of naming two individual artists comically links cultural past and present. Given surrounding context, it operates as well as a debunking mechanism, as a hidden joke that, when apprehended by the informed reader, promotes uncrowning laughter at the expense of popular icons.

Germán García was a Cuban singer who, in the late 1950s, had a hit romantic song in which he rhapsodized about Varadero, calling it — among other things — "blue beach of illusions." This metaphor became lexicalized due to the composition's success, and Germán García's meteoric career flourished until the advent of the Cuban Revolution. Even though he immigrated to the United States in the early 1960s, García's efforts to rekindle his languishing fame within the Miami community met only with failure. It was as if he himself had become lexicalized, a metaphor for an irretrievable past, a name tied exclusively to a paradise lost, to a legendary Cuban beach. Hence, when Mirta refers to him she is denoting a bygone era, she is waxing nostalgic within a humorous context. Germán García operates as cultural signifier in a chain that degrades emotion in carnivalesque fashion.

The second icon identified is Julio Iglesias, Julio to his enthusiastic Hispanic devotees. In a manner of speaking, he embodies a present that is full of past, not only because of his traditional crooning style but also because of his penchant to perform old classics and nostalgic love songs. Iglesias has also gained fame for singing duets with noted American recording artists Willie Nelson, Stevie Wonder and Diana Ross as well as the Mexican Pedro Vargas. When she anticipates a ludicrously cooperative effort between Iglesias and García, Mirta links epochs in aberrant manner and implies an affinity for sentimental singing styles. Consequently, by being part of grotesque speech and objectives, this type of music and their interpreters become the object of derision, of debasing laughter. Song titles often appear interpolated in character speech with a similarly degrading purpose. In a pornographic short story authored by Mirta, the male protagonist identifies himself as a "Universal Soldier" (113), hence evoking Buffy Sainte-Marie's folk ballad of political protest. According to the announcer of a television program named "Only in America," perhaps after the early sixties hit by Jay and the Americans, a group of Cuban ladies intone "God Bless America" for the benefit of the roving camera. They are led in song by one of the novel's most important characters, María de los Angeles López de Rodríguez (Mima), the plantain chip magnate, who accompanies them with castanets. According to the narrator, Captain Carter — a farcical police inspector who stars in the lengthy chapter entitled "Who killed C.R.?" — perceives Mirta, his love interest, as a "Venus in Blue Jeans" (186), parodically inverting the stereotype which this Jimmy Clanton tune suggests. The provocative young female has been comically transformed into a ridiculously clad senior citizen. Later, a depressed Carter hums the trite and mood-reflective "My Old Kentucky Home" (187), whose melancholic softness is understood as grotesque given the surrounding situation.

With regard to Spanish song titles, mocking allusions naturally entail an additional twist. Translated in literal fashion, they constitute bizarre utterances that invoke immediate laughter due both to the context and to either awareness or unawareness of the referent. A case in point is the names of musical albums, Cuban artists and specific songs that a character reads during preparation for the dancing conclusion to "The Good Night," a chapter which provides a satiric Larra-like depiction of Christmas Eve's celebrations.[3] Jesusito says to his family members: "I brought also a few records: 'The Big Dances of Anthony M. Romeu,' 'Fajardo and His Stars,' 'Congas and Carnival from the Orient,' and Jacinto's favorites, 'The Moor Woman from Syria' by Little Barbaro X, and 'They are from the Hills' by the Moorkiller Trio" (48-49). The debasing effect of word-by-word translation is noticeable both to the initiated and the uninitiated. Cuba's Oriente province, by becoming the Orient, evolves into a misleading signifier whose comic impact is self-evident. "La mora de Siria," a famous romantic ballad, appears in English as a distorted image, a reflection on a concave mirror. "Son de la loma," a classic *son oriental* from the late 1920s, suffers an identical fate. Its name seems strange and hence, humorous. Equally strange, of course, are the effects of literal translation upon such personal names as that of pop singer Barbarito Diez, here transformed into a minute version of Malcolm X, and that of the musical group "El Trío Matamoros." Through the exploitation of linguistic inflexibility, Fernández succeeds in promoting that carnivalesque laughter which debunks cultural symbols.

By appropriating pop song lyrics, character speech gains a tripartite alienness. Voices speak abnormally in musical terms, referring the reader to a whole pre-

---

[3]I allude above all to Mariano José de Larra's famous *artículo de costumbres*, "El castellano viejo" ("The Old Castilian"), where he satirizes in slap-stick fashion nineteenth-century birthday celebrations among the nascent Spanish bourgeoisie. Fernández appears to have had this text in mind when concocting "The Good Night."

text whose meaning their words degrade given the profane nature of the real text. Secondly, the recognizable quality of borrowed utterances operates against the characters themselves, trivializing their discursive acts. Thirdly, by falling victim to the repetition of empty signifiers they have learned by rote within a bilingual ambience, these literary entities reveal their cultural hybridity, their ambiguous ethnicity, their internal chaos. Fernández himself has argued in carnivalesque style that his is "a tribute . . . to a dying era. The work is funny, but here is also a certain sadness."[4] And a dying era is characterized, as Bakhtin has aptly affirmed, by change and renewal, by a general feeling of crisis that reflects itself in language, in social attitudes, in political realities. As in Fernández's text, carnival idiom confronts these tragicomic stages:

> with the sense of the gay relativity of the prevailing truths and authorities. We find here a characteristic logic, the peculiar logic of the "inside out" (*à l'envers*), of the "turnabout," of a continual shifting from top to bottom, from bottom to rear, of numerous parodies and travesties, humiliations, profanations, comic crownings and uncrownings. (Rabelais 11)

In *Raining Backwards,* borrowed lyrics are reflective of flux, of turmoil within displaced persons who depend ambivalently upon diverse codes.

Allusions to pop songs are intercalated in narrative discourse and character speech without identification or admission of their use as grafts, or loaned words. Among quoted lines figure some from such familiar compositions as "The Star Spangled Banner," "Unchained Melody," "On Top of Old Smokie," Morris Albert's "Feelings," The Cyrkle's mid-sixties hit "Red Rubber Ball," and "My Country 'Tis of Thee." To illustrate their textual effect, however, one need only to focus on the correspondence between advice columnist Dr. Helen Kings and lovestruck heroine, Caridad "Connie" Rodríguez. The latter, who is assassinated by a resentful cheerleader captain and Tongue Brigade leader, appropriately named Mary Lou (perhaps after the Ricky Nelson hit tune, "Hello, Mary Lou"), writes to a pop psychologist seeking counseling about her relationship with Bill Cloonan, her American boyfriend, who consequently emblematizes incipient miscegenation. In her letter, she intersperses words from Billy Joel's "She's got a way" with her own fictional language. Connie states:

---

[4]In *Rabelais and His World*, Bakhtin writes that, in the Renaissance, carnival images, "saturated with time and the utopian future, reflecting the people's hopes and strivings . . . became the expression of the general gay funeral of a dying era, of the old power and old truths" (99). Fernández's fictional world-view may be identified with such a carnivalesque tradition.

> I'm very much in love with my boyfriend, Bill, but *he has left me three times before and I don't know what to do* . Now we're together again, but I *just know he's getting ready to leave me again* . . . . Last time he left me, I let him come back because he wrote me many love notes begging me to have him back . . . . In his notes, Bill . . . said *to give him one more chance to keep him satisfied, to tell him that my sweet love hasn't died* . . . Dr. Kings . . . . *He's got a way about him and I just don't know what it is!* (91; my italics)

Dr. Kings' response in her column, jokingly titled "Times of Trouble" after "Let It Be," The Beatles' anthem to marijuana ("When I find myself in times of trouble, / Mother Mary comes to me, / Speaking words of wisdom: / 'Let it be, let it be"), is based partly on a Billie Holiday hit, "My Man." The columnist writes: "The truth of the matter is that he's your man and you love him so. Dear Confused, *so what's the difference if you say you'll go back to him?*" (101; my italics). Character speech, then, becomes entwined with pop lyrics with the result that it degrades as it is degraded by the trite reference. The voice that employs borrowed words in a ridiculous surrounding immerses the pre-text itself within parody, vividly underlining the musical composition's own frivolity.

When the quoted text was originally written in Spanish, translation introduces that additional parodic effect already mentioned in the discussion of cited titles. It suffices to reproduce the "thoughtful birthday wishes" that Dr. Helen Kings receives after she turns forty. Among the notes are homages from Cuban composers, two of whose names appear comically distorted. Ernesto Lecuona becomes Ernie Lecuona while Eduardo Sánchez de Fuentes is transformed into Eddie Fuentes. The quoted lines are "To live without your words is too much loneliness" (195), from Sánchez de Fuentes "Vivir sin ti"; "I wish I could kiss you, burning with fever, and drink the nectar of your mouth" (195), from Félix B. Caignet's "El néctar de tu boca"; "In the path of my sad life, I found a flower" (195), from Oscar Hernández's "Lágrimas negras"; and "Like the lullaby of the palm trees on the plain, like the trilling of the mockingbird in the thicket, like the blue of the sky, that's what you are" (196), from Ernesto Lecuona's "Como el arrullo de palmas." Interspersed with these fragments is an alien signifier, suggestive of prevailing biculturalism. Mirta Vergara's arcane memory produces a clashing expression of praise: "You are my soul and my inspiration" (196). That her static mind invokes The Righteous Brothers' sixties hit is indicative of cultural mixture, of the evolving times. In general, the translation of lines from Cuban popular songs that, in exile, have become symbolic of a paradisiac past, that automatically triggers nostalgia, debunks the pre-text's poetic nature, elucidating more clearly their blatant sentimentality. As a result, the neurotic longing for a bygone era is equally demythologized.

Finally, in at least one instance the allusion to a particular pop song motivates a novelistic episode. The Merengues are a celebrated singing group within the fictional Miami community. Their fame proceeds from two compositions. One is their upbeat version of a Mexican classic, José Alfredo Jiménez's *ranchera*, "Tú y las nubes," translated as "You and the Clouds" in Fernández's book. Their interpretation suggests ironic inversion, for this sentimental love song does not lend itself to boisterous *merengue* style. It's as if they had taken one step further than Celia Cruz's already far-fetched transformation of the song[5] to create a text that parodies a pre-text that parodies an original pre-text. The English version, of course, further degrades José Alfredo Jiménez's intensely melodramatic lyrics: "I'm flying low. My love is in the dumps and you so high and so high, looking at my grief and laughing, knowing that I'm a man and will have to tell you: I love you. You and the clouds drive me crazy, you and the clouds are going to kill me" (166). In a manner of speaking, then, this endeavor metaphorically represents the novelist's own creative attitude.

The second song, however, is the one that promotes fictional anecdote. Alberto Beltrán, a Dominican singer from the late fifties, gained renown because of a humorous composition entitled "El negrito del batey." In *Raining Backwards*, the Merengues interpret this song in English, creating a text that does not function within the racially stratified American society. What in the Island was read as the transparent comical effort of a black musician, in the United States is perceived as a manifestation of ethnic prejudice. Translated as "The Little Blackman from the Sugar Mill," its words read as follows:

> They call me the little blackman from the sugar mill, because for me work is the worst enemy. I leave working to the ox because God made work as a punishment. I like to eat crispy merengue with a nifty black mama. I also like to dance sideways, dance very tightly with my succulent black lady. (173-74)

---

[5]In a late 1970's album recorded with Puerto Rican musician Willie Colón, Celia Cruz sang "Tú y las nubes" in *guaracha* beat. This effort supposes a type of danceable parody of José Alfredo Jiménez's serious love song.

Due to the recalcitrant discrimination such lyrics imply, the song is banned by authorities. Indeed, the Merengues are accused of being a white supremacist group. However, their denouncers fail to realize that they are all black: four Dominicans and three Haitians (174). This grotesque episode underlines cultural distinctions that prevent absolute assimilation. Antagonistic poles must clash before they merge, which is why Fernández's novels always communicate a sense of crisis, of dangerous instability

Raining Backwards must be read, accordingly, as a polyphonic construct in which voices allude unconsciously to popular music. These references constitute ambiguous cultural signifiers which show both integration and rejection, conformity and unconformity. They emblematize a past rapidly mixing with a present that augurs an undefined future. Fernández summarizes his novel in the ensuing manner: "This is a book about human beings, it's about a vanishing society. When I was writing this book, I wanted to leave some sort of record of a generation that's dying, that's disintegrating" (Photos 13). By elucidating an effervescent cultural hybridity almost unhinged in nature, the analyzed grafts enhance the topsy-turvy atmosphere of a microcosm akin to a vociferous and ill-fated *conga* line.

WORKS CITED

Bakhtin, Mikhail. *The Dialogic Imagination: Four Essays*. Ed. Michael Holquist. Trans. Caryl Emerson and Michael Holquist. Austin: U of Texas, 1981.

——. *Problems of Dostoevsky's Poetics*. Ed. and trans. Caryl Emerson. Minneapolis: U of Minnesota, 1984.

——. *Rabelais and His World*. Trans. Hélène Iswolsky. Bloomington: Indiana U, 1984.

Culler, Jonathan. *On Deconstruction: Theory and Criticism after Structuralism*. Ithaca: Cornell UP, 1982.

Fernández, Roberto G. *La montaña rusa*. Houston: Arte Público Press, 1985.

——. *Raining Backwards*. Houston: Arte Público Press, 1988.

——. *La vida es un special*. Miami: Universal, 1981.

Kristeva, Julia. *Desire in Language: A Semiotic Approach to Literature and Art*. Ed. Leon S. Roudiez. Trans. Thomas Gora, Alice Jardine, and Leon S. Roudiez. New York: Columbia UP, 1980.

Larra, Mariano José de. *Artículos*. Elda-Alicante: Nueva Generación Editores, 1982.

Photos, Lisa."Exploring the Myths." *Vista*, 29 Oct. 1988: 13.

"A Surging New Spirit." *Time*, 11 July 1988:47.

LAUREN W. YODER

Developing Identity in the Caribbean: Writing about History in the Novels of Daniel Maximin

According to Edouard Glissant, one of the major Caribbean novelists and literary theoreticians of our day, history and literature are interdependent, for history provides a source of inspiration, and literature gives new life to events of the past. Both are essential to enable a people to understand its cultural identity. Glissant affirms that self-expression is a path toward attaining that understanding. "Sterility," he claims, "can be pushed away by the flow of history, improperly known yesterday, but which, as it is unveiled, fertilizes our being with a flood of unsuspected possibilities, of new hopes" (*L'Intention poétique,* 187).[1] Historical foundations of a people nourish creative literature, and literature in turn helps select and unveil essential elements of history, developing a "collective memory," which, says Glissant in the same essay, is lacking and urgently needed in the Caribbean.

The quest to understand the past in order to know oneself and one's culture is at the heart of both novels by the contemporary Guadeloupean novelist Daniel Maximin, *L'Isolé Soleil* (*Isolated Sun*), and *Soufrières* (*Sulphur Mines,* or in the singular, La Soufrière, the name of the volcano that dominates the island of Guadeloupe). In these two novels he reserves a prominent place for references to literature as well as to other forms of art such as painting and music which often seem to be the key to developing that understanding. Beyond being simply gratuitous allusions to other works of art, these references constitute an essential part of the framework of the two novels. They also speak to the nature of the human experience and to the role of art forms in that experience. Specifically, the use of art forms in *L'Isolé Soleil* and *Soufrières* reflects the freedom of the human spirit and the desire to communicate the relationship of the past to the present and to give tentative and renewable form to the life of individuals in the Caribbean.

In 1973 at a colloquium whose theme was the role and function of the African critic and which brought together in Cameroon writers from Africa and the

---

[1] All translations from the French are by the author of the article.

Caribbean, Daniel Maximin made several interesting observations which suggest how he saw the role of the black writer in the 70s. He reminded the audience, in a manner reminiscent of the Russian critic Mikhail Bakhtin's view that dialogue is the essential component of true humanity, that any writer must always be conscious of why he or she is writing and who the public is. And he continued by saying that such questions must always be "the foundation for the action and writing of the black intelligentsia who have undertaken the quest for a new history, a new people, and a new individual" (*African Critic* 316). Here, as he does in his novels, Daniel Maximin stresses the importance of reflecting on history in order to understand one's culture and to be fully self-aware.

L'Isolé Soleil is a personalized recreation of two centuries of the history of Guadeloupe. Not attempting to be objective history, the narration moves back and forth in time between real historical events and their interpretation by personae from the twentieth century. The primary historical events take place during the days and weeks of Guadeloupean resistance to the efforts by Napoleon's envoy Richepanse to turn the clock back and re-establish slavery on the island, and specifically the mass suicide engineered by Louis Delgrès in 1802 when it became clear to him that the alternative meant a return to slavery. The main characters are the old slave woman Miss Bea and her son Jonathan, who lived at the end of the eighteenth century, and Marie-Gabriel and Adrien, two young aspiring writers of the twentieth century.

Soufrières is the story of five different days over the span of five months leading up to the eruption in 1976 of the volcano La Soufrière on the island of Guadeloupe. However, the title, a plural noun, shows that the novel is more than simply the story of one specific volcano's eruption. It is also the record of the essential background of Caribbean life brought to the surface by the narrative, the story of the hopes and desires of various individuals, including Adrien and Marie-Gabriel from *L'Isolé Soleil,* each with his or her own personal "bubbling volcano," each needing to come to an understanding of the past before being free to face the future with confidence.

Though the subjects of the two novels seem at first glance different, they are in fact very complementary, and we can see the second as a continuation of the first in several ways. First of all, both have as their point of departure a specific and real historical event. Secondly, the major characters in *Soufrières* were already present in *L'Isolé Soleil* as those who reflected on the historical events of the preceding centuries. And thirdly, apparent in both novels is these characters' preoccupation with writing, with the interplay of literature and history, and with the goal of using that interplay to help them understand themselves and their place in the twentieth century.

Other signs point to the many links between the two. There are several repeated phrases, including the expression "isolé soleil," and "beau sang giclé" (beautiful spurting blood), shared by both works, and parallel events reflect the thematic continuity of the two novels. For example, near the end of both narrations a death of a friend saddens the other characters. In both cases the person who dies is named Toussaint, though the manner of death is different. The first Toussaint in *L'Isolé Soleil* dies during an attack on the governor's residence in 1943, the second is killed when his Citroën 2-CV hits a tree after the volcano's eruption.

The fundamental themes of the two novels are interrelated. In both, the same basic questions are posed: How is a twentieth-century Caribbean man or woman defined by geography and history? What is the nature of relationships between parents and children? Between the past and the present? Between violence and self-expression? Between liberty and the desire for order? Between word and deed? It seems then appropriate to look at *Soufrières* as an extension of *L'Isolé Soleil* and to examine the related themes of history and writing, of deed and word, of past and present identity in both of the novels. A close reading of the preface of each novel provides insights useful for understanding the preoccupations of the author and for signaling the dominant centers of interest in the narrative.

In *L'Isolé Soleil,* the four short paragraphs of the preface can be read as a prose poem, full of images and surprises, with suggestions rather than explanations. The preface opens with a flock of wounded hummingbirds landing in open seas and ends with a second image of flight, an image composed of leaves (or probably pages, since there is a reference in the first paragraph to an "empty page") floating skyward. As an example of the numerous semantic levels of the words used in these novels, we should also point out that leaves can also be read as leaves on the genealogical tree. After all, a major emphasis of the novel is the attempt to understand one's past; in particular one's family and one's place in it.

In between the opening image of the hummingbirds and the closing image of leaves lifted skyward three major semantic clusters emerge. The first is grouped around the word "history" (*histoire*), and is composed primarily of negative terms, reflecting the violence, pain and anguish of early Caribbean history, terms such as "ruins," "broken branches," "blood-letting," "fear," and "sweat" (*IS* 9). The second is more positive and is centered on the relationship between male and female, on a spirit of cooperation, on a spirit of family. One of the word plays enjoyed by the two characters Adrien and Marie-Gabriel in *L'Isolé Soleil* is the play on the personal pronouns "*il/elle*" ("he/she") which can be easily transformed into "*île*" (island) and "*aile*" (wing), both of which appear at least twice in the preface. The islands, represented by the image of the flock of wounded birds resting on the water to regain their strength, must work together in order to change their destiny. Their history is shown to be not simply a series of individual histories; rather it is the "history of an archipelago," and must include everyone living there: "attentive to our four different races, our seven different languages, and our dozens of bloodlines." The third semantic cluster is grouped around words, around the spoken and the written word, around "shouts of misery and joy . . . held in the throats of men and women who write about themselves." This progression in the preface of *L'Isolé Soleil* suggests that hope can arise out of the pain of the past and that it can be consolidated by self-expression.

In this novel, one of the purposes of writing is to create what one character calls "desire," and which we might explain as energy and will, a desire and energy which can in turn induce social change. In an image calling to mind the ruins on the hills of Guadeloupe of sugar mills with their broken vanes, Maximin says in the preface: "desire is to history as vanes are to the windmill." Just as the vanes of the mill, if repaired, could set the wheels of the mill in motion, so could desire and political will, if reborn and anchored in the hearts of citizens, trigger the wheels of history, of change, and of the development of self-understanding.

A glance at the preface of Maximin's second novel, *Soufrières,* confirms the close thematic relationship between the two novels. In the final four paragraphs of the longer preface to *Soufrières,* we see once again the key thematic centers of the first preface: "the hummingbird," "notebook/novel," and "sea/volcano/sky." The primal elements air, earth, water, and fire which compose the geographical elements of the sea, the volcano and the sky are closely associated with the themes of death and rebirth. We note, for example, the references to "the end (*la fin*) and to the verb "to die" (*mourir*). But death is clearly not portrayed here as final. In a phrase not coincidentally reminiscent of the Senegalese Birago Diop's poem in his tale "Sarzan," where he admonishes his compatriots to listen to the voice of the ancestors in the sounds of nature, we have a reference to the continuing presence of one's ancestors: "Before dying, you are able to see once more those who have died without ever leaving." Furthermore the preface conveys the impression of a re-creation, of a new Garden of Eden which has yet to be contaminated by men and women: "Human footprints will have stopped at the beaches and at the edge of the craters." Only after this psychological return to paradise is rebirth to a new identity possible, in much the same way that in the Gospel of John the seed cannot live unless it first dies. By the use of the words "birth" (*naissance*) and "true life" (*vraie vie*) the prose poem that composes the preface suggests that indeed new life can and will arise from the ashes of the mass suicide of the Guadeloupean troops under the command of Delgrès, from the volcanic ash that covers Basse-Terre after the eruption of la Soufrière, and from the ashes of the character Marie-Gabriel's home called "The Flame Tree" (*Les Flamboyants*).

In keeping with the theme of death and rebirth, we also have in the preface of *Soufrières* a strong repeated image of the hummingbird. Still wounded as in the preface to *L'Isolé Soleil*, a hummingbird takes refuge between the pages of Marie-Gabriel's working notebook of ideas, the notebook she is using to prepare for writing her novel. At the end of this preface, as the notebook opens up, the hummingbird, which earlier represented the Caribbean islands, soars skyward "with a smile, freed by the hibiscus flower open to the sun."

It is not by chance that the hummingbird finds its healing and inspiration in the notebook, an obvious symbol for artistic creation based on events in real life. The hope expressed in the first preface was that "songs" and "poems" and "words" would rewrite history to bring people together in order to understand themselves and each other. And in the second the "notebook," a "novel," and "a word of love" achieve a link between the poet, the islands, her past, and consequently, her future.

The preface of *Soufrières* echoes the preface of *L'Isolé Soleil* in other ways as well. In the earlier novel, the final sentence of the preface begins with the image "words are leaves/pages taken flight at the risk of losing their roots" (*les mots sont des feuilles envolées au risque de leurs racines*), suggesting that writing does involve risks (perhaps the risks of deforming or clouding the past and consequently of destroying one's real roots). The preface of *Soufrières,* almost as if it were the continuation of the earlier preface, begins in this way: " . . . and the page/leaf takes flight, risking its greenness" (*et la feuille prend son vol au risque de sa verdure*). And on the first page of the narrative, "a leaf/page takes flight" (*S* 15), in this case the leaf of a mango tree whose function is to provide shade for Angela's house. Indeed, the exact same phrase returns in the postscript of *L'Isolé Soleil,* signed by "Daniel" in which the narrator/author expresses the desire for synthesis, for solidarity, and for continuity. Marie-Gabriel herself in the course of the novel combines the images from the two prefaces in the following statement: "And how much memory is essential for knowledge? And especially now that the story of her roots is nearing its end, why would the leaf/page fly off risking its greenness?" (*S* 64). Given the importance of the symbol of trees in Maximin's work, especially in the preface to the second novel and to Marie-Gabriel's "writing tree," (*arbre d'écriture*) in the first, it is clear that sometimes words are synonymous with leaves. Indeed, the old music teacher Adrienne Roussy comments on the value of writing and perhaps unconsciously on the tree theme by saying that "paper is simply wood. Wood rots, but words do not" (*S* 193). On the obviously physical level, leaves of a book are of course related to leaves on a tree. The theme of trees is also closely linked with the historical and genealogical purposes of the novels, with the leaves from the genealogical tree, since Maximin traces the history of Guadeloupe over two centuries from father or mother through daughter or son. Furthermore, tree leaves have another symbolic relationship in these novels. Some leaves are authentic and have a clear and conscious identity. Others are more ambiguous because they present two different colors, depending on the way one looks at them. In *L'Isolé Soleil,* "non-authentic" Caribbean people, those who have concentrated more on imitating other cultures than on understanding themselves, are presented as resembling the leaves of a tree called the cannonwood (*bois-canon*): "The freed Negroes suffer from the fear of being like the leaves of the *bois-canon* tree, for they are green on top and white underneath" (*IS* 42). Consequently, the darker color green represents black identity. Most trees of course bear only one kind of fruit or have only one kind of leaf. Marie-Gabriel imagines that her writing is like a tree which bears both sweet fruit and bitter, comforting and personal, which is at the same time stimulating, disquieting, and universal. And, she says, stressing the fundamental feminine nature of her literary activity: "trees would be women in secret, and volcanoes would be too. Trees are a synthesis, and volcanoes too, of earth, air, fire, and water" (*IS* 229).

Back in 1973 at the Yaounde Colloquium, nine years before the publication of his novels, Maximin began to establish the guidelines he felt were essential for an effective writer. The literary critic, he said at that time, and by extension the writer, corresponds faithfully to an earlier definition of the intellectual, who must be "sometimes a decoration, sometimes a mediation, sometimes a catalyst" (*African Critic* 318). On the theoretical level, then, writing has three functions, which may or may not overlap. First, writing creates beauty, presumably by giving new form to life. Secondly, writing is a link which encourages self-understanding, a link between past and present, a link between individuals, or a link between the everyday and the eternal. And thirdly, writing, by developing self-awareness at both the individual and community levels, does encourage people to act — to act socially, politically, or artistically.

Before examining the functions of writing and the role of the poet/writer as expressed in Maximin's two novels, let us look for a moment at the references to literature and the occurrences of writing as an activity in the novels themselves.

In the catalog of literary references, an important place belongs to oral literature, including riddles (*IS* 210), proverbs (*IS* 45), and tales. The Caribbean folktales which appear in these novels provide a grounding in tradition and have an extension into other parts of the novels. Siméa, the mother of Marie-Gabriel, translates creole tales and uses them to help the little girl Angela in the psychiatric hospital recover the use of language which she had lost when she saw her fisherman father killed by a surfacing Nazi submarine during the second world war. The most frequent references to animal characters in Caribbean folklore are to the evil "Soldier Fish," (*Poisson-Armé*) representing the forces that enslave and endanger liberty, and the valiant "Colibri," which, given the other references in the novels to the hummingbird, represents courage, freedom, and the soaring of human imagination. The submarine, which by surfacing capsizes Angela's father's fishing boat, is referred to as a "poisson-armé," and by extension reference to the dangerous fish also evokes the unwise use of military force by policemen and soldiers. Such use of force is always contemptible, whether it be the invasion by the troops of General Richepanse at the beginning of the nineteenth century or the violence during the years of Petainist France when, at carnival time in Saint Claude the character Toussaint is shot.

The appearance of the folk hero "colibri" is frequent elsewhere in the novels as well. In addition to representing the courage and freedom of the island's people, the colibri appears to be as well the symbol for communication, for literary creativity. The narrator points out in fact in *Soufrières* that birds are probably one source of original human language: "children's first words imitate birds" (*S* 33). It is not surprising then that the character Angela is able to sing before she is able to speak properly. The story of the folk hero Pélamanlou/Pélamanli is also significant, for in the version of the Caribbean tale told by Marie-Gabriel's father, a version that underlines the importance of music, the child with the flute and his twin manage to charm the Seven-Headed Beast with their alternate playing so that he is unable to stop dancing and finally falls over dead, powerless over the twins and their music.

The major twentieth-century characters in *L'Isolé Soleil* and almost everyone in *Soufrières* seem to live and breathe literature. We see this preoccupation specifically in Adrien's letters to Marie-Gabriel, in the activity surrounding the production of plays, in the younger Toussaint's mania for quoting poetry, and in Siméa's journal. In Siméa's 1939 journal, two major areas of interest are surrealist poetry and black poetry, including the poetry of the Harlem Renaissance and the reawakening of authentic Caribbean poetry with Léon Damas and Aimé Césaire. It is clear that surrealism leaves an important legacy by its strong emphasis upon images, and the new black poetry showed that poetry could be both openly militant and richly evocative. Adrien cites in a letter a comment Damas made to him one evening, showing the dual nature of poetry in its role of defining identity: "A poem is useful; it's strong and fragile as graffiti on a large wall" (*S* 20).

References to the theater are also important in *Soufrières*. Adrien writes home from France at length about the play *Solitude la mulâtresse* (*Solitude the Mulatto Woman*) presented at the Avignon theater festival. And the principal project of the secondary school students and their teachers is the preparation of a play, *La Danse de la femme-volcan* (*The Dance of the Volcano Woman*). This play, a collective and partially subconscious effort to participate in the real activity of the real Soufrière, is based in turn upon *La Danse de la forêt* (*The Dance of the Forest*), a play by the Nigerian writer Wole Soyinka.

Not only do the characters make constant reference to literature, they are also directly involved themselves in the act of writing. Much of the communication between characters is in the form of letters, and at least seven people keep "notebooks": Jonathan, Marie-Gabriel, Adrien, Angela, Elisa, Louis-Gabriel, and Rosan. These notebooks serve different purposes of course, but in general, the major quality of the notebook genre is its provisional nature. In the same fashion, the identity of an adolescent or the identity of a cultural community learning to understand itself is provisional. That is, as opposed to a literary work in final publishable literary form, what is written in a notebook is always open to change and modification once reactions from other individuals are gleaned. In this way the characters in Maximin's novels look at words and ideas as did Mikhail Bakhtin, who felt that dialogue between individuals and groups captures the essence of humanity and freedom. Morson points out that Bakhtin:

> continually sought and found unexpected ways to show that people never utter a final word, only a penultimate one . . . Humanity is defined by its "unfinalizedness" [*nezaversennost'*]. Whether existence is wholly determined or partially free, whether knowledge is possible or impossible, we retain the capacity to surprise ourselves and others. (vii)

By the same token, plays on words also show a similar preoccupation with freedom. As we have pointed out, words are valued by Maximin and by the characters in his novels precisely because they can suggest multiple meanings and elicit varied responses.

For Jonathan, the notebook/journal was a preparation for his stand with Delgrès against slavery. For Marie-Gabriel it is the source-book for the novel she is writing. For Elisa, a notebook becomes a less-threatening replacement for speaking ("paper-speak," [*le parler-papier*]). And for Rosan, the agricultural agent who works near the foot of the volcano, his journal is the center of his life as an amateur scientist. In it he records all of the activity of La Soufrière in the days and weeks before its eruption. In every case, keeping a notebook is an essential way of understanding oneself as well as understanding the natural and social environment and one's place in that environment.

Words, the stuff of literature, seem sometimes to take on a life of their own in Maximin's novels. This life may be the magical power of incantation, as in 1802 when Miss Bea helps Delgrès decide whether to use force or ruse in combatting Richepanse and the French armies. Some of the same incantatory words are used by Angela when she tries to calm the child Elisa who, reminded of the death of her brother during another political demonstration, goes into a frenzy upon seeing the policeman massed to prevent a political demonstration during carnival time (*S* 97).

Words also take on special meaning as names, and confer on individuals qualities of the meaning inherent in them in a manner reminiscent of the importance of given names in most African societies, where one's name is an essential part of one's identity. Or even in the tradition of the Old Testament, where naming the trees and the animals is a way of understanding the relationship among them. One has only to look at the title of the first novel, *L'Isolé Soleil,* to see that except for the accent mark the first word is contained in the second as is the second in the first. That is, the identity of the first is wrapped up in the second, as the second is subsumed in the first. Furthermore, in *Soufrières,* in keeping with his desire for synthesis and amalgamation, the narrator reminds the reader who hasn't noticed before that the word incorporates both male and female: "*Soufrières: soeurs et frères mêlés*" (Soufrières: sisters and brothers intermingled: *S* 273). This synthesis at the end of *Soufrières* echoes a passage in the first novel where the three friends Toussaint, Siméa, and Louis-Gabriel take a hike up the mountain to gather strength from the volcano on the morning of the planned insurrection at carnival time in 1943. At the top of the mountain, near the fuming crater, the narrator addresses the three characters: "Before you go back down, the name Soufrière offers you its richness" (*IS* 230). And in a shared ritual expressing their faith in the power of words to define their individual identities, each chose several words made directly from the letters of Soufrière: Toussaint composed words such as "*refus*" (refusal), Gaby, "*frère et soeur*" (brother and sister), and Siméa composed the message "*soufrière: oui, frères, oser fuir*" (yes, brothers, dare to flee: *IS* 231). Later that day Toussaint is killed and Gaby flees into exile.

Daniel Maximin points out by rearranging letters in this way that words are always more meaningful than they seem, and that their meanings are open-ended. They are polysemic, and therefore characters and reader alike must be willing to open themselves up to the seemingly frivolous yet serious game of discovering hidden meanings, hidden meanings that help explain the essential identity of each individual.

As a further example of the polyvalence of words, the author and the characters delight in rearranging letters in names to make other words. One of the journals Marie-Gabriel keeps as she begins to think about writing her novel is called "*L'Aire de la Mer*" (The Sea's Domain). Changing the phrase slightly (though the sounds are absolutely identical) as he chooses a title for the fifth section of *L'Isolé Soleil,* Maximin calls it "*L'Air de la Mère*" (The Mother's Air). In a similar manner, Siméa and the musician Louis-Gabriel explore words beginning with "S" because they can help unveil the identity of Siméa, which of course begins with the same letter. They choose words linked to the four elements: *Soufrière, Source, Sable, Sérénade* (Soufrière (volcano), spring, sand, serenade). Though the verbal banter seems like simple game-playing, Siméa makes it clear that there is a deeper meaning. "Chance," she says, "expresses as much the identity we seek as the one we flee, rather than the identity we really possess." In other words, the identity expressed by these words is a developing, dynamic, and multi-faceted identity, not something static. In high school, Adrien and Marie-Gabriel play a similar game based on their given names. For example, in the double name Marie-Gabriel they find words such as "*arbre, mère, mirage, abri*" (tree, mother, mirage, shelter), and in the name Adrien they discover "*aire, nid, ire, aide*" (domain, nest, anger, help).

Rearranging letters in their names is a way of reaffirming the liberty of self-expression and self-determination. Siméa laments in her journal all the European names by which the islands and their cities are known, and she explains how important a reaffirmation of names can be in developing pride in oneself and in affirming identity: "Our history has only first names to inscribe into our memories. We are not the masters of the names of our islands, our cities, our streets" (*IS* 187). She goes on to explain the origin of her own name. Her father, she says, "no doubt wanted be to have many friends, so he constructed my name Siméa from the word 'friends' " (*IS* 187). In a similar way, Marie-Gabriel suggests that she was named Marie because the name contains the verb "*aimer*" (to love).

Indeed, the case of the child Elisa is especially interesting when seen in light of the importance of names. She is practically mute, refusing to speak because of the horrible scene of her brother's death. Her first words are her own given name, which she repeats in order to gain confidence in herself and to express her feelings to other people. Angela, who herself had been brought in mute to the psychiatric hospital following a psychologically traumatic experience of injustice, reminds Elisa in a strange image of the importance of her name. "Protect your name carefully, my daughter! Your name is like a sack suspended from a branch. Even if the branch breaks, the sack won't fall. It's your name!" (*IS* 27).

In a limited but fundamental sense, Elisa is representative of Marie-Gabriel the apprentice novelist, and perhaps even of Caribbean literary production. She begins by learning to know herself and recover her own identity and progresses to the point where she can express the end of her own exile and the beginning of her own creativity. Marie-Gabriel, by writing, digs into her own past and into the past of her family in order to understand her own identity. In a letter to Elisa she shows how close her feelings must be to Elisa's: "With the sun in my eyes, I walked into my forbidden forest as confidently as you do when you climb alone in the morning up to the heart of the volcano" (*S* 115). She recognizes, as she writes to Elisa, that she is using images from the "story of her own rebirth" (*S* 116) and she realizes as well that she herself has become a link in the chain of Caribbean history, perhaps even the spiritual reincarnation of a long line of valiant women that have been characters in *L'Isolé Soleil* and *Soufrières*: "a little girl with her heart pinched over her notebook, changing names at the crossroads: Ti-Carole, Angela, Eve, Ariel, Gerty, Inès, Siméa, Marie-Gabriel, Elisa, anchoring and drifting names, names of the future and the remembered past, a necklace of things desired adorning the neck of the Caribbean mother" (*S* 117). The reference to "*désirades*" (desired things) reminds the reader that the first section of *L'Isolé Soleil* is entitled "*Désirades,*" and that the island of Guadeloupe is presented as a slave mother who has just given birth to a daughter, the island of Désirade, and who, like the mother strangling her daughter to prevent her from suffering the indignities of slavery, seems to be pushing the island slowly off back across the Atlantic toward the East, toward Africa.

What do the characters in the novels themselves say about the importance of writing? We can extrapolate several specific reasons for the activity of writing, and by extension, of reading, because we remember that letters are exchanged, private journals are uncovered, and even drafts of novels are passed around for commentary. First of all, writing is useful to renew history. Secondly, it can be political in aim, to encourage social or political change. Thirdly, writing and reading can awaken imagination and facilitate dreams. In the fourth place, writing can heal by restoring faith in one's identity, by revitalizing individual and collective hope.

We have already pointed out the importance of history and historical events, especially in *L'Isolé Soleil*. The characters, especially Adrien and Marie-Gabriel, struggle with the meaning of events in the Caribbean, and in particular with the collective suicide of Louis Delgrès. Would it not have been better, they wonder, for him to have fought with his troops against Richepanse until the bitter end? Or was the defiant act of suicide more useful as a symbol to future generations to encourage them never to accept slavery in any form?

In any case, a vision from the past and an understanding of that vision must penetrate the whole person, as the narrator admonishes in *L'Isolé Soleil:* "you will give your memory in trust to your loins, to your heart and to your eyes, out of reach of the forgetfulness of lips that keep our secrets caged up" (*IS* 61). In Jonathan's notebook, that admonition is repeated several times in substantially the same terms (*IS* 61-75). True memory is anchored in the womb as a sign that an individual descends directly, both culturally and physically, from a real ancestor. It must also be anchored in the heart as a sign that memory is a basis for courage, and in the eyes signifying that memory also resides in the intellect and is transmitted through the written word.

As she gathers material for her novel, Marie-Gabriel recognizes the difficulties, physical as well as intellectual, of rewriting history. After all, most of the documents explaining the eighteenth and nineteenth centuries are kept in France. The young novelist suggests that such documents are kept away purposefully, in order to preserve mastery, mastery over the future as they have guaranteed over the past (*IS* 106). Marie-Gabriel recognizes the importance of anchoring her narration in nature in order for it to maintain its veracity and trustworthiness. Tropical nature, and especially the volcano itself, becomes a character in the novels rather than simply a background for action, "like a character . . . who demonstrates both open rebellion and cowardly acts" (*IS* 18).

In one sense, the important thing about a historical novel is that it makes history alive and reminds people of events. In some cases the reawakening of history also means a fundamental rewriting of historical perspective. In others, it is sufficient to bring new life to events which have long since died in popular memory.

Marie-Gabriel goes about reawakening history on both the personal and the collective level. Her father, Louis-Gabriel, wrote to her just before his death in a plane crash at the summit of the Soufrière while returning from Europe. Her father was a musician, and the project of his dreams was to rewrite the history of the Caribbean in music (*IS* 15). Thus his death is associated in her mind with the death of Delgrès. Even while her writing project is still secret, Marie-Gabriel writes to preserve the memory of both men: "you secretly jot down ideas and images for the novel that you plan to write in order to bring back to life from our history, from the eruption by Delgrès up to the eruption of the Boeing, those fathers who have disappeared" (*IS* 15). However, Marie-Gabriel wants to be sure that she writes something more substantial than sentimental childhood memories, for fear that they might "put people to sleep like lullabies" (*IS* 24). She would place in the same category as those lullabies sentimental poetry written in celebration of heroic historical figures, fearing that such poetry is insufficiently oriented toward action.

Secondly, then, to complement its goal of reawakening the past, writing can encourage social and political change. In order to effect social change, one must first understand social and political structures. Portraying these structures in literature is one way of developing and communicating such understanding. The writer is privileged, because he or she has been forced to struggle with word choice and images, in much the same way that Elisa uses her personal notebooks to expand her exploration of the world around her and to concretize her grasp of what she observes.

Political treatises, incitements to act in specific circumstances, are another example in these novels of writing which is directly and clearly useful. In 1802, with the arrival of the French troops to turn back the clock and reintroduce slavery, Louis Delgrès wrote a tract which was tacked up in streets all over town (*IS* 47), affirming and confirming his intention of resisting Napoléon's plan to re-enslave plantation workers. In the same way, on the creative level of writing, says Léon Damas in the reported conversation already referred to in *Soufrières* (20), a poem can be useful in the same political sense of graffiti on walls. "Antillean people," affirms Marie-Gabriel, "are slumbering volcanoes that we need to awaken with stories about zombies, monkeys, bamboo, rum, music and cutlasses" (*IS* 24). In other words, the writer must not be reticent about including all facets of life, the beautiful as well as the more violent. And it is especially important to use those themes and situations that are specific to the Caribbean, such as life on the sugar plantation and its vestiges. There is however a danger in writing a novel full only of grievances, for such prose suggests that one is writing to awaken the conscience of someone more powerful who might be able to change the situation, to appeal to a paternal authority. And indeed, one of Marie-Gabriel's tenets is: "You must not compose a book of complaints, because they would need to be submitted to a king" (*IS* 19).

One of the recurring motifs in *Soufrières* is the painting *The Jungle* by the Cuban painter Wifredo Lam, whose exposition Adrien visited in Paris and writes about to Marie-Gabriel. Seeing the freedom and life expressed in the painting, Adrien is reminded that the role of the painter and the role of the poet are similar. Both can reawaken Caribbean identity and pride by pointing to the specificity of the Caribbean experience and can confirm that the Caribbean is able after years of uncertainty to stand solidly on its own legs: "Yes, it so happens that men who juggled their destiny of jungle and misery, riddled with doubts, with contradictory demands on them, thanks to their nervous gropings, to incoherence, to lightening flashes, have finally discovered themselves" (*S* 73). Wilfredo Lam's painting becomes a point of reference for the girl Elisa who herself, as we have pointed out, can be seen as representative of the awakening of the Caribbean, because she learns self-awareness and self-expression thanks to the "salutary invention of paper-speak" (*S* 254). In what has become a ritual for her, she sits staring at the painting for long moments, drawing strength from its vibrant life and from the short dedication composed by Adrien: "Every naked footprint on the sand guarantees desire a future" (*S* 254).

One of the social changes that a writer can encourage, particularly a woman writer such as the character Marie-Gabriel, is to revalorize the position of women in society. According to Marie-Gabriel, reflecting on the story of Delgrès, men tend to see the world too often only in terms of heroes. Consequently, normal living and normal interactions between people fail to receive the attention they should. She explains her reaction to history as defined by males in a letter to Adrien: "I am struck as well by the growing feeling that history is only men's lies. Lies in relationship to the way in which women live their history" (*IS* 198).

If writing and words can encourage social change, then they are also vehicles of personal healing and collective hope. The act of writing itself is salutary for

Marie-Gabriel, for after her father's death it allows her to unburden herself, to work out her grief, to express her love. Indeed, love is closely linked to creative writing, especially in the first few pages of *L'Isolé Soleil,* where Marie-Gabriel reacts to her father's death in the plane wreck, imagining what she calls a "novel from beyond love" (*IS* 17), which would replace the letters and photos that her father would send every year on her birthday from across the sea. In a similar fashion, Adrien, writing to himself on the airplane returning to Guadeloupe, also recognizes that writing is an act of love: "You know how to write about love. Loving itself is not enough. You need to say that you love" (*S* 196).

And for Elisa as well, working with words helps her to make right what has gone wrong, make whole what has been splintered and partial, helps her affirm her identity and blossom into full humanity. Hence the importance of her "paper-speak" throughout *Soufrières*. Elisa expresses her healing and her wholeness in the final scene of the book during the burning of Les Flamboyants, the family home of Marie-Gabriel, under the smoking volcano. She carries off from the fire two items that are important symbolically: Wifredo Lam's painting, and a bag of records belonging to Marie-Gabriel's father. She completes her collection by picking up the notebook belonging to Marie-Gabriel. The common thread running through each of these art forms is their reaffirmation of the Caribbean identity. Lam reaffirms the life and vigor of the island peoples; Louis-Gabriel's music was an attempt to lay bare the soul of the culture, and Marie-Gabriel's notebook affirmed making sense out of a history that is both heroically national and intimately personal.

The combination of these art forms enabled Elisa to regain hope, to live with the memories of her childhood, transforming even negative and painful experiences into fertile ground with the potential for positive growth. To express this hope she scribbles several lines on the last page of Marie-Gabriel's notebook: "Thus exile moves on, carrying clumsy seeds to birds born in time which never sleep in the fertile spaces of joggled childhood memories" (*S* 278). The infusion of hope helps one understand the past, and Maximin suggests that the hope which helps understand the past can also help modify the future. The three lines that end the novel are presented as a poem, and juxtaposed as they are with the old creole round that the tape recorder sings sweetly to Elisa, who finally feels that she has found her place in the world ("nicely positioned between sky and earth"), they can be taken as representing an old creole song, suggesting hope and healing just as the old traditional songs instilled identity and understanding:

> When the thread of the days
> follows the needle of hope,
> its patches up destiny. (*S* 279)

As Siméa expresses in her journal: "A page of poetry . . . will always be able to express . . . the essence hidden in a passing moment, an eternity of dreams, an instant of true life" (*IS* 139). Writing, along with other art forms, is able to capture eternity, linking meaningfully for individuals and for countries the events of the past, the experiences of the present, and the hopes of the future.

Understanding the contemporary culture of the Caribbean and developing an awareness of the Antillean identity depends on the interplay between history and writing about that history. Writing, the act of placing words on paper in the various forms we see in these two novels, encourages not only reflection, but also action. But most of all, writing by the characters in Maximin's novels is an affirmation of their self, of their community, and of their culture.

WORKS CITED

Glissant, Edouard. *L'Intention poétique.* Paris: Editions du Seuil, 1969.

Maximin, Daniel. "Critique de l'activité critique dans le Tiers Monde noir," *The African Critic and his People as Producers of Civilization.* Paris: Présence Africaine, 1977.

——. *L'Isolé Soleil.* Paris: Editions du Seuil, 1981.

——. *Soufrières.* Paris: Editions du Seuil, 1987.

Morson, Gary S. *Bakhtin: Essays and Dialogues on his Work.* Chicago: U of Chicago P, 1986.

MARGARET K. BASS

Race, Class, and Gender in Four West Indian Novels: *Pitch Lake, Corentyne Thunder, The Hills Were Joyful Together, Wide Sargasso Sea*

In George Lamming's autobiographical novel, *In the Castle of My Skin,* G., the narrator talks about being unable to describe adequately a feeling that he and his friends have about something that they have just seen. The feeling is "a big, big feeling," and G. laments the fact that he and the other boys do not know enough words to relate the magnitude of it. G. says: "We had to say something was like something else, and whatever we said didn't convey all we felt" (153). G.'s statement expresses my frustration as I discuss the question of identity in these four West Indian novels. I do not want to say that they are like something else because they are not. It would be all too easy to define these novels by comparing them to their more familiar American and British counterparts. While comparative studies certainly have their value, such a study would not, I think, give these novels the recognition which they deserve as classics from an established literary tradition.

The quest for an identity, the desire to discover who I am and how I relate to the society in which I live, is certainly not a theme that is exclusive to West Indian novels. It is, of course, a universal quest and a theme in many novels. However, history and geography combine to make this universal struggle manifest itself in very particular ways for the West Indian people.

Michael Gilkes says that the "angst of identity is the most central and urgent theme of West Indian literature" (96). This angst is most assuredly related to West Indian history — a history shared by writers from diverse backgrounds and different islands. George Lamming, in *The Pleasures of Exile*, succinctly chronicles the "discovery" of the West Indies:

> Their [the Caribbean Islands] history has been similar, a sad and hopeful epic of discovery and migration. First Columbus, coaxing and bullying his crew to find India by a western route, choosing that name from his mistake and a legend of his time . . . . Next the full European descent, urged

> by both adventure and greed; Spain, France, England, Holland as well as the Danes and Swedes, and a tiny, almost forgotten rock-pool of Germans!
>
> All arrived in this Caribbean Sea like an epidemic ignorant of its specific target . . . . And all have remained in the complexions of their descendants who now inhabit these lands.
>
> The indigenous Carib and Arawak Indians, living by their own lights long before the European adventure, gradually disappear in a blind, wild forest of blood. That mischievous gift, the sugar cane, is introduced, and a fantastic human migration moves to the New World of the Caribbean; deported crooks and criminals, defeated soldiers and Royalist gentlemen fleeing from Europe, slaves from the West Coast of Africa, East Indians, Chinese, Corsicans and Portuguese. The list is always incomplete, but they all move and meet on an unfamiliar soil, in a violent rhythm of race and religion. (17)

It is this myriad of customs and cultures meeting and moving on "unfamiliar soil" which makes the history of the West Indies so distinctive. People left or were compelled to leave fully developed civilizations and were forced to merge — to create a culture where there was none. This seems to me a most astonishing feat. Such a tremendous achievement makes ludicrous V. S. Naipaul's statement that "history is built around achievement and creation; and nothing was created in the West Indies" (*Middle Passage* 29). West Indians and West Indian culture were created in the West Indies and from this coalescence of nations comes a rich literary tradition. With the creation of a new culture comes a mandatory relinquishing of the old. No matter how people tried, it was impossible to fully preserve African or Indian or Portuguese culture in the new land. One offshoot of this merging and rending is a kind of cultural schizophrenia or a feeling of belonging to two worlds, and another is a feeling of rootlessness — a feeling of belonging to no world at all. The central figures in *Pitch Lake, Corentyne Thunder, The Hills Were Joyful Together,* and *Wide Sargasso Sea* experience one of these feelings.

Edward Brathwaite in "Timehri" says that "the problem of and for West Indian artists and intellectuals is that having been born and educated within this fragmented culture, they start out in the world without a sense of 'wholeness' " (*Is Massa Day Dead* 30). This sense of fragmentation is reflected in the authors' works and is the basis for the frequent declarations of ethnic heritage and racial purity that we find in the novels. Since the characters believe that they have no roots, they define themselves only in terms of race, gender, and social class. No character defines himself or herself as West Indian, and that is an important omission.

The intense desire for a separate and specific identity moved a young Barbadian man to challenge my use of the term Anglophone West Indian literature: "The English speaking islands are not at all alike," he said. "We see the world differently. Any Bajan would be insulted if you called him a Jamaican and vice versa." My friend's observation was quite correct. Each island *is* different. However, Barbados, Jamaica, Trinidad, and the other formerly British colonies are far more alike than different. The colonizers had a perversive influence over the slaves whom they simultaneously oppressed and forced to conform to a British way of living. The islands became merely extensions of the "Mother Country." It is important to note here that the British, unlike the French, were not assimilationists. Hence, the slaves and immigrants were never accepted by the British as British and consequently could not define themselves as such. They were, quite simply, British subjects — like the British in custom but not British. C. L. R. James, in an essay entitled "The Old World and the New," discusses the impact of colonization:

> [T]here is far more in common between me and ninety-nine percent of Englishmen than between the Englishman and the Italian, the Englishman and the German, and the Englishman and the French. To begin with, we use the same language . . . . We use the same books, we have similar social attitudes, the same basic ideas, even the same religion . . . .
> (*Rendezvous* 203)

The Anglophone islands, like siblings from the same family, have their own personalities and cultures. They have grown and become independent and self-governing, but they still remain inextricably linked because of their common history of British colonialism and their common language. What is the West Indian novel? Lamming defines it simply as "a novel written by the West Indian about the West Indian reality" (*Pleasures* 38). *Pitch Lake, Corentyne Thunder, The Hills Were Joyful Together,* and *Wide Sargasso Sea* are about that reality.

The question of racial identity in the West Indies is a complex one. The centuries of intermingling and intermarriage among the races in the West Indies has intensified the "angst of identity." "White" characters in the novels vociferously proclaim their racial purity. For people of color, the question of ethnic heritage becomes more complicated. Characters seem to place themselves on V. S.

Naipaul's color chart to determine how nearly white they are. Naipaul claims that West Indians divide people into categories of "white, fusty, musty, dusty, tea, coffee, cocoa, light black, black and dark black" (*Middle Passage* 68). The novels reflect this preoccupation with skin color — a seemingly necessary preoccupation when we consider that power and prestige wane as one moves further away from "white" on the spectrum of skin color. To be "pure white" in the West Indies is to be part of an extremely privileged and powerful minority group. In *Wide Sargasso Sea* Antoinette Cosway is a Creole, a white West Indian. Since she was born in the West Indies, she is not a *real* white woman in the eyes of those who live in her community, particularly the blacks. "I never looked at any strange negro," she says. "They called us white cockroaches" (23). Antoinette constantly tries to distinguish herself from the black servants who work on her family's run-down plantation, but she cannot escape the taunting accusations that she is a "white cockroach." Antoinette's life and destiny are shaped by her feeling of inferiority. She is ostracized and denied participation in any community. Antoinette even feels separate from her *genuinely* white British husband. Antoinette's West Indian cultural background gives her a bond with blacks which her husband cannot comprehend. For example, Antoinette understands *patois,* the language spoken by the indigenous and predominantly black population. One day, Amelie, a young black servant, sings a song in patois which deeply disturbs Antoinette. She tells her husband the meaning of the song:

> It was a song about a white cockroach. That's me. That's what they call all of us who were here before their own people in Africa sold them to the slave traders. And I've heard English women call us white niggers. So between you I often wonder who I am and where is my country and where do I belong and why was I ever born at all. (103)

Antoinette expresses anguish and uncertainty in this passage, but she asserts her superiority to those of African descent. She also absolves herself and her ancestors from participation in one of the first injustices committed against the African people during the slave trade. She reminds us that Africans were sold to slave traders by other Africans, but more important than this, she reminds us that her ancestors were in Jamaica long before the slaves were brought there. Antoinette claims Jamaica not as *her* country, but as the country of her ancestors. That claim, which implicitly recaptures the island from the blacks, only brings Antoinette shame and further alienation from the British residents of the island.

Even though she is white, Antoinette cannot be both Jamaican and British.

The issues of race and class are so closely intertwined in these West Indian novels that it is impossible to discuss just one of these aspects of identity in isolation. Rhys makes it clear that Antoinette Cosway wants to be seen as "pure white." However, that desire is coupled with the desire to be part of a particular class and a specific social and racial community. Because she is a Creole, she revolves in the world without social connections. She is white and West Indian and, according to Rhys's rendering, that is to be a part of nothing at all.

The characterization of Joe da Costa in *Pitch Lake* brings the interrelatedness of class and race to the fore. At the beginning of the novel, Joe, the twenty-two year old son of a Portuguese rum-shopkeeper, seethes because "he had wasted so many years of his life in selling rum and cigarettes to common niggers and coolies, who were not fit even to tie his shoelaces" (14). Joe feels nothing but contempt for the blacks and East Indians in San Fernando. He feels the same contempt for his father for running such a lowly business. The rum-shopkeepers are on the lowest social strata in the Portuguese community. The Portuguese, Joe says to himself, "of all the white communities in the island were the most despised: they made themselves too cheap by running the shops of the island and coming into contact with common coloured people" (15). Part of Joe's hostility stems from his own feeling of inferiority. Joe is the son of immigrants, and he is not considered quite as white as the British. His father is from Madeira, an island owned by Portugal but closer geographically to Northern Africa. This fact, in a culture that is acutely concerned about origin and ethnic background, cannot be overlooked.

The remainder of Pitch Lake focuses on Joe's struggle to move from one social class to another. He leaves the rum-shop and goes to the city to live with a brother and sister-in-law who are decidedly and self-consciously upper middle-class. Try as he may, Joe can never fit in. He is readily accepted by the community, but Joe's personality is the major impediment to his social climb. He cannot rise above who he really is. He enjoys socializing with the lower classes, particularly lower-class women. Joe's unsavory associates are, not insignificantly, all people of color. Much as he castigates himself for his behavior, Joe cannot change even though he is given every opportunity for a better life. Joe is more like those whom he scorns than those whom he aspires to emulate.

In *Corentyne Thunder* the question of race is almost completely obscured by the issue of class, but it is there. All of the major characters in the novel are East Indians except Big Man Weldon. Big Man is white, or at least appears so, and it is he who causes the division in Ramgolall's family. Ramgolall is a peasant "cow-minder" who lives a life that remains untouched by what most would call civilization. His daughter, Sosee, runs away with Big Man Weldon. Although they never marry, Sosee and Big Man live together for many years as husband and wife. Because of his whiteness and his wealth, Sosee believes that she has been socially elevated merely because of her association with Big Man. She refuses to acknowledge the existence of her father and younger half-sisters, and she does not want her half-white children to identify with them. Mittelholzer vividly shows how ludicrous Sosee's sense of superiority is when she speaks. Sosee's dialect stands in stark contrast to the standard English spoken by her husband and children. Of her half-sisters, Beena and Kattree, she says: "Aw! All-you stop all dah family talk, na? We na wan' hear 'bout Beena an' Kattree, Beena an' Kattree not on your level of sociologity" (55). Mittelholzer also points up Sosee's lower-class nature in the description of her that is filtered through the consciousness of the narrator and Big Man: "She was bare-footed. Her hair hung greasily behind her in a loosely plaited pigtail . . . . She wore no corsets and her fleshy belly protruded in the front of her dress and smelt like curry and Sunlight soap" (32). More than seventeen years of cohabitation have not made Sosee a middle-class woman. Although she has access to money and every conceivable material possession, she still lives as she did in Ramgolall's mud house. Sosee, like Joe, carries her class within her, and the contempt which she feels for her father and siblings, Big Man feels for her: "And Sosee, Sosee was only the plump, lazy mother of his children. For her he felt apathy, or disgust, or anger" (40).

Race does not initially appear to be an issue in *The Hills Were Joyful Together* because almost all of the characters are black. Indeed, race is only an issue in that, as George Lamming puts it, "To be black, in the West Indies, is to be poor . . ." (*Pleasures* 33). The characters in the novel are members of Kingston's lowest class, and Mais suggests, as Lamming says, that the conditions described in the novel are experienced solely by the black majority population. There are no identity crises in this novel. Each character knows what he or she is without question, and that is poor and black. The major concern in the barrack-yard is simply survival. Mais's description of life in the yard is reminiscent of Lamming's description of the village in *In the Castle of My Skin*. In the introduction to his novel Lamming writes:

> The book is crowded with names and people, and although each character is accorded a most vivid presence and force of personality, we are rarely concerned with the prolonged exploration of an individual consciousness. It is the collective human substance of the village itself which commands our attention. The village, you might say, is the central character. (x)

I quote Lamming here because his remarks seem to apply to many West Indian novelists who use the black population, the largest and poorest racial group in the West Indies, as their subject matter. The novels emphasize, as does *The Hills Were Joyful Together*, the plight of the oppressed underclass. Although we follow with interest the lives of Rema and Surjue, Shag and Euphemia in Mais's novel, our attentions are drawn toward the community as a whole. We focus on the collective struggle to live and love in the yard. The total absence of privacy in the yard adds to the feeling that the residents are members of one big family. The physical make-up of the yard and the poor quality and proximity of the small "apartments" makes private family matters public affairs. Everybody in the yard knows what is going on in everybody else's house.

The Hills Were Joyful Together has graphic descriptions of every conceivable kind of violence and scenes where characters experience unbelievable pain and suffering. Mais does not intend to portray the baseness of the lower class. Mais shows us, rather, that the people in the lower class are victims, and that poverty can reduce the human to the inhuman. Violence becomes, among the lower-classes, an expression of power. It gives an otherwise powerless people a temporary feeling of control over a particular life or a particular situation.

Mais's narrative is deeply moving and very effective. We suffer with Rema as she makes her descent into madness. We are horrified by Shag's brutal murder of Euphemia, the woman he once loved, but it is Surjue's demise which is emblematic of the fate of all those who reside in the yard. Surjue, who has been imprisoned for some months, searches for a way to escape. He has heard that Rema, the woman he loves, is ill. After much planning, Surjue's nearly successful attempt to escape is thwarted. Just as he is about to go over the prison wall, he is killed. It becomes clear to us that all of the residents of the yard are trapped. There is no way out for them, and most die as violently as they lived.

The relationships between the sexes in the novels, specifically the treatment of women, break down some of the barriers between race and class among male characters. Men of all classes and racial groups are bound by their domineering and abusive attitudes toward women. Women play major roles in all of the novels, but whatever their social class, all women are abused and treated as inferiors and sexual objects. Class only determines the form of abuse to which the women in the novels are subjected. Antoinette Cosway's marriage to the unnamed English gentleman is arranged. He receives thirty thousand pounds from her step-brother to marry her. Of his marriage the Englishman says: "It was all very brightly coloured, very strange, but it meant nothing to me. Nor did she, the girl I was to marry. When at last I met her I bowed, smiled, kissed her hand, danced with her. I played the part I was expected to play" (*Sargasso* 76). While Antoinette's husband cannot be held totally responsible for her tragic ending, his unloving and superior attitude toward one who so desperately needs love and validation surely contributes to her eventual insanity. Her husband never physically abuses her, for physical abuse is "appropriate" only among the lower classes. He does, however, subject her to extreme mental abuse.

We have noted that Big Man Weldon, in *Corentyne Thunder,* has no love for Sosee. For him, she has simply been the vessel that carried and bore his children. Sosee, of a different race and class, is not respectable enough to marry. She is, very simply, treated like a servant in Big Man's house:

> In the back of his mind he saw her only as a kind of slave — a healthy female slave to satisfy his sexual needs and to reproduce his kind. Somehow, he never thought of the children as belonging partly to her. He had always thought of them as being wholly his, as though he had taken them from his body as complete seeds and planted them in her as fertile soil. (94)

Geoffry, eldest son of Sosee and Big Man, views women in exactly the same way that his father does. This ambitious, egocentric lad is sexually involved with two girls in the novel. When he impregnates a schoolmate, Clara Macleod, his only concerns are the possible interference with his own life goals and the disappointment of his father, whom he seems to love dearly. Geoffry wants his father to arrange an abortion for Clara. This will free him from any responsibility and save her from disgrace. Big Man agrees to rescue them both and tells Geoffry that he is not at all disappointed in him for doing what is "natural." Clara's social class dictates Geoffry's response to her pregnancy. In contrast, Geoffry feels only a momentary pang of guilt about his sexual activity with his "half aunt" Kattree. The familial relationship is obscured by the distance that their class difference has placed between them. Geoffry neither loves Kattree nor has any concern about the possibility that she may become pregnant. Kattree does become pregnant, but her pregnancy brings no disgrace on Geoffry. He never considers Kattree's possible shame, for Kattree is not fully human.

Geoffry's attitude toward Clara and Kattree is essentially the same. They are both inferior objects to be used for his pleasure. He responds differently to Clara's pregnancy only because social mores dictate what he must do for a "respectable" girl from the "upper-class."

In *Pitch Lake,* Joe da Costa is flattered by the attentions of Cora Goveia, a member of Port of Spain's Portuguese upper middle class. She is a woman unlike any he has ever known. She is flirtatious but chaste, and this confuses Joe. He is accustomed to lower-class women who have few sexual inhibitions. Joe has had a previous long-term liaison with Maria, a colored woman from the lower class in San Fernando. His desire to move up requires that he rid himself of Maria, and he does so with little concern for the effect it will have on her. When he becomes attracted to Stella, the maid employed by the sister-in-law with whom Joe lives, he justifies the relationship by convincing himself that he is her protector. Joe eventually decides that he is in love with Stella, who is orphaned and of questionable racial background. Joe's relationships with Stella and Cora continue simultaneously until he and Cora become engaged. At this point, he treats Stella as he treated Maria, blaming her for his own weakness, immorality, and indiscretion. Stella's pregnancy complicates Joe's life to an unbearable degree and he kills her. On the surface, it appears that Joe respects Cora more than Maria or Stella; that he sees her as a person rather than an object. Cora's social class clearly dictates the limits of Joe's sexual behavior with her. However, she is merely the stepladder that Joe thinks he can use to climb to social respectability.

There is little verbal communication between men and women in *The Hills Were Joyful Together*. Plenty of semi-serious banter goes on between the sexes, but other than that, the men give a series of commands to which the women respond. The women are, for the most part, extremely aggressive. They curse and physically attack when they are wronged. However, they receive more mental and physical abuse than they give. Men see women, again, as their personal property to do with as they please. The rule of the yard is to keep the women in line, and the male is head of the household. Sensitive and loving men are thought to be namby-pamby. Everyone is aware of Euphemia's clandestine relationship with Bajun Man except Shag, the gentle man with whom she lives. The neighbors joke about Shag's unmanly trust in Euphemia. When Shag discovers Bajun Man in his home, he is emotionally shattered because he truly loves Euphemia. When Shag eventually hacks her to death with a machete, residents of the yard are horrified. However, the message that the narrative relays is that justice has somehow been served. Shag commits a very manly act.

There are no social prescriptions for life in the yard and no concern about society's laws or mores. The yard has its own laws, for its residents are not really considered members of society. They are society's blight. Men and women are like soldiers at war with one another and with the conditions of life itself.

We can conclude that, in these West Indian novels, color and ethnic background determine social class and class determines social mores and the kinds of relationships that exist between men and women. The characters in these novels do not really define themselves. They assert what they are not rather than who they are. No character defines himself or herself as Jamaican or Trinidadian, or, as I said earlier, West Indian. Characters are simply male or female, black or nearly white, rich or poor. We get no clear sense that any character has a personal identity, or perhaps I should say an identity based on internal qualities rather than external features. I think that this inability to define the self as self relates to the fragmentation and rootlessness about which Brathwaite speaks. The identification of the self is related to the recognition of a place called home — a feeling of home. For example, many of the colonial Americans defined themselves in relation to the new country that was evolving and developing. Benjamin Franklin's autobiography is quite simply the story of the birth of early America. Franklin had a sense of national identity even before his country became independent, and his idea of what it meant to be an American helped him to define what it meant to be Benjamin Franklin. He felt, as Brathwaite says, "a sense of 'wholeness.' " The characters in these novels have no feeling of national and inter-island identity. Without that sense of belonging — that particular and peculiar tie to a space called home, the individual struggle to define the self becomes intensified. Antoinette, Joe, and Sosee grasp for whatever they can in order to connect with a community and a social group. The tenants in the barrack-yard, Ramgolall, Beena, and Kattree are defined by the society at large because of their poverty. They can never move beyond the basic concern with survival. All of the characters begin without "a sense of 'wholeness'," and without this foundation upon which they can create a self, they remain caught in the web of non-being. They never move beyond their racial, class, and sexual identities.

WORKS CITED

Brathwaite, Edward. "Timehri," *Is Massa Day Dead?* Ed. Orde Coombs. New York: Anchor P, 1974. 29-44.

Gilkes, Michael. "Edgar Mittelholzer," *West Indian Literature*. Ed. Bruce King. London: Macmillan, 1979. 95-110.

James, C. L. R. *At the Rendezvous of Victory*. London: Allison & Busby, 1984.

Lamming, George. *In the Castle of My Skin*. 1953. New York: Schocken Books, 1983.

——. *The Pleasures of Exile*. 1960. London: Allison & Busby, 1984.

Mais, Roger. *The Hills Were Joyful Together*. 1953. London: Heinemann, 1981.

Mendes, Alfred. *Pitch Lake*. 1934. London: New Beacon, 1980.

Mittelholzer, Edgar. *Corentyne Thunder*. 1941. London: Heinemann, 1970.

Naipaul, V. S. *The Middle Passage*. 1962. New York: Vintage, 1980.

Rhys, Jean. *Wide Sargasso Sea*. New York: Popular Library, 1966.

ELIZABETH A. WHEELER

Riddym Ravings: Female and National Identity in Jamaican Creole Poetry

> For the most part, speaking is associated with men, and most of the social types and speech acts and events are regarded as appropriately male activity. This is not to say that women are not expected to talk, but engaging in the kind of nonsense behavior characteristic of public communicative interaction attacks the fabric of female respectability canons in many ways. Furthermore, it is assumed that women primarily speak in their yards and house and therefore engage in the kind of two-person interactions of commess [gossip].
>
> (Roger Abrahams, *The Man-of-Words in the West Indies* 124)

> Look how long Jamaica oman
> — Modder, sister, wife, sweetheart —
> Outa road an eena yard deh pon
> A dominate her part!
>
> Louise Bennett, "Jamaica Oman" (*Poems* 21)

In listening for gender differences in Jamaican creole poetry, one hears not subtle nuances but flagrant contradictions. Both speakers above map out two kinds of symbolic space in Caribbean life: the yard and the crossroads. These are more than literal geographic realms; they appear in myth and help define cultural identity. Roger Abrahams, the American anthropologist, reserves both oral performance and public space for men. For him, the crossroads and the rum shop host a male public speech that counters all female domestic values. To women he reserves the yard, a private space for private speech. Literary critic Carole Boyce Davies would agree with Abrahams that the male voice dominates Caribbean oral performance. She also notes negative images of women within men's performances:

> This tendency towards the "putting a woman in her place" seems to dominate the entire Caribbean oral tradition. The oral literature — which provides a tremendous amount of material for the study of the development of traditional and contemporary attitudes to women, and of women towards themselves — consistently portrays the woman, in the worst extreme, as an evil despicable entity or at best, as a malleable, unthinking, submerged personage. In at least three categories of the earliest material available — the proverb, the folktale and the major song form, the calypso — woman's image is almost uniformly negative. (Davies 165)

On the other hand, for the Jamaican poet Louise Bennett, woman speaks and acts confidently "Outa road and eena yard." Obviously, men and women hotly contest this symbolic space.

It was Louise Bennett who, in the 1930s and 1940s, first wrote exclusively in the Jamaican creole language. She inspired the dub poets, whose work is recited and recorded, often to a background of reggae music. Sometimes dub poetry is published in book form; however, it is usually preserved only on tape. The printed version of Jean Breeze's "Riddym Ravings" was originally a poster to advertise her audio cassette.

Until *Riddym Ravings* in 1984, Louise Bennett's recorded successors had all been male. Recently, other women dub poets, such as Lillian Allen, have joined Breeze. The absence of women raises interesting questions about dub poetry. Has Caribbean oral performance been exclusively male until now? Is Breeze the exception that proves the rule? Or does Breeze continue a long tradition of female public speech? In other words, is Roger Abrahams right or wrong? I think we can answer "yes" to all these questions. While Breeze must overturn male conventions in her dub poetry, she also has at her disposal a rich arsenal of Jamaican women's voices. The personages speak up loud and clear in Louise Bennett's poetry: tramriders, cleaning ladies, voters, concertgoers, candysellers.

In evaluating Abrahams' statement, we should remember that Jamaicans have a very different sense of privacy from Northern Europeans or many Americans. Tropical people live out in their yards, adjacent to the road. Crammed into Kingston public housing, many Jamaicans don't have the luxury of privacy. Therefore, even the "two-person interactions" of gossip take on a decidedly public cast. While Bennett's *personae* gossip frequently, they gossip in loud voices and large circles about events that affect the whole community. Furthermore, women's public speech has a class dimension. Jamaican women who work in offices or hotels generally maintain a quiet demeanor. However, marketwomen are not only chatty but engage in time-honored ritual wordplay: "Hairnet, scissors, fine teeth comb!/Weh de nice lady deh?/Buy a scissors from me noh lady?/Hair pin? Toot' pase? Goh wey!" ("South Parade Peddler" *Jamaica* 27).[1]

---

[1]Hairnet, scissors, fine tooth comb! / What about the nice lady there? / Won't you buy a scissors from me, lady? / Hair pin? Toothpaste? Go away!

Before an in-depth analysis of Jean Breeze's work, it will be necessary to discuss Jamaican oral poetry in general. Many genres call back and forth to each other, from political epic to rapid-fire nonsense rhymes. Because Jamaican folk culture was publicly despised for centuries, oral poetry still flourishes in defiance of formal written culture. The Jamaican school system still teaches British customs, down to the starched uniforms and weekly floggings. Although people learn standard English, it remains estranged from their daily lives. While Albert Lord draws a dividing line between literate and oral cultures, Jamaica shows how the two can live side-by-side for centuries without gaining the least respect for each other.

Inheriting this colonial legacy, a poet makes a political statement if he or she writes in Jamaican creole. Louise Bennett became a popular hero; her picture appeared on children's school notebooks, as pop stars do in this country. One could argue that Bennett removed the creole language to a separate sphere by writing it down. However, she never became a purely literary figure. She had her own radio show for many decades, speaking her poems out loud from everyday speech. In a similar way, contemporary dub poetry promotes a proud sense of black community among all Jamaicans. It is no accident that dub poetry has strong ties with Rastafarianism, the African-oriented religion founded in Jamaica. As Albert Lord writes, "The roots of oral traditional narrative are not artistic but religious in the broadest sense" (Lord 67).

Cassettes of dub and reggae music permeate Jamaica, and so does live performance. A taxi driver or sidewalk vendor is likely to break out into rhyme at any moment. Jamaicans place a high value on verbal dexterity; it can even lead to stardom. In the oral poetry variously called rub-a-dub style, dance hall music or DJ toasting, the opportunity to tape an album arises out of live improvisational contests held in Kingston, Negril or Montego Bay. Each town has its stars, and their tapes retain this local identification and subject matter. Performers use the word "dub" because they overdub their voices on top of recorded or live music. They are called DJs because they talk over the other tracks, like a radio disk jockey.

What is the Jamaican language of dub poetry? Dub poets write in what Edward Kamau Brathwaite calls "nation language": not Jamaican dialect *per se* but "the submerged area of that dialect which is much more closely allied to the

African aspect of experience in the Caribbean . . . in its contours, its rhythm and timbre, its sound explosions, it is not English, even though the words, as you hear them, might be English to a greater or lesser degree" (Brathwaite 13). Brathwaite points to rhythm as a key feature of Afro-Caribbean usage. Indeed, when one listens to dub poetry it is the rhythm that strikes the ear as clearly African. Oku Onoura, a leading practitioner of the art, calls a dub piece "a poem with a built-in reggae rhythm" (Morris 150).

Brathwaite does not clearly define what is African about nation language. However, I can make some speculations based on my own knowledge of Yoruba. While Jamaican speech uses English words, it breaks them apart to fit African rhythm and syntax. The result is a language so far from English it is incomprehensible to non-Jamaican English speakers. Let's take for example Jean Breeze's repeated formula in "Riddym Ravings": "De fus time dem kar me go a Bellevue"; "a dat time dem grab mi an kar mi back a Bellevue"; "an is back eena Bellevue dem kar mi."

Jamaican either chops off or lengthens words so that they will glide into one another, as in African speech. For instance, "in" becomes "eena"; "carry me" becomes "kar mi." It also adds words to fit African rhythm and syntax: "go a Bellevue"; "when mi see dem a go home wid." The word "fi," a common interjection, seems to come straight from Yoruba "fi," meaning "by, to, or with." Breeze says, "a tear up newspaper fi talk to." In Yoruba one would say, "Dodo ni nwon fi jeun" (They had fried plantains to eat). The use of "dem" for "they" and "mi" for "I" bears some relation to the Yoruba use of object for subject: "Inu mi dun" (I am happy; literally, my insides are sweet to me). Other African aspects of Jamaican grammar include using present tense to convey past action, and forming the possessive without apostrophes ("de Chinaman backlat").

Beyond linguistic comparisons, the heart of the matter lies in Brathwaite's phrase "African aspect of experience" — the key word being experience. Africanism has to do not only with grammar, but also with methods of adaptation in the live context of experience. Tracing such patterns in informal settings, Roger Abrahams shows how extremely English festivities — caroling, mumming, acting out *St. George and the Dragon* — are reworked entirely according to West African patterns of call-and-response and competitive showmanship (Abrahams

121). Brathwaites's concept of multiple aspects of experience in the Caribbean translates into multiple voices and adaptations.

Having discussed dub poetry in general, I want to move into more specific analysis of Jean Breeze's *Riddym Ravings*. Breeze seems to feel that rhythm is a hallmark of her work and of Caribbean life, for she ushers us into the album with "Rhythm So Sweet." This marching tune combines political optimism with pop infectiousness, as if Breeze were Jamaica's answer to John Philip Souza. While Breeze clearly writes within the Rastafarian tradition, she employs here not heavy "dread" but a lighter, overtly feminine style. Almost like cheerleaders, Breeze and her female chorus encourage the "soldiers marching home" to "lick up your fork and pick up your hoe." In this way, Jamaica will defeat Babylon, the Rastafarian term for all foreign, decadent influences.

Belying Roger Abrahams' theory, Breeze describes not the opposition but the interrelationship between the yard and the crossroads. Both men and women plant and harvest in the hills; they renew energy by dancing at the rum shop in town. The beats and rhymes of the DJ, encouraging them to dance, become a force that clears the way and sends "Babylon forces in retreat":

> Musical tradition come to free up de nation
> 'Cause we know de situation
> Pure hunger and frustration
> So forward, forward on we go
> Marching to the sound of the dub mento.

I have referred to the yard and the road as symbolic spaces, but rhythm itself can become symbolic space. The sound system, meaning not only reggae music, the DJ and the amplifiers but also the floor and the crowd, takes on great significance in Jamaica and in Great Britain's West Indian communities as well. Describing the Brixton riots of 1979, dub poet Linton Kwesi Johnson conveys that it was the sound system, pumping out Jamaican power, that incited the crowd to "righteous righteous war" ("Five nights of bleeding," Johnson).

Jean Breeze associates the beat with militancy and community; however, in the *a cappella* poem "Riddym Ravings," the centerpiece of the album, she pushes the concept even further. For the Mad Woman protagonist, the DJ personifies the very possibility of an alternative voice. Maintaining any voice at all is an active struggle. The poem raises so many of the issues and employs so many of the voices of dub poetry, it will be the main topic of discussion.

The woman's role in the yard or in the crossroads becomes completely irrelevant here, for the speaker is homeless, attached to no community at all. The urban grit Breeze evokes here provides necessary contrast to the optimism of "Rhythm So Sweet." The voiceover of "Riddym Ravings" sounds entirely lifelike, as if a sociologist had taken a tape recorder to a park bench and prompted the woman to speak. The Mad Woman begins her story *in medias res*. As we might expect, most of it concerns her struggle to survive: to find something to eat, a place to wash herself. She is subject to continual harassment:

An mi foot start wanda falla fly
to de garbage pan eena de Chinaman backlat
dem nearly chap aff mi han eena de butcha shap
fi de piece a ratten poke
ah de same time de mawga gal in front a mi
drap de laas piece a ripe banana
an MI — ben dung — pick i-up — an nyam 'i
a dat time dem grab mi an kar mi back a Bellevue . . . [2]

Although this "Mad Woman's Poem" is surreal, it is also entirely realistic. In Los Angeles, for instance, homeless people have been herded off the streets with bulldozers. Being homeless *is* surreal, and Breeze's Mad Woman speaks just right.

Just as Breeze had spoken elsewhere of "creativity on a hungry belly," here the material and the mental collude with each other (Heartbeat Records 4). The woman hears voices *because* she's been sleeping outside after an eviction. Both the doctor *and* the landlord operate on her brain. The fact that Bellevue in Kingston is both a mental hospital and a poorhouse reinforces the connection:

De fus time dem kar me go a Bellevue
was fi di dactar an de lanlord operate
and tek de radio out a me head,
troo dem seize de bed
weh did a gimme cancer
an mek me talk to nobady
An di same night wen dem trow mi out fe no pay de rent
mi haffi sleep outadoor wid de Channel One riddym box
an de DJ fly up eena mi head mi hear ima play seh
Eh, Eh,
No feel no way
Town is a place dat ah really kean stay
Dem kudda — ribbit mi han

---

[2]And my foot started to fly / to the garbage pan in the Chinaman's back lot / they nearly chopped off my hand in the butcher shop / for the piece of rotten pork / at the same time the skinny gal in front of me / dropped the last piece of ripe banana / and I — bent down — picked it up — and ate it / at the same time they grabbed me and carried me / back to Bellevue . . .

Eh — ribbit mi toe
Mi waan go a country go look mango.[3]

Why is it a DJ voice that flies up into her head? This was a fascinating choice for Breeze to make. Out of all the varieties of Jamaican popular music and oral poetry, from reggae to dub, DJ toasting (speaking over recorded beats) is the most flamboyantly macho. Yellowman, one of the most famous DJs, croons: "Girl, you can't do what the guys do, you know, and still be a lady" ("Still Be a Lady," Yellowman). With his gold chains and extravagant self-praise, Yellowman is a typical Jamaican DJ. His role of "love man" contains an element of self-parody, for Yellowman is a homely albino. However, his looks do not detract from his verbal dexterity: his intricate slang, his rude good humor, his showmanship:

Every muckle make a mickle, every mickle make a muckle.
You never knew Yellow could mek a good couple.
De 'igha de mountain, de coola de breeze.
De yonga de couple, de tighter de 'queeze!
("Mi Believe," Yellowman)[4]

In "Hustler Skank," another cut from the album, Breeze does a hilarious parody of the DJ's manly swagger. In "Riddym Ravings" she appropriates the male voice in a different way. She uses madness, a time-honored literary strategy for women, one evident in Caribbean fiction from Jean Rhys to Erna Brodber. The DJ voice is only in the Mad Woman's head; she does not literally attempt to perform. This voice sounds nothing at all like a typical male DJ. A reggae beat underscores the vocal, but Breeze sings delicately, without showing off. In contrast to the bold public persona of most DJs, this voice is small, plaintive, intimate — and decidedly female.

In the DJ's refrain, the Mad Woman warbles a country tune instead of reciting, as she does the rest of the time. The simplicity of "Mi waan go a country go look mango" makes a stark contrast with the Mad Woman's complex troubles. When Breeze says "ribbit" she means "bind up," but she is also reworking the DJ term

---

[3]The first time they carried me to Bellevue / was for the doctor and the landlord to operate / and take the radio out of my head, / true, they seized the bed / which gave me cancer / and made me talk to nobody / And the same night they threw me out for not paying the rent / I had to sleep outdoors with the Channel One rhythm box / and the DJ flew up into my head, I heard him play, say / Eh, Eh, / No feel no way / Town is a place that I really can't stay / They cut up — bind up my hand / Eh — bind up my toe / I want to go to the country, go look at the mango.

[4]The higher the mountain, the cooler the breeze. / The younger the couple, the tighter the squeeze!

"repeat." DJs use the word "repeat" continuously as a way of gathering momentum to their patter.

By using the DJ voice within her *a cappella* poem, Breeze plays with the categories of Jamaican oral poetry. Even supporters of dub poetry can find DJ music unacceptable. It has been criticized as too commercial, lacking deep thought and educational value. Claudius Hilliman, reviewing dub poet Mikey Smith's album *Mi Cyaan Believe It,* praised its militant stand against oppression: "In this way it departs from the repetitiveness and vulgar commercialism that tends to affect black popular music" (Hilliman 162). Tomlin G. Ellis of Poets in Unity stresses the DJ's responsibility to offer meaning to youth. He points out the ubiquitousness of Jamaican music and the possibility of educational lyrics:

> Let's face it: this country we have a lot of young people. Everyone hears this. You hear it on the radio, on the streets, the minivans. A lot of these guys carry cassettes, with dance hall music and thing. I think children should be brought up on good lyrics . . . A lot of the songs that come out now are probably 4 or 5 lines, and it repeat again, and because the reggae music is so good it will be a hit. But I feel that if the lyrics are stronger, it will have a better opportunity. So I think the lyrics is what will work for the poets now. (Heartbeat 3)

A former teacher herself, Jean Breeze also finds a didactic purpose for her poetry: "Is like class, you know, a different sort of teaching" (Heartbeat 4).

However, perhaps the strength of the DJ voice lies in its ragamuffin status, unofficial and undidactic even by alternative standards. Against all the official voices in "Riddym Ravings," the DJ voice is the only symbolic space the Mad Woman can occupy and trust. As Ellis notes, DJ music is everywhere. It decolonizes public space and repatriates it with noise. Its improvisational demands make it both transitory and vital: you can't pin a DJ down to any preconceived notion of form.

The structure of meaning in "Riddym Ravings" depends upon a structural element of DJ music. The DJ exhorts a crowd to dance through the basic *modus operandi* of African music, call-and-response. Yellowman poignantly invokes this form when he calls distant Jamaican pasieros (comrades) into dialogue: "Brixton pasiero I hear you. London pasiero I hear you. Liverpool pasiero I hear you" ("Jamaica Nice," Yellowman). Breeze's Mad Woman reveals the deepest meaning of this activity, for she attempts to construct a self through dialogue with another. She is always looking for someone to talk to. In Bellevue the doctor and the landlord "did a gimme cancer/and mek me talk to nobady." She sits down "eena Parade/a tear up newspaper fi talk to." The lack of dialogue pains her as much as the lack of food. Her first blow on moving to the city was that no one answered her:

> Wen mi fus come a town
> mi use to tell everey bady "mawnin"
> but as de likkle rosiness gawn outa mi face
> nobady nah ansa mi
> silence tun rags roun mi bady in midst a all de dead people dem
> a bawl about de caast of livin'. . . . [5]

She thinks the conductor behaves harshly because he can't hear her, even though they occupy the same reality: the rhythm in her head is the same one the bus driver plays on a cassette:

> an di canductar bwoy a halla out seh,
> "Dutty gal, kum affa di bus"
> Ah troo im noh hear di riddym eena mi head
> ame as de tape weh di bus driva a play, seh . . . [6]
> (Chorus)

While the doctor and the landlord have no voices, the bus driver and her neighbors speak in moralistic tones. The driver responds sharply, as if to a dog or child. The Mad Woman passes along the insults of the "two mawga (skinny) gal" in her own voice: "Who kudda breed smaddy like me?" (Who could breed somebody like me?). The Mad Woman is troubled by their aspersions and because she is dirty. Here she displays a womanly concern with respectability. The Mad Woman fights back with invective, contrasting her own "pure nice man" with "de likkle dutty bway dem when mi see dem a go home wid" (the little dirty boys I see them go home with). Respectability and gossip are an inseparable duo. In fighting off gossip, the Mad Woman seems to involve herself in a particularly female problematic — as suggested by the title of Louise Bennett's book *Jamaica Labrish,* "labrish" being a local word for gossip.

I once asked a Jamaican why he didn't make money by teaching outsiders his language. He said, "No way. They tricked us with language before." In the history of slavery, duplicity plays a central part. Turning a negative into a positive,

---

[5]When I first came to town / I used to say "morning" to everybody / but as the little rosiness went out of my face / nobody answered me / silence wound rags round my body in the midst of all dead people who / bawled about the cost of living . . .

[6]and the conductor boy hollered out, saying, / "Dirty gal, get off the bus" / Ah, true, he doesn't hear the rhythm in my head / same as the tape the bus diver plays, say . . .

Jamaicans celebrate duplicity in the figure of Anansi, the spider trickster. Comparing the female sensibility in Louise Bennett's poetry with middle-class feminism, Carolyn Cooper writes:

> The existential jungle, the repository of the accumulated waste of the society, becomes in the folk iconography the locus of transformation . . . Cunning, rather than overt male/female confrontation is the preferred strategy for maintaining equanimity. (Cooper 14)

The Mad Woman must employ such cunning to keep hold of the DJ voice. The first time the doctor and the landlord take the plug out of her head, "as ah ketch back out a street/ah push een back de plug," she reports with glee.[7] The next time, the doctor and the landlord perform more drastic surgery — but the Mad Woman doesn't give up without a fight:

> but wen dem tink seh mi unda chlorofarm
> dem put i'dung careless
> an wen dem gawn
> mi tek di radio — an mi push i'up eena mi belly
> fi keep de baby company,
> far even if mi noh mek i'
> Mi waan my baby know dis yah riddym yah
> fram befo she bawn[8]

The attempt to silence the voice of urban despair only amplifies and multiplies it. The "locus of transformation" is the womb. The Mad Woman forms a link with the future. She has remembered her distant parents and grandmother with affection and pride; now, through her baby, she has a chance to reestablish some family connection.

Then, in the devastating end of "Riddym Ravings," death, performance, pain and birth all become equivalent in one flash of artificial lightning:

> An same time
> de dactar and de lanlord
> tigger de electric shack
> an mi hear di DJ vice bawl out, seh
> "MURTHER."
> PULL UP MISSA OPERATOR!

The DJ voice becomes protestor and historian, bearing witness to oppression,

---

[7]as I got back out on the street / I pushed the plug back in

[8]but when they think I'm under chloroform / they put it down careless / and when they're gone / I take the radio — and I push it up in my belly / to keep the baby company / for even if I don't make it / I want my baby to know this rhythm / from before she's born /

calling for it to "pull up" [stop] and recording the event for the future. The place of violence becomes the site of regeneration. The DJ bawls out "MURTHER" as if it were a birth cry. With this outcry, the radio and the baby are born at once. Breeze's spelling suggests "mother" as well as "murder." The moment of killing/birth is also a performance. Although the words do not appear in the printed version of the lyrics, Breeze says that the doctor and the landlord operate "in de theater." "Murder" is the word the crowd yells when a DJ gives a great performance. Just as DJ music is electronically transmitted, the outcry is triggered by electric shock.

Throughout "Riddym Ravings," Breeze's voice ranges from giggling to quavering, as if it were impossible to hit the right tone. This impossibility parallels Breeze's view that it is impossible to live a decent life in the big city of Kingston. In an interview she described her agrarian populism:

> There is a portion of country youth really move out of the rural situation and go into the urban situation every year in search of employment which is definitely not available any longer in the urban situation. As a result, now, the rural areas are depopulated, in terms of ages between, say, 17 and 35. They are merely populated by grandparents and the younger youth who are at home with the grandparents while the parents go in search of work. Now the overpopulation now in the urban areas have resulted in most of the suffering and tribulation that you hear our artists and so on talking about. So what I am trying to promote here is really a return to the whole agrarian culture, which was the primary culture of the black man. It is one of the primary solutions of all of the problems that we are dealing with in the country right now. (Heartbeat 3-4)

Creole poetry came into being in the transition from rural poverty to urban slum. In 1938, Louise Bennett commented on the transition in "Writing Home." The poem reflects the speaker's optimism about the city and his continued ties to home. He mentions his mother's ambitions for him, which she believes attainable through schooling and standard English. But "Writing Home" is drenched in dramatic irony. Although unemployed, the speaker is thrilled to be striking with a newly-formed union:

> So wid em at me back ah hope to do all right
> An all ah do at present is strike wid all me might.
> Ah did soh glad yuh did force me fe teck de zamination
> Far now ah can demands a job fe suit me edication.
>
> Soh a mus say good-bye for ah gwine stap write now

Teck good care a-yahself, and look afta me cow.
(Bennett *Jamaica* 117)[9]

Ironically, rejecting the mother's urban ambitions is the only way to rediscover the mother land and the mother tongue as well. With a background of waterfall, flute and birdsong, Jean Breeze recites in "Repatriation to Love": "For Love created I among the cool ferns of a river's morning." Elsewhere, she scolds the audience in heavy dialect: "Go `ome to ya madda she will `elp you min' de yout' " ("Going Home").[10] The motherland also means Africa, in a tragically half-remembered way. In a political protest, Breeze echoes the Mad Woman's shame and endangerment:

My heartbeat kept me awake last night
Like an ancient talking drum
Saying remember
Why don't you remember?
Madda Africa
Madda Eart'
Madda Africa
Madda Eart'

Leave Eart' alone
She ain't done no wrong
Say, can't you understand?

The earth-as-mother image appears frequently in Caribbean poetry of all kinds. In *Mother Poem,* Edward Kamau Brathwaite writes of his "mother Barbados," equating her with the submerged African culture hidden like underground springs in limestone. In "Say, Natty-Natty," Mikey Smith criticizes the selling of Jamaican culture to tourists. He ties culture to earth to mother: "Remember yard is yah mumma, /pon groun yuh sleep . . . " ("Say, Natty-Natty," Smith).[11]

Jean Breeze's vision of change is close to Brathwaite's and Smith's. As Carolyn Cooper writes, "In the Jamaican context, class, rather than gender is the functional determinant of power" (Cooper 15). Breeze refers to agrarian culture as the "primary culture of the black man," as if that definition included black women, too (Heartbeat 3-4). Breeze embraces not feminism but a vision of

---

[9]So with them at my back I hope to do all right / And all I do at present is strike with all my might. / I'm so glad you did force me to take the examination / For now I can demand a job to suit my education. /

So I must say goodbye for I'm going to stop writing now / Take good care of yourself, and look after my cow.

[10]Go home to your mother she will help you mind the youth.

[11]Remember the yard is your mother, upon the ground you sleep.

Caribbean brothers and sisters united against imperialism. The creole language of her poetry represents opposition to the British-style English of Jamaica's white and light-skinned rulers. It also opposes the encroachments of the United States, whom she calls the "Big Time Tief" [thief]. While the Mad Woman copes with her personal tragedy, Breeze's other poems protest the larger forces that bring tragedy to many Jamaican men and women.

However, in her protest Breeze employs a traditionally female variety of public address: the abuse of the marketwoman. Louise Bennett's candy seller excoriates anyone who won't buy from her: "Me noh ha nutten dah-gi way. /Gi de lady pass fe come, /Wey yuh noh go jine de air force? /Dem have plenty use fe bum" ("Candy Seller," Bennett *Jamaica* 28).[12] Similarly, in "Big Time Tief" Breeze excoriates global deadbeats. Personifying the "developed" nations as folk known to all, she gossips about them: "We know dem by the score . . . You don' know dem? Lord!" she laughs. By insulting them, she declares them part of her community and holds them accountable to her standards.

To conclude my close reading of *Riddym Ravings,* I want to return to Roger Abrahams' theory of gender roles in Caribbean oral performance. Following the anthropologist Peter J. Miller, Abrahams sketches a clear dichotomy between male *reputation* (acting tough, speaking creole) and female *respectability* (attending to household matters, learning standard English). He points out a " 'duality of cultural patterning' between positive (usually European) forms and negative (usually old-fashioned, country, or African) ones:"

> These bad performances, regarded as appropriately masculine, embody male reputation values . . . only when playing is sanctioned are the sporty ones permitted to perform before the community as a whole, and then only by dressing up or dressing down, taking unaccustomed roles into which they channel their antinormative (i.e., antihousehold) nonsense . . . Playing then means playing bad, playing black, playing lower class.
>
> (Abrahams 151)

Although Breeze critiques the machismo of the 'sporty' performer, she does so not to defend the household or to defend Standard English. Rather, she critiques him from another vantage point *within* Jamaican language. Abrahams regards the male "nonsense" voice as the dominant voice of Creole performance. Breeze

---

[12] I don't have nothing to give away. / Let the lady come forward. / Why don't you join the air force? / They've got plenty of use for bums.

takes on this voice, both literally and figuratively. In "Hustler Skank," she parodies the DJ's outlaw persona.

Just as her Mad Woman sounds authentic, so does her Hustler, and it is hilarious to hear a woman talk this way. She throws in interlocutions in a narcotic drawl ("Whatcha know?") and Rastafarian terminology ("I dread," "Yes I," and "Irie," which means "cool" or "fine"). She combines things a hustler might actually say with devastating parodies thereon, as in the last line here:

Hear me, I dread!
Love star!
Yes I is a city fulla superstar,
You ida sing reggae music or you pos' go noir.
An' if you cyan mek it inna ida one
You jus' jine a posse an' 'ave some fun.
Herb-man posse a really de bes'
Tree-piece suit — nuttin' less!
Specially if hem alla sell cocaine
You jus' turn 'im pimp an' go muck up some brain.
Whatcha know?
You see me, me just want get rich quick
Only ting mus' work hard is my dick.[13]

The Hustler's goal is stardom through reggae music or Rasta style, two aspects of Jamaican culture that have become tourist attractions. Dealing drugs is another way of making money while seemingly remaining independent of the system. The Hustler glorifies his dealing and dread-talk as a variety of black militancy, while in reality he only "want get rich quick." Jean Breeze does not make fun of him for "playing *bad*, playing black, playing lower class," or for using Jamaican language. Rather, she criticizes him because he can't resist the blandishments of mainstream culture. You could say she criticizes him for not being bad *enough*. Without altering his boasting manner in the slightest, the Hustler betrays his real relationship to power. His cool Rasta talk has become just another way to shuffle:

Is de same man we work for, you damn blasted fool!
When you say, "Yes, sir, Mr. Alston,"
I just say, "Comin', Mr. Cool.
On my way, Mr. Cool.

---

[13]Hear me, I dread! / Love star! / Yes I is a city full of superstars, / You either sing reggae music or you should go *noir*. / And if you can't make it in either one / You just join a posse (gang) and have some fun. / Herb-man posse (marijuana dealers) really the best / Three-piece suit — nothing less! / Specially if they all sell cocaine / You just turn into pimps and go muck up some brain. / Whatcha know? / You see I, I just want to get rich quick / Only thing must work hard is my dick.

Yes, boss. Irie, boss.
ON MY WAY, BOSS."

Within the many-voiced sound system of Jamaican oral poetry, Jean Breeze curses, drawls, wails and laughs — showing how well the woman-of-words plays her part.

WORKS CITED

Abrahams, Roger. *The Man-of-Words in the West Indies*. Baltimore: Johns Hopkins UP, 1983.

Bennett, Louise. *Jamaica Labrish*. Kingston: Sangster's Book Stores, 1966.

——. *Selected Poems*. Kingston: Sangster's Book Stores, 1982.

Brathwaite, Edward Kamau. *The History of the Voice: The Development of Nation Language in the Anglophone Caribbean*. London and Port of Spain: New Beacon P, 1984.

Brodber, Erna. "Perceptions of Caribbean Women: Towards a Documentation of Stereotypes." *Institute of Social and Economic Research,* U of the West Indies, Cave Hill, Barbados, 1982.

Cooper, Carolyn. " 'That Cunny Jamma Oman': The Female Sensibility in the Poetry of Louise Bennett." *Bulletin of Eastern Caribbean Affairs* (Barbados) 11:1 (March-April 1985): 13-27.

Davies, Carole Boyce. " 'Woman Is a Nation. . . ': Women in Caribbean Oral Literature." in Davies and Elaine Savory Fido, eds., *Out of the Kumbla: Caribbean Women and Literature*. Trenton, NJ: Africa World P, 1990, 165-194.

Heartbeat Records. *Word Soun' 'Ave Power: Reggae Poetry*. Interview booklet accompanying record. Cambridge, MA: 1983.

Hilliman, Claudius. Review of Mikey Smith's *Mi Cyaan Believe It. The Race Today Review* XIV:5 (1983): 162.

Lord, Albert B. *The Singer of Tales*. Cambridge: Harvard UP, 1960.

Morris, Mervyn. "Dub Poets," *The Race Today Review* XIV:5 (1983), pp. 150-160.

Wilson, Peter J. *Crab Antics: The Social Anthropology of English-speaking Negro Societies in the Caribbean*. New Haven: Yale UP, 1973.

Discography

Breeze, Sister [Jean]. *Riddym Ravings*. New York: Reachout International A-153, 1987.

Johnson, Linton Kwesi. *Forces of Victory*. London: Island 9566, 1979.

Smith, Michael. *Mi Cyaan Believe It*. London: Island 9717, 1983.

Yellowman. *King Yellowman*. New York: CBS CK 39301, 1984.

TEJUMOLA OLANIYAN

Corporeal/Discursive Bodies and the Subject: *Dream on Monkey Mountain* and the Poetics of Identity

Writing on the region that from 1492 "rapidly became the dramatic proscenium of the European invasion and domination of the Americas," F. W. Knight and C. A. Palmer argue that "the modern Caribbean states represent a unique and challenging experience on the history of mankind" (1). Part of the experience they challenge is the Old World fable of mythical origins and stable, unreflexive identities. The islands are not just the creations of *known* history, but this history is also their very constitution. The inhabitants were virtually *unknown*, practically *did not exist*, before the "European intrusion" that "abruptly interrupted the original pattern of their historical development . . . severely altered their physical environment . . . diversified their diet, complicated their epidemiological systems, produced new biological strains, and linked them inextricably to the wider world beyond the Atlantic Ocean" (1). These combined experiences of slavery and colonialism have conspired to produce a situation in imperial dominance in which over ninety percent of the population, oppressors and the oppressed alike, are, in the legal parlance of today's nation-states, "aliens," from far-flung locations in Europe, Africa, and Asia. They stayed, endured, but were never to be free from the enervating afflictions of a known history, a history of dates.

Edward Brathwaite, the distinguished Barbadian poet, testifies to the perpetual stress of adjustment to such a terrain by offsprings of both planter and slave, when he writes that at least for the artist, "[t]he most significant feature of West Indian life and imagination since Emancipation has been its sense of rootlessness, of not belonging to the landscape" (2-3). The quest for *roots*, for *rootedness*, is the quest for "identity," a plebeian term for a shifting set of markers proposed or flaunted as distinguishing an individual or group from others. What this disarming "definition" masks is of course the generative paradox that is at the heart of all identity quests. The core question in an individual's or group's "search" for identity and difference is always of a "second-order" character, though it rarely presents itself as such: it is not a question of whether one is what one is — after all, one must *be* in order to be able to raise a question — but whether one is what one is supposed to be, according to some determined order of expectation in space and time. Thus behind and alongside the language of primordia characteristic of many identity quests (e.g. "rootlessness"), is often language of far less primordial motivations, such as responses to ongoing domination or imperialism.

It is such an emphasis on the social basis of identity that you will find in the writings of Caribbean scholars and artists such as Rex Nettleford, Edouard Glissant, and the important collections of essays edited by Orde Coombs and John Hearne. Amilcar Cabral is right then when he describes the crucial formative factor of identity as the "social condition . . . arising from economic, political, social and cultural aspects which are characteristic of the growth and history of the society in question" (65-66).

In the area of literary practice, the ubiquitous discourse of identity is inflected in attempts at fashioning literary and artistic forms that are subtended by the cultural matrix of the Caribbean and that cannot be said to be mere imitations of Euro-American literary traditions. This at least is the hope and driving aspiration. In this essay, I shall investigate how this drama is played out in a text by Derek Walcott, the leading West Indian dramatist and poet. I consider his *Dream on Monkey Mountain*[1] a poignant dramatization of the construction of identity and formation of subjectivity by the dominated in the context of the Caribbean. The central character, Makak (monkey) begins as the exemplary victim of the colonial hegemonic discourse, living fully his constitution — his subjection — as "black, ugly, poor [and so] worse than nothing" (237), and then gradually negotiating his way towards self-definition.

In investigating the structuration of the Makaks in that kind of setting (colonial and postcolonial), I will quickly identify two opposing models of articulation. The first takes the "black" body as existing entirely outside discourse; the "black" body *is,* without any discursive mediation. Corporeality or morphology of the "black" body becomes that body's definition, in terms which are neither just corporeal nor morphological but most crucially, cultural. Biology is stretched,

[1]Derek Walcott, *Dream on Monkey Mountain and Other Plays* (New York: Farrar, Strauss and Giroux, 1970). Henceforth cited in the text by page number and prefixed by *Dream* where necessary.

violently beyond limits, to perform the tasks of hermeneutics. We give two examples:

> I am apt to suspect the negroes, and in general all the other species of men (for there are four or five different kinds) to be naturally inferior to the whites. There never was a *civilized* nation of any other *complexion* than *white*, nor even any individual eminent either in action or speculation. No ingenious manufactures amongst them, no arts, no sciences. (Hume, in Gates 10; emphasis added)

> Father Labak reports that a Negro carpenter, whom he reproached for haughty treatment toward his wives, answered: "You whites are indeed fools, for first you make great concessions to your wives, and afterward you complain when they drive you mad." And it might be that there was something in this which perhaps deserved to be considered; but in short, this fellow was *quite black* from head to foot, *a clear proof* that what he said was *stupid.* (Kant, in Gates 10-11; emphasis added)

Of course this theory is dated and, and some would rather wish it lay buried in the recesses of history. However, it is important to us here as a conception that was not only hegemonic for the past two centuries but whose contours can still be traced today even if in extremely subtle forms.

Many theorists have recently been more than willing to deconstruct this position, revealing its "essentialism," and emphasizing the importance of discourse in the constitution of the subject. This brings us to the second model which conceives the body as existing only within discourse. The argument is that there is no unchanging essence by which any subject can be distinguished, and reality is non-existent outside the parameters of discourse. Corporeality is fiction; what there are are only discursive bodies, and there is absolutely no relation between these and any "reality" outside them. "We attempt to explain how discourse may be conceived . . . " asserts Barry Hindess and Paul Hirst, "when it is not supposed that it corresponds to or appropriates unities of being external to it in a relation of 'knowledge' " (in Macdonell 71-72). Meaning is relative: it is locked only within the particular discourse in which it exists; there could be several discourses, and with contradictory relations between them, but they never really aggregate to produce any degree of stability for the subject to find a position. They not only keep their differences but they are also always in constant flux. Diane Macdonell explains and quotes Hirst: " 'Reality' is made up of the referents and constructs of all different discourses. Everything is dispersed and plural: one has . . . to accept the *difference* of the referents of discourse, the potential infinity of referents"

(73). If the "black" body is real, then it is so only in discourse; a signifier without a stable determinate referent. The extremism of this postulate is underscored by Michele Barrett's exasperated response, in her "Ideology and the Cultural Production of Gender," to its appropriation by some feminist theorists: "Are we really to see the Peterloo massacre, the storming of the Winter Palace in Petrograd, the Long March, the Grunwick picket [and we add, the Middle Passage] as the struggle of discourses?" (72).

We really have no choice between these approaches. "Black" body is certainly not "all there is" but neither is it a fiction without any "reality." It pre-dates discourse and thereby foreshadows a specific subjectivity for the "owner" under specific circumstances. What discourse does, writes Kaja Silverman in a different context, is "first to territorialize and then to map meaning onto bodies" (*"Histoire"* 65). In fact, Amilcar Cabral has earlier finely grasped that corporeal and discursive bodies operate *dialectically* to structure the subject:

> In fact, if it is correct that the biological element (inherited genetic patrimony) is the inescapable physical basis of the existence and continuing growth of identity, it is no less correct that the sociological element is the factor which gives it objective substance by giving content and form, and allowing confrontation and comparison between individuals and groups. (65)

I conceive, then — and this is what I think *Dream on Monkey Mountain* suggests — the relation between corporeal and discursive bodies as one of *mutual* determination, influence, interaction, and reinforcement. Many of Silverman's points are relevant to my argument:

> [N]ot only is the subject's relation to his or her body lived out through the mediation of discourse, but that body is itself coerced and molded by both representation and signification. Discursive bodies lean upon and mold real bodies in complex and manifold ways . . . While the subject's history may not be narrowly *determined* by his or her biological identity, there is scarcely a moment within that history which is uninfluenced by it. Although it cannot always be assigned with absolute certainty it usually has considerable bearing on how one is culturally "recognized," and hence on the social positions to which one has access, even when one's identifications run completely counter to that "recognition." (*Acoustic Mirror* 146-48)

The Structures of Hegemony

The main excuse for dragging Makak into the vortex of visibility — the prison — is that he is "Drunk and disorderly" (*Dream* 215). This is not exactly the case. He is taken as drunk and disorderly because he had begun to reconstitute his corporeality through and with a new kind of discourse. He had a dream that he is "the direct descendant of African Kings, a healer of leprosy and the Saviour of his race" (225). He claims that God spoke to him directly — "in the form of a woman" (226) — and that at a point in the dream, he felt he was "God self, walking through cloud" (227). This is how Corporal Lestrade, the representative preserver of the law and the order of "Her Majesty's Government" (217), the "agent of normality" (Foucault 293-308), records the offense in his book of charges: "You claimed that with the camera of your eye you had taken a photograph of God and all that you could see was blackness" (225). The didascalia, or stage direction, tells us that "the judges rise in horror" (225), horror at the potentially disruptive effect of this dream on the 'order' and the discourse which props it. Only Lestrade is able to go beyond the gestural to verbalize the horror:

> Blackness, my lords. What did the prisoner imply? That God was neither white nor black but nothing? That God was not white but black, that he had lost his faith? Or . . . or . . . what? (225).

Notice already the effects of the counter-discourse: manic insecurity and uncertainty evinced by the string of rhetorical questions, the ellipses, and the general implicit hankering for the restoration of a destabilized meaning. It surprises none then that Makak's dream is officially described as "vile, ambitious, and obscene" (224). But what exactly is the order being destabilized? What are its contours? This will be none other than a narration of how the hegemonic order constitutes Makak as a spoken subject (i.e., forces him to occupy a spoken position in the operations of discourse).[2]

This order operates through a Manichean opposition between blackness and whiteness. "White" is the solvent of all values; and the entrenched symbol for all positive attributes, while "black" is its irredeemable opposite. *With* the aid of the law, which Lestrade insightfully defines as "a whore" that "will adjust her price" (280), blackness automatically consigns the body to the receiving ends of discourse in the world of the play. And this law, we are told in unmistakable terms, is the law of the "white man": "I am an instrument of the law . . . I got the white man work to do" (279). According to this law, to be black is to be "[a]nimals,

[2]"Discourse always requires a speaking position (a position from which power-knowledge is exercised) and a spoken subject (a position brought into existence through the exercise of power-knowledge)" (Silverman "Histoire" 66-67).

beasts, savages, cannibals, niggers" (216). According to Lestrade's theory of evolution, God created the human being as ape; after some time however, some tribes of this ape straightened their backs and began to walk upright: only one tribe "lingered behind, and that was the nigger" (217).

The major black characters are therefore mapped and territorialized as ugly beasts not only directly but also by association: monkey, mouse, tiger, and mosquito. Makak is not only a monkey, he is also a *charcoal* burner, and lives in the "forest" (236), in the jungle, on Monkey *mountain*. He is the other, the obverse face of civilization. The cell in which he is locked becomes a "stinking zoo" (216) and Lestrade, the *keeper*, wants "a transfer to civilization" (281). In addition, whatever operates in Africa his ancestral home is nothing but "the law of the jungle" (280).

In one telling moment, we not only see the process of the "robotization" of Makak but also its immediate effects. Before his mock trial, Lestrade takes him through a grueling drill. As "the CORPORAL, like an animal tamer, cracks out his orders" (222) — sit, stand, kneel, turn, and so on — Makak responds like an automaton. The chorus to all this is "Everything I say this monkey does do / I don't know what to say this monkey won't do" (223). At the end of it all, Makak, we are told, flops down "wearily" (223), a zombie.

The law effectively prevents Makak from contesting these meanings; he is simply the passive, obliging surface on which they are inscribed. When he is brought into the prison, he has totally forgotten his name, and his "race" is "I am tired" (219). His corporeality is cartographed not only physically but this process also produces in him a supportive (i.e., quietistic) consciousness. He adores whiteness — the only thing his reality tells him is worth striving for — and secretly keeps a white mask in his work bag. He has psychologically absorbed the relations of power that map his corporeality. He not only believes he is ugly and a beast, but actually lives and *voices* this subjection: "Is thirty years now I have look in no mirror, / Not a pool of cold water, when I must drink, / I stir my hands first, to breakup my image" (226). His case tends dangerously close to that classic stage of self-subjection narrated by Foucault:

> The efficiency of power, its constraining force has, in a sense, passed over to the other side — to the side of its surface of application. He who is subjected to a field of visibility, and who knows it, assumes responsibility for the constraints of power; he makes them play spontaneously upon him-

> self; he inscribes in himself the power relation in which he simultaneously plays both roles; he becomes the principle of his own subjection. By this very fact, the external power may throw off its physical weight; it tends to the non-corporeal; and, the more it approaches this limit, the more constant, profound and permanent are its effects: it is a perpetual victory that avoids any physical confrontation and which is always decided in advance. (202-03)

Lestrade is correct, after all: "In some places the law does not allow you to be black, not even black but tinged with black" (280). However, no hegemony is total, and this play makes the point obvious. The reality of Makak's revolt indicates there are some areas of experience and consciousness not yet accessible to regimentation.

Negotiating Subjection

Makak's particular strategy of negotiating the dominant discourse is the reverse discourse, a method of "subversion through inversion" whereby the *outcast* authenticates herself/himself by "replacing the negative representations [that constitutes her/him] with more positive ones, appropriated from the dominant" (Dollimore 182).

With the dream — where he encounters a white woman who tells him he is neither ugly nor "nothing" but a worthy human being, a descendant of emperors and kings in great Africa — as catalyst, Makak begins to invert / reverse the dominant discourse: to discursively negate his negative representations. In the first place, the woman he sees in his dream, whom he takes in his arms (236), is not only the "loveliest" and most beautiful in the world (227), but she is also *white* (Moustique swears Makak is mentally unbalanced to have dreamt up such an abomination, 236). Above all, this white woman is celestial: "Like the moon walking along her own road" (227).

The woman not only tells him he is a handsome man with a royal ancestry: "She say I should not live so any more, here in the forest, frighten of people because I think I ugly. She say that I come from the family of lions and kings" (236), but also, and more importantly, that he is not a monkey: "That Makak is not my name" (236). We say the latter is more important because "monkey" is, in the dominant discourse, his implacable badge, the signifier of his subjection, his "nothingness" and his spoken-ness.

It is not surprising then that Makak describes the morning of his dream as "resurrection morning" (226). Of course, the "powers that be" see this attempt at self-reconstitution as nothing other than "the rage for whiteness that does drive niggers mad" (228). In fact, Makak is so gripped with the possibilities for self-definition opening up that he emphatically denies he has only dreamt them. Henceforth, he stops at nothing but the superlative: from a "nothing," he becomes a prince, a"lion," a "God's warrior" (226, 240). He co-owns only an overworked ass but "[s]addle my horse!," he roars, in preparation for the journey to Africa (240). From the zombie who flops down"wearily" in the mock trial scene, Makak now strides with his spear in agile agitation (241-42). He does not hesitate much before he stabs the corporal in order to escape from the prison (285), after all — he has explained earlier, "If we dead, . . . is not better to die, fighting like men, than to hide in this forest?" (242).

The immediate effect of this reverse discourse is that it turns up the gaze of the supervised on the supervisor and makes "orderly" government difficult. The crowning example is the jail-break. Again, it is Lestrade that brilliantly expresses the implication:

> Attempting to escape. Attempting to escape from the prison of their lives. That's the most dangerous crime. It brings about revolution. (287)

The function of this strategy of resistance — inversion — is to transform Makak from a non-entity to a king, a political figure. This is exactly what happened. His "royal" experience in Africa, however, tells him that his vision of that continent is extremely idealized. He finds the tribes "devouring" one another when he had supposed them united because they are racially homogeneous (305).[3] The tribes, led by the converted Lestrade, now the chief ideologue of "black consciousness," are more of praise-singers than effective monitors of their leader (308-11). Once in control of power, their preoccupation seems to be with revenge, and this they pursue with reckless abandon:

> We have no time for patient reforms. Mindless as the hawk, impetuous as lions, as dried of compassion as the bowels of a jackal. Elsewhere, the swiftness of justice is barbarously slow, but our progress cannot stop to think. (311)

A trial is set up. Makak, in kingly splendor, sits enthroned. History is dragged out from the deepest recesses and accused of having trampled "blackness" underfoot.

[3]Walcott writes, revealingly, of "Makak's trip back to Africa where he found the tribes slaughtering each other (Ibos were being slaughtered by their Nigerian brothers while I wrote the play: a familiar human tragedy, of course, for civil wars are going on all over the world). Makak recognizes that human cruelty is raceless" (Rodman 249).

Aristotle, Shakespeare, Galileo, Lincoln, Drake, Tarzan, Cecil Rhodes, Wilberforce, Mandrake the Magician, and so on, are all sentenced to the gallows, because they are "indubitably . . . white" (312). The enemies of the present — from the Pope, the United States, apartheid South Africa, the Ku Klux Klan, and so on — "fearing revenge," offer apologies and hands of fellowship; the tribes, of course, reject all (312-14). However, Makak begins to interrogate his vision when Moustique alleged that he — Makak — is only a puppet now, surrounded by power-hungry hounds, and that the original dream has been corrupted (314-15). Let us not mistake Moustique for a visionary; he deserves his two deaths because he started the corruption: he began selling the dream for profit when it had barely taken shape (250-55, 265-69).

Makak's suspicion of his vision (316-19) is an implicit critique of reverse discourse as a method of resistance. It dawns on him that his dream of a pristine, glorious Africa is ironically an acceptance still of whiteness as a measure of value (i.e., to *exhibit* his black heritage, to counterpose it to whiteness in the fashion of a binary opposition, not necessarily because he believes in it). And remember it is a *white* woman that set him on the wild utopian chase. In other words, Makak's reverse discourse is operating within, and therefore already circumscribed by, the Manichean terrains of the dominant discourse.

It would be crude, however, to belittle Makak's resistance because of this limitation. It is the kind of contradiction to be found in a revisionist politics. Even then, such a strategy sometimes proves to be quite subversive and therefore indispensable as a *stage* to more effective forms of resistance. I find Dollimore relevant:

> Jacques Derrida reminds us that binary oppositions are "a violent hierarchy" where one of the two terms forcefully governs the other. A crucial stage in their deconstruction involves an overturning, an inversion "which brings low what is high." The political effect of ignoring this stage, of trying to jump beyond the hierarchy into a world quite free of it is simply to leave it intact in the only world we have. Both the reversal of authentic/inauthentic opposition . . . and the subversion of authenticity itself . . . are different aspects of overturning in Derrida's sense. Moreover they are stages in a *process* of resistance. (190)

Ultimately, however, Makak did go beyond an inversion of the dominant discourse. He confronts the apparition of the white woman that catalyzes his epic quest for Africa. "Why have you caused me all the pain?" he queries her. As

Lestrade appropriately cuts in, the woman's "vision is exhausted" (316). What remains is to get rid of her. Her *theory* of *negritude*, her message of an innocent Africa, is discovered to be, in the last instance, a Greek gift: another, and more insidious, form of enslavement. We shall have to quote Lestrade, addressing Makak, in some detail:

> She . . . was but an image of your longing . . . as fatal as leprosy . . . destroy her; otherwise . . . [y]ou will come out in blotches, . . . neither one thing nor the other . . . kill her! . . . She is the mirror of the moon that this ape look into and find himself unbearable . . . She is . . . the mother of civilization, and the confounder of blackness. I too have longed for her. She is the colour of law, religion, paper, art, and if you want peace, if you want to discover the beautiful depth of your blackness, nigger, chop her head! . . . She is the white light that paralysed your mind, that led you into this confusion. It is you who created her, so kill her! (318-19)

And the result?

> MAKAK: [Removing his robe] Now, O God, now I am free [He holds the curved sword in both hands and brings it down. The WOMAN is beheaded]. (320)

Makak rejects the deception by beheading the white goddess. And it is significant that he steps *out* of the charade of a splendor-filled imperial Africa — by "[r]emoving his robe" — before performing the decisive act. The challenge of resistance is no longer just to invert the hegemonic discourse, but to radically alter the terrain of production of discourse and the relations of the subordinated to it. With Makak's final act — a rejection of black/white essentializing discourses — the dominant discourse's main supporting pillar, Manicheism, becomes an obsolete tool. "Our mistake," writes Walcott of Caribbeans, "has been to try to align our real power, a human thing, with the hallucination of *sharing* it, either with Africa or America. Going back to Africa is assuming an inferiority. We must look *inside*. West India exists but we must find it." He then defended Makak's treatment of the white woman: "Getting rid of his overwhelming awe of everything white is the first thing a colonial must take. The error is that when you translate this into *political* terms, it leads — wrongly, disastrously — into acts of murder, and eventually genocide" (Rodman 240, 249).

The dream, or nightmare, serves as a spiritual cleansing for Makak. The signal of his reformed consciousness is that in the end he not only smartly named himself (321), but also rejected the white mask found in his bag (324). From being a slave to whiteness and then to an imaginary Africa, he is now his "real" West Indian self — a cultural mulatto — without any illusions: "Lord, I have been washed from shore to shore, as a tree in the ocean. The branches of my fingers, the roots of my feet, could grip nothing, but now, God, they have found ground" (326). Even the elements celebrate this rebirth: the sun appears in all its bright glory (325) as Makak is freed from prison, the symbolic prison of mental enslavement. This political gesture may be "small" but it is the pre-condition for any clear-sighted struggle in the social sphere.

Writing the Self?

It is interesting to note that Walcott went through a similar experience toward negotiating a distinct cultural matrix for his theatre. Just like Makak's, three stages of the "journey" — really, the growth of his consciousness — can be identified: European, African, and West Indian. As a fact of his Western education, Walcott started out, as he says, as a "natural assimilator" *(Dream* 4) of the "great" tradition of English literature. The literature of the "mother country" provided the challenge and the inspiration to fill the literary desert that was the Caribbean, and create a viable extension of those "masterpieces" which he considered as universal classics. Walcott's earliest play, *Flight and Sanctuary*, written in 1946 when he was 16 years old, best represents this phase. The play was written entirely in verse, and neither in setting, characterization, language nor storyline was it typically West Indian (Hill 31-32). Finally convinced of his Englishness, the young dramatist knocked at the doors of this "Great Tradition" but was rudely turned back — by F. R. Leavis. Let Walcott himself tell us of his embarrassment:

> I saw myself legitimately prolonging the mighty line of Marlowe, of Milton, but my sense of inheritance was stronger because it came from estrangement. I would soon learn that every tribe hoards its culture as fiercely as its prejudices, that English literature, even in the theatre, was hallowed ground and trespass, that colonial literatures could grow to resemble it closely, but could never be considered its legitimate heir. There was folk poetry, colonial poetry, Commonwealth verse, etc., and their function, as far as their mother country was concerned, was filial and tributary. (31)

Walcott retraced his steps and gradually "began" an "African phase." Makak too dreamt of a royal ancestry in Africa. Both never found a comfortable position in this stage. Outside of an escapist dance of self-deception, any *unproblematic* claim to Africa for cultural and spiritual succor was virtually impossible. Walcott writes: "If one went in search of the African experience, carrying the luggage of a few phrases and a crude map, where would it end? We had no language for the bush and there was a conflicting grammar in the pace of our movement" (57). In dramatic and theatrical terms, this quandary is demonstrated concretely when Walcott directed one of Soyinka's plays with his company, The Trinidad Theatre Workshop:

> When we produced Soyinka's masterpiece *The Road,* one truth, like the murderous headlamps of his mammy-wagons, transfixed us, and this was that our frenzy goes by another name, that it is this naming, ironically enough, which weakens our effort at being African. We tried, in the words of his Professor, to "hold the god captive," but for us, Afro-Christians, the naming of the god estranged him. Ogun was an exotic for us, not a force. We could pretend to enter his power but he would never possess us, for our invocations were not prayer but devices . . . only blasphemy was left. (8-9)

Finally, Walcott, like Makak, had to reject the "African dream." "West Indies exists," the author assures himself, "but we must find it. It's a mosaic, you might say" (Rodman 240). For Walcott therefore, an "authentic" cultural identity for the Caribbean cannot be forged outside the parameters of conscious hybridity; a "mulatto style" to confront his schizophrenia and rootlessness, a "bastard" aesthetics for a "bastard" reality:

> [W]hat is needed is not new names for old things, but the faith of using the old names anew, so that mongrel as I am, something prickles in me when I see the word Ashanti as with the word Warwickshire, both separately intimating my grandfather's roots, both baptising this neither proud nor ashamed bastard, this hybrid, this West Indian. (10)

The Subjectivity of the Text

What we need to examine next is the formal artistic configurations of the construction of Makak's identity. What we discover is that as the main character seems to be inventing himself, the text itself appears to be on a similar mission. The text is intricately structured upon an elaborate system of oppositions and tensions between such disparate elements as the material poverty of the setting and the intellectual richness of the dramatic discourse, clarity and ambiguity of symbols and metaphors, Creole and Queen's English, inside and outside theatrical spaces, seriousness and horseplay or buffoonery, animal and human characters, poetry and prose passages, stylistic complexity and popular theme, dream and wakefulness or reality, history and fable, and raw folk forms and extensive, sophisticated "foreign" high-brow allusions and borrowings. I shall pick the first, and the last two, for further discussion.

Except, perhaps, in the "Apotheosis" where an atmosphere of material splendor and opulence is created, the play virtually operates on the barest material theatrical accoutrements. Maybe little is to be expected from a setting that is either a cell, a country road, a forest, a hut or a village market. And what is more, the didascalia pay only a *minimal* attention to the materiality of the scenes. The "style should be spare, essential as the details of a dream," the playwright insists (208). Borrowing Grotowski's phrase, this instruction intimates the playwright's agenda for "The Poor Theatre" which he asserts:

> has never been more applicable to our own situation here in the islands, both as economics and as chord of compassion for theatre artists, playwrights, actors, musicians and craftsmen continue to labour under embittering conditions. Our culture needs preservation and resurgence, our crises need an epiphany, a spiritual definition, and an art that can emerge from our poverty, creating its own elation. (Nettleford 33-34)

Hence the emphasis in the play is on the actor's body as the chief theatrical resource, its capability to switch roles and create spectacle. The quest is "for a staging that would be easy under some backyard tree as with the devices of the rich theatre. The wealth of this bareness is in the nakedness of spirit, in the pliant and magical metamorphoses of the body" (Nettleford 36-37). It is upon this material bare-ness of the play's setting — "A West Indian Island" (210) — that Walcott erects a dramatic discourse that has all the trappings of affluence: poetic, highly textured and theatrically and intellectually challenging; an extensive canvas bearing etches of disparate philosophical, theological and artistic systems and traditions from several parts of the world. I shall return to say more about this extensive reach.

The second set of oppositions is that between history and fable. The play as fable is not only evident in its self-advertisement as a dream but also in the assignation of animal names to the characters, the symbolic use of masks, the journey to "Africa of the mind" and the corporal's consistent theatrical overkill and rhetorical excess. History, however, retains an equally strong pull, and the most obvious evidence of this is the effusion of "definite references" of the extratextual variety (Issacharoff 84-94) that threaten to drown the play: Africa, Lion of Judah, Esau, Ashanti, Moses, Sharpeville, Marlowe, Ibo, Pushkin, and so on. Besides, the play can hardly deny that it could stand, symbolically, as a history of the Afro-Caribbean.

Walcott has an unhidden preference for history as fable or myth rather than as chronology. To be fixated with the rational and chronological idea of history, he says, is to fetter the creative intellect with sociological detail, with the statistics of oppression and exploitation and the likes. This attitude can only produce a "literature of revenge," a morbid aesthetics distinguished by its substitution of querulousness for art:

> In the New World servitude to the muse of history has produced a literature of recrimination and despair, a literature of revenge written by the descendants of slaves or a literature of remorse written by the descendants of masters. Because this literature serves historical truth, it yellows into polemic or evaporates into pathos . . . This shame and awe of history possess poets of the Third World who think of language as enslavement and who, in a rage for identity, respect only incoherence or nostalgia.
>
> ("Muse" 2)

On the contrary, what is appropriate for the New World writer is to conceive history as fable, as myth subject to the fashioning hands of the artist: "The truly tough aesthetic of the New world neither explains nor forgives history. It refuses to recognize it as a creative or culpable force . . . [it] reject[s] ethnic ancestry for faith in elemental man" ("Muse" 2-5). This attitude identifies and celebrates the shared sensibility between such poles as Prospero and Caliban, Crusoe and Friday; rather than enervate its will contemplating the shipwreck, adopts the "Adamic" vision, accepting the challenge of creating a world anew. It is significant to note that the play does not subscribe to this extremist critical position by its author; in it, history does not in any way exclude the fabulous — in fact, the latter serves as a competent strategy for exorcizing the onerous burden of the former.

And finally the tension between the play's folk elements — the characters, songs, dances, raw humor, and the extensive borrowings and sophisticated allusions. This is, perhaps, an indication of Walcott's rejection of "stylistic careerism" — the wholesale and uncritical adoption of models from any *one* of the cultural tributaries that feed the Caribbean. The ideal, he says and as his work shows, is to be a "traitor," "the mulatto of style" (*Dream* 9), free to borrow not only from Aeschylus, Shakespeare, Brecht and Soyinka but also from ancient Japanese and Chinese theatres, contemporary American opera and West Indian folktale. In *Dream on Monkey Mountain*, critics have directed attention to the Strindbergian trait of the production note, Brechtian estranging effects such as Lestrade's direct addresses to the audience, the author's claim of some indebtedness to the Kabuki theatre, and other influences from Plato, Kierkegaard, Lorca, Buchner, Cervantes, and Christian theology (the last is the most pervasive, e.g. Makak as a Christ figure, Tigre and Souris as the two thieves, and so on). "I am a kind of split writer," Walcott confesses, "The mimetic, the narrative, and dance element is strong on one side, and the literary, the classical tradition is strong on the other (Hamner 64).[4]

The Caribbean Condition

The problem remains how to articulate this hybrid aesthetics in order to evaluate its relevance to the construction of cultural identity in the Caribbean context. In this respect, in the light of the play's creative plunder of disparate and most often canonical philosophical systems and artistic traditions, we identify its organizing principle as "coherent deformation." There is the extensive parody of the established law by none other than its officer; a parody that subtly but accurately reveals the law's alpine weight on the dominated (*Dream* 215-26). Makak is black, poor and "ugly as sin," but he is the Christ, complete with healing power (216, 250), and the two thieves (especially in the cell scenes) in the characters of Souris and Tigre. Makak is also Moses, coming down from the mountain with good tidings (248). Or one might look in another direction and see him as Don Quixote, and Moustique as his Sancho Panza, set to exorcise the age-old oppression of their kind (231-56); but neither Makak-Moustique nor their goal could be said to be exactly quixotic. And what could this speech by Lestrade signify if not that that famous, lofty Declaration of Independence still remains little more than mere rhetoric for some category of people?

> Your rights? Listen, nigger! according to this world you have the inalienable right to life, liberty, and three green figs. No more, maybe less. You can do what you want with your life, you can hardly call this liberty, and as for the pursuit of happiness, you never hear the expression, give a nigger an inch and he'll take a mile? (279)

"Coherent deformation," Allen Weiss explains, "is the process whereby the form, the facticity of the world is shattered by praxis, with the result that a new meaning ensues. The 'coherency' maintains the equivalence between signs; the

[4]For a discussion of Walcott's borrowings, see Hamner, chapter 3. I am also referring to notes on Wole Soyinka's discussion of Walcott in a class lecture, Cornell University, Ithaca, 11/29/88.

'deformation' achieves the differences between signs" (20). Weiss quotes Merleau-Ponty: "It is just this 'coherent deformation' of available significations which arranges them in a new sense and takes not only the hearers but the speaking subject as well through a decisive step" (20). The subversive character of coherent deformation is that it undermines the stability of signs, destroys the established order of meaning and classification, and opens up the possibility of a realignment of forces. As a politico-symbolic response to "the obstinate fact of a society that has been deeply historically segmented" (Nettleford xxiii), perhaps such interventions are direly necessary. But only as a means that must constantly interrogate itself. For instance, while it may be clear that the play allies itself with the mood of change and regeneration, especially as it concerns the plebeian, it is not exactly certain that it is in a form they can master (Brecht 107-15). For example, Slade Hopkinson, who played Corporal Lestrade when the play went on a West Indian tour in 1968, reported that while they performed to full houses of "'the mass of the people'" in the several islands — which evinced that they knew "what the play was about," he would nevertheless "not suggest . . . that all these people 'understood' the very great complexity of the play in all its poetic and psychological detail." And among the "educated," Hopkinson continues, the play has a reputation of being "powerful but inaccessibly abstruse and high-brow" (78). If indeed, "West Indian militancy lies in art" (*Dream* 18) as Walcott asserts, then it is another challenge for an oppositional practice such as his to more properly define its audience and to constantly re-vision itself in relation to that audience.

Dream on Monkey Mountain is more than the story of Makak, or Walcott, it is the epic of the constitution of cultural identity for the Caribbean, as the playwright envisions it. In the struggle to attain a speaking position within discourse, the play suggests conceiving the relationship between corporeal and discursive bodies as close and mutually affective. The corporeality of the West Indian is that s/he is a hybrid, a cultural mulatto. It is within this space that the theatre of Walcott speaks.

WORKS CITED

Barrett, Michele. "Ideology and the Cultural Production of Gender." In Newton & Rosenfelt.

Brathwaite, Edward. "Timehri." In Orde Coombs, ed. *Is Massa Day Dead?: Black Moods in the Caribbean*. New York: Anchor P, 1974.
Brecht, Bertolt. "The Popular and the Realistic." *Brecht on Theatre*. Trans. John Willet. New York: Hill and Wang, 1964.
Cabral, Amilcar. *Return to the Source*. New York: Monthly Review Press, 1973.
Dollimore, Jonathan. "The dominant and the deviant: a violent dialectic." *Critical Quarterly* 28:1 & 2 (1986): 179-192.
Foucault, Michel. *Discipline and Punish*. Trans. Alan Sheridan. New York: Vintage, 1979.
Gates, Jr., H. L., ed. *Race, Writing and Difference*. Chicago: U of Chicago P, 1985.
Glissant, Edouard. *Caribbean Discourse*. Trans. J. M. Dash. Charlottesville: UP of Virginia, 1989.
Hamner, Robert D. *Derek Walcott*. Boston: Twayne, 1981.
Hearne, J., ed. *Carifesta Forum: An Anthology of 20 Caribbean Voices*. Kingston, Jamaica: Institute of Jamaica, 1976.
Hill, Errol. "The Emergence of A National Drama in the West Indies." *Caribbean Quarterly* 18:4 (1972): 9-40.
Hopkinson, Slade. "*Dream on Monkey Mountain* and the Popular Response: A few questions." *Caribbean Quarterly* 23: 2 & 3 (1979): 77-79.
Hume, David. "Of National Characters" (1748). Cited by Gates.
Issacharoff, Michael. "How Playscripts Refer: Some Preliminary Considerations." In Whiteside & Issacharoff.
Kant, Immanuel. *Observations on the Feeling of the Beautiful and the Sublime* (1764). Cited by Gates.
Knight, F. W. and C. A. Palmer, ed. "The Caribbean: A Regional Overview." *The Modern Caribbean*. Chapel Hill: U of North Carolina P, 1989.
Macdonell, Diane. *Theories of Discourse*. Oxford: Blackwell, 1986.
Nettleford, Rex. *Caribbean Cultural Identity: The Case of Jamaica*. UCLA: Center for Afro-American Studies & Latin American Center Publications, 1978.
Newton, Judith & D. Rosenfelt, eds. *Feminist Criticism and Social Change*. New York: Methuen, 1985.
Rodman, Selden. *Tongues of Fallen Angels*. New York: New Directions, 1972.
Silverman, Kaja. *The Acoustic Mirror*. Bloomington: Indiana UP, 1988.
Silverman, Kaja. "*Histoire d'O:* The story of a Disciplined and Punished Body." *Enclitic* 7:2 (1983): 63-81.
Walcott, Derek. *Dream on Monkey Mountain and Other Plays*. New York: Farrar, Straus and Giroux, 1970.
Walcott, Derek. "The Muse of History." In Coombs
Weiss, Allen S. "Ideology and the problem of Style: The Errant Text." *Enclitic* 7:2 (1983): 17-23.
Whiteside A. & M. Issacharoff, eds. *On Referring in Literature*. Bloomington: Indiana UP, 1987.

ASHTON NICHOLS

Colonizing Consciousness: Culture and Identity in Walcott's *Another Life* and Wordsworth's *Prelude*

Derek Walcott's *Another Life* has become one of the most significant works of contemporary poetry from the Caribbean. Walcott's book length autobiographical poem has been praised for its powerful lyricism, its evocative characterizations, and its effective depiction of the colonial and post-colonial situation in the Caribbean basin.[1] Perhaps the most enthusiastic praise the poem has received comes from Kenneth Ramchand, who described the 1973 publication of *Another Life* as the "literary event of the West Indian year." Ramchand went on to claim that the poem "contains more metrical variety and experimentation, and . . . is more compressed and less self-indulgent than the only other poem in English that approaches it for stature, but the most convenient way of suggesting its richness and importance is to describe it as Walcott's and the West Indian's *The Prelude*"(131). Whether or not we agree completely with Ramchand's evaluation, he points to a connection that is both significant and suggestive. A careful comparison of Walcott's *Another Life* and Wordsworth's *Prelude* suggests how much Walcott owes to the Wordsworthian tradition of verse autobiography, and also how our understanding of Wordsworth's poem deepens when seen in light of its Caribbean counterpart. More importantly, a reading of Walcott's poem alongside Wordsworth's reveals the role of culture in the development of identity, particularly as that process occurs in autobiographical texts.

If it is true that Walcott is a sort of Caribbean Wordsworth, then Wordsworth is an earlier version of a colonized consciousness like the one described in Walcott's poem. Reading Walcott in light of Wordsworth suggests that colonization is

[1]For comprehensive responses to *Another Life* see particularly Baugh, Brown, and Lieberman. Clara Thomas compares *Another Life* to Margaret Laurence's *The Diviners* and notes that Walcott's complex Caribbean context compels him to "go beyond his own racial past to record and commemorate the Carib Indians who held the land before the white men came, and who leaped from the rock at Sauteurs rather than be enslaved" (265). J. A. Ramsaran analyzes the important interplay between Caribbean and Mediterranean sources in Walcott's poem.

perhaps the central metaphor for any literary account of a coming into consciousness. Every autobiography to some extent records the desire to aesthetically shape one's experience and the realization that one is, at the same time, being culturally shaped by that same experience. Identity, in Walcott's and Wordsworth's poems, emerges out of an interaction between sociocultural forces and an aesthetic posture that seeks to critique all cultural identifications. The resulting autobiographical voice — whether Wordsworth's or Walcott's — seeks an "artistic" position free from social limitations, while at the same time revealing the complex forces that prevent such a culturally neutral position from ever emerging.

While Ramchand may have been the first to cite the connection between *Another Life* and *The Prelude*, he did not develop the Wordsworthian side of his parallel. Edward Baugh extends Ramchands's comparison in "The Poem as Autobiographical Novel: Derek Walcott's *Another Life* in relation to Wordsworth's *Prelude* and Joyce's *Portrait*," an essay that is thorough and convincing in its analysis of the structure of *Another Life*, but which likewise never develops the details of the comparison to Wordsworth.[2] Walcott's poem is, in fact, a subtly transformed and modernized version of *The Prelude*. The intertextual relation between these two poems helps us to understand the cultural context of all of those autobiographical writings that employ a primarily lyrical mode. In addition, Wordsworth's earlier text reveals the forces of intellectual colonization at work in a Caribbean context like Walcott's.

Stylistically, Walcott's poem owes obvious debts to Yeats, Pound, Eliot, and Whitman. But the real source texts for *Another Life* are Walcott's early autobiographical poem, "Epitaph for the Young," and Wordsworth's "Poem to Coleridge".[3] Walcott's "Poem to St. Omer," as *Another Life* might be called, not only draws on the tradition of the dedicatory poetic autobiography. His poem enriches that tradition by describing a complex artistic sensibility that emerges out of its relationship to a variety of colonizing cultural forces: art and literature

---

[2]See also Travis Lane, who likewise notes the connection to Wordsworth, but sees Walcott's version as "a different" growth of the poet's mind.

[3]Hamner notes that "Epitaph for the Young" (1949) includes many of the details of *Another Life* in a cruder, more imitative form (xv-xvi). Baugh claims that Walcott's "Leaving School" essay seems to have begun the autobiographical process that led to *Another Life (Memory as Vision* 3-4).

of the past and present, the natural environment, the society on the island of St. Lucia, the teacher (Harry Simmons), the first and lost love (Anna/Andreuille), and the fellow artist (Gregorias/Dunstan St.Omer).

Walcott's cryptic title has most often been explained by referring to the "divided child" described in book one of the poem. Thus the conflicting worlds of Walcott's ancestral and hereditary past — the white world of the colonizing British and the black world of the St. Lucian slaves — like the racially divided world of his Caribbean present, represent, each to the other, "another life": "my white grandfather's face . . . my black grandfather's voice" (64).[4] As Lloyd Brown has noted, the poet struggles to incorporate the dual racial and cultural sides of his identity and the result is a kind of tense unity: "this new integrated consciousness constitutes *another* life, the mature completeness within which the poet accepts the diverse sources of his selfhood" (136). Brown sees this as part of a more characteristically West Indian dilemma: "the quest for national consciousness and identity is not only a localized cultural act, but it is also a reflection of every individual's need to achieve a sense of complete or creative selfhood; and on this basis the individual or national consciousness of the West Indian is developed in response to a universal need" (136-37).[5]

Walcott reveals one sort of cultural debt by using Matthew Arnold's "To Marguerite . . . Continued" as the epigraph to part four of his own poem. The Arnoldian passage suggests the gulf that separates Walcott as an adult from the earlier sources of his inspiration. Adulthood has produced yet "another" life, a literary and Westernized Walcott who feels that an "estranging sea" now divides him from his teacher, best friend, and first love, all of whom stood for so much in the earlier sections of the poem. On these terms, the "other" life is the memory of childhood that can only be regained fleetingly in adulthood. The mature artist begins to sense that this earlier life is as much a creation of the present as it is a recreation of the past.

---

[4]Quotations are given with page numbers from the Three Continents Press edition of *Another Life*. Robert Hamner provides an extremely useful introduction and chronology in this edition.The most recent publication of the poem occurs in *Collected Poems: 1948-84*. All Wordsworth citations, except as indicated, are taken from the 1805 version of *The Prelude* as it appears in the Wordsworth, Abrams, and Gill edition.

[5]Brown argues that in Walcott's case "the poet's growth or personal odyssey involves a fusion of the divided self into a unified consciousness without obliterating the distinctive nature of the experiences that he has inherited from either world"(136).

The adult autobiographer gives the people he remembers from his youth "a stature / disproportionate to their cramped lives," primarily because he remembers them as they seemed to him then, when he beheld them at "knee-height" (40). In those early days, the adults' "thunderous exchanges / rumbled like gods about another life" (40). Here Walcott adopts an additional ambiguous use of "another" to suggest the Caribbean adults' sense of worlds beyond what seemed to them their limited cultural realm. Years would have to pass before Walcott could see the things he read of in the literature of the "outside" world: "an orchestra, / a train, a theatre, the spark-coloured leaves / of autumn" (40). In a Caribbean world without orchestras, trains, theaters, or autumn, how could the young child understand the things he read of, described in books with such "processional arrogance." Nor could he understand the cultural forces that produced the "cramped" lives he would never imagine describing in pejorative terms until much later. Walcott's analysis suggests one way that colonization works in the Caribbean context. Language creates a sense of unknown European modes of experience that come to be identified with a local absence, a cultural shortcoming. Born into this unjustly diminished Caribbean world, of racially mixed ancestry, and so far removed from the European world of which he read as he matured, how could he be anything but "a divided child?" (40).

Such a world of personal division, however, is not unique to a culturally divided consciousness in the Caribbean. Walcott actually produces a much more typical account of personal identity. He describes the experience of any self-conscious individual, any person who develops a sense of the gulf that separates aspirations from reality, the world of possibility from the world of actuality. Wordsworth recounts just such a self early in his own autobiography, *The Prelude*. Thinking of the days of his youth from the uneasy vantage point of adulthood he says: "I seem / Two consciousnesses — conscious of myself, / And of some other being" (II, 31-33). Wordsworth here describes the "vacancy" that separates him as an adult from the days of his most vivid childhood memories. Yet the power of these memories is still able to produce a "self-presence" of the earlier identity in the adult poet's mind. No matter how far Wordsworth moves from the experiences of childhood, they continue to exert a power that helps to unify an unstable and divided self. Another life — "some other being" — is drawn from the past in order to define the present life. Identity is created in part by being remembered.

The two Wordsworths, "myself / And some other being," have more in common with the divided child described by Walcott than we might first imagine. Wordsworth, the middle class, rural son of a father who died early in his life, describes a world of natural objects that become particularly valuable to him. His sympathies enlarge as "the common range of visible things" grows "dear" (II, 182). Yet he also draws strength from the culture around him: from local legends, fairy tales, and a wide range of significant experiences that eventually lead him to transform his thoughts into the raw material for artistic creation. Walcott likewise loses his father at an early age and grows up surrounded by the need to draw his identity from the culture around him. This task is complicated by his mixed racial and middle-class ancestry, his provincialism, and his sense of a Caribbean environment which cuts him off from the rest of the world. At the same time, however, this apparent lack of historical and cultural context gives him a clean slate on which to inscribe a version of himself. Caribbean provincialism, Walcott would later say, was an asset, because it allowed him to have a more complete "communion with things that the metropolitan writers no longer care about" (Jacobs 9). These links with a non-urban sense of "family, earth, and history" are strikingly similar to the feeling Wordsworth describes when he leaves the sophistication of Cambridge and London to return to the Lake District and begin writing his own autobiographical poem.[6]

Walcott claims that his first affections for artistic representation were not derived from reality but from art itself. The epigraph from Malraux with which Walcott opens his poem notes that the painter Giotto was "more deeply moved by the sight of works of art than by that of the things which they portray" (3). Walcott begins his own poem by citing his early attempts to become a painter. He depicts painting as a way of learning to see and thus come to love one's surroundings. The pictures painted by his teacher Harry Simmons, and the world of art they represent, are depicted as "another life, / a landscape locked in amber, the rare / gleam" (5). This image reminds us of Wordsworth's claim, in his epiphany

[6]Note Wordsworth's claim to Sir George Beaumont that he began his autobiographical poem because he was "unprepared to treat any more arduous subject." "I had nothing to do but describe what I had felt and thought," Wordsworth says, intentionally distancing himself from the sophisticated conceits of metropolitan poets of the late eighteenth century (Wordsworth, Abrams, Gill 534).

of the drowned man, that the childhood sight of a dead body caused him no fear, because he had "seen" such sights before in stories he had heard or read. Wordsworth describes the dead man, whose body rose up through the water with a "ghastly face":

> And yet no vulgar fear,
> Young as I was, a child not nine years old,
> Possessed me, for my inner eye had seen
> Such sights before among the shining streams
> Of fairyland, the forest of romance — . (V, 472-77)

For Wordsworth, as for Walcott, the world of art helps to stabilize experience by making it recognizable. Because the child has imagined death before, his actual confrontation with a corpse produces "a spirit hallowing what I saw / With decoration and ideal grace." The result is primarily aesthetic; the image comes to possess a "dignity, a smoothness, like the words / Of Grecian art and purest poesy" (V, 478-81).

The similarities between Walcott's St. Lucia and Wordsworth's Lake District are obvious but also startling. Natural beauty in both environments contributes to the emerging identity of the literary artist. The human world, although rich and diverse, seems often secondary to the child's sense of his own psychic interactions with his environment. Both poets sense, however, that the world of natural objects may actually assume a secondary role in the psyche, secondary to the effort that transforms nature into artistic representation. The jutting mountains, deep valleys, and unpopulated landscapes of Walcott's childhood remind us of precise details of Wordsworth's Lake District. In both cases, however, it is the ability to create aesthetic images out of these natural objects that forms the basis for the relationship between art and identity.

Walcott introduces his own autobiographical subject with the painterly sights of a literary sea, "where the pages of the sea /are a book left open" (5) and, like Wordsworth, connects his own first experience of death with a vision of water. At the funeral of a neighborhood child, Walcott recalls how:

> The world
> Stopped swaying and settled in its place.
> A black lace glove swallowed his hand.
> The engine of the sea began again. (9)

Walcott has been waiting for the dead child to rise up, like Wordsworth's drowned man, as a spirit: "the live child waited /for the other to escape, a flute / of frail, seraphic mist." But the only sounds and sights that arrive are associated with voices in shells and the rolling of the sea. Wordsworth, no less significantly, begins the earliest versions of the poem that would become *The Prelude* with the waterish sounds of the river Derwent: "Was it for this / That one, the fairest of all rivers, loved / To blend his murmurs with my nurse's song" (1799, I, 1-3). This water sends a "voice" that flows through the child's dreams, making a "ceaseless music" that gives the young consciousness a knowledge "of the calm / Which Nature breathes among the fields and groves" (1799, I, 14-15).

Walcott provides one of the climaxes to his book-length poem with another image of water, this time associated with the literary imagination that produces books:

> So, I shall repeat myself,
> prayer, same prayer, towards fire, same fire,
> as the sun repeats itself and the thundering waters
>
> for what else is there
> but books, books and the sea,
> verandas and the pages of the sea. (139-40)

Walcott then cites a series of adult memories which retain a precise value as a function of their connection to his past. "Holiest" of all of these images, he claims, is "the break of the blue sea below the trees" (140). Walcott's lines are subtly reminiscent of Wordsworth's climactic description of the sea in the closing book of *The Prelude*. Having scaled Mount Snowdon, Wordsworth sees at his feet an ocean of mist and beyond that "the real sea," which renders up a "roar of waters, torrents, streams/ Innumerable, roaring with one voice" (XIII, 49, 58-59). The crack in the mist through which this sound rises becomes an analogue for Wordsworth's own creative imagination.

Walcott produces yet another echo of this imagery in the description of his first memorable departure from the island of his birth. He leaves behind the people who have been most important to him — Gregorias and Anna — and, as the plane rises into the sky, he gains a perspective remarkably similar to Wordsworth's atop Snowdon:

> I watched the island narrowing, the fine
> writing of foam around the precipices, then
> the roads as small and casual as twine
> thrown on its mountains, I watched till the plane
> turned to the final north and turned above
> the open channel with the grey sea between

> the fishermen's islets until all that I love
> folded in cloud. I watched the shallow green
> breaking in places where there would be reef.
> (108-09)

Thus the sight of water, like the sound of water, serves in both Walcott and Wordsworth to unify disparate sense impressions into a unity of natural and psychological process.

Many of Walcott's specific details echo Wordsworthian images or evoke a Romantic sense of the self emerging into consciousness through its natural and cultural surroundings: "Across the pebbled back yard, woodsmoke thins, / epiphany of ascension. The soul, like fire, / abhors what it consumes" (12). Walcott, like Wordsworth in the preface to *Lyrical Ballads*, is powerfully affected by the language of ordinary people. In Walcott's case, however, this language is the "Jacobean English" of the King James Bible. In Walcott's colonized ears this English "rang, new minted, / the speech of simple men, / evangelists, reformers, abolitionists" (23). The patois of Walcott's Caribbean culture combines with the language of the European culture he is appropriating through books to produce a new and powerful voice — his own.

Like Wordsworth, Walcott records the artistic difficulties attendant on adopting a narrowly dogmatic approach to religion.The emerging St. Lucian artist finds in the natural world a religion deeper than any organized faith, a religion that connects him with his African origins. The "pragmatic / Methodism" of his infancy gives way to a sacramental view of the entire world, grounded in the tribal authority of the wilderness — "the bush" (24-25). Walcott once noted that "Whether you wanted to accept them or not, the earth emanated influences which you could either put down as folk superstition or, as a poet, accept as a possible truth" (Hamner xiii). Walcott begins to hear in seashells and in wind-blown water the same kind of voices Wordsworth heard in mountain rocks and the wind through dry grass. Wordsworth tells of "low breathings," "strange utterances," and "unknown modes of being" that fill his increasingly sensitized mind, leading to a "sense of God, or whatsoe'er is dim / Or vast in its own being" (XIII, 72-73). Walcott's sense, derived from the power of these earth-emanated influences, leads him away from the desire to "be a preacher" and "write great hymns" (24), toward a longing for an aesthetic harmony that will unite culture and identity into an artistic unity. In the case of both poets, one result of this transmuted religious longing is the writing of autobiography. The mundane can thus be seen as revelatory in secular, literary terms.

Walcott's description of the way an ordinary sight can become remarkable is reminiscent of the Wordsworth of the Lucy poems, "The Solitary Reaper," and "Resolution and Independence":

> Beside the road,
> a beautiful, brown Indian
> girl in rags. Sheaves
> of brown rice held in brown,
> brittle hands, watching us
> with that earth-deep darkness
> in her gaze. She was
> the new Persephone,
> dazed, ignorant,
> waiting to be named. (73)

The poet takes the mundane materials of his ordinary world and transforms them into a new myth. "The radiance of sharing extends to the simplest objects" (15), Walcott claims. The "inventory of accidents" that become significant in our mind causes us, if we can intensify their value artistically, to "weep for dumb things"(15). But Walcott's thoughts, like Wordsworth's, sometimes lie deeper than tears.

Any doubt that Walcott has Wordsworth in mind as he writes *Another Life* is dispelled when he ironically invokes "intimations of immortality" to describe his first "immoral" longing for "Other men's wives" (101). Earlier in the same section, Walcott describes the desire "never to leave" his isle in strictly Wordsworthian terms:

> to sit and watch the twilight in this harbour
> igniting other lives, watching the herring-gulls rehearse
> with each dusk their cycle of departure,
> to watch the visionary glare
> tarnish to tin. (100)

In this powerful image, which is also reminiscent of Wallace Stevens's "The Idea of Order at Key West," we hear the Wordsworth of the "Intimations Ode": "Whither is fled the visionary gleam?" As Wordsworth's gleam fades with adulthood, so Walcott's tarnishes into a diminished, but still powerful vision.

The connection between Gregorias (Dunstan St. Omer) and Coleridge forms another important link between *Another Life* and *The Prelude*. Though Walcott's poem is not dedicated to St. Omer, Gregorias appears as the focus of part two of the poem, "Homage to Gregorias," and remains a powerful influence on the developing consciousness of the narrator. In Walcott's case, the primary source of intellectual influence seems to be a composite figure of St. Omer and Harry Simmons, the art teacher. In Walcott's description of St. Omer/Gregorias, however, we hear direct echoes of the Wordsworth-Coleridge collaboration. Gregorias is the figure of the inspired artist whose soul is intensified by his own emotional and aesthetic vision. As a painter, Gregorias has "abandoned apprenticeship / To the errors of his own soul"(56). As Walcott's closest friend, Gregorias comes to embody the unrestrained imaginative and intellectual energy that Wordsworth so often ascribed to Coleridge.

The young Walcott, like Wordsworth, claims to be galvanized by a more purely verbal imagination. As a result, he finds himself caught — unlike Gregorias — in the realm of the metaphoric, seeking always the "paradoxical flash of an instant" which might nevertheless reveal a "crystal of ambiguities" (56). Walcott envies Gregorias the "explosion of impulse" that characterizes his work, but realizes that the same explosion is partly responsible for grotesqueness and "aboriginal force" (57), the destructive qualities that form part of Gregorias' artistic spirit. The potential danger of the unrestrained imagination has a clear parallel in Wordsworth's view of Coleridge. This dangerous force manifests itself in Coleridge's imaginative and narcotic excesses, as it does in the drunken rantings which lead Gregorias' canvas to be "crucified against a tree" (50).

We might also argue that the Anna of Walcott's poem, based on Andreuille Alcée, has an analogue in the one unspoken influence in Wordsworth's *Prelude*. Wordsworth's own first love affair, with Annette Vallon, produced an illegitimate child and a sense of guilt that led the poet to expunge all direct accounts of her memory from his autobiography. But the details of this relationship find their way into "Vaudracour and Julia," a fictionalized account of two lovers that appeared in Book IX of *The Prelude* until 1832, when it was removed and published as a separate poem. In Walcott's case, the influence of Anna/Andreuille clearly equals that of the best friend and the art teacher. Anna is depicted in the strongest possible terms: "The disc of the world turned / slowly, she was its centre" (83), "There have been / other silences, none as deep. There has since/ been possession, none as sure" (97). Of Vaudracour's love for Julia, Wordsworth says, "he beheld / A vision, and he loved the thing he saw . . . all paradise / Could by the simple opening of a door / Let itself in upon him" (IX, 582-83, 591-93).

Walcott's aesthetic identity, like Wordsworth's, takes shape not only through a sensitivity to these powerful human influences, but also through Walcott's version of "spots of time," epiphanic moments of psychic intensity that fuse thought, feeling, and language into an apparent unity. Such a process is particularly important to any poet worried about unifying the scattered elements of culture into a unified version of the self. If the disparate phenomena of perception can be fused by the mind into a unity, then perhaps the fragmentary contents of memory can be united with a powerful sense of the present to produce an integrated aesthetic consciousness. Georges Gusdorf, one of the foremost theoreticians of autobiography, sheds light on this process when he claims that all self-life writing "is a second reading of experience, and it is truer than the first because it adds to experience itself consciousness of it. In the immediate moment, the agitation of things ordinarily surrounds me too much for me to be able to see it in its entirety" (Olney 38).[7] As autobiographers, Walcott and Wordsworth read themselves into history by making a history for themselves. This process results from fusing a sense of cultural and communal identity with an equally powerful sense of one's uniqueness as revealed in certain powerful, personal moments.

Writing an autobiography in poetry rather than in prose suggests a lyrical and atemporal approach to experience, an emphasis on significant moments rather than on a more linear narrative chronology of the self. In both *Another Life* and *The Prelude* we find the poet living in a culture that contributes to this lyrical tendency. In Walcott's case, the fragmentation of Caribbean culture — the diversity of its racial, ethnic, and social histories — like the diversity of individual West Indian lives, leads to an emphasis on distinctly personal moments. Discrete individuals must then search to find a place for themselves in a larger cultural unity. This phenomenon is evident, for example, in Walcott's alphabetic list of the diverse residents of Castries: Ajax, Berthilia, Choiseul, Darnley . . . Weekes, Xodus, Zandoli. In Wordsworth's case, the revolutionary movements of the late eighteenth and early nineteenth centuries, augmented by fragmentations of religious, scientific, and cultural unity, produce a similar emphasis on the solitary

[7]Gusdorf adds that when I see myself as a legitimate subject for autobiography, "the recapitulation of ages of existence, of landscapes and encounters, obliges me to situate what I am in the perspective of what I have been" (Olney 38).

individual seeking integration into a larger world that seems increasingly destabilized.

As Gusdorf notes, autobiography emerges only when "at the cost of a cultural revolution humanity must have emerged from the mythic framework of traditional teachings and must have entered into the perilous domain of history" (Olney 30). Both Walcott and Wordsworth inhabit a world that has left a traditional past to embark on a much less certain future. The Caribbean author seeks stability in the face of a chaotic society that often seems to lack a history. The English Romantic longs for a stable new order in the wake of the convulsions of culture that resulted from the Enlightenment. For the twentieth-century Caribbean writer, no less than for his English Romantic counterpart, epiphanic moments become one way of steadying personal identity on the unstable sea of cultural history.

Perhaps the most Wordsworthian epiphany in *Another Life* occurs at the climax of section one, when the "divided child" experiences a spot of time that leads to the sense of a self at once engendered and made meaningful through art. I quote this entire passage because it reflects so well on the interaction between culture, identity, and authorship in Walcott's poem:

> About the August of my fourteenth year
> I lost myself somewhere above a valley
> owned by a spinster-farmer, my dead father's friend.
> At the hill's edge there was a scarp
> with bushes and boulders stuck in its side.
> Afternoon light ripened the valley,
> rifling smoke climbed from small labourers' houses,
> and I dissolved into a trance.
>
> I was seized by a pity more profound
> than my young body could bear, I climbed
> with the labouring smoke,
> I drowned in labouring breakers of bright cloud,
> then uncontrollably I began to weep,
> inwardly, without tears, with a serene extinction
> of all sense; I felt compelled to kneel,
> I wept for nothing and for everything,
> I wept for the earth of the hill under my knees,
> for the grass, the pebbles, for the cooking smoke
> above the labourers' houses like a cry,
> for unheard avalanches of white cloud,
> but "darker grows the valley, more and more forgetting."
> (41-42)

This passage derives in important ways from a whole series of Romantic texts and assumptions. More importantly, it reflects Walcott's unique ability to force traditional Romantic images to yield up a new and enhanced power. Walcott's description of his younger self reminds us of Wordsworth waiting on the "highest summit" of a "crag" for the horses that would take him home to learn of his father's death, and also of the "blasted tree," and "stone wall" (XI, 349, 355, 377-78), the images of which remain connected in his memory for a lifetime. Walcott's "serene extinction / of all sense" recalls Wordsworth's crossing of the Alps in *The Prelude*, where Wordsworth describes a glory in himself evident only "when the light of sense / Goes out in flashes that have shewn to us / The invisible world (VI, 534-36).

Walcott's epiphanic trance likewise reminds us of Shelley's dedicatory epiphany in *Laon and Cythna* (later *The Revolt of Islam*). Shelley records an "hour" in his youth that burst his "spirit's sleep": "a fresh May-dawn it was, / When I walked forth upon the glittering grass, / And wept, I knew not why" (22-24). Shelley's weeping originates in his sudden recognition that he lives in "a world of woes," a land where the "strong still tyrannise" and the selfish rule amid "harsh and grating strife." He now longs to dedicate himself to a life of artistic creation that will reveal these injustices.

Walcott ends his own dedicatory epiphany with a quote from George Meredith's "Love in the Valley," and with a powerful image of his commitment to an artistic purpose wider than solipsistic self-recognition. The forgetfulness that comes with darkness is possible, according to Meredith's poem, only "if forgetting could be willed" (38).[8] But we cannot forget the sources of our strength or the memories that tie us to our past. Walcott concludes this passage with an image that would have been unavailable to the culture that produced Wordsworth, Shelley, or Meredith:

> For their lights still shine through the hovels like litmus,
> the smoking lamp still slowly says its prayer,
> the poor still move behind their tinted scrim,
> the taste of water is still shared everywhere,
> but in that ship of night, locked in together,

[8]Meredith's "Love in the Valley," is a sustained meditation on lost love and the problematic possibilities of recovery. The line Walcott quotes introduces the conclusion to an early stanza in the poem: "Darker grows the valley, more and more forgetting: / So it were with me if forgetting could be willed. / Tell the grassy hollow that holds the bubbling well-spring, / Tell it to forget the source that keeps it filled."

through which, like chains, a little light might leak,
something still fastens us forever to the poor. (42)

Recalling the Middle Passage of his black ancestors, whose only access to the New World came via slave ships, Walcott drops all first person pronouns and evokes a powerful sense of a shared community. His uncontrollable weeping on the hillside has reminded him that for all his attempts to seek a European identity, he is part of a world of suffering unknown to the artistic masters he would serve. Walcott achieves one of the fullest realizations of his own poetic voice by embracing the conflicting sides of his cultural identity. His black grandfathers and white grandfathers merge in this powerful epiphanic recognition, an image that links the language of Wordsworth and Shelley with the memory of slaves chained in the hold of a Middle Passage vessel.

At one other point in *Another Life* Walcott achieves comparable poetic energy by reflecting on his ancestral past. He imagines himself as a child, putting a seashell to his ear and hearing a sound that betokens another world. The child:

who puts the shell's howl to his ear,
hears nothing, hears everything
that the historian cannot hear, the howls
of all the races that crossed the water,
the howls of grandfathers drowned
in that intricately swivelled Babel,
hears the fellaheen, the Madrasi, the Mandingo, the Ashanti.
(136)

Walcott goes on to recall the countless Chinese and Indians who were also brought to Caribbean shores against their wills. For all of these subjected cultures and races "the crossing of the water has erased their memories." Of course it is now Walcott the poet who hears imaginative sounds in a shell. Transformed into poetry, such sounds are able to return the memory of these enslaved souls to the West Indians who descend from them. In the process, Walcott also recalls Wordsworthian sounds: "rocks that muttered close upon our ears — / Black drizzling crags that spake by the wayside / As if a voice were in them" (VI, 562-64). The ancestral echoes Walcott hears and records are, perhaps not surprisingly, a remade version of Wordsworth's "workings of one mind, the features / Of the same face." Walcott finds a way of speaking for himself by speaking for countless others, producing, as a result, a newly minted Caribbean account of "[t]he types and symbols of eternity" (VI, 568-69, 571).

Just as Wordsworth ends *The Prelude* by turning once again to his best friend

Coleridge, so Walcott ends by returning to Gregorias, his own best friend from childhood, the painter whose "explosion of impulse" helped Walcott to form his personal artistic credo. Like Coleridge, Gregorias sometimes dances "with that destructive frenzy / that made our years one fire" (144). But in these earlier days the two aspiring artists, even when "lit" (drunk) felt themselves to be "the light of the world!" (145). Their aesthetic collaboration fired sparks in both developing minds. This is Walcott's repetition of the modern conceit that reclaims an ancient connection between poets and divinity. It is likewise a final echo of Wordsworth's affirmation of the primacy of self-awareness: "to my soul I say / 'I recognise thy glory' " (VI, 531-32), and later, "All that took place within me came and went / As in a moment, and I only now / Remember that it was a thing divine" (VIII, 708-10).

The self creates itself by recreating its past. In Walcott's Caribbean world this process is particularly important, since the colonial individual so often seems to lack a viable sense of history. Identity emerges from the interplay between memory, culture, and a cultural memory that can perhaps only be imagined in the poet's most supremely creative moments. But this process is no less at work in a poet from a colonizing culture like Wordsworth. Wordsworth also feels cut off from a stable, idealized past. He too feels alienated from his fellow human beings and from an increasingly unstable world. Otherwise why would both Walcott and Wordsworth work so hard to establish a literary version of a secure identity, to establish verbal contact with others by way of autobiography?

Avrom Fleishman, in *Figures of Autobiography*, answers a question that applies equally well to Walcott and Wordsworth:

> Where does the language of self writing come from? From the community's narrative discourse, to be sure, especially from those authoritative texts which embody the prevailing schema of a life — whether simply human, heroic, or divine . . . Life stories, like lives, are modeled after idols of the tribe and constitute a subgroup sometimes difficult to distinguish from its other narratives of history and fiction. (479)[9]

---

[9]See also John Pilling, who connects the Wordsworthian autobiographical impulse with an important strain in modern literature. According to Pilling, the author and the reader of works that chart the "growth of the poet's mind," "coexist in a peculiar allegiance; for both of them the object (and the objectification) transcends the subject. This is, it seems to me, one of the special satisfactions to be derived from this particular branch of 'post-Romantic' literature, and one of the most interesting evidences of the twentieth century's continuing struggle with the legacy of Romanticism. Just as many of the great figures of twentieth-century literature in traditional forms

Poetic autobiographers consistently cross the boundary between the imagined story of their own lives and the recreated history of their tribes. What emerges from a parallel reading of *Another Life* and *The Prelude* is not merely a matter of direct poetic influence, nor a simple tracing of common structures and imagery, but a remarkable sense of the similarities between identity formation in two vastly different worlds. The worlds that characterize this difference — the English Lake District of the late eighteenth century and the island of St. Lucia in the early twentieth century — yield up, via these texts, two strikingly similar poetic developments. The adult autobiographer has been produced and controlled — we might more accurately say "colonized" — by a whole series of cultural forces: material, social, economic, emotional. These forces, embodied in childhood and reimagined by the adult, determine the individual's sense of identity, but also produce a concurrent uncertainty about that identity. Autobiography seeks to situate the self in a specific cultural context. At the same time, the self resists that situation, seeking a reinvigorated version of culture. In Walcott's Caribbean, no less than in Wordsworth's Lake District, the reformation of culture is tied to the formation of identity.

WORKS CITED

Baugh, Edward. *Derek Walcott: Memory as Vision: 'Another Life'*. London: Longman, 1978.

——. "The Poem as Autobiographical Novel: Derek Walcott's '*Another Life*' in Relation to Wordsworth's 'Prelude' and Joyce's 'Portrait.' " In *Awakened Conscience: Studies in Commonwealth Literature*. Ed. C. D. Narasimhaiah. New Delhi: Sterling Publishers, 1978. 226-35.

Brown, Lloyd W. *West Indian Poetry*. Boston: Twayne, 1978.

Fleishman, Avrom. *Figures of Autobiography: The Language of Self-Writing in Victorian and Modern England*. Berkeley: U of California P, 1983.

Hamner, Robert D. "Introduction." *Another Life*. Washington, D. C.: Three

---

(Joyce, Eliot, Wyndham Lewis, Ezra Pound, Paul Valery, Rilke) have sought to go beyond the self and proposed a modern version of 'classicism,' so — and precisely where one might least expect it — these modern 'Preludes' are oriented outwards, in what Henry James very aptly calls an 'act of life' " (119). Roger Rosenblatt connects a related phenomenon with an aspect of minority autobiography. "All autobiography is minority autobiography," he writes, insofar as every autobiographer feels unique and, to some extent, uniquely isolated. As a result, "the autobiographer wishes the reader to be alone and counts on it because whatever may separate them from each other, their states of loneliness are mutually recognizable. For the black autobiographer this is a central connection; he is after all not a minority in relation to his lonely reader. They are equal in the exchange" (Olney 169, 180).

Continents Press, 1982: xi-xxvii.

Jacobs, Carl. "There's No Bitterness in Our Literature." *Sunday Guardian* (Trinidad), 22 May 1966: 9.

Lane, M. Travis. "A Different Growth of a Poet's Mind: Derek Walcott's *Another Life*." *Ariel* 9 (1978): 65-78.

Lieberman, Laurence. "New Poetry: The Muse of History." *Yale Review* 63 (1973): 113-136.

Meredith, George. *The Pre-Raphaelites and Their Circle*. Ed. Cecil Lang. Chicago: U of Chicago P, 1975.

Olney, James. *Autobiography: Essays Theoretical and Critical*. Princeton: Princeton UP, 1980.

Pilling, John. *Autobiography and Imagination: Studies in Self-Scrutiny*. London: Routledge & Kegan Paul, 1981.

Ramchand, Kenneth. "Bibliography for 1973: The West Indies." *The Journal of Commonwealth Literature* 9:2 (1974): 129-33.

Ramsaran, J. A. "Derek Walcott: New World Mediterranean Poet " *World Literature Written in English* 21:1 (1982): 133-147.

Shelley, P. B. *Shelley's Poetry and Prose*. Ed. Donald Reiman and Sharon Powers. New York: Norton, 1977.

Thomas, Clara. "Commonwealth Albums: Family Resemblance in Derek Walcott's *Another Life* and Margaret Laurence's *The Diviners*." *World Literature Written in English* 21:2 (1982): 262-68.

Walcott, Derek. *Another Life*. 2nd ed. Washington, D. C.: Three Continents Press, 1982.

——. *Collected Poems:* 1948-1984. New York: Farrar, Straus & Giroux, 1986.

Wordsworth, William. *The Prelude: 1799, 1805, 1850*. Ed. Jonathan Wordsworth, M. H. Abrams, and Stephen Gill. New York: Norton, 1979.

RENU JUNEJA

Culture and Identity in Lovelace's *The Wine of Astonishment*

In his preface to Frantz Fanon's *The Wretched of the Earth,* Jean Paul Sartre describes the last days of colonialism in French Africa:

> In certain districts they make use of that last resort — possession by spirits. Formerly this was a religious experience in all its simplicity, a certain communion of the faithful with sacred things; now they make of it a weapon against humiliation and despair; Mumbo-Jumbo and all the idols of the tribe come down among them, rule over their violence and waste it in trances until it is exhausted. (19)

Sartre's observations, both accurate to a degree yet incomplete, recognize the underlying connections between religious practice and political aspirations. Feelings that could have inspired political violence are now being sublimated in the ceremonies of possession. Even while Sartre laments the loss of purity of the religious experience, he acknowledges that religion becomes a means of bolstering dignity and pride, "a weapon against humiliation and despair," among people ground down by colonial powers. In dismissing it as mumbo jumbo and waste, however, Sartre fails to see the effectiveness of such modified religious practices as legitimate tools both of resistance and of collective reconstruction of identity now dislodged by colonialism.

Recent scholarship on religious cults of Africa and the new world now indicates that such religious movements are acts of resistance whose meaning is unambiguous even if seldom consciously perceived.[1] This is true of those syncretist movements where Christianity blends with or is transformed by existing religious practices and beliefs. If structures of dominance within a given society are supported by a hidden ideology which permeates, however unconsciously, all levels of culture, then resistance to such authority can also manifest itself through subversion of publicly sanctioned codes and conventions.[2] An ideological or political

[1]See, for instance, the work of B.G.M. Sundkler, *Bantu Prophets in South Africa*; Wim van Binsberger, "Religious Innovation and Political Conflict in Zambia"; and Jean Comaroff, *Body of Power, Spirit of Resistance.*

[2]See, for instance, Roland Barthes, *Mythologies* and Louis Althusser, *For Marx.*

struggle can thus render itself as a struggle for appropriation of rituals and symbols of religious discourse. More specifically, in syncretist religious movements of Africa or the new world, Christian symbols are appropriated and made to carry a different meaning. Thus, Sundkler, in his work on South African Christianity, records the seeming ease of internalization of forms of the Western church but also a simultaneous inner resistance to cultural domination through transformation of these forms (19). Indeed, as Dick Hebdige has pointed out, a "struggle between different discourses, different definitions and meanings within ideology is therefore always, at the same time, a struggle within signification, a struggle for possession of the sign which extends to even the most mundane areas of everyday life" (17).

In systematically presenting the Spiritual Baptists as a counterculture within colonial Trinidad, Earl Lovelace's novel *The Wine of Astonishment*, makes explicit this underlying connection between religion and ideology. Lovelace's remarkable achievement lies in his sure decoding of ordinary forms of cultural expression among these descendents of ex-slaves as coherent, if oblique, acts of resistance against the dominant colonial culture. But the novel does much more. It also reveals these avenues of resistance as part of a vital process whereby a subjugated people construct and express an identity distinct from that of the colonial masters. That is, the language of ritual, of dance and music, of ordinary forms of self-expression among the villagers of Bonasse serves not merely to repudiate the hegemony of the existing order, it also serves as a vehicle for self-representation and self-realization. To use, now, the language of the novel, it allows the villagers to *become* a people, to remain a people. Denied the right to practice ceremonies natural to their worship, the people, fears Eva, the novel's narrator, will lose their identity: "What was we becoming?" she wonders (48). This ability to express themselves in cultural forms natural to them, she rightly understands, is also the power to shape a collective identity, to *become* a people. It transforms them from mere victims of cultural oppression, mere ciphers or Naipaul's mimic men, into purposive agents of their own destiny.

Lovelace's fictional account of the struggles of the Spiritual Baptists of Bonasse closely follows the circumstances of the Spiritual Baptists, or Shouters, as they are called in Trinidad, during the period of ban against their religious practices. In 1917, with the passing of the *Shouters Prohibition Ordinance*, the colonial government made it illegal for the Shouters to worship in a manner natural to them, a law which remained in effect for over thirty years. The Shouters were a revivalist Christian sect whose natural manner of worship included handclapping, dancing, stamping, loud singing of hymns all leading to possession by the spirit and speaking in tongues. The Shouters were banned because they were viewed by the establishment as an "unmitigated nuisance," because their method of worship violated colonial notions of respectability and civilized behavior appropriate for "a well-conducted community" (Herskovits 343).

The well-conducted community worshipped in established churches which in Trinidad were predominantly Anglican and Roman Catholic. Unlike missionary Christianity, sects like the Spiritual Baptists were products of a cultural transaction between the African inheritance of the slaves and the new religion acquired in the new world. Bastide points to many African survivals in the religious practice of the Shouters (165). The ecclesiastical organization of the Baptists, for instance, incorporates both African and Christian concepts. Within the community of Baptists there are leaders, preachers, and masters fulfilling functions not very different from those of Christian priesthood. But there are also leaders with the gift of healing and of foretelling the future. Entry to the sect is through initiation involving the Christian ritual of baptism but the initiation, as in Africa, takes place in the bush. The initiate receives a gift or power in a manner reminiscent of African religions.

Perhaps the most significant departure from establishment Christianity is the ritual around the center post of the church, around which members dance until they achieve possession or the entry of the spirit within them. Charles Kingsley describes a religious ceremony he witnessed in Trinidad at the end of the nineteenth century where he saw blacks dancing around what he calls a fetish:

> Martin now began to chant a monotonous African song accompanying with the tom-tom. Gradually he began to quicken the measure; quicker went the words; quicker beat the drum; and suddenly one of the women sprang into the open space in front of the Fetish . . . . And now the whole of the woman's body seemed electrified with it; and, as if catching the infection, a man now joined her in the mad dance. Couple after couple entered the arena, and a true sorcerers' sabbath began. (243)

Kingsley had seen, in a dimly lit hut, a center post having the appearance of a man but the head of a cock. Variations of the center post, with or without decorations, are to be found today in the Haitian Vodun, the Bahian *candomblés*, and the

Trinidadian Shango indicating commonalty of tradition. The specific links between the Yoruba based Shango and the Spiritual Baptists have been noted by Simpson who also points out the frequency with which Shango leaders become affiliated with the Spiritual Baptists (78).[3]

Like many other new world Christian sects, the Spiritual Baptists practice a Christianity significantly transformed and adapted to suit the needs of people with African ancestry. The transformation indicates that the slaves did not passively absorb the new culture imposed on them. Such transformations are evidence of both creativity and resistance. The symbolic content of such rituals is a coded message to the community, and often in direct opposition to the dominant system. Jean Comaroff, writing of African Christianity, sees the widespread syncretist movements as, frequently, "subversive *bricolages*, that is, they are motivated by an opposition to the dominant system" (198). This political, defiant aspect is equally present in the Caribbean syncretist religions. As Bastide points out, during colonialism myalism was a secret anti-white society (102). With the present day Rastafarians, this hostility to established powers, those middle-class inheritors of colonial power and Western values, is an explicit dimension. Caught in Babylon, they crave for deliverance through a black Christianity clearly at odds with the established religion, their opposition expressed through symbols like dreadlocks and the use of the weed. Unlike the Rastas, the Baptists have no explicit political credo, but their political aspirations are equally closely intertwined with religion. In their account of Toco village in Trinidad, Herskovits and Herskovits report, for instance, that one of their informants identifies the whole range of his economic and social disabilities with restrictions on worship imposed on the Shouters. And when discussing the case of Shouters, this informant moves on "to tell of the objectives of the Garvey movement or of the struggle of Haile Selassie against European powers" (186).

In *The Wine of Astonishment*, matters of religion clearly nest into politics. As the novel moves back and forth over thirty years, it focuses on the attempts of

---

[3]The similarities include possession, baptism, mourning rites, and the practice of healing. Simpson records the history of Mother Q who visits a Shango priest for healing, having been a cripple for three years and practically blind. She is given a Spiritual Baptist baptism, mourns, and receives "The Yoruba gift." During mourning, she has travelled spiritually to Africa and has seen Yoruba work there. After this experience, she practices healing and regards herself both as a Spiritual Baptist and a Shango leader (78).

Bonasse's Baptists to first defy the ban, and when this fails, to lift it through permissible political action. In a repressive situation, acts of public defiance usually result in failure and greater repression. As the peaceful, typically law abiding Baptists are forced to recognize, their lack of political power makes their defiance, however necessary as an act of self-definition, largely futile: "When you break the law," says Eva, "you don't hurt the law, you don't change the law, you just make the law more the law; you stiffen the heart of the magistrate and set yourself to dodge and peep and every step you make, look over your shoulder for the police" (64).

Through the contrasting histories and personalities of two young men, the novel explores alternative ways of dealing with an oppressive law. Bolo, in whom the African tradition of the warrior is still alive, is first the catalyst of communal defiance and then the sole agent of violent rebellion where rebellion takes the form of becoming a "badjohn." His persistent breaking of the law, finally self-destructive, is both a raging mockery of the forms and values of colonial authority and a desperate attempt to force his community to recognize that continuing submission or accommodation will erode its identity as "a people." Rejecting Bolo's way, the Spiritual Baptists choose a different way of taking law into their own hands. They work to have one of their own, Ivan Morton, elected into the Legislative Council in an effort to have the law affected from within. The failure of this strategy, caused by Ivan Morton's betrayal of his community, represents the dangers of cooption. In travelling the road to power, the aspirants may so fully internalize the norms of those in authority that they no longer see themselves as a part of their original community.

The pressure of these events radicalizes the consciousness of these people. First the younger men acquire a new political awareness. They gather at the local rumshop, whose owner, Buntin, encourages talk "about the war or God or Marcus Garvey" (75). Revolution and religion are linked together. Buntin's shop is decorated by pictures of Marcus Garvey, Joe Louis, Jack Johnson and Haile Selassie, and by a sign, composed by Buntin, which articulates a renewed awareness of racial identity through religious metaphors: "I am black and comely / O ye daughters of Jerusalem, / As the tents of Kedar / As the Curtains of Solomon" (75). Finally, even the older generation, specifically Eva and Bee, come to see the religious issues in larger, political terms. They are frustrated by Ivan Morton's failure to understand "that to free the church is to free us":

> If he can't understand that the church is the root for us to grow out from, the church is Africa in us, black in us, if he can't understand that the church is the thing, the instrument to make us legal and legitimate and to free him, Ivan Morton, himself too, if he can't understand that, Bee say, then he don't have any understanding of himself or of black people . . . Ivan Morton really don't understand why . . . we should first want to see ourselves as black . . . he don't understand that to say Trinidadian or West Indian don't by itself describe our condition. (133)

Eva's distinction between nationality and ethnicity, between being Trinidadian and being black is, of course, a poignant comment on the inadequacies of nationalism as a metaphor for identity among people of the new nations created in the wake of colonialism. Artificially carved states have run roughshod over ethnic identities of people, or, as in the West Indies, plantation economies built on slave and indentured labor have forcibly brought together people of varied ethnic origins. While Eva expresses no overt hostility against the other subgroups — the Indians and the Chinese — she clearly excludes them from her notion of the people. More importantly, Eva sees her church both as a metaphor for political freedom — "make them legal and legitimate" and so free them — and for identity — "the church is Africa in us, black in us."

We may ask now what makes the Spiritual Baptist church so apt an embodiment of these people's opposition to existing hegemonies and of their efforts towards self-realization? The Anglican and Catholic Churches are clearly the white people's churches, and the split between the established churches and others like the Baptists occurs along both class and race lines. The colored bourgeoisie, ambitious for jobs and advancement, "must kneel down in front of white saints" (32). The black peasants and proletariat continue to worship in ways most congenial to them, clearly recognizing that lack of financial or other support from the government for their church makes it fully their own. "Black people own" this church, says Eva, "Government ain't spent one cent helping us to build it or to put bench in it or anything" (32). While the Anglican and Catholic clergy are usually of a different racial stock, the Baptist Church is free of "white priests or latin ceremonies" (32). Herskovits and Herskovits remark on the feeling of participation and ownership common among the Baptists. The Anglicans and Catholics must "obey rules concerning dogma, ritual, and organization that are laid down far from Toco [the village under observation], regulations that communicants can only obey, and in the establishment and alteration of which they have no voice" (182). In contrast, Eva's language about her church is constantly the language of ownership: "We have this church in the village. We have this church. The walls make out of mud . . . But is our own" (32).

But ownership is not simply a matter of organization and financial independence. Most fundamentally, ownership is a matter of using a ritual language expressive of these people's selves and needs, and therefore also at odds with the values of the established order. As Eva says, "we touch black people soul" (32). The primary signifier of difference in ideology is the phenomenon of possession. Villagers of Toco believe that the capacity to catch the spirit, and the tendency, lies among all black people even those who choose to follow the Anglican and Catholic ways of worship: "When the parson talk," says a Tocoan, "sometimes you feel the spirit come to you. It's like an injection. A shiver pass over the body. It happen if you are an Anglican. Happen if you are a Catholic. But if the priest see you shiver, he not glad" (Herskovits 175). In contrast, among the Spiritual Baptists, catching of the spirit signifies the true way of worship, the sweetness and the power of which makes the Catholic or Anglican way appear "lifeless" (64).

For Eva, two feelings mark catching of the spirit — joy and power. Speaking of the church, she says, "it was nice . . . to have a place to be together, where you could hear your own voice shouting hallelujah and feel the Spirit spreading over the Church as the brethren sing and dance and catch the power" (33). After the ban, and after a long period of repression of their natural way of worship, the Baptists of Bonasse break the law and allow themselves to catch the spirit. Eva's lyrical description of this moment invites close analysis because Lovelace packs the description with highly charged ideological content:

> Like a strong wind, like a mighty water, like a river of fire, like a thousand doves with wings. It come, the Spirit. And I was clapping my hands and singing. And it catch Bee up and spin him round and bow him down and It hold him up and walk him down from the pulpit to the Centre Post . . . and he turn and walk down to Old Mother Raymond, Bolo mother, and hold up her hands and salute her in the Spirit, and her Spirit take her up and she begin to talk to him in unknown tongue . . . Sister Lucas . . . walk to them . . . in that sweet, graceful, noble walk that black women alone have from generations of carrying on their heads buckets of water and baskets of cocoa, and she go to the Centre Post . . . all over the church people was get-

ting up with their Spirit on them and we meet there in the centre of the church and we hold hands and salute one another. (61-62)

We may note that Bee, the leader of the congregation, leaves the high pulpit and comes down to the center post signifying the equality of relationships that characterize the Spiritual Baptists. Within the hierarchical Anglican and Catholic churches, the priest, ensconced in authority as much of class and race as ecclesiastical, duplicates the inequalities of the wider society. Among the Baptists, although one man or woman may be designated the leader due to his or her special gift, many members of the congregation, from the moment of their baptism, bring equally vital gifts and powers. Some are provers, others judges or pumpers or healers or divers or philosophers (see Herskovits 196). More importantly, insofar as catching the spirit signifies explicit identification with God, all who catch the spirit are raised together into a new equality in power. Such a phenomenon reverses hierarchical and linear systems of order. Significantly, all participants dance around the center post in circular motion. Eva describes them as holding hands and saluting one another. The circular movement and the holding of hands dissolves all distinctions. And the saluting gesture, reserved within Western hierarchies for those in authority, acknowledges the sharing of power through this infusion by the spirit. Through a moment of possession by a potent God, these dispossessed people have acquired dignity and status. In fact, the very marks of dispossession, slave and plantation labor of carrying water and cocoa, are now transformed into sources of grace and nobility.

The transformation is achieved not only through a renewed sense of power, but also through a transfusing joy. "When the body is fill with joy," reports one villager from Toco, "it move, it shake. If I got up one mornin' and didn't feel like shoutin', then I know the Lord is not with me" (Herskovits 199). The affective aspect of worship remains central to religious movements like the Spiritual Baptists. Bastide believes that this affective dimension to the religions of new world blacks arises in response to oppression because religion now becomes a channel for needs of security and emotional enhancement (204).[4] The Christian missionaries may have preached brotherhood but they usually made their black congregations feel inferior. Elements within these new religions redress the situation by com-

---

[4]Thus, according to Bastide, African religion is practical, and the trance itself is merely ritualistic in purpose, practiced "as a gesture rather than for affective ends" (204).

bating cultural and emotional deprivation. In providing this psychological uplift, these religions also strengthen the inner resistance to oppression. The hymns of Eva's people use the vocabulary of freedom and oppression: "The Lion of Judah shall break every chain" (62). The process of rising up in spirit is also the process of political resistance. Eva marvels at the effect of their stolen moment of catching the spirit: "see . . . how we rise, how *we rise up*, how we dance and sing and how we break the law like the law was nothing" (63, italics mine).

The transforming, affective power of the ritual of possession within black syncretist churches is best appreciated through comparison with white revivalism. For instance, in white churches, the entranced are few but there are many onlookers. The communal, participatory, and equalizing aspect of catching the spirit is thus lacking. The testifying that takes place during possession in white churches is prompted by fears of hell and damnation (see Bastide 163). In concentrating on sinfulness, such religions reinforce the sense of distance between God and humanity. Even when manifested in people, the power remains awful and frightening. In fact, the dominant sentiment propelling the congregation is not joy or hope but fear. As Bastide points out, the body movements of the white revivalists are violent and convulsive. The moment of possession begins to approximate the experience of hysteria (163). In contrast, the shaking and dancing of black revivalists has rhythm and grace signifying the possession of self, not its disintegration.

Lovelace's prose carefully recreates the distinctive dynamic of possession among the Spiritual Baptists. Eva describes Sister Lucas as dancing "around like a bird going to fly" (62). At the end of the ritual, she speaks of "a cleanness and a lightness" that has "come over the church," "and we was fresh and wash like new grass in the morning" (62). This sense of release and transformation linked here with the image of cleansing is a recurring motif embedded in many of the ritual practices of the Baptists. Most notable, of course, is the centrality of baptism to their religion. Whereas, among the established churches baptismal immersion has been truncated to a brief symbolic gesture within a larger ceremony, with the Baptists full immersion in living water remains the focal point of the ritual. The baptismal rite is again communal, with the whole community participating so that the attendants far outnumber the participants (see Herskovits 202-03). It lasts through the night, and involves triple immersion in the sea or a river. By conducting the ceremony under open skies and in living waters, the Baptists reinforce the connection between this ritual and the power to catch the spirit which, as Eva recounts, comes like "strong wind, like a mighty water, like a river of fire" (61).

In fact, before the immersion the eyes of the candidates are bound for several hours and opened only when they are marched to the water (Herskovits 202-3). The ceremony of baptism is usually followed by the rites of the Mourning Ground where a period of sensory deprivation is followed by the participant receiving his or her special gift. As an informant tells Herskovits, "Go there [to the Mourning Ground], and ol' person die, new person born" (204). Those mourning are envisaged as "travelling a path to glory" (Herskovits 206). Somebody will get a vision," says Eva:

> and he come to us and we baptise him in the river and put him out on the Mournin' Ground to pray and fast and wait for the Lord to send him a sign so he will know if his mission is to be a shepherd to the sheep, or a nurse, or if he call to be a prover . . . or if he is to be a warrior. (32)

Clearly, these rites empower the people. They reform the psyche so that the former identity is dissolved and a new, more powerful, more gifted and healed identity is allowed to emerge. As Mircea Eliade has said, "Rituals *act*, they perform, modulate, transform" (Beane 164). We may note, as well, the practice of healing among the Baptists and other syncretist religions. The physical affliction suffered by the body is viewed as an expression of a deeper, existential state. When religion heals the sense of estrangement, of powerlessness, it can also heal the body's ailments. The power which transforms an individual's or a community's psyche can also transform the body physical. In condoning slave labor and economic deprivation, the missionary churches had separated body and spirit. These new churches restore that connection.

Eva's people have linked hands and come together in spirit. The individual psyche, thus renewed through healing rituals, gathers even greater strength in affirming communal ties within the church. Among the Spiritual Baptists, the holding of hands and the circular dance around the center post enact their deeply cherished sense of themselves as a community. Lovelace underscores this integrative function of religion by making his narrator constantly refer to the Bonasee Baptists as "the people," "our people." Within the congregation, members are addressed by kin terms and given affection and help appropriate to an extended family. For Eva, the community extends even beyond church membership to include all those blacks in the village who have shared a common history of oppression. So Ivan Morton's mother may have dropped from the church when Ivan joins the Catholic school, but for Eva she still remains one of them. Eva does, however, draw clear distinctions between "we" and those others who have lost their affiliation by sharing the power and values of the establishment — the red-nigger (light-skinned) magistrate who harangues the Baptists for practicing religion in the barbarous, heathen way of Africa, or Prince, the policeman, who relishes exercising brutal power against his own people, or Mitchell who, in the manner of the Yankee capitalists subjugating with the power of the dollar, begins to exploit his own people. When Eva sees the community disintegrating, she worries that they have become "a lot of people, but [they] ain't a people" (136). Her organic metaphors speak of a failure to keep alive their tradition, of the people as a tree no longer nourished by juices drawn from the roots (136).

As Bastide argues, the black churches, whether in Africa or the new world, are seldom simply religious organizations. They have become the focal points of a community's social life (205). Typically, in situations where people feel themselves excluded or alienated from avenues of justice provided by those in power, they chose to regulate themselves. Herskovits and Herskovits have observed this desire among the Shouters to stay away from established powers. One man comments that they [the Shouters] "Don' like court at all; try to settle between ourselves" (199). Among the Bonasse Baptists of the novel, Bee is not merely the church leader, he also assumes, and is accorded, communal leadership in matters that have no direct bearing on the church. He is the one to whom Brother Primus runs when Bolo abducts his daughters. And had not Primus suffered a failure of nerve and invited the police, the novel clearly implies, Bee may have succeeded in persuading Bolo that violence against his own people, even when motivated by an urgent desire to jolt his people into recognition of need for action and self-assertion, remains a futile, self-destructive gesture. Bee, as Lovelace conceives of his role as a church leader, must deal with problems which are, in the last resort, political.

This distinction between "us" and "them" is encoded not only in ritual practice and communal organization but also in ordinary expressive choice of style, body movements, and even allocations of physical space. Just as within the church building the center post unites and equalizes the congregation, so too the location of the church itself functions to re-center the sacred. The church may be nestled among the houses of the congregation, a house like other houses with no ostentatious markers to separate it from the daily lives of the people — like Eva's church with its "roof covered with carrat leaves: a simple hut with no steeple or cross" (32). Such a church stands at the heart of this alternative community which usually finds itself on the spatial periphery of sections where wealth and power reside, away, that is, in Trinidad from the great estate or the bureaucratic centers of government. Initially, the church of Eva's people occupies a central place in their community, is situated on its main street. Later, the Baptists, under pressure from local authorities, are forced to move to the edge of the village, "far up in a wilderness place" (34). A similar spatial pattern is recorded by Herskovits and Herskovits for Toco Village. The Anglican church occupies the center of the village; the Catholic church stands in gracious preeminence on a hill; and the Shouters' church stands at the edge of the village (167-87). The imagery of space makes visible the disharmonious relationship between the structures of authority and the Spiritual Baptists, and the underlying conflict in values this disharmony implies.[5]

In his novel, Lovelace notes the distinct religious uniform of the Baptists. The church leader wears a white gown, and ties his head with three cloths — white, black, and yellow — "the yellow signifying the light and the glory of ascension and the white the resurrection and the black the earth that keep us for all these years" (143). Eva does not interpret the symbolic meaning of the colors of gowns worn by the rest of the congregation — browns, greens, whites, and blues — and indeed the meaning assigned, according to Herskovits and Herskovits, may differ from congregation to congregation. But even in the brief interpretation Eva offers us, we can see the ennobling of black, and the representation, in a fresh combination, of the two grounds of these people's existence: their validation of their labor and their hopes for transformation via grandeur available through religious faith. Lovelace also notes that the uniforms have merited disapproval from the establishment. Eva has thought that they would have to bury Bee in his white gown "because it didn't look he would get a chance to wear it while he was living" (143). If the authorities had banned the Spiritual Baptists because they found their method of praying too loud and unseemly and the phenomenon of spirit possession too barbarous, they had little reason to restrict the dress of the Shouters. Af-

[5]I owe this perception to Werbner's work on Zionist churches in Africa. In particular, see Richard P. Werbner, "The Argument of Images."

ter all, the Shouters were allowed to pray as long as they followed the decorum of the Anglican or Catholic churches, a manner which Bee, with delicious irony, designates "this heathen way" (85).

Can we surmise that the authorities had sensed a form of resistance in the dress code? Lovelace does not make such a connection explicit perhaps because such an understanding is not available to his narrator, Eva. Comaroff, when analyzing similar religious uniforms of the South African Zionists, has remarked that these robes "reverse, in color and line, the functional severity of Western garb; they seem thereby to protest the values and pragmatic implications of proletarianization (221). The flowing robes blur gender distinction and soften contour. They seem another manifestation of the circular, curving lines of ritual. In recalling the pomp of Anglican or Catholic ceremonies (Bee carries a shepherd's staff), the uniforms also function as signs of grandeur, and like the ceremony of baptism, elevate and reconstitute the wearer. The Baptists have appropriated some of the symbols of colonial power, a fact that could not but offend the authorities, and reconstituted them into signs of transcendence. Eva's description of the community dressed in regalia, walking to church, is suffused with pride: "And is [something] to see us walking up the street" (143).

In Lovelace's novel, those who are spirited, have the capacity to catch the spirit, are also marked by the manner in which they possess their bodies. That is, the body, the tabernacle for the spirit, becomes an instrument for self-expression, a vehicle, however unconscious, of expressing affiliation. To the white colonists, the free, uninhibited body movements of the slaves may well have seemed a visible and offensive sign of their raw, unformed, undisciplined nature. Writing in the middle of the last century, Edward Underhill deems the swaying movement of people in church an expression of their too easy excitability and of their inability to exercise rational self-control. He is speaking to a church group when, toward the end of his speech, "some symptoms of excitement betrayed the emotional character of the people, and I rather hastily concluded [his address]. One woman swayed her body from side to side, and was scarcely held on her seat by her neighbors" (48). The "wild" dances of the blacks, whether performed in social or religious contexts, violated white notions of decorum and seemly behavior appropriate to a "well-conducted community." The dancing, in fact, was usually viewed as sexually provocative and as a prelude to debauchery.[6] On the other hand, for the blacks, attempts to regulate their bodily movements by the ruling class — whether through restrictions on movement from one place to another during slavery or restrictions on how the body moves — are palpable signs of oppression. For both blacks and whites in the Caribbean, certain styles of holding or moving the body among blacks are clearly linked to their African ancestry. Those blacks who adopt white cultural norms also modify their style of movement.

Given these assumptions about style and movement, we may conclude, as does Lovelace, that rhythmic opulence and swagger of a black body are a sign of resistance to imposed cultural norms. Within the novel, this swagger is evoked most consciously in descriptions of stickfighters, in whom, according to Eva, the spirit of the African Warrior still survives.[7] The spirit flows most visibly in Bolo, the stickfighting champion of the village, and to an extent the counterculture hero: "for him stickfighting was more the dance, the adventure, the ceremony to show off the beauty of the warrior" (21). His speed and rhythm, Eva concludes, is an offering to the people to remind them of the vitality within themselves and their traditions. "As if," says Eva, "what he really want was for people to see in him a beauty that wasn't his alone, was theirs, ours, to let us know that we in this wilderness country was people, too, with drums and song and warriors" (22). "His spirit [rears] up inside" Bolo, making his walk a "quick-stepping prancing" (44). The adjective that Eva repeatedly uses about Bolo's movements, and about others who move with spirit, is smoothness, as if there are no rough edges here, only curves. His stride is "free easy," his walk "smooth fluent joyful" (27). The same fluidity and smoothness characterize Eulalie before she loses her spirited freedom after becoming pregnant by, and then being rejected by, Ivan. Eva's evocative descriptions of both underscore a surging vitality, what Eva calls "aliveness" (44). Even Eulalie's clothes come alive with her body's motion: "Her skirt hit her hips and the cloth dance up . . . as if it is not cloth at all but a living thing" (44).

---

[6]Commenting on the festivities of the plantation blacks, Bryan Edwards concludes that "their songs are fraught with obscene ribaldry and accompanied with dances in the highest degree licentious and wanton" (87). See also William Jones, *The Diary of Rev. William Jones*, 1777-1821 and Gardner, *A History of Jamaica*, 99-100.

[7]Stickfighting derives from a stick dance called Kalinda, probably of African origins. The stickdance involved a mock combat, and stickfighting as it evolved became both a dance and a combat. See Errol Hill, *The Trinidad Carnival*, 23.

When Ivan Morton rejects Eulalie in favor of the "light-skin" lady, the full implications of this contrast, and of his choice, are evoked through descriptions of movement. Both Ivan and his wife have a stiffness in bearing, a labored quality to their walk suggesting their acceptance of white cultural norms. On the way to his church, Ivan walks slowly to keep from perspiring while his wife walks with "her white veil falling over the stiff black curls on her pressed hair, her two careful knees barely bothering the cloth of her dress" (50). The white veil is both physical and metaphoric; the blackness within her has stiffened in her effort to become white. Just as the Anglican and the Catholic ways of worship are "lifeless" (64) ways for these people, because empty of spirit, so too the movements of Ivan and his wife are lifeless because the body is empty of spirit. Bolo's transformation from the warrior hero to the "badjohn" is also signified through a stiffening of movements, through the body losing its circular smoothness. While Bolo's new stiffness is not born of imitation of white ways, it nevertheless speaks of distortion of spirit. Initially, the stiffness is only a stiffening of resolve to oppose authority, and thus a manifestation of spirit. Bolo stiffens, for instance, as he stands "in the middle of the road, tall, stiff," ready to challenge Prince (67). Gradually, however, the tall, unbending stiffness of Bolo (49) reveals a hardening within that isolates him from his community.

In designating stickfighting a ceremony, Eva has linked it to other ceremonies within the community where the spirit manifests itself. Lovelace makes explicit connections between different manifestations of spirit by using this common terminology and by making Eva gradually recognize that what happens within the church is something that finds expression in other cultural forms of the community. And in each instance, these ways of self-expression among these people are signs of their difference, their distinct identity as a people rooted in their distinct history.

This spirit flows through Clem, the singer of stickfighting and bongo songs and later the calypsonian. It's there when Clem tells stories to children. There is a hint that these are stories of jumbies or ghosts, spirits of the dead still interacting with the living, stories that frighten children, but serve as reminders of their different heritage. The spirit is with Clem when he sits within "the circle of men ringing bamboo joints on the ground and dancing the bongo," the spirit and the men "dipping and leaping up like the flames of a flambeau lighting up the ring" (28). Clem's singing is also identified with those elements which constitute group identity. When Clem was "in Bonasse singing, with all the changes, we had a feeling that the village was still our own. Now he wasn't there we feel more and more that it don't belong to us" (29).

These connections between religious practice and other cultural forms are developed most emphatically at the end of the novel. The ban against the Spiritual Baptists has been lifted; the congregation has gathered for worship at a newly visible and redecorated church. Brother Alfred has trimmed the mango trees around the church "to unhide it from the world, to show it without shame at last to the village" (143). The church has a fresh coat of paint and flowers around it, and within burn incense and candles "lighting in every corner, and at the Centre Post there is the bell and the bowl of flowers . . . and the holy water, and on the benches is the sisters and brothers in their colours" (143). Bee preaches a fine sermon and rings the bell and sprinkles the water, but nothing happens. The spirit does not come. There is another attempt to "unlock" the spirits by repeating the ritual, but "the Spirit wouldn't come" (144).

Eva and Bee walk home silent and saddened, when Eva hears the music of the steelband: "I listening to the music; for the music that those boys playing on the steelband have in it the same Spirit that we miss in our church: the same Spirit" (146). Eva discovers the same sanctity and the same capacity to lift the soul in this music as in the ritual within the church. Her heart swells as if "it is like resurrection morning" and both Bee and Eva bow their heads "like if we passing in front of something holy" (146). Lovelace's insistent identification of Baptist worship and steelband music highlights his understanding that religion is a cultural expression and fulfills the same needs, serves the same function, as other cultural forms. The evolutionary history of the steelband deserves brief capitulation because it reveals, like the syncretized Christianity of the Baptists, the struggle of a people to shape their culture, and their success in shaping a distinct culture during colonial oppression.

The steelband, for those unfamiliar with the music, is an orchestra consisting of instruments forged from old oil drums (pans), tempered and tuned by hammering sections to carry a true tone when hit. This mode of playing music evolved in response to the banning of African drums during carnival. Much as they had responded to the Spiritual Baptists, the authorities found the playing of African drums barbarous, heathen, and also politically subversive.[8] In the following comment by the editor of *Fair Play and Trinidad News*, written in 1883, we may note that the terms of disapproval are similar to those used by the Attorney General in banning the Shouters:

> To the ear of the European philharmonist there is no music in it but a dull and monotonous reiteration of sound rendered the more objectionable by the distance to which it is carried by the muscular vigor of the performers and the immense reverberating capacity of the instrument. The state of civilization of people whose members can be set in movement by the repetition of such barbarous sound can easily be gauged.

Not only did the steelband embody the resilience and startling creativity of an economically deprived people, it also retained those elements of resistance that had been associated with other cultural survivals from the African past like stick-fighting and Anansi stories. Initially, the steelbands were actually bands of angry young men gathering around the yards of slums like Laventille hills and East Dry River surrounding the affluent Port of Spain. Their music was their means of sublimating their anger and frustration, of honing their despair into an instrument of resistance rather than succumbing to it. They adopted names like Renegades, Desperadoes, Invaders, and elicited fierce loyalty from the members of their community.[9] Just as they have elicited, and continue to elicit, distaste from those travelling what Naipaul has called "the weary road to whiteness" (88). Naipaul, a traveller familiar with the road and an accurate observer of his own colonization, registers this distaste in *The Middle Passage*, his account of his first visit back to Trinidad after years of escape to England: "The steel band used to be regarded as a high manifestation of West Indian Culture, and it was a sound I detested" (43).

The colonial government had, of course, been equally hostile towards these manifestations of West Indian culture. It had banned the carnival for many years, thus effectively banning stickfighting and steelband music. And it had banned the Spiritual Baptists. Its rhetoric of justification acknowledged the dissonance between ruling class norms and the values embodied in these cultural forms. The act

---

[8]The "Musical Ordinance" of 1883, banning the playing of drums, was a response to the Canboulay Riots of 1881, supposedly more explosive because of fanning of passions by the music of the African drums.

[9]For more information on the evolution of the steelband see my article on "The Trinidad Carnival."

of banning, a political ploy, acknowledged the subversive nature of these cultural expressions. Lovelace's novel, as we have seen, carefully establishes the mutuality of various cultural forms as well as the political dimension of culture. It also leads us a step further into attempting complex assessments of various forms of resistance.

Given the centrality of religion in the novel, the question of effectiveness is framed in terms of a search for a savior, for the best means of saving the people. Ivan Morton is the first character to be explicitly identified as the savior, although this identification is obviously ironic. After being elected to the council, Ivan rides up and down the streets of Bonasse in his big car: "He wave, moving one hand across and just in front his face like a Catholic priest blessing his congregation, giving a thrill to all we . . . who see him as the savior" (5). Yet what makes Ivan capable of saving the people, his education, also alienates him from them. Western education, like Western religion, had been viewed by the ruling class as an instrument of civilizing the people. Within the colonial context, then, education and civilization mean adopting white culture, travelling the weary road to whiteness. After the election, when Bee approaches Ivan for his help to save the Baptists from harassment, Ivan is unsympathetic because he too now views the Baptists from the perspective of the ruling class: "We can't change our colour," he tells Bee, "but we can change our attitude. We can't be white, but we can act white" (13). Education, Bee decides, makes people "forget where they come from" (14).

Ivan's movement away from his origins is represented as an active disowning of his ancestral house, so that once again movement in space connotes ideology. Ivan moves into the big house occupied previously by the owners of the estate. On one level this is salutary. Black people are taking over the possessions and positions of white colonists. Yet as the novel indicates, *this* act of possession is also a dispossession. For Ivan moves out of his father's house without taking a single piece of furniture, "As if Ivan Morton was saying to the world that the house his father leave to him was nothing" (10). Eva, very shrewdly, speaks of the big estate house as being "like a old church with God gone from it that nobody want any more to worship in" (8). At least nobody should want to worship in it, but Ivan does.

But education, although it may lead to false gods, is not to be dismissed quite so easily. As Eva recognizes, the process of change to which these people are subject is inexorable: "What was happening was that the warrior was dying in the village as the chief figure. The scholar, the boy with education, was taking over" (46). The battle the people are fighting is still the old one, the "battle to be somebody" (46). Education is now the new avenue to this goal. Whatever education may be doing to the "heart inside [the children]," there is no other way at the moment. "But what else to do?" asks Eva (79). The trials and tribulations came down harder when "you don't have education" (11).

Interestingly, and with no overt irony, Lovelace identifies the dying warrior, Bolo, also with Christ. This village hero is slowly transformed into the village badjohn, his rage fueled by his growing conviction that his people have become so enslaved that they are now incapable of self-assertion. In the machismo vocabulary of this warrior, his people have lost their manhood. The novel asks us to see Bolo's deliberate idleness and loafing as expressions of alienated labor. The crimes directed against Mitchell in particular function as explicit rebellion against exploitation. Bolo's madness, then, is part of his mission to provoke the village men to face up to the "man-challenge" of the warriorhood they have inherited from Africa (101). The hero has turned against his own people, because, as he tell Bee, "We ain't no people . . . A people does be going somewhere . . . Where you going to that I could, if I want to, go with you?" (120).

As Bee sees it, Bolo finally chooses himself to become "the victim and the sacrifice, make him Christ who they let the soldiers crucify on the cross because they didn't care enough" (129). Yet, the rhetoric of martyrdom which Bee uses to explain Bolo's actions cannot, in the final reckoning, elevate Bolo to the status of a savior for Bolo's strategy has been as ineffective in saving the people as the path chosen by Ivan Morton. Bolo's violence and Ivan's accommodation, Lovelace suggests, are understandable although ineffective responses to the same condition of helplessness. Bolo's anguished cry of explanation, "I want to be a man too" (119), leads Eva to recognize that perhaps Ivan has become what he is also because "his manness was so important to him and because we didn't, don't have no world . . . with power where he could be a man in, where his manness could come out legitimate just from being himself" (135).

The Spiritual Baptist church can provide a legitimate avenue for this selfhood these people seek but the church has become illegitimate. Bee, the leader of the church, could be the savior. Early in the novel he too is identified with Christ as he stands "his arms back on the cross like Jesus crucify in front the door" (3). The novel, in fact, opens with Eva's self-conscious assertion of the ideology of suffering as strength that will save the people. The strong suffer the most, she tells the children when they ask if God is vexed with them. They are suffering because they can bear it, "because out of all the shoulders in the world our shoulders could bear more weight, and out of all the flesh in the world our flesh could hold more pain" (1-2). But in separating religion from politics such a conception of history is problematic. It implies the success of early missionary teaching which had encouraged acceptance of suffering rather than rebellion. It merely reinforces a people's inability to challenge and reverse domination.

How then are we to assess the effectiveness of religious movements like the Spiritual Baptists? Jean Comaroff, in dealing with South African Zionists, asks: "Are such movements merely finely wrought self-delusions, so entrapped within structures of domination that they unwittingly put their imaginative power at the disposal of the regime they protest?" (261). Lovelace's response in *The Wine of Astonishment* is sufficiently complex. Bolo's challenge to the Spiritual Baptists' implies that the church has become merely a liminal refuge, that the quietism of the church is inherently dangerous and will lead to erosion of that very sense of distinct identity which it seeks to nourish. The church is, through Bolo's challenge, led to breaking the law and so entering the political arena. Within the historical framework that Lovelace faithfully follows, this attempt ends in failure. When the church finally becomes free, this freedom has not been won through the actions of the people. Yet the novel seems to suggest some hope. The church has, for a while, united the people; it has given them some competence to act. The actions may have had little practical effectiveness but they have helped in shaping a collective self-consciousness.

Lovelace charts this emerging consciousness through Eva. When the novel ends, Eva's initial quietism, her faith in the strength of mere suffering, has been transformed. It is no longer enough for her "just to be here to bear . . . but we have to rise too" (140). Bolo's restlessness continues to haunt the people of Bonasse, and Eva welcomes this badjohn kind of restlessness from her son Taffy who has left for Port of Spain. She accepts with sympathy and understanding her son Winston's desire to become a policeman and continues to encourage, despite Ivan

Morton's betrayal, her youngest son's path to achievement through education. She cannot, will not, deny the cultural actualities of her world, for to deny them will undermine personal effectiveness in her hybrid, colonial society. Ultimately, the novel suggests, these people must cherish their blackness but must also learn to cope with their changing, Western dominated world.

In this novel, Clem, the calypsonian, provides the model for successful coping. He is able to maintain his integrity even when responding to change. He tells the raging Bolo, "When I take up my guitar, I don't sing for them, I sing for me" (25). Above all, he is capable of taking his African inheritance and transforming it into something new, something more resilient. He takes the old music, the stick-fighting tunes and the bongo songs, and puts new words to it and sings it as calypso. And so the spirit Eva and Bee miss in their church survives in the calypso and in the steelband music. The politics of liberation are subtle and various. Resistance need not be the all or nothing phenomenon it becomes with Bolo. The collective reconstruction achieved through syncretist religions like those of the Baptists and through other cultural forms is also a form of resistance. Certainly, Lovelace implies in *The Wine of Astonishment*, it may even be, given the political reality, the more enduring and viable means of transcending political and cultural oppression.

WORKS CITED

Althusser, Louis. *For Marx*. London: Allen Lane, 1967.

Barthes, Roland. *Mythologies*. New York: Paladin, 1972.

Bastide, Roger. *African Civilizations in the New World*. New York: Harper, 1971.

Beane, Wendell C., and William G. Doty, eds. *Myths, Rites, Symbols: A Mircea Eliade Reader*. New York: Harper, 1976.

Comaroff, Jean. *Body of Power, Spirit of Resistance*. Chicago: U of Chicago P, 1985.

Edwards, Bryan. *The History, Civil and Commercial, of the British Colonies in the West Indies*. vol. 2. London: John Stockdale, 1801-1819. 3 vols.

Fair Play and Trinidad News, March 1, 1883.

Gardner, W. J. *The History of Jamaica*. London: Stock, 1873.

Hebdige, Dick. *Subculture: The Meaning of Style*. London: Methuen, 1979.

Herskovits, Melville J., and Frances S. Herskovits. *Trinidad Village*. New York: Knopf, 1947.

Hill, Errol. *The Trinidad Carnival: Mandate for a National Theatre*. Austin: U of Texas P, 1972.

Jones, William, *The Diary of Rev. William Jones*. Ed. O. F. Christie. London: Brentano's. 1929.

Juneja, Renu. "The Trinidad Carnival: Ritual, Performance." *Journal of Popular Culture*. 21.4 (1981): 87-98.

Kingsley, Charles. *At Last: A Christmas in the West Indies*. New York: Macmillan, 1971.

Lovelace, Earl. *The Wine of Astonishment*. London: Heinemann, 1982.

Naipaul, V. S. *The Middle Passage*. 1960. Harmondsworth, Middlesex: Penguin, 1985.

Sartre, Jean Paul, Introduction. *The Wretched of the Earth*. By Frantz Fanon. 1961. New York: Grove, 1968.

Simpson, George E. *Religious Cults of the Caribbean: Trinidad, Jamaica, and Haiti*. 1965. Puerto Rico: Institute of Caribbean Studies, U of Puerto Rico, 1980.

Sundkler, B. G. M. *Bantu Prophets in South Africa*. Rev. ed. London: Oxford UP, 1961.

Underhill, Edward B. *The West Indies: Their Social and Religious Condition*. London: Jackson, Walford, and Hodder, 1862.

van Binsberger, Wim M. J. "Religious Innovation and Political Conflict in Zambia." *African Perspectives 1976/2. Religious Innovation in Modern African Society*. Eds. Wim M. J. van Binsberger and R. Buitenhuis. Leiden: Afrika-Studierscentrum, 1977. 101-35.

Werbner, Richard P. "The Argument of Images: From Zion to Wilderness in African Churches." *Theoretical Explorations in African Religions*. Eds. W. M. J. van Binsberger and Matthew Schoffeleers. London: Routledge, 1985. 253-85.

CHEZIA THOMPSON-CAGER

Earl Lovelace's Bad Johns, Street Princes, and the Masters of Schools

Resistance, or the act of forcibly confronting individual or institutional acts of terrorism and/or disfranchisement, is an ingrained part of the survival conditioning of peoples of African descent in the New World. Earl Lovelace uses the theme of resistance to deconstruct the essential nature of economic and cultural oppression in post-colonial Trinidad, and the primary vehicles carrying this theme of resistance are the Street Prince, the Bad John, and the Masters of Schools. The acts of resistance in Lovelace's characterizations reveal the real self of the literary *personae* and provide a model for questioning accumulated stereotypes of Africans, African-Americans and West Indians in European and Euro-American literature.

Earl Lovelace writes eloquently of a culture of resistance that has grown out of West Indian communities in Trinidad. The character Aldrick, in *The Dragon Can't Dance,* expresses the attitude of defiance which characterizes the lifestyle of many real people throughout the New World; although it is noticeably missing in traditional literary archetypes. Aldrick is clear about his goal when he says: "Make no peace with slavery. Make no peace for you have survived" (Lovelace 179). Focussing on the impact of the Street Prince, the Bad John and the Masters of Schools, as innovators of this resistance pattern in a Trinidadian culture of poverty raises a number of questions about the motives and methods which West Indian men (with African and Native American ancestry) use to assert their personhood, as members of the urban and rural poor (Rodman 4).

In *Resistance and Caribbean Literature*, Selwyn Cudjoe defines resistance as any act or complex of acts designed to rid a people of its oppressors, be they slave masters or multi-national companies (Cudjoe 19). This paper utilizes a modified version of that definition which recognizes resistance as a series of decisions and acts that produce a counter-movement to mainstream culture and politics in any society. The intent of that movement is to change the society in ways that benefit the masses (as opposed to the bourgeoisie), by providing for greater freedom of expression and more opportunities for the pursuit of happiness. Cudjoe's delineation of resistance utilizes a more anthropologically-based definition that puts *cultural resistance, socioeconomic resistance* and *political resistance* in separate categories because their behavioral manifestations are different. Cultural resistance is generally expressed in the folkways, art and religion of a people. While socioeconomic resistance is expressed in socially subversive acts such as work sabotage, suicide, murder, abortion etc., and political resistance is centered in acts that encourage political change such as revolts, rebellions, and revolutions in either the process of government, a change in administration or both (Cudjoe 19).

Lovelace expands these definitions of resistance to include the politically or socially enslaved — which does not necessarily mean the individual or group members were slaves during the Atlantic Slave Trade era. He creates new examples of culture specific models of resistance in his novels and plays. This essay considers West Indian culture in Trinidad as an example of African culture, as it appears throughout the diaspora. The three literary figures of the Street Prince, The Bad John and The Masters of Schools are presented in a unique manner as the representation of a transplanted legacy, whose synthesis process has shaped the West Indian environment and genetic bloodline. The characters attempt to establish their rights to political and social enfranchisement against the wishes of the dominant culture. As Michael Lieber clarifies it:

> Since the economies, and the accompanying politics, of the Caribbean have, from their inception, been highly capitalistic in organization, class-based stratification has arisen to an elaborate degree . . . In the past those styles associated with a European-focused elite have constituted the mainstream, while those associated with Afro-Caribbean mass of the population have been denigrated and forced to respond to the intrusions of the mainstream. (2-3)

This concept of mainstreaming is equally applicable to societies of color in the United States, as well as to the lives of poor people in both societies. Both groups are victims of their political and hierarchical relationship with the European power establishment that created and perpetuates their position in the total society. Color and caste work to keep them out of the mainstream; media and education attempt to force them to accept mainstream behavior and values. And yet Earl Lovelace's characters in their different ways struggle against disfranchisement. They benignly resist accepting the legacy of the plantation system (which utilized first African slave labor and then East Indian indentured labor) to create new ways to approach the quest of discovering their identities and realizing their strengths.

The strategies that Lovelace's characters employ do not fit within the pattern of appropriate behavior as sanctioned by mainstream society. The strategies of resistance usually require defying or breaking the law in an attempt to resist dehumanization. The three primary types which recur in his work — The Bad John, The Street Prince and The Masters of Schools — can be found as historical and contemporary personalities in the general population. In each case, their interpretation of what the correct law is determines the characters' sense of social responsibility and degree of resistance or non-resistance to the mainstream culture or politics.

The Bad John, as a twentieth-century social prototype, takes his name from the fictional character developed by John Wayne. These cowboy heroes have phenomenal physical strength, are irresistibly attractive to women, have superhuman sexual prowess, are fierce fighters in battle and do not tolerate affronts to their personal integrity. They are also never particularly well-educated and are given to being not particularly conversant as a part of their ideal of male mystic — the classical strong, silent type. They drink and smoke, as a part of the test of physical constitution for this prototype. They think of themselves as the new warrior class in the twentieth century. However, their frustration at being marginalized in mainstream society expresses itself in acts of violence against members of their society and against members of mainstream society, when they can access them. They cannot function as positive role models or effective political entities in Trinidad.

The Street Prince is an older social prototype. Originating in the imagery of "a man of the people" portrayals, the Street Prince is greatly loved by his community. His reputation and his ability to elicit resources from members of society depends upon his ability to represent and defend the interests of the community. He is a prince because he is the unanimous choice of a community, but because he is without wealth and is the recipient of the kindness and charity of the community in which he lives, he can be seen as a kind of hustler and street person who lives by his wits. The proliferation of Bad Johns and Street Princes, as documented in Michael Lieber's case studies in *Street Life* expands our view of the economic plight and function of the Bad John and Street Prince in real life.

The Master of Schools is a recent social prototype. While it is certainly connected to the advent of black men successfully matriculating through the esteemed educational institutions in the Western World — i.e., Oxford and Harvard — its primary impetus comes from the rise of the West Indian Schoolmaster. The ultimate historical example of the power of ascension of the schoolmasters was the election of Dr. Eric Williams, a university history professor, to the office of Prime Minister of Trinidad. (A similar feat has not been replicated in the American political system.) The concept of *principal*, in the American school system, and *schoolmaster*, in the English school system are not socially equal. The schoolmaster is accorded by his society great moral conviction, purity of motive, and behavioral insight that combines the best of parenting skills with the temperament and wisdom of a priest. The schoolmaster is a valued community resource, when he understands his role as mentor and nurturer and is assigned many rights and privileges not given to the American principal — who is seen as a manager in a particular job position.

When the schoolmaster does not understand his community support role and uses the school and his control of access to education as a forum to impress his accomplishments and will upon the community, I call him a Master of Schools. The Master of Schools uses schools as a political forum from which to rule the members of the community — members he considers inferior to his own illustrious being. He is a being born of Darwinism and Capitalism, who views the community as a domain in which he is lord and progenitor. These three literary figures have no female gender counterpart in West Indian literature, we observe.

Lovelace creates characters that gesture to us that a people can unite to survive in the twentieth century. In his most recent (1982) novel, *The Wine of Astonishment,* he combines the distinctly separate gestures of resistance of the Master of Schools, in the character of Ivan Morton, and the Street Prince turned Bad John, in the form of the character Bolo. In his 1981 novel, *The Dragon Can't Dance,* the gestures of resistance in Street Prince Aldrick Prospect, and Bad John Fisheye are distinctly different, though they are similarly unemployed and on public charity. Because their definitions of manhood are the same, we find them linked in strategic places in the plot of the novel. The Master of Schools in the novel, *The Schoolmaster,* offers us a different lesson on how resistance determines our fate. Like Ivan Morton in *Dragon,* his intent to control his life and to have an effect on the lives of others is clear. Both these characters are images of what must change in the society to improve life for everyone. In literature, some characters resist acculturation and domination overtly. The political systems within which Lovelace lives and writes requires more sophisticated strategies of varying kinds. Hence, Cudjoe's categories of resistance as *cultural, socioeconomic* and *political* become a useful device to use to construct a comparison of the three Lovelace male characters as prototypes. Lovelace's work suggests a community pyramid of power that consists of the before-mentioned selected male behavioral models. The novels suggest that the collective power represented by the pyramid is the reason that Afro-West Indian communities in Trinidad have survived with the vitality that they have. This essay extends that argument to African-American communities throughout the "New World."

Cultural resistance is seen in Aldrick's ability in *Dragon,* to enter the mask of "The Dragon" and unify the community as one voice, like Bee's ability, in *Wine,* to use the enchantments and rituals of the Spiritual Baptist as a unifying force for the poor black people of Bonasse. Cultural resistance is the ability of a people to define themselves in their own terms and use those terms to enhance their psychological, spiritual and physical health in a continuously hostile environment. This cultural resistance forms the first of three faces of the pyramid of power. Without it the other two faces of resistance are ineffective.

Ivan Morton's community position in *Wine,* and the Schoolmaster's community position, in *Schoolmaster,* form the second face of political resistance. Both infiltrate mainstream culture and become self-consciously acculturated to its behavioral logic as a way of reducing the amount of oppression and stress that they have to personally bear daily from mainstream cultural carriers. In doing so, they provide acceptable models of male behavior for others to emulate and provide a negotiating medium between mainstream or in this case post-colonial power networks and the grassroots society. This political resistance forms the second face of resistance in the pyramid of power.

Bolo's community position, in *Wine,* and Fisheye's community position, in *Dragon,* represent the living poverty of the lower economic class's day-to-day struggle to survive and affirm themselves. They are literary descendants of the ancient warrior class whose protective love for the people was a way of acting out their love for themselves.

However, as Bad Johns that ancient energy turns in upon itself, as an expression of their hatred for the state of their people and thus their hatred of their own state. The result is a continuum of actual or ritualized violence that keeps the mainstream society aware of the elements of social unrest. Bolo and Fisheye know what they can do to "improve their status" in society. They know (and reject) how necessary acculturation is to their survival. Their socioeconomic resistance forms the third face of resistance in the pyramid of power.

The base on which the three walls rest is the society, which strategically uses color and economic caste as a way of differentiating between people's political and social rights. Together, these figures suggest that Africans in the New World are always in a state of resistance. Their legacy does not allow them to "make peace with slavery," the bureaucracy or the social mores that keep them second class citizens in the later twentieth century. In both African-American and Caribbean Literature, the process of resistance is in the "ideological content" that informs the artistic structure of the plot and characterization.

In *Wine,* Lovelace recreates the historical details of the Spiritual Baptist Church's resistance to the "Shouters Prohibition" that was in force from 1913 to 1951. This law, passed by the Trinidadian parliament, made it illegal to worship in the manner of the Spiritual Baptist. The Spiritual Baptist's worship services resembled those of the Sanctified and Holy Ghost Pentecostal Churches in America. All of their patterns of worship were and remain fundamentally African worship rituals — unlike the European aesthetic forms of Anglican or Catholic worship rituals. Because they resembled fundamental African patterns of worship, the Spiritual Baptist's existence was unacceptable to the members of middle and upper economic social levels in Trinidad, who had resigned themselves to the continuance of British cultural and economic exploitation. So Parliament (dominated by these acculturated groups) denied the Spiritual Baptists the right to use their ritual of affirmation because they saw the church as a significant threat to mainstream society. Political analysis suggests that they were persecuted because Parliament saw that this way of worshipping (practiced by the poor and lower-socioeconomic class Trinidadians) was a way of organizing — a form of resistance.

In 1951, due in part to the work of the Honorable T. U. B. Butler, this law was repealed. The speech delivered by him at the parliamentary session which repealed "The Shouters Prohibition" provides the non-Trinidadian with significant insight into the controversy surrounding the Spiritual Baptists. At that time the Minister of Eduction and Social Services argued that there were three ways of justifying the continuation of "The Shouters Prohibition": if the churches disturbed the public peace, or provided some sort of outlet for perverse behavior, or thirdly, facilitated "gross, degrading, or immoral" practices, then they deserved "permanent and unqualified suppression." T. U. B. Butler's reply was the essence of Lovelace's later fictional statement about the Spiritual Baptists:

> Mr. Speaker and honorable members, as one of those persons, Sir, who have for the past 15 years been consistently bringing to the notice of Government the injustice placed upon this religious body, I rise to support the Bill before the House with all my soul, and with all the vote that I possess . . . . I want to say, Sir, that His Majesty's most loyal subjects are staunch followers of the Spiritual Baptist faith and even though the Inspector General and Attorney General of 1917 or the Attorney General of yesterday and today may have referred to them as Shouters, we know them as Baptists — as spiritual teachers.
>
> When the Ordinance was passed in this colony against the wishes of these people in 1917, the Baptist religion was as old as the hills . . . . When I speak about a body of people whose love of God and their fellow men is second to none in this Christian country, so I want to dissociate myself from the idea that as a religious body they have committed the wrongs alleged.
>
> This ban was placed upon the religious body to prevent them from serving God in the way they know best. But despite that, they have still served their God. I have not known them ever to hide to practice their religion clandestinely although they have been made to suffer . . . many of these people have gone to jail . . . they openly carried on the ancient practices of their ancient religion and so it is not really true to say that they went clandestinely about it.
>
> (Transcript of Trinidadian Parliamentary discussion, Friday March 30, 1951: 1370-1376).

Lovelace, in his treatment of this issue, writes in the feminine voice of Eva, mother of three children and wife of the minister of a Spiritual Baptist Church in Bonasse. Her first person narration relates her vision of a community under siege, so that her epiphanies are our epiphanies as well. This is especially true in her relationships with men. A deconstruction of Eva's views reveals a man describing the way he believes women see or would like women to see men. Of interest is that an earlier draft of the novel (in the Lovelace Archives in Trinidad) contains another feminine narrator. In that draft, the wife (of the schoolmaster-turned-politician Ivan Morton) describes the same events from a completely opposing point of view, as a member of the bourgeoisie.

Eva explains that the difference between Ivan's level of resistance to the system and the members of the Spiritual Baptist Church's level of resistance is his desire and his mother's desire for him to be equal to the ruling class of his society. For them acculturation equals freedom from restriction and persecution. It is not an unusual formula for success for Africans in the New World. Therefore, when Ivan's Spiritual Baptist education becomes a liability to his successful pursuit of status and money, Eva tells us that his single-parent, washerwoman mother told him to "Turn Catholic." That process involves more than a change of religions or schools. It involves a redefinition of the essential self that will sever its identity from the previous group and reverse its political orientation to insure Ivan Morton's entry into the bourgeoisie.

Modern Trinidad has the physical and aesthetic educational system that it inherited from the Catholics (who came with Columbus) and the British (who captured the island during the Napoleonic wars). Eva's remarks about Ivan Morton "turning Catholic" remind us that when a society cannot educate its own members to uphold the priorities and values of the group, it either faces extinction or is forced to adapt to a system which may not uphold its moral or cultural creeds.

Lovelace's elimination of the schoolmaster's wife in the published novel focuses the reader's attention entirely on the numerical majority: the working, rural and urban poor. Their numerical dominance reflects ironically on their cultural inequity and political disfranchisement in Trinidadian society during this period. Ivan Morton's acculturation strategy is designed to separate him from the Spiritual Baptist's state of helplessness under the law. He pursues an alliance with the colonial and Catholic power structure because he believes that it will give him maximum control over what happens to him and his family. This alliance requires him to disassociate himself from his grass roots origin. Hence, he despoils a much beloved, brown-skinned, village belle, consciously marries a light-skinned girl from another town and moves into the abandoned sugar plantation mansion, where he reigns until the next election. Only the need to be re-elected forces him to act on behalf of the people to assist in repealing "The Shouters' Prohibition."

The laws against the Spiritual Baptist made them very conspicuous and at risk because their cultural resistance tested the boundaries of the political power enforced by the police, the courts, the Church and the formal education hierarchy. Ivan Morton's real struggle is against the poverty and ridicule of his youth — not against the Spiritual Baptist Church. His desire to control his destiny and the destiny of his people is reflected in his conversation with the Minister Bee (Eva's husband). He accuses Bee of being an agent of regressive evolution for continuing the church services of the Spiritual Baptist. Ivan Morton, as a schoolmaster and politician, represents a figure of resistance that utilizes acculturation as a survival strategy.

Eva realized too late that her husband, the Minister Bee, and Bolo are each resisting the force of historic change which comes in the form of the American armed forces' occupation of Trinidad during World War II, and the consequent massive migration to the city and to America:

> But when I look at it, I see that what happen with Eulalie [the village belle] was showing something bigger that was happening in the village right under our nose. What was happening was that the warrior was dying in the village as the chief figure. The scholar, the boy with education, was taking over and if we was thinking, we wouldn't be surprised for now education was getting popular as the way to win the battle to be somebody; and the warriors, the men to fight real fights, was just something to remember, for they never win no battle and if they do anything, is to bring us more trouble. (*Wine* 46)

Eva and Bee's younger son Taffy represents a whole generation that is trying to figure out how to live in the modern society that they can clearly see coming, but for which they can't find new definitions. The fear that Taffy feels is the same fear that prompts Bolo and Fisheye to resist violently. A disruptive person in school, Taffy is left to learn tailoring as a trade, but his mother can see that learning tailoring will not resolve his need to resist status quo values, as he pursues his own definition of manhood:

> Of all my children he is the one that give me the most trouble to bring into this world, and the way it looking, he going to be the one to send me to my grave quick. Because Taffy have this knife that he grind down from hacksaw and put a handle to, that he always throwing, sticking on the door, in trees, in anything. He have this knife and he have this way about him, this attitude, this gam, this thing in him that the world does beat out of man before he reach eighteen years, but that ain't beat out of Taffy yet . . . . (*Wine* 53)

Taffy's predilection for unemployment is a major factor of socioeconomic resistance in Trinidad. Farley Braithwaite notes the following:

> The data present a picture of some deprivation among the unemployed. Firstly, they show that the mean income among the same was approximately $98.05 [Trinidadian dollars] per month [or $40.00 per month in American dollars] . . . Secondly, that 48 or 31.2% of our respondents did not have any regular source of income. Thirdly, that 93 or 60.4% got less than $100.00 [Trinidadian dollars] per month [or about $41.00 per month in American dollars]. (22)

The data indicate that more than 50% of the population survives on less than $14.44 per week. Taffy lives in that kind of struggling, working poverty. His assertiveness, daring, grace and sensuality are all the hallmarks of a blossoming Bad John who will wage war as a reason to live. His promise of violence, like the violence that erupts in the characterization of Bolo, is a direct response to the helpless of his father (as parent and community leader) against the brutality of the police chief Prince. Bolo's decision to turn to violence was his personal strategy of resistance against the community's decision to empower the wrong man (Ivan Morton) as chief. Constantine Patron's act of murder in *Schoolmaster* will be generated by the same cause.

Lovelace uses Constantine Patron to question how a schoolmaster, a leader of the community, is chosen. The novel chronicles the folly of any community's willingness to hand over all rights of power to anyone without any initiation into the society, for which he or she will be providing direction. Like Ivan Morton, the Schoolmaster's political resistance to identifying with the masses that he serves and his push to have them imitate mainstream culture as much as possible, is a part of his strategy for assimilating the power to control his destiny as an African in the New World. Benn, the alcoholic donkey trailsman, who guides people through the narrow unpaved passage leading into Bonasse, indicates that the Schoolmaster is clearly not of the community:

> He is black, yes. But not my own people. Priest [white, Irish, Catholic, male person], he is closer to your people. I think he is your people. He learned in your schools, and he wears the clothes the way you wear them, and talks the way you talk, and his thinking is that of your people. He is yours, priest. He is not mine. (*Schoolmaster* 66)

As with Eva in *Wine,* and Sylvia in *Dragon,* it is the insight of the feminine character that reveals the dichotomies of clashing realities in Trinidadian society. Christiana is one of the few townspeople who can read and write well. Her father (Paulaine Dandrade) is a very powerful community leader; even so, she becomes engaged to an illiterate laborer on her father's plantation. However, neither male can protect her against the dominating Schoolmaster. Christiana does not resist physical rape; it is a metaphor for the moral rape of the trusting village people by the Schoolmaster, who clearly sets himself above the law he pretends to represent. When the townspeople learn of Christiana's suicide (an act of socioeconomic resistance) in response to her secret rape and pregnancy, they are galvanized in a way that contrasts with their dispersion earlier in the novel. Constantine Patron kills the Schoolmaster to keep him from deliberately walking away to forget what he has done to Christiana. The townspeople will approve and confirm Constantine's decision, that the Schoolmaster must die for his crime. The returning priest will find "one people" who are decidedly more skeptical about church and education than they were before. As critic Kenneth Ramchand states in the introduction to the novel:

> What Lovelace is really saying . . . is that the kind of education and progress coming to these islands (for the novel is parabolical, Kumaca stands for the island), and the selfhood of those whose responsibility and privilege it is to be the means of that coming are closely related matters; if we fail to take this into account, there will be no moral authority, only pappyshow, betrayal and dreadful autumn for the Patriarch. (Introduction xi)

Bolo in *Wine* means to make that prophecy come true with a vengeance. He starts out in the novel much like Robert Winston or Rat does in real life in Port of Spain (Lieber 43). Rat is a Street Prince who is also a hustler, not a Bad John. Like Bolo's community, Rat's community loves him and grants him the affection of a native son, who is always true to his roots. He is tall and comely and has the fictional Bolo's magical appeal to women. Rat always has others constantly doing him favors. Consequently, both Bolo and Rat are well taken care of without the necessity of the aggression of the Bad John. The good Street Prince does not need coercion or deception to get what he needs to live. The Street Prince's cultural resistance is an ancient way of living by willingly sharing wealth communally with the members of his group. He conscientiously refuses to act solely in his individual interest because he realizes that he is dependent on the trust and generosity of others.

It is this affection between his community under siege and Bolo that forces him to confront the elders of the community. He confronts those who would protect and cherish his community in a stance that clearly challenges the idea that one person — Prince, the police chief, or one organization — the judicial power of the parliamentary system — can subdue "a people." Bolo's metamorphosis from Street Prince to Bad John, and Fisheye's metamorphosis from Strong Man to Bad John bespeaks a violent resistance movement growing in the rural and urban poor.

Both Bolo and Aldrick are artists in the proletarian tradition. Fisheye has no craft or talent aside from fighting and laboring. Both Aldrick and Bolo use their art form to facilitate their personality changes from passive to aggressive — from an enslaved being to a liberated person. Lovelace's literary sensitivity and aesthetic values emanate from the socioeconomic, political, and most importantly, cultural conditions of his people. It is the striking, acute immediacy and the musicality of the language, together with the timely historical perspective that triggers the reader's response.

Aldrick, Bolo, and Fisheye as Dragon and Bad Johns are the fiercest forces of resistance in the pyramid of power. Together they represent one side of an ancient sphere of power, the power "to turn beast" and wreak havoc upon one's enemies. They hold the power of Dionysus — Lord of Carnival / Lord of the Mas'. His is the power to destroy as an act of re-creation and the power to dance as an act of power. In *Dragon,* dancing becomes a metaphor for successful adaption itself. To dance is to be able to successfully balance the forces of the world and move them in a graceful pattern to reflect life's beauty and vitality. To dance is to live, to experience the fullest realization of one's humanity and one's right to move in a world ordered by Death and Time, who are obligated to no one. "Dancing is a chant that cuts off the power of the devil" (*Dragon* 13-14). The Bad John and the Dragon openly combat the attempts of the oppressive elements of society to imprison them in "the void of timeless estrangement" — of having no control over their bodies, minds, or behavior" (Barthold 75-76).

Fisheye is predisposed to be a Bad John, out of his frustration at inheriting a national economy depressed by the impact of the (East) Indian immigration. Unemployment is high and wages are low in rural areas. He also understands that Trinidad's economy has been undermined by foreign interest in Trinidad's rich oil resources. These problems are compounded by the continuing struggle for effective self-government by a new middle class leadership that supervises widespread poverty in urban areas. Fisheye migrates from the country to the city. His fictional failure to adapt is modeled on the lives of real men who attempted that transition. Richard Granger or "Dum Dum" (as in Dum-dum bullets) is one of Michael Lieber's case studies in *Street Life*. Lieber's description of Granger merges fiction with fact as we recognize Fisheye:

> Dum-Dum . . . was a 'bad john' — a tough, flamboyant, violent, bullyish sort of man, more attracted to violent crime than to non-violent hustle . . . . Dum-Dum was a big powerful man, with a husky, threatening voice and moody, excitable, aggressive disposition. (44)

Fisheye represents the majority of those who form the labor pool in Trinidad, in that he is unskilled and uneducated. His love for physical work, that could be put to use on the country plantations, cannot easily be channeled into another kind of work in the city. He is a strong man with no arena in which to act, until he proves the worth of his masculinity by joining the Calvary Hill Gang as warrior supreme. The gang provides him with a home, work and a purpose for living. Its ritualized violence orders his life and makes him a celebrity.

The legitimation of the gangs and their transformation into artistic ensembles of steel bands kills the violent element of gang warfare. Fisheye is left with no arena to act out his frustration and his powerlessness. His inability to see the political wisdom of his woman's advice to unite the gangs and attack the political structure, leads him to be a petty criminal and bully. Fisheye turns to crime and terrorizing the neighborhood as a way of life.

Fisheye's final act of resistance, involving several kidnapped police officers and stealing a police van for several days, will get him a jail sentence — a prison dance — or a place where he is fed regularly, housed adequately, and allowed the luxury of an intellectual dialogue on the nature of resistance with Street Prince *extraordinaire* and Dragon Master, Aldrick Prospect. Fisheye's Black, Oxford trained lawyer articulates the power structure's view of Aldrick's and Fisheye's act of resistance (or revolutionary dance) as the futile action of an impotent, desperate people who wanted nothing more than to have their personhood affirmed:

> The authorities trusted these men to fail, that is why they made no move to stop them . . . The action undertaken by these men was an attempt to not even seize power, as we have seen, but to affirm a personhood for themselves, and beyond themselves, to proclaim a personhood for people deprived and illegitimized as they: the people of the Hill, of the slums and shanty towns. (*Dragon* 183)

The lawyer speaks from inside the sociopolitical-economic system that Fisheye is resisting. The lawyer and the Schoolmaster are brothers in a power pact made in their successful initiation into the secrets of formal education, which free them from the necessity of having to resist the power of disfranchisement and degradation in Trinidad.

Christiana's father, Paulaine Dandrade in *Schoolmaster*, is the primary catalyst for establishing a formal education system (under the auspices of the Catholic Church in Kumaca, Trinidad); but his vision is incomplete. Aldrick Prospect's vision in *Dragon*, of what he has escaped by being a Street Prince and Dragon, by resisting either the discussion or the reality of formal education and traditional work, is incomplete. In both cases it takes a teenage girl to help Aldrick and Paulaine to discover and complete their visions.

Growing up in the shadow of his frequently absent father, Sam the Miracle Man, Aldrick inherited his "sense of miracle and manness, this surviving on nothing and standing up still on your own two feet to be counted as somebody in a world where people were people, were human, by the account of their property" (*Dragon* 41). As an apprentice to his Street Prince uncle, Uncle Freddie, he learned the words, "take it easy," and he learned how to transform linear time into the cyclical phenomenal time that ruled life on the hill — a life where there were no prospects and a limited number of predictable futures. It was the life that Aldrick chose over struggling against his caste and color to be accepted by mainstream society. It was his decision to accept the legacy of the anger and the injustice of slavery in Trinidad. Lovelace describes his twentieth-century environment as follows:

> . . . asserting their humanness in the most wonderful acts of sabotage they could imagine and perform, making a religion of laziness and neglect and stupidity and waste; singing hosannahs for flood and hurricane and earthquake, praying for damage and pestilence: continuing it still after Emancipation, that emancipated them to a more profound idleness and waste when, refusing to be grist for the mill of the colonial machinery that kept on grinding in its belly people to spit out sugar and cocoa and copra, they turned up this hill to pitch camp here on the eyebrow of the enemy, to cultivate again with no less fervor the religion with its Trinity of Idleness, Laziness, and Waste, so that Aldrick Prospect an aristocrat in this tradition, not knowing where his next meal was coming from, would get up at midday from sleep, yawn, stretch, then start to think of where he might get something to eat, his brain working in the same smooth, unhurried, nonchalance with which he moved his feet, a slow, cruising crawl which he quickened only at Carnival. (*Dragon* 10-11)

Aldrick's resistance is aimed at simplifying time by denying the linear time that controls traditional employment and regularized family life. As the Street Prince, he is "hustler supreme" and as such is a kind of heroic leader of the resistance movement. As master hustler he is clever, cool, and attuned to what is happening in his environment while carefully maintaining a certain quality of physical and emotional distance from all events and people. For Aldrick, resisting linear time means foregoing the commitment of a meaningful relationship that would create a family. His social relationship to all members of the community was pre-determined by the ancient legacy that ties the Dragon to the community. The Dragon is the manifestation of their will to be rebellious, to resist accepting their designated status as underprivileged:

> Once upon a time the entire Carnival was expressions of rebellion . . . Suddenly they were all gone, outlawed from the city or just died, gone, and he felt alone . . . The dragon alone was left to carry the message. (*Dragon* 121)

Aldrick uses the art form of the making of the Dragon to argue for change that will produce a society that does not take power and voice away from any people. What the Oxford lawyer describes emptily as a dragon dance is the ancestral symbol of revolt, the power "to turn beast," to have the strength to wage war; it is the preserved dignity and spirit of "the hill" and its residents' stance or gesture of resistance. Lovelace also uses his character Cyril Village to invoke the power of another cultural art form, stickfighting, in his play "My Name is Village," to rediscover the dignity and spirit that the "the Dragon" preserves. Cyril is ridiculed by his wife and ignored as a model of manliness by his young son Roy. Roy is practicing at being a Bad John and is at the point in his adolescence where he is easily influenced by what appears to be a successful negative model of masculinity, Mr. Towntest. Roy has warrior blood like Bolo and Fisheye. He wants to join the guerrillas hiding from the police in the hills or he would like to be a soldier in a big war. Strength in armed struggle is Roy's concept of an exciting and meaningful life. His bad behavior is in fact a cry for help in addressing his frustration while waiting for someone else to change things.

Cyril Village recaptures his ability to once again resist all of the same forces facing Roy, as he summons the power of resistance in a mock stickfight with the night watchman. Alcoholism aside, he announces, "Village fighting again, all shit cut out. I fighting again" ("My Name is Village" 111). The declaration is meant to put all of the enemies of village life and welfare on notice, that the people will fight to protect their families and their values. Cyril marches forward to dismiss the negative part of the Bad John spirit without killing Roy's warriorhood or his ability to resist disfranchisement and discrimination. Roy will reapproach the village belle, Elena, and say in Lovelace's beautiful, lyric language:

> I sorry! I sorry for true. Look I bring these flowers for you . . . A man is flowers too and I sorry . . . ("My Name is Village" 117).

Roy, like Taffy, in *Wine,* avoids both Bolo's and Fisheye's fate because the fabric of his family and cultural legacy is strong enough to provide direction for him, when he needs it most. For the moment, he resolves the dialect of being a West Indian, male youth at odds with the mainstream, urban culture. Cyril's ability to resist being defined as politically or culturally dysfunctional (because he is not European and has not been absorbed into the mainstream culture), provides a model of resistance for Roy to build upon. Aldrick's statement as the Dragon and Street Prince forms the oratorical center of Lovelace's lesson on resistance:

> "Make no peace with slavery," Aldrick cried. "Make no peace, for you have survived . . . We have to live as people. We have to rise up. But how do you rise up when your brothers are making peace for a few dollars? When sisters are selling their children? How can you rise up with rent to pay and children to school, and watch your hunger march across your yard and camp inside your house?" (*Dragon* 179)

New World history teaches us that we are only capable of "making peace with slavery," surviving and evolving as individuals of color, when we work to insure the survival and evolution of the group.

In the distant past, carnival was a collective expression of the folk's resistance against disenfranchisement. The folk are the people whose traditions Aldrick knows he must uphold by breaking the law. The laws prohibiting the Spiritual Baptists from worshipping in a more joyful, active and traditionally African manner are wrong and inhumane; Bee knows that he must uphold that folk tradition as High Priest, leader and father by breaking the law and encouraging others to worship God in their own way. When neither the church nor the government will protect the people's right to self-identify, self-determination and education, both Bolo and Constantine Patron know that they must uphold that tradition of resistance as warrior and elder by breaking the law and resisting mainstream terrorism. If we understand their actions, then Lovelace's lesson to us is clear. He says in a petition to Prime Minister Eric Williams, "We believe that progress in a community is not measured only by what government provides but chiefly by what the community is prepared to do for itself, to solve its own problem." The Bad John, Street Prince and Master of Schools are three critical figures in the community's hierarchy of power, its ability to do for itself. Experiencing them though Lovelace's vision helps us to create a clearer picture of how they can be managed in more effective ways to strengthen the Black community's potential for united action and resistance against forces which oppress its growth and enlightenment. These men are the mirror of our collective failure and success and must be acknowledged as we continue the struggle to be, with the spirit to go forward — the spirit of our ancestors who created a way out of no way for us to travel.

WORKS CITED

Barthold, Bonnie. *Black Time*. New Haven: Yale UP, 1981.

Braithwaite, Farley. *Unemployment and Social Life: A Sociological Study of The Unemployed in Trinidad.* Bridgetown, Barbados: Antilles Publications, 1983.

Cudjoe, Selwyn R. *Resistance and Caribbean Literature.* Chicago: Ohio UP, 1980.

Lieber, Michael. *Street Life: Life and Afro-American Culture in Urban Trinidad.* Boston: Hall, 1981.

Lovelace, Earl. *The Schoolmaster*. London: Heinemann, 1979.

——. *The Dragon Can't Dance*. London: Longman's, 1981.

——. *The Wine of Astonishment*. London: Heinemann, 1982.

——. "My Name Is Village." In "*Jestina's Calypso and Other Plays*. London: Heinemann, 1984.

Ramchand, Kenneth. "Introduction." In *The Schoolmaster* cited above.

Rodman, Hyman. *Lower-Class Families: The Culture of Poverty in Negro Trinidad.* London: Oxford UP, 1971.

Transcript of Trinidadian Parliamentary discussion Friday, March 30, 1951, Relative to the Repeal of The Shouters' Prohibition, pp. 1370-1376.

III

Continental Culture and Identity

VICKI ADAMS

Milan Kundera: The Search for Self in a Post-Modern World

Carlos Fuentes has said that the most urgent poles of contemporary narrative are found in Latin America and in Central Europe (256), and the modern reader automatically thinks of Gabriel García Márquez and Milan Kundera. This paper will look at one of these well-known authors, Milan Kundera, in terms of the Slavic soul representing its geographic standing between East (the land of orthodoxy or ideology), and West (the land of nihilism). Kundera is interesting in this connection because he resists either camp: what he calls the angelic laughter of certainty, of truth, of ideology, and the demonic laughter of infinite relativism, cynicism, and nihilism we have heard so much about in Western philosophy.

Milan Kundera, the Czech writer who has been living in Paris for more than twenty years, and writing for a foreign audience because his books were banned in his own land, does lean toward the abyss (nihilism), does favor what R. B. Gill has called "epicurean accommodation" (90), does opt for the novel of relative truths, but somehow has managed to keep a foothold on the cliff overhanging the modern abyss of nothingness. His particular foothold seems to be a rediscovery of his folk culture, as the comforts found in his early Moravian roots offer him touchstones of identity perhaps not available to other contemporary writers. His philosophical novels offer a compromise between memory and forgetting, between irony and commitment. What might be so fetching about this writer is that, instead of arriving at the modern conclusion that life has less and less meaning in a post-Derridian world, he celebrates those very weaknesses that make us human (angst, confusion, hopelessness, uncertainty, and especially, man's simplicity) as synonymous with beauty. Thus, he turns the modern philosophical world topsy-turvy, because aesthetics has a way of turning to ethics in his post modern fiction . . . his post-structuralist worldview emphasizes the beauty of the uncertainty. Unlike other modern spokesmen of a bleak and dreary reality, his acceptance of relative truths seems to be a manifestation of a wry Kunderian accommodation to man's powerlessness in post-Stalinist Central Europe.

The goal of this paper is to underscore the role of Kundera's folk heritage in the formation of his world view in his search for self and, in doing that, to consider the source of his international appeal. The investigation will first of all consider Kundera as firmly in the post-modernist camp and then look at some of Kundera's own theoretical statements on fiction and the novel (including revelatory excerpts from six of his novels). Attempting to show how his chosen form of expression — the novel — is the only one capable of expressing his concept of identity in a post-modern world, a transition will then be made from the seemingly value-free post-modern viewpoint to Kundera's other side — where his individual characters are called upon to make choices, and where the destinies of "Der Volk" matter intensely. The transition will use some very recent ideas of Derrida and Lyotard to pose the obvious question: How can a novelist, clearly so post-modern in his techniques and philosophical thrust, be at the same time a heralder of the beauty in a life chock full of irony and chaos?

Jacques Derrida offers a justification for deconstructionist thought in our world that Kundera will echo in both his novels and his own critical writings. If the truth of reason is really our own experience of it, it is relative anyway. So, we need new kinds of "knowledge" to deal with this relative world, new unheard of thoughts, "qui se cherchent à travers la memoire des vieux signes." [sought from the memories of old signs] (*La voix et la phénomène* 115). This is precisely what Kundera will discover in his folk culture — memories of old signs — which will offer the possibility of an identity, a spiritual or psychological homeland waiting to be repossessed by him.

In terms of history (and Kundera is mainly concerned with man's relationship to the past, to history), his theory was already introduced by Foucault's deconstructionist views that it is just possible that history is made up of interpretation, not fact; that any sign/event is already an interpretation of another sign/event (see Descombes 117). The goal of history has always been the triumph of meaning, annihilation of the negative, the presence of a truth; but, when this happens, according to the deconstructionists, there is nothing left to do, nothing more to learn. Kundera's view of history has more to do with disorder than triumph of meaning. While his sentimental side yearns for a safe, unchanging, constantly returning, idyllic past, his skepticism tells us that Foucault's view was right: alternative accounts are possible when authorities in Czechoslovakia tear down the old heroic monuments, give the streets new Russian names, and fabricate in the schools a tidy and sentimental account of Czech history. Kundera writes his fiction to awaken doubts or skepticism as an alternative. He insists that the novel is the form to express this doubt, or contradiction. The novel teaches us to comprehend other peoples' truths and the limitations of our own truth, so the novel should be deeply non-ideological: "it is as essential to our insanely ideological world as is bread" (*Le Monde* 16). In another article, "Man Thinks, God Laughs," he says that the novel's wisdom is different from that of philosophy — it is born of the spirit of humor. The novel contradicts ideological certitudes: "Like Penelope, it undoes each night the tapestry that . . . philosophy and learned men wove the day before" (11). Life is seen rationally, as a:

> glowing trajectory of causes and effects, failures, and successes, and man, setting his impatient gaze on the causal chain of his actions, accelerates further his mad race toward death. (12)

Kundera sees human existence (its beauty) located "where the bridge between a cause and an effect is ruptured" (12). At this juncture, there is liberty, digression, the incalculable, a lack of reason, the opposite of eighteenth-century rationalism and Liebniz. So the art born of God's laughter — the novel — is the "art that has managed to create the . . . imaginative realm where no one is the possessor of the truth, and there everyone has the right to be understood" (12). Clearly, Foucault's view of history as interpretation, or as "alternative accounts" is manifested in this 1985 essay by Kundera.

In Kundera's own fiction, one strongly senses a deconstructionist view of the modern world and an example of Kundera's attempt to deal with the concept of identity in this deconstructed world of his novels. In his 1973 *Life is Elsewhere,* the theme is that the poetic viewpoint should not dominate one's life because it is incapable of irony; its only goal is beauty. Because lyricism is never ironic, it risks being totalitarian. In this novel, Jaromil, the young poet, cannot draw human faces, giving the reader a metaphor for an ideology — where only causes, and not individuals, exist, where nuance and irony are absent. At one point the narrator says of Jaromil:

> The raw simplicity of the statement made him happy because it placed him in the ranks of those direct and simple men who laughed at nuances and whose wisdom lies in their understanding of the ridiculously simple essentials of life. (119)

Speaking later in the novel of the "adult world" of relativity, Kundera compares it with poetic form:

> In rhyme and rhythm reside a certain magical power. An amorphous world becomes at once orderly, lucid and clear, and beautiful when squeezed into regular meters. Death is chaotic, but if it is in rhyme, it is orderly. (179)

He goes on later to say: "The adult world knows perfectly well that the absolute is an illusion, that nothing human is either great or eternal" (206).

In *Laughable Loves* (1974) Kundera portrays love as a meaningless game, but one area of life where we are convinced we have some control, one area (along with religion) where we try to find our essence, our peculiar identity. Man has little control over most spheres of life, but in love, there is a sense of relative freedom, and that being so, women became, for one of his characters, the "one legitimate criterion of his life's destiny" (32). Women became, for the protagonist, a way of choosing his identity in a society where he was, in every other way, powerless to express himself. Later in the same story, however, the same character complains:

> All at once I understood that it had only been my illusion that we ourselves saddle events, and are able to control their course. The truth is that they aren't our stories at all, that they are foisted upon us from somewhere outside, that we are not to blame for the queer path they follow. (88)

The interesting, diverse group of characters in *The Farewell Party* (1976) try to control their destinies in a fertility clinic where sex is used to trick destiny. They gather to say good-bye to a comrade who has gotten permission to emigrate, and the themes are similar to those in his other novels. One character says: "We really had no choices," after he had carried with him what he thought was a suicide pill for years, feeling that at least in the end, if things turned bad, he could decide his own life or death. The doctor who gave him the pill explains: " . . . the fake pill allowed him to turn his life into a noble myth" (77), the myth of some control over his destiny. Kundera has also created characters in his novels who equate order with identity, who need to have the authorities establish their identities. An outspoken, and very ideological nurse at the clinic dislikes the emigré's face because it looks "ironic" to her, and she hates irony. All irony was, for her, "like an armed watchman guarding the portal to her future, disdainfully refusing her admittance" (82). Admittance to what? To Kundera's adulthood of irony, or uncertainty, to real life? Kundera asks, "What motivates people to totalitarianism?

The longing for order, the desire to turn the human world into an inorganic one?" (85). This kind of Kunderian character needs her identity established for her; she fears that in freedom, in the chaos of uncertainty, she will not know who she is. For Kundera, real life is disorder, chaos, while a willfully imposed order is akin to death.

Kundera's two most successful novels are *The Book of Laughter and Forgetting,* published in 1978, and *The Unbearable Lightness of Being,* published in 1984. Both texts are concerned with man's relationship to history and both texts resist a single reading. Both texts need to be considered in any discussion of problems of identity because Kundera himself has equated the absurd chaos in historical events with an individual's life. The two novels keep insisting that understanding the absurdity, the lack of a rational structure in historical events is just one more way to understand his concept of individual identity. Both are inaccessible to our human understanding. The structuralists' view of history is just as mistaken as the poetic view of individual identity: rational cause and effect in history is just as illusory as is the absolute (he would say, childish) concept of apprehending one's individual identity, of knowing who we really are. Control over history and individual identity is a fiction. Both novels place their protagonists in a world where the border is warped between reality and art, or between history and the fantastic, between memory and forgetting. *The Book of Laughter and Forgetting* is called by David Lodge, "a masterpiece of post-modernist fiction" (111). The novel offers several separate stories, some having the same characters which flow (or, as Lodge puts it, "leak") into each other. Themes, motifs and author's comments are repeated. It is a novel in the form of variations, which is not so much manipulation of chronology or point of view as it is a disruption between author and narrator. Milan Kundera keeps leaping over his narrator to appear overtly in the stories. It is in *Laughter and Forgetting* that Kundera moves back and forth from the historical to the fantastic, where previously introduced motifs and fantastic events are brought together with real facts. (We think of Marquez's magical realism here, and the broader connection between Central Europe and Latin American literature in our era.) As Lodge has said: "The outrages of modern history in those regimes are of such a scale that only the 'overt lie' of the fantastic and the grotesque can represent them" (119).

It is in both *The Book of Laughter and Forgetting* and *The Unbearable*

Lightness of Being that Kundera clearly portrays history as a narrated story, and shows the fabrication of what is called the truth, or shows history as an interpretation. In the more recent novel, Kundera's most philosophical novel to date, he considers such questions as individual responsibility, Nietzsche's 'eternal return,' and chance and coincidence in life. Again, familiar motifs are here: erotic trickery in order to outwit fate, self deception, the limits of human lucidity, and the games of history. The now-familiar technique of mixing history and the fantastic is rampant in this story. The characters have a goal of making decisions, but, since Kundera rejects Nietzsche's eternal return, his characters cannot learn from repeated events, and thus, decisions or actions cannot weigh heavily on them. We are, like his characters, relieved of that responsibility of learning from history. Robert interprets Kundera's sense of "lightness of being" in this way: "If reality were like clockwork, history would have been infinitely organized. Any accident would have affected the whole: there would have to be individual responsibility in history" (45). If individuals are as light and meaningless as historical events, if individuals have no responsibility for these events (as Kundera's narrator suspects in this novel) then how can we determine who we are, where we fit into the scheme of society's fate, its progress, its demise? Kundera jumps into his novel to tell us that history is as light as an individual's life. In fact, as early as 1958, Kundera would write:

> . . . les mécanismes psychologiques qui fonctionnent dans les grands événements historiques (apparemment incroyables et inhumains) sont les mêmes qui régissent les situations intimes (tout à fait banales et humaines.).
> [. . . the psychological mechanisms which function in the grand (and apparently inhuman and unbelievable) historic events are the same which rule intimate (and completely banal and human) situations.].
>
> (Quelque part la derrière 58)

Whether readers understand the novel's quartet of Tereza, Tomas, Sabina and Franz as representing weightiness or lightness, (or probably, as structures or variations on a theme), it is clear that Kundera's fictional mode is now more philosophical than political. He uses Nietzsche as an introduction to Tomas's philosophical quandary between weightiness and lightness, and the reader is led through the philosophical maze of questions concerning individual identity in this world either devoid of individual responsibility or filled to overflowing with personal responsibility. Tomas keeps fluctuating between the negation of both social and personal responsibility, and accepting the burden of Teresa's ponderous love, his country's shame, and his medical work (where he, as a surgeon, claims to be able to find another's identity with the act of cutting open another's body). Tomas finally chooses the responsibility of another's life (weightiness), marries Teresa and moves to a farm commune, and thus has his identity given to him by his circumstances. By Kundera's ironic slight of hand, however, Tomas has also managed to choose lightness of being: he has moved from city to simple country life; he has given up a very controlled medical profession (the weightiness of his beloved work); and, he is now free and away from authorities, living a simpler, rather idyllic life of limited responsibility, freer to define who he is. Kundera has ended his novel ironically; the reader may choose the philosophical stance he prefers as he finishes the novel. Has the protagonist found an identity, or given up the search?

After having looked at Kundera's oeuvre in terms of his being solidly based in the post-modern intellectual camp, it would be beneficial to digress briefly for the purpose of coming at a conclusion from another angle. The original question of this investigation was: How does Milan Kundera, who is solidly post-modern in his theoretical stance and in his fiction, who espouses a modernist (some say, nihilistic or anti-humanist) credo of lack of certainties in life, lack of high tragedy in human events, how does this very modern writer manage to convey the bittersweet beauty inherent in the sometimes absurd, often meaningless lives in his books? How does he successfully shun, as R. C. Porter claims he does, both the literature of incoherence and the literature of absolute ideas? (91). The following brief digression is meant to put his seemingly janus-faced contribution into an historical context.

First of all, intellectuals from Central Europe have always been engaged, have always had an ethical motivation for their theoretical output. The charges of an "arid formalism or political escapism" which members of literature departments level against post-modern theoreticians are just not applicable to Slavic writers. "In the Slavic world, structuralism is seen not as the cerebral play of a few armchair theoreticians, but as a clearcut political stance . . ." (Steiner 6). For Kundera, whose nostalgia yearns for the Bohemia of pre-history, who sees his whole oeuvre, "comme une longue méditation sur le fin possible de l'humanité européene" [as a long meditation on the possible end of European civilization] ('Un occident kidnappé' " 16), literary theory must be attached to the ethical; and, in fact, the importance of this art (modern literature from Prague, Budapest or Warsaw) does not lie in the fact that it criticizes this or that political regime, but "that it offers new testimony about mankind in a social or political setting which people here in the West cannot even imagine" (*Comedy is Everywhere* 6).

Secondly, even Jacques Derrida admits to an ethical, even political thrust of modern literary theory when he writes in *Ecriture et la différence* that the only way to do battle with Western metaphysical absolutism is through stratagem or strategy (59). Sounding particularly political, he suggests playing a "double game" or double agent, "serving two sides" or feigning obedience to a system of rule while simultaneously trying to undermine its rule by posing unsolvable problems. He continues: "The question here is to pretend to speak the master's language in order to kill him" (133). This sounds like the strategy of any minority, and defeated group (i.e., Kundera's citizens in post-1969 occupied Czechoslovakia). The key to keeping one's identity intact is that "arriére pensée" (133), a mental reservation, held back so that one does not buy into the ideology completely. Kundera calls it a moment of pause before we give an arbitrary significance to a word. So, Derrida concludes, modern theories need not be so alienated from ethical concerns; they can be, on the contrary, "active interventions" (*Critical Inquiries* 168). An artist need not be enclosed in some "prison house of language," (165) but rather engaged in very political, ethical pursuits. Milan Kundera elegantly makes that bridge or crossover from aesthetics to ethics, and his motivation is clear in this borrowed quote from a 1983 article: "Only in opposing history can you oppose today's history" (Un occident kidnappé 15). By questioning an individual's responsibility in historical events, the individual can better define his responsibility and his essence in contemporary events.

Francois Lyotard, author of *The Post-Modern Condition* and several other texts considering that state of contemporary knowledge, has said that post-modern knowledge refines our sensitivity to differences and reinforces our ability to tolerate the incommensurable. Milan Kundera's work is a product of this post-scientific era, an era, according to Lyotard, in which narrative knowledge will be more valuable to us than scientific knowledge. Since, according to most post-modern theorists, language is no longer a system of signs, but "tricks or games," or, to quote Jameson's forward to this text, "a conflictual relationship between tricksters" (xi), Kundera's themes of linguistic and historical trickery of sleight of hand are definitely post-modern. But also, Kundera shares with these new theorists the goal of generating new ideas, new kinds of knowledge, and ultimately, a new way of looking at man. Kundera's art offers a way of seeking one's identity in this post-modern world of extremes. He suggests, in his novels, another alternative — beyond those of nihilism or absolute truth.

Each age has its dominant way of the sign, and the things they signify, says Foucault in *The Archeology of Knowledge*. Lyotard, in *The Post-Modern Condition,* claims that there are scientific periods of history, but now, there is a revival of the narrative view of truth. He insists that scientific knowledge is based on narrative truth anyway, that theories are just disguised narratives (*Instructions paiennes* 28), that philosophy too was just a seductive tale (*The Post-Modern Condition* 29). He gives as examples Plato's "Myth of the Cave," a non-scientific narrative used to inaugurate science, or Descartes resorting to what he calls the "story of the mind" in his *Discourses,* or even Aristotle suggesting that scientific knowledge is composed only of arguments (i.e., dialectics). For Lyotard, narrative is not just a new field of research, but a mode of thinking, fully as legitimate as that of abstract logic.

Another urgent level of Lyotard's text proposes that the narrative must generate the illusion of an imaginary resolution of real contradictions. It is on this level that a real correspondence between Kundera and Lyotard can be made: using as his backdrop real contradictions, (social, political and historical), Kundera creates illusions (a fiction) of imaginary resolutions, or he emphasizes the imaginary aspects of his resolutions. That, then, is another function of mixing the fantastic with the real in these novels. The very idea of "idyll" on which Kundera relies so often, is his "illusion of a resolution." Carlos Fuentes calls Kundera's notion of idyll, "a Communist offering to forget the past, a false remembering," (263). His characters are desperately looking back (into prehistory?), through the memory of "old signs" to find themselves. It is this concept of idyll that will be exploited to suggest a dreamy, almost mythic, remembering of early Moravian folk culture as sedative to the barrage of absurdities in the post-modern world. Kundera defines idyll this way in *The Unbearable Lightness of Being:* " . . . an image . . . like a memory of Paradise" (295) or " . . . a looking back to Paradise" (296). But, Kundera's ultimate message is that the good old days cannot return because there never was an original, or a model to imitate. The concept of an original is only a disabled metaphor. The narrative, or history, had always already begun, and it changed a little each time in the telling, so now history is a story that never ends. What is myth, but a collection of stories endlessly retold, and Lyotard would add that all discourse is narrative, so really we live in an age when reason or truth is transformed into *mythos* (myth) and thus all history is myth (*Instructions paiennes* 28).

Many of Kundera's contemporaries in Czechoslovakia see him portraying Central Europe as "a Europe raped by Asia . . . a spiritual graveyard maintained by governments of forgetting," and his idea of history as an "inexhaustible store of cruel jokes" (Havel 83). For Havel, Kundera's history is a "deity capable of deceiving and destroying us, playing tricks on us," and thus real life is elsewhere, outside of history. Real life, for Kundera as well as for other post-modern theorists like Lyotard, is in myth, or in narration, or in interpretation.

In 1964, Kundera wrote *The Joke,* a cult book for the intelligentsia in Czechoslovakia, and the book that resulted in his expulsion from his homeland and emigration to France. This early novel seems to embody his later themes of history as myth and, at the same time, to provide the rationale for proclaiming Kundera as a modern humanist. The novel deals with folk culture and prehistory in an absurd environment. Ludvic, a clever university student, sends a post-card to his girlfriend (a passionate Stalinist), and as a joke says, "optimism is the opium of the people . . . long live Trotsky" (26). The result is his expulsion from the university and the Party, and years of labor in the mines. Years later, after a completely unsatisfactory life as a result of that one joke, he is in his hometown, and witnesses the legendary "Ride of the Kings," a folk tradition that will illustrate to him "our world of ever-accelerating forgetting." He writes:

> Suddenly I saw it all clearly. People willingly deceive themselves with a double false faith. They believe in eternal memory (of men, deeds, things) . . . and in rectification (of deeds, errors, sins, injustice). Both are shams. The truth lies at the opposite end of the scale: everything will be forgotten, and nothing will be rectified. All rectification will be taken over by oblivion. No one will rectify wrongs; all wrongs will be forgotten. (245)

While watching the "Ride of the Kings," however, Kundera's narrator (whose son was chosen to be this year's King in the parade) reflects on the origin of the legend of the King's Ride:

> Where did it come from and what does it mean? Does it perhaps date back to pagan times . . . The "Ride of the Kings" is a mysterious rite; no one knows what it signifies, what its message is . . . perhaps the Ride of Kings is beautiful to us at least partly because the message it was meant to communicate has long been lost, leaving the gestures, colors, and words to stand out all the more clearly. (221)

It is in Moravia, Kundera's ancestral land, where he:

> had the sensation of hearing verse in the most primitive sense of the word, the kind of verse I could never hear on the radio or on TV . . . it was a sublime and polyphonic music — each of the heralds declaimed his verse in a monotone, but each on his own individual note, so the voices combined willy-nilly into chords. (221)

This music of variation describes also Kundera's technique of theme building already noted.

Kundera's sense of myth (of history as myth), which his protagonist seems to find in his folk culture, is the key to his love of humanity. Perhaps he believes it is futile to seek to shape the future, or to recapture the past, but it is in these rare moments when his characters fall back beyond history into myth, that Kundera reveals his own nostalgia for human solidarity, some common past which is an amalgam of truth and legend. The narrator's thoughts, while playing the final folk concert after the "Ride of the Kings" is played out, are moving. He says, "I felt a long-forgotten sense of companionship come over me" (262). He and three friends are playing in a noisy cafe filling up with a young, boisterous audience; but, says the narrator:

> We managed to forget what was going on around us and create a magic circle of music; it was like being walled off from the drunks in a glass cabin at the bottom of the sea . . . I felt happy inside of the songs . . . where sorrow wasn't playful, laughter wasn't mocking, love wasn't laughable . . . where love is still love, pain, pain and values free from devastation. (265)

This a rare instance, among all of Kundera's novels, where the author describes a freedom from irony, where the author feels no irony, and this instance is in myth, in Kundera's rediscovery of his folk culture. This is Kundera's nostalgia, his own kitsch, his own way of forgetting history — through folk tradition, legend or myth. Predictably, however, he immediately counters with:

> I was equally aware that my home was not of this world . . . that everything we sang and played was only a memory, a monument, a recreation in images of something that no longer was, and I felt the firm ground of my homeland sinking under my feet, felt myself falling . . . into the depths where love is love and pain, pain, and I said to myself that my only real

> home was this descent, this searching eager fall, and I gave myself up to it, savoring the sensuous vertigo. (265)

Here is Kundera, the master of "epicurean accommodation"; he has chosen accommodation to an absurd world, not denial or revolt, and he is instantly a post-modern writer. For an instant, I think, we see what is the core of his attraction for modern readers, why he is not a nihilist, why he is not an ideologue. It is his method of accommodation to modern angst.

In his choice of accommodation, Kundera leaves room for the importance of the individual; while institutions and political systems may be absurd, individuals are not. In *The Unbearable Lightness of Being,* Kundera is constantly studying individual life, how concrete it is, how varied it is, how beautiful it can be. Most of his characters in this novel have no outside system of reference, so they must constantly make decisions. Human life is celebrated in this novel in all its chaotic progress, and, as Robert has described it, in all its existential contingency (45). The protagonist's life turns on coincidences; the very beauty of life, however, is in these coincidences.

The characters in this novel live in a non-tragic mode of fiction, in their own brand of twentieth-century folk culture. Kundera sees his characters as central European, representing the flip-side of European history, its outsiders, its victims. It is this historical disenchantment which is the source of their non-tragic character which "se moque de la grandeur et de la gloire" [mocks grandeur and glory] (Un occident kidnappé 15). In Kundera's post-Stalinist Central Europe there are few of the elements of high tragedy like grandeur, high status, or fatal flaw, so it is understandable that what is left is a sense of humor, a sense of humor which allows one to see other points of view, and to seek a measure of values on a human scale.[1] But Kundera also finds beauty in man's sense of discomfort in the modern ideological world. Fuentes explains that while "Central Europe took care to demonstrate that a man need not be an insect in order to be treated as such," there is, when one reads Kundera, a change in Kafka's scenario: "The cockroach

---

[1]Bruce Donahue in "Laughter and Ironic Humor" has highlighted the difference between a sense of humor which allows one to demystify one's myths, and thus become more human, and laughter — a malicious laughter which blinds one to other points of view.

R. B. Gill, in the previously-noted 1984 article in *Critique,* has differentiated between laughter and comedy, whereby laughter is healthier in our demonic modern world because, unlike traditional comedy, it provides no transformed world but, instead, "adjusts the psyche to an aberration in his world rather than attempting to change it" (90).

no longer thinks he knows; now he knows he thinks" (265). He suggests that even if the future has already taken place and it stinks, maybe the answer for Kundera is "an internal utopia," a real space of untouchable life (267). Herein may lie the core of his constant preoccupation with sex and love. Kundera wrote in *The Book of Laughter and Forgetting:*

> The symphony is a musical epic. We might compare it to a journey leading through the boundless reaches of the external world, on and on, farther and farther. Variations also constitute a journey, but not through the external world. You recall Pascal's pensee about how man lives between the abyss of the infinitely large and the infinitely small. The journey of the variation form leads to that second infinity, the infinity of internal variety concealed in all things. (164)

While there is nothing new in this approach to modern life, Kundera is fresh in his ability to see beauty in our very post-modern condition: the common folk, be he comrade, poet, peasant or professor, swimming in a disconnected world, uncertain of its past, of what is its real present, wallowing sometimes in irony, reveling in coincidence. It is Kafka sans insects, with flesh and blood characters in a modern communist society, striving for some sense of joy and vitality. His is neither the literature of incoherence, nor the fiction of ideology. He is capable of satirizing loss of memory, but still offering unlimited possibilities of choices to his characters. He talks about the "semantic hoax" by which the same word can be endowed with the opposite meaning, or with a meaning just a little off, the same successive approximations which he and Lyotard and Derrida use to describe communication in general. I suppose we are talking here about a metonymic and not a metaphoric relation (an associational and not an exact correspondence), and that it applies to Kundera's treatment of historic truth, meaning in language, and possibilities of knowing. Kundera's very ethical goal seems to be to "discover the yet unknown avenues that depart from history and lead us to realities we had hardly suspected" (Fuentes 267). What is pleasing about this goal is that it celebrates our very post-modern condition; instead of wallowing in the hopelessness of it all, it celebrates our very lack of connection to external codes, to institutions, and heralds the yet unknown possibilities for men — unconnected, demystified, and deconstructed. Kundera's (and Derrida's and Lyotard's) contribution might be as simple as the suggestion that the invariable is only one way of looking at things, that others do exist. Perhaps Kundera's folk culture offers not a collision with these post-modern forces, but an instance of beautiful accommodation.

WORKS CITED

Deleuze, Georges. *Nietzche et la philosophie*. Paris: Presses Universitaires de France, 1962. (See p. 72 for comments on 'Eternal Return.')

Derrida, Jacques. *L'écriture et la différence*. Paris: Seuil, 1967. Trans. Alan Bass. *Writing and Difference*. Chicago: U of Chicago P, 1978.

——. *La voix et le phénomène*. Paris: Presses Universitaires de France, 1967.

——. "Response to Anne McClintock and Rob Nixon." Trans. Peggy Kamuf. *Critical Inquiry* 13:1 (Autumn 1986): 155-170.

Descombes, Vincent. *Modern French Philosophy*. Trans. L. Scott-Fox and J. M. Harping. Cambridge: CUP, 1980.

Donahue, Bruce. "Laughter and Ironic Humor in Milan Kundera." *Studies in Modern Fiction* 25 (Winter 1984): 67-76.

Foucault, Michel. *L'archeologie du savoir*. Paris: 1969. Trans. *The Archeology of Knowledge*. A. M. Sheridan Smith. London: Tavistock, 1974.

Fuentes, Carlos. "The Other K." *Tri-Quarterly* 51 (Spring 1981): 256-267.

Gill, A. B. "Bargaining in Good Faith." *Critique* (Winter 1984): 77-91.

Havel, Vaclav. "Doing Without Utopias." Trans. G. Brair. *Times Literary Supplement*, Jan. 23, 1987: 81-83.

Kundera, Milan. *The Book of Laughter and Forgetting*. Trans. Michael Heim. New York: Knopf, 1981.

——. "Comedy is Everywhere." *Index on Censorship* 6 (November/December 1977).

——. *The Farewell Party*. Trans. Peter Kussi. New York: Knopf, 1976.

——. "Interview." *Le Monde* 23 (January 1976).

——. *The Joke*. Trans. Michael Heim. New York: Harper & Row, 1982.

——. *Laughable Loves*. Trans. Suzanne Rappaport. New York: Knopf, 1974.

——. *Life is Elsewhere*. Trans. Peter Kussi. New York: Knopf, 1974.

——. "Man Thinks, God Laughs." *New York Review of Books* 32 (June 13 1985): 111-112.

——. "Un occident kidnappé." *Le debat* 27 (November 1983): 3-22.

——. "Quelque part la derrière." *Le debat* 8 (January 1981): 50-63.

——. *The Unbearable Lightness of Being*. Trans. Michael Heim. New York: Harper and Row, 1984.

Lodge, David. "Milan Kundera and the Idea of Author in Modern Criticism." *Critical Quarterly* 26:1 & 2 (Spring 1984): 105-121.

Lyotard, Jean Francois. *Instructions paiennes*. Paris: Editions Galeles, 1977.

——. *The Post-Modern Condition: A Report on Knowledge*. Trans. G. Bennington and R. Massumi. Vol. 10 of *Theory and History of Literature*. Minneapolis: U of Minnesota P, 1984.

Porter, R. C. *Milan Kundera: A Voice from Central Europe*. Denmark: Arkona P, 1981.

Robert, Daniel. "L'après-histoire: 'le live du rire et de l'oublie' et 'l'insoutenable légèreté de l'être' de Milan Kundera." *Passage du temps, L'ordre de la Transition*. Jean Bessière. Paris: Presses Universitaires de France, 1985: 37-53.

Steiner, Peter. "Slavic Literary Studies Yesterday and Tomorrow." *Profession '87*. New York: Modern Language Association, 1987: 2-9.

Weiss, Jason. "An Interview With Milan Kundera." *New England Review and Breadloaf Quarterly* 8:3 (Spring 1986): 405-10.

RENATE GERULAITIS

Anatomy of a Bestseller: The Making of an Identity

Christine Brückner's Quin(d)t trilogy follows the fortunes and misfortunes of a Pomeranian noble family from World War I to the present. It belongs to the tradition of family novels as they are part of the German literary heritage, with Maximiliane von Quindt's life reflecting Germany's turbulent history of those years. The title of the first of the three novels, *Jauche und Levkojen (Liquid Manure and Gillyflowers)* is a Theodor Fontane quote and serves as a signal to the reader as well as a self-definition for both author and novel; this novel follows the family fortunes from World War I to 1945, when Maximiliane, the protagonist of all three, with her four children joins the great trek to the West while her grandparents commit suicide rather than leave the family estate. The world depicted in *Jauche und Levkojen* is patriarchal, hierarchical and whole; love of the soil and devotion to the fatherland inform the value system of the von Quindts, who will do anything to preserve their estate at Poenichen in Pomerania. This means above all making marriages that will guarantee the continuation of the line. *Nirgendwo ist Poenichen (Nowhere is Poenichen)* follows Maximiliane and her brood, now five, from the trials and tribulations of resettling in the West to Maximiliane's visit to Poenichen, now Polish, a visit that shows how irretrievable the loss of that bygone world is. This visit to the past liberates and emancipates Maximiliane. *Die Quints (The Quints),* finally, describes the lives of Maximiliane's children as adults and her own ultimate withdrawal to a *Heidekloster,* a Protestant convent for single women in the heath of Northern Germany. Together, the three novels show the impact of historical events on the lives of a family, and how these events force the female protagonist, a survivor, to gain true stature. The Nazi period and World War II each created very specific cultures; Maximiliane and her children needed to adapt in order to survive. Yet Maximiliane could never deny her aristocratic heritage. The culture of the landed nobility as transmitted to her by her grandfather was both a justification for, and the cause of, her unconventionality.

The question is: what makes these novels so popular? Wherein lies their appeal, besides the violence, sex and nostalgia for the past? The answer is that they reaffirm values and convictions held dear by millions of Germans but frowned upon by the guardians of high culture. These novels dare to advocate and admire that which is officially unacceptable.

This paper will investigate the schemata according to which the novels were written and which guaranteed their success. It will trace Maximilane's coming of age during the Nazi period; it will show her courage and ability to cope during her family's flight from Pomerania in 1945; it will show her ability to survive in the post-World War II period and its unique culture of homelessness and materialism. It will analyze the social and political subversion inherent in Maximiliane's value system and philosophy that inform these bestsellers and their precarious perching on the thin line separating works of high literary quality and works of popular culture. It is the aura of profundity with which the author manipulates what is, essentially, kitsch that explains her propulsion to preeminence. The most astounding result yielded by the analysis is a heroine who does not change. She is a law unto herself; historical calamities and personal hardships and deprivations do not touch her. Her aristocratic background has given her enough self-assurance to weather any storm with which her very unaristocratic life confronts her.

Maximiliane has been hailed as a modern Mother Courage, and the author as a feminist and a writer of high literary quality. This study will show that Maximiliane and the author are none of these.

Reviewers and Christine Brückner herself like to mention Theodor Fontane as one of the great influences on Brückner's work (Schmitt 1318). This claim is overreaching and applies to the subject matter only. Like Fontane, Brückner writes about the landed gentry in the East of what used to be Germany and is now part of Poland, and like Fontane she follows one family through three generations. But here the similarities end. In the execution of her theme, Brückner is of a different caliber, far closer to William von Simpsons's two family novels *Die Barrings (The Barrings) and Der Enkel (The Grandson),* 1937 and 1939 respectively, than she is to Fontane. While the latter places his characters squarely in situations where the closed culture of their world, the landed aristocracy, conflicts with, or even clashes with, historical and sociological change, Brückner's Maximiliane has no consciousness of her acculturation even though she lives through great historical and sociological upheavals. Since she does not change, there is presumed to be no need to articulate this acculturation. Yet Maximiliane acts in all three volumes just as the popular mind would expect a member of her class to act. As will be discussed below, this very lack of self-awareness in a heroine is a trademark of German popular culture. This tradition helps to explain Brückner's extraordinary popularity and her place among the so-called *Auflagen-Millionäre,* authors with printings of over a million copies (Schmitt 1317). Her millions of primarily female readers identify with Maximiliane von Quin(d)t, assuming that she is a female role model and archetype of the kind long popular in German culture, both popular and high, the earth mother, what is called in this trilogy the *Muttertier* (mother animal) (*J & L* 11). But instead of being an archetype, Maximiliane is a cultural stereotype, like the grandmothers in the movie *The Tin Drum* and the popular German TV series *Heimat.* Like them, Maximiliane is taciturn and nonreflective, a maternal type whose mere presence and actions rather than anything she says make her impact and reflect a cultural idol. We never know what she thinks, if she does think, or how she judges anything. What makes her a maternal idol is the fact that what she does seems right even though it very often isn't. But it always serves the purpose of protecting or defending her young. No male protagonist could act so consistently unethically and be so assured of the readers' admiration.

So far, the attention paid Christine Brückner and her work has been largely restricted to newspaper reviews except for a dissertation in comparative literature. In 1987 German television presented a program about her, a portrait of the author. Nothing could better illustrate her extraordinary popularity than this TV special. From the first publication of *Jauche und Levkojen (Liquid Manure and Gillyflowers)* in 1975 to October 31, 1987, the three volumes of the saga of Maximiliane von Quin(d)t had a total printing of 1,205,000 volumes (personal correspondence). A reviewer in the *Börsenblatt* called her " . . . einen der ganz großen Publikumserfolge der Nachkriegszeit . . . " (one of the truly great publishing successes of the post-war period [Schmitt 1317]). What is truly astonishing is that her readership seems to be age-neutral. When Christine Brückner holds public readings, those attending represent all age groups (personal correspondence). No formal analysis of her readership on the basis of sex is available, but my hunch is that women would be more interested in these novels than men.

Maximiliane as protagonist is axiomatic for the schemata on which the trilogy is based. She has been called a Mother Courage (Ross 104) and the trilogy a *Bildungsroman* (developmental novel [Martin 254]). Both are misnomers and testify to a misunderstanding of both the model and the equivalent. Mother Courage is not a lovable person; Maximiliane definitely is. Brecht's protagonist is a materialist, Brückner's definitely is not. "Das brauchen wir nicht," (we don't need that) is her standard reply at a time and in a country, Germany after World War II, when conspicuous consumption was at a premium. Therein lies the attraction for the reader: in a time of blatant materialism one nevertheless appreciates and values the opposite, a woman whose economic behavior conforms not with one's own actions but with one's notion of the good old days when higher ideals supposedly reigned. The trilogy is not a developmental novel because the characteristic ingredients are absent, to wit: cultural influences (von Wilpert) in the sense of high culture and the causal and educative effects of experiences on personal growth (Herd and Obermayer). On the contrary, Maximiliane is a static character who does not grow and remains unchanged by her experiences. Interestingly, one would have to claim withdrawal from the world as the cultural goal towards which the character is developing if one wanted to sustain that claim. Instead, it is more in the nature of a reward, a peace earned after an eventful and very hard life. This entry into a Protestant convent at the end is only one, even if the most spectacular, of the many episodes with a pronounced anti-modern attitude. This anti-modern attitude has been part of German culture, and specifically popular culture, for a very long time.

In 1977, upon publication of the second of the novels, a reviewer commented that Brückner once more had successfully navigated a novel through the iron curtain that in West Germany separates novels of entertainment from art novels (Ross 104). The dissertation mentioned above also refers to the "high literary quality" (Martin 1) of these novels. To be sure, the panorama, both historical and geographical, is larger and more generous than is common in popular fiction. In particular, however, it is the note of irony that hovers over these novels which sets them apart from most popular fiction. Irony, however, serves several purposes: it allows one to make statements without committing oneself to them; it creates an aura of sophistication and erudition, and it permits Brückner to be the spokesperson for all sides to a question. As she herself said in the TV program, her Poenichen-trilogy was written from two perspectives: that of the refugees who fled the approaching Red Army at the end of World War II and that of those in Germany who did not have to flee but who had lived through the years of relentless bombing (*Frauengeschichten*). Both groups tended to view each other with resentment, suspicion and envy. Both groups, therefore, can read her and identify with its characters and situations; the novel itself does not have a point of view.

Brückner's favorite stylistic device is the use of aphorisms. They frequently lend a touch of irony to the narrative and create the impression of sophistication. The speech of cultured Germans is always interwoven with quotations from the classics or the Bible, often slightly changed to fit a particular context but still clearly recognizable. Maximiliane's grandfather, the old baron, peppered his speech with aphorisms, so-called *Quindt-Essenzen* (the word play works in both English and German), whose function was to express meaning that was not shown but needed to be explained. As Maximiliane grows older, she develops the same habits of speech, but instead of *Quindt-Essenzen* she produces *Maximen:* "words are no worse than deeds," (*J & L* 129); "A fool in Christ is still better than a fool in Hitler," (*J & K* 189) or "What you don't say can't be misunderstood," (*J & L* 224) are *Quindt-Essenzen*. The maxims tend to be more practical. "You don't have to do everything you could do" (*Q* 132); "It's in the nature of human beings that they don't stumble over a mountain but over an ant heap" (*Q* 173); or "You can do more than pass on a tradition . . . you can create new ones" (*Q* 209). These few samples may stand for the many; they are on every page and create the philosophical patina of these novels. The reader would recognize the *Quindt-Essenzen* and the *Maximen* for what they are supposed to be: a sign of an upper-class upbringing. Being educated and cultured is a sign of class and a goal espoused by both high and popular culture in Germany.

In the TV interview mentioned above, Christine Brückner says that she had chosen the landed nobility for her characters because they were hit hardest of all the refugees created by World War II (*Frauengeschichten*). They had lost their estates in the Eastern parts of what was then Germany and with this loss came the loss of status and, consequently, of identity. Former ladies of the manor found themselves working in menial jobs in the West, nobody according them the respect to which they were used. Maximiliane finds herself in this position. As a refugee she and her children are barely tolerated and treated with contempt by some of the West Germans they encounter. But, being a true aristocrat in upbringing, Maximiliane remains who she is; she does not need others to confirm her. Brückner's readers would recognize, and approve of, this trait.

The nobility is a favorite subject of popular culture and fiction in Germany. Popular magazines report on the comings and goings of the members of both domestic and foreign aristocratic families in great detail and regularly. Nothing could better explain the dynamics of these novels that are everything to everyone, in which every point of view and its opposite hold sway. Thus the preponderance of stereotypes, a few of which will be discussed in the following.

The first of these is the old juxtaposition of country vs. city, a cultural stereotype that became a determining factor in Maximiliane's upbringing. Her father had married a city girl who never felt at home in Poenichen and who, upon being widowed in World War I, returned to Berlin, abandoning her infant daughter to her in-laws. In turn, Maximiliane married a man from Königsberg, a rabid Nazi who used Maximiliane as a brood mare to populate the East and whose fanaticism never abated. He spent his time in Berlin and came to Poenichen rarely and then only to copulate. The few Nazis in Poenichen were relatively harmless; it was in Berlin that real atrocities took place: the son of the baron's valet was arrested there and sent to the Oranienburg concentration camp; Maximiliane's mother, who had married a Jewish psychiatrist, was persecuted there. In both cases the old von Quindt came to the rescue. He allowed the former concentration camp inmate to live on the estate, and he gave his daughter-in-law Vera the financial means to leave Germany. As the admirable protagonist of the first of the three novels, it is imperative that Herr von Quindt be an anti-Nazi. His collaboration with the Nazis and the motives for this collaboration will be discussed later. The old baron's decision in the 1930s to shun the capital as much as possible is an illustration of the anti-urban and pro-country attitude that permeates the entire trilogy. This happens early in the saga (*J & L* 149). Maximiliane's retirement to a convent in the heath of Northern Germany comes at the close, these two episodes serving as a frame to the trilogy.

The juxtaposition of urban life and values vs. rural ones has a long tradition in German popular culture. The German movie industry still produces large numbers of films depicting an idyllic country or mountain village into which an intruder, a representative of the urban culture, brings destruction and unrest and who is destroyed in the end so that the village can resume its life as it was before. Romances, too, still exploit the theme of country vs. city. Nothing illustrates this deeply imbedded cultural attitude better than the 1985 13-part TV series, *Heimat* (*Home*) made in response to the American TV series *Holocaust*. It traces the history of a farming family, again for three generations, in a remote part of Germany from the beginning of the Nazi period to the present. In the village the effects of fascism are quite harmless in contrast to the nearby cities where we are shown a much more brutal side. In addition to the dichotomy of country versus city, there is a rather strong and long-standing antipathy towards modernity and machines mentioned above and discussed in more detail later.

Another stereotype encountered repeatedly refers to the influence of race, a vague belief in racial and class determinism, not just in looks but also in character, temperament, and attitudes. Thus Edda, the child fathered illegitimately by Maximiliane's husband but brought up by Maximiliane, is a true and rather crude materialist reflecting her natural mother's petit-bourgeois background, not Maximiliane's aristocratic and therefore generous nature. Edda is the only one of the children who cries from hunger, supposedly typical for one of her mother's class. None of the truly aristocratic children do. While Edda's older half-siblings go to college because they want an education, she is intent on making money. Mirka, born because Maximiliane had been raped by a Kirgizian, not only has the facial features that will make her a top model later in life, she also has the stoic and passive nature attributed to that race. Class and race seem inextricably fused in these novels and act as causal explanations for human behavior.

Maximiliane is a protagonist who shares with female protagonists in German literature since the eighteenth century a seemingly typical taciturnity (Gerulaitis 401-12). As mentioned above, we never find out what Maximiliane is thinking; she speaks sparingly and is never judgmental. She never chides her juvenile-delinquent son who is dispatched from the scene through a fatal automobile accident in a timely fashion before he can become a full-fledged criminal. An envious dependent who had been in charge of the exodus from Poenichen in 1945 and who had abandoned Maximiliane and her small children one fine morning with most of the Poenichen possessions never hears an accusatory word.

Maximiliane certainly was not predestined for her role in life; motherhood, the war and circumstances forced her into a heroic mold. She becomes a figure larger than life: she gets herself and her children through the trials of the flight to the West; she makes it possible that they survive the hunger and rubble years; when all her children have grown up and left home, she becomes the receptionist of a hotel to which her aristocratic name lends class; and finally she withdraws to the serene life of a canoness, a member of a Protestant convent. Maximiliane accomplishes all that primarily, but not exclusively, by hard work and perseverance. She also uses stealth, deception, and forgery, all without the slightest doubt as to the rightness of her course. She is a law unto herself, in fact above the law. She does whatever seems to be in the best interest of her children or herself; right and wrong seem irrelevant. Three examples may stand for many: she identifies herself as the widow of a high Nazi official or a war widow depending on the political orientation of her vis-à-vis. When her husband's daughter Edda needs a birth certificate attesting to an impeccable aristocratic lineage, Maximiliane forges the certificate. And finally, she gets accepted into the convent on the assumption that she is an unmarried elderly lady. Consequently her children have to turn into nieces and nephews when they visit her. In other words, Maximiliane perpetuates the myth and caters to the admiration of the singular person who is a law unto her/himself and who must be measured with a different yardstick than ordinary people. This concept is deeply imbedded in German culture, from the heroes of medieval epics to Goethe's Faust to some of Thomas Mann's characters.

The three novels hover precariously between feminism and anti-feminism in attitude. Edda, this illegitimate daughter of a petit-bourgeois mother, is the best example of an emancipated woman, weighed down with all the clichés of the past: she is efficient but brusque; she is successful but greedy; her children use bad language. But worst of all, her efficiency has emasculated her husband who — consequently — becomes an alcoholic! Even the children are shown defending their father against the mother's attacks on him; one can hardly imagine a more damning piece of evidence against the kind of woman Edda supposedly represents.

The woman who most closely resembles what seems to be the ideal woman in these novels is Inga Brandes, the new owner of the hotel in which Maximiliane works. Maximiliane calls her her *Wahltochter* (daughter of choice [i.e., the daughter she would have chosen] *Q* 207). Who is this woman? She has a degree in hotel management and is every bit as efficient and successful as Edda, but her personality is not brittle; she is warm and feminine and does not compete with her husband whom she adores. She loves children and animals; in other words a conventional type in a conventional woman's profession, but modernized to include an academic degree.

One rather interesting and revealing opinion referred to several times in the course of these novels concerns the role of women in wartime and bears dealing with in some detail. Maximiliane's oldest son, Joachim, is trying desperately to understand his fanatical father whom he does not even remember. In his search for the memory of his father, Joachim withdraws to a cottage in Sweden in order to read and do research on the historical time in which his father lived so that he could write a biography of him. He hoped this would make his father real to him:

> Against his will he developed something like compassion and understanding for the accused during this time of research. The distance grew smaller; in the same way the distance to his mother grew, to all women, whose naïveté and good-naturedness seemed to him unintelligible, even criminal. They had prevented nothing, had always only been intent on saving what could be saved. For a while it looked as if his book would become an accusation against women, who collaborated, who made war possible because they jumped into the breach and only waited to take over the position of the men but later had less guilt to carry. He could not remember having seen women among the defendants at the Nuremberg war crimes trials. (*Q* 36).

The above paragraph is paradigmatic for the opinions expressed in the trilogy and the way they are expressed. On the one hand, the enormous compliment to women for their power over war and peace and for their competence; on the other, the imputation of lowly motives for that competence (i.e., they only wanted to usurp men's places, and then shirked the responsibility for their actions). Thus, the damning cancels the praise, and we are left with nothing.

Joachim's father, who, in fact, was a caricature of a Nazi, elicits sympathy and understanding in his son. Joachim, the most loveable of Maximiliane's children, the only one with whom her relationship is free of tension, whom the reader certainly finds admirable, comes to that conclusion by studying the context in which his father lived. To understand is to forgive. Joachim then burns all his books about Nazism and World War II as well as the photographs showing his father with Hitler (*Q* 110). An era and its demons have been laid to rest, a very reassuring solution for the reader, particularly the German reader over 55.

The groundwork had been laid. The old baron was an anti-Nazi, as mentioned above. Nevertheless, he voted for the NSDAP. But the reader is shown that he had no choice; it wasn't personal cowardice, it was the responsibility for Poenichen (*Q* 153). The baron was quoted as saying, "You have to be able to afford a conviction" (*Q* 148), a sentiment that gets everyone off the hook. It is implied also that only the golden party book of Maximiliane's husband protected the estate. Maximiliane had joined the Nazi girls' organization, loved the parades and mindlessly sang the songs. When her mother gained notoriety in Berlin for being married to a Jew, Maximiliane denied knowing her, and she did that in Hermannswerder, the Pietist boarding school she attended. Maximiliane knew she would be expelled otherwise. It should be quite obvious that the impeccable credentials of an institution founded in Count Zinsendorf's name guarantee the omnipresence of Nazism as well as the need to protect all institutions, even religious ones, against the possible reprisals by the regime. In comparison, personal membership and mild, harmless participation seem less serious. Therein lies absolution for the readership.

At the end of the trilogy, Maximiliane's favorite child, her son Joachim, becomes a member of parliament. He was a published author, a poet, married to Inga, the perfect woman. The subtext of this young politician whom the reader is supposed to admire and approve of is quite subversive. During his first speech on the campaign trail he describes himself as being neither a parliamentarian nor a member of the extra-parliamentary opposition (*Q* 148). In an interview he speaks of himself as above or between the parties, claiming that a commitment to a political party is a voluntary putting on of blinders, clearly undesirable (*Q* 144). In other words, like his maternal grandfather before him and like his mother, Joachim trades on his personality as a guarantor of his honest convictions (*Q* 148). I would suggest that this negative attitude toward party politics and politicians is widespread and thus reflects reader attitudes as do a certain disdain for those who play by the rules and the admiration for those who are a law unto themselves. Nevertheless, Joachim not only seeks a seat in parliament, he is elected, so that as in previous examples the political message has something for everyone, democrat and anti-democrat alike.

Equally subversive is the juxtaposition of fact and meaning. As hotel receptionist, Maximiliane was wont to write quotes on the menus like watchwords, but disregarded their source or accuracy. A librarian once corrected them and cited their attributions, with the following result, "The sentence had gained in accuracy but not in intelligibility" (*Q* 38). It is a cheap shot because it juxtaposes accuracy and intelligibility as if they were mutually exclusive. When Joachim begins the search for his father, we read, " . . . [he] had acquired some standard works about World War II; his library was not large; *he wanted to preserve his naïveté* as much as possible" (*Q* 35; emphasis added). These two examples illustrate once more the disdain for rules. Maximiliane, like her favorite son later, sees herself as above the petty rules and regulations binding other people. By virtue of her personality, she is free of ordinary concerns. It isn't that she articulates this belief. She has it as her birthright but is unaware of it. Her identification with those whom the culture will permit to act out these attitudes is self-understood.

The attraction of Christine Brückner's trilogy lies in her catering to certain values deeply imbedded in German mass culture: in politics personality is more important than and above affiliation — the name of Bismarck accompanies the plot like a leitmotif; factual information is of limited use; not everyone is subject to the law; feminism needs sweetening with traditional femininity; feeling and instinct are superior to ratiocination. An anti-modern and anti-technology attitude permeates all three novels. In the execution, too, we find the typical characteristics of a bestseller: overdrawn characters, sentimentality, avoidance of controversy by supporting at least two sides of every question. Besides, there is the fact of the nobility and the occasional snobbery that permits. The many literary and cultural allusions that are carefully identified when they are not obvious can only serve as veneer and cannot disguise the nature of the trilogy. In Maximiliane von Quindt, Christine Brückner has created a character formed by four distinct and different cultures: the landed nobility in Pomerania, the Nazi era, World War II, and the so-called rubble years. Though Maximiliane could not have developed in the specific way she did at any other time, Brückner endows her with qualities reflecting cultural values held dear by large numbers of Germans, values that are part both of high and popular culture. Consequently, readers see themselves mirrored in their feelings and in their failings, they identify and feel exonerated regardless of their persuasion. The author, who craves harmony and abhors destruction and confrontation (*Frauengeschichten*) correctly assumes that large numbers of readers do too. The sales statistics bear her out.

WORKS CITED

Brückner, Christine. *Jauche und Levkojen*. Ullstein Buch 20077. Frankfurt/Main: Ullstein Verlag. 1980. Abbreviated in the text as *J & L*. All translations are mine.

Brückner, Christine. *Die Quints*. Frankfurt/Main: Ullstein Verlag. 1985. Abbreviated in the text as *Q*. All translations are mine.

"Christine Brückner." Dir. Konstantin Pauly. *Frauengeschichten*. ARD and Radio Bremen. 8 Sept. 1987.

Gerulaitis, Renate. "Gretchen's Fickle Lovers." *Michigan Academician* XV (1983): 401-12.

Herd, E. W., and August Obermayer, eds. *A Glossary of German Literary Terms*. Otago German Studies 2. Dunedin, New Zealand: University of Otago. 1983.

Kröners Taschenbuchausgabe 231. Stuttgart: Alfred Kröner Verlag, 1959.

Martin, Elaine. "Uncommon Women and the Common Experience: Fiction of Four Contemporary French and German Women Writers." Diss. Indiana University, 1981.

Ross, Werner. "Eine charmante Mutter Courage. Christine Brückners zweiter Poenichen-Roman." *Süddeutsche Zeitung* 22-23 Oct. 1977: 104.

Schmitt, W. Christian. "Auflagen-Millionäre — zu Besuch bei den Königen der Backlist." *Börsenblatt* 15 May 1984: 1317f.

Verlag Ullstein GmbH. 9 Nov. 1987. Personal correspondence.

Von Wilpert, Gero. *Sachwörterbuch der deutschen Literatur*.

MAX E. NOORDHOORN

Wilhelm Busch's *Max und Moritz:* A German Tale of Innocence and Experience

Wilhelm Busch's *Max und Moritz,* subtitled *The Story of Two Rascals in Seven Pranks,*[1] has since its publication in 1865 not merely become the most popular children's book in Germany but ranks high on the all-time list of German books translated in other languages, following only Goethe's *Faust,* Marx's *Das Kapital,* and some of Grimm's *Fairy Tales.*[2] Before proceding to an analysis of the work, a brief background sketch of the children's literature popular at the time of its inception and of Busch's work up to this time seems to be appropriate.

From the mid-nineteenth century on, German children's literature was dominated by the middle-class picture book which initially attempted to portray the middle-class world in a fairly realistic manner but gradually came to depict a

---

[1]I have only listed the major critical editions of Busch's works used here, since the German copyright expired in 1959 and too many editions of individual works have appeared to be mentioned. Wilhelm Busch, *Gesamtausgabe*, ed. Friedrich Bohne. 4 vols (Wiesbaden: Emil Vollmer, 1968). This is a facsimile edition of the historical-critical edition published by the Standard-Verlag in Hamburg in 1959. *Max und Moritz* appears in vol. 1, 343-89; the notes detailing its history and Busch's letters about it appear in vol. 1, 578-79. This is the edition referred to in the paper. Wilhelm Busch, *Sämtliche Werke*, ed. Otte Noldeke. 8 vols. Munich: Braun & Schneider, 1943 has *Max und Moritz* in vol. 3, 5-51. It reproduces 2 pages of the original M.S. in color, 9, 11. I also consulted an edition with colored illustrations as it was sold during Busch's lifetime: Wilhelm Busch, *Max und Moritz Eine Bubengeschichte in sieben Streichen,* 22nd edition. (Munich: Braun & Schneider, 188?). On the work's external changes see Ute Liebert, "120 Jahre Max und Moritz," *Wilhelm-Busch-Jahrbuch,* 1985, 19-26. The subtitle is translated by Roome in Wilhelm Busch, *Max and Maurice: The Story of Two Rascals in Seven Pranks,* tr. Walter Roome, (Montreal: Mansfield Book Mart, 1961). I preferred the English edition of Arndt which features a very good introduction: *The Genius of Wilhelm Busch: Comedy of Frustration,* ed. and tr. Walter Arndt (Berkeley: U of California P, 1982). *Max and Moritz* appears on 25-35.

[2]Manfred Görlach, "Literatur zu Wilhelm Busch," *Wilhelm-Busch-Jahrbuch,* 1985, 68-75, see 69. This journal is published by the Wilhelm-Busch-Gesellschaft, and lists periodically all articles and bibliographies on Busch. It will hereafter be referred to as *Jahrbuch.* By the same author see also "Bibliographie der Max-und-Moritz-Übersetzungen (Stand: November 1981)," *Jahrbuch,* 1981, 28-40 and "Bibliographie aller Wilhelm Busch gewidmeten Beiträge in den Mitteilungen und Jahrbüchern der Wilhelm-Busch-Gesellschaft (seit 1931)," *Jahrbuch,* 1981, 41-69. Walter Pape, *Wilhelm Busch* (Stuttgart: Metzler, 1977) has a select bibliography of *Max und Moritz,* 35-38.

world which became ever more idyllic, and ultimately presented a rather narrow and highly idealized section of reality. Identification of the readers with the characters and values portrayed seemed to be implied in these works with their conscious depiction of everyday life with their pronounced anecdotal, prettifying and illustrative tendency. Central to these books was the peaceful and contemplative nature of German middle-class existence. Childhood was seen as a realm of cheerfulness and serenity. The world of the child was meant to mirror the great outside world but was filled with happiness and freedom from care. Thus childhood was perceived as representing a paradisaical human condition and all things serious and problematical were kept out of this utopia that was deemed to be real. Illustrations showing children, adults and tame animals as role models played an important role and contributed to the prettified image of the middle-class depicted. In reality, however, the picture books contain a rather narrow slice of reality and it is doubtful whether the reality after 1850 is really portrayed in texts and pictures (Doderer, "Das bürgerliche Bilderbuch," 189-215). Ironically, this genre art had probably come into being as a reaction to the idealization, stylization and symbolization of nature and the environment of the Romantic poetic picture book which became popular after 1840, yet never achieved the popularity of the middle-class picture book (*Ibid.*, 190). The poetic picture book conceived of the child as a symbol of naievete and innocence, and the great Romantic heritage of fairy-tale, folk poetry and medieval epic materials were celebrated in word and picture to appeal to the imaginative faculties of the child (Doderer, "Das Poetische Bilderbuch," 99-103). Although no sharp distinction was made between the middle-class and poetic picture books, Doderer sees the latter as tending to poeticize the world and as being more literary in character whereas the former laid claim to portraying reality more closely. As such the middle-class picture books were reflections of a definite way of thinking aimed at the self-portrayal of bourgeois ideas in a particularly tangible and pure form ("Das bürgerliche Bilderbuch," 183).

Yet, no matter how much the middle-class and romantic-poetic books dominated the market, there were some works, determined by a rational and anti-sentimental caricatural style which were enormously successful. The two major representatives of this trend were Heinrich Hoffmann and Wilhelm Busch. The former is known for the second most popular children's book in German,

Struwwelpeter (1845), aimed at three to six year olds, which became so popular that it led to a whole genre called "Struwwelpetriade." The stories are short, self-contained narrative structures in which pictures and verse make the morals abundantly clear. The purposely flat and amateurish outline technique of drawing, the avoidance of elaborate description and explanation, and the restriction to only rendering the most significant story line moments allow even the child who cannot read to follow the story. Mistakes by children often leading to dire consequences are depicted; the endings of the stories often contain a surprising and witty turn which remove them from the child's everyday experience and move it into the sphere of the unrealistic. The author wanted to evoke fairy tale like, gruesome, exaggerated mental images. He equated the Germanic child with the Germanic nation from whose education and consciousness, he claimed, not even the educators of the nation could eradicate the stories of Little Red Riding Hood being swallowed by the wolf or of Snow White being poisoned by her wicked stepmother (Müller 141-58). Thus his own tale of "Suppenkaspar" shows in a few pictures how Kaspar, a robust little boy, turns into an emaciated stick of a boy and dies — all within the space of several days — because of his obstinate refusal to eat his soup. Hoffmann uses caricature and grotesque distortion to explain the existing Biedermeier catalog of virtues such as obedience, orderliness, cleanliness, and consideration of others. His stories are visible proof that bad behavior fails to achieve anything and may indeed be dangerous (Doderer, "Das bürgerliche Bilderbuch," 219).

Only the first of Busch's larger picture stories, *Max und Moritz,* attained world stature and like Struwwelpeter tells a story in picture and verse with consistent action and its consequences, thereby revealing a didactic background and letting the reader recognize in grotesque distortion a moral or the ridiculing of an apparent moral. Doderer finds that Busch criticizes society in a fairly indirect manner, "per negationem" as it were, by discovering the sympathetic and alluring in what middle-class society deems malicious behavior, and by having his audience take pleasure in the destruction of that safe world which the middle-class picture book idealized and protected (*Ibid.,* 219-23).

Wilhelm Busch got his start as illustrator and writer by publishing his first contributions in the *Fliegende Blätter (Flying Leaves)* which were pictorial strips, appearing with or without a text. These strips can be traced back to the thirteenth century and reached their zenith in the nineteenth. The most significant production center was Munich where the company of Braun and Schneider published the famous *Fliegende Blätter* from 1844 on and the series *Münchener Bilderbogen* from 1849 till 1898. The quality of these popular strips was of an unusually high nature since Munich boasted of an extraordinary number of well-known artists who used the wood engraving process to produce strips which could be had in black and white or colored versions, and could be bound together to create continuing series. The majority of the strips, aimed at the middle-class audience depicted harmonious idylls and displayed a stylization similar to that encountered in the middle-class picture books. The cheerful entertaining strips and stories — among them 50 strips by Busch — were very popular and apparently were a draw for the lower classes as well (Baumgärtner 67-72, 78-84).

Folksong, fairy tale and legend which Busch collected served, as he himself mentioned, as an inspiration for his works (*Briefe* 1: 265-66). In this he seems to have to have continued the German and European tradition begun by Herder during the Storm-und-Stress era, continued by Goethe, until it reached its popular high point during German Romanticism which brought forth the seminal collections of German folksongs by Arnim and Brentano, and of fairy tales by the brothers Grimm which in turn culminated in the creation of the great Romantic Art folksongs and fairy tales. It is likely that Busch too yearned for the supposed German values of sincerity of emotion, honesty, loyalty and true faith and their fortright and naive expression in these traditional literary forms. And perhaps he turned to collecting them for the same reasons as had his predecessors: the impossibility for the educated classes to participate in a meaningful way in public and political life which caused them to resort to academic and cultural pursuits as an outlet for their intellectual and creative impulses (Korff, 4: 152-72). But, as Lotzke remarks, Busch deviates in his own work from a mere recreation of traditional forms by injecting heterogeneous elements such as rationalistic explanations, realistic descriptive details, and a level of style and sophistication into his works which ultimately lead to the perception of alienation and the creation of the grotesque. In this interpretation, Lotze follows Wolfgang Kayser's lead who sees the essence of the grotesque as "the estranged world," and as "a play with the absurd." This characteristic is particularly obvious in the objectification of human beings, e.g., the headless skater in "Der harte Winter" who gets a job carrying boards where his head doesn't interfere or poor Peter in "Eispeter" who melts into a puddle, is spooned into a jug labeled with his name and three crosses, and stored in the pantry between the cheese and the pickles.[3] Another related, alienating and recurring theme in Busch's works is that of "die Tücke des Objekts" (the malice of the inanimate object) as Friedrich Theodor Vischer called it, where the animosity, inherent in objects — the effect of evil spirits inhabiting all objects — is prominently featured. Lotze views both Vischer and Busch as employing laughter to cope with the threat posed by man's hostile and irrational environment and therefore their works represent Kayser's final interpretation of the grotesque: "an attempt to invoke and subdue the demonic aspects of the world."[4]

These deviations seem to represent a way of coping with a world in which the much vaunted harmony and simplicity, originally perceived by many Romantic writers, were no longer seen to prevail, and they might well be indicative of a deep pessimism which quite unexpectedly and incongruously is expressed in a humorous way by its author in works which at first glance seem to be inappropriate vehicles for the expression of social criticism and philosophic doubt: picture books ostensibly written for the delectation and edification of German children.
Busch's pictorial narratives achieve their peculiarly individual effect through image and verse and the interplay of both. The former, dependent on the woodcut technique, evolved between 1858 and 1864 into what the famed cartoonist Thomas Theodor Heine called "a shorthand of graphic representation" (34-37) which distilled the essence of form and motion into bold lines, while suppressing three-dimensional representation, light and shadow, and background particulars. Novotny sees movement as the essence of the pictures which is brought about by exaggeration and modification of reality, particularly of gesture, proportion and perspective. He also regards the outline drawing technique as contributing to the super-plasticity of Busch's figures which combine both the naturalistic and the fantastic (29-49). Glockner defines Busch's technique as the "paradoxical combination of extreme realism and extreme abstraction" (15). Thus it is not surprising that this unusual mixture leads to the perceiver taking distance from

[3]Dieter P. Lotze, *Wilhelm Busch* (Boston: Twayne, 1979) 22-25. See also Wolfgang Kayser, *Das Groteske in Malerei und Dichtung* (Munich: Rowohlt, 1960) and by the same author *Wilhelm Buschs grotesker Humor* (Göttingen: Vandenhoeck & Ruprecht, 1958).

[4]Lotze, 25-26. For the discussion of *Max und Moritz*, see 42-49. Rudolph Dirk's *Katzenjammer Kids* were patterned after Busch and first appeared in 1897, see Lotze 48-49.

that which is depicted. Busch himself was very much aware of this in his observation that laughter is "an expression of relative comfort," and that he used only "Phantasiehanseln" ("imaginary Jacks") which could be set up depending on one's needs to say and do what one wanted them to do. He continues by stating that such "Konturwesen" ("outline beings") can easily be freed from the law of gravity and especially if they are not beautiful, can suffer greatly before we feel any pain. One may look at the objects and float in "comfortable self-assurance above the sufferings of the world" (4: 210).

A similar means of creating distance may be observed in the verses accompanying the majority of Busch's pictorial stories. Rhymed couplets in iambic and trochaic meter predominate. Characteristic of Busch's verse is the "technique of disillusionment" (Lotze 38-41) which employs many of the same means Heinrich Heine had used such as the juxtaposition of apparently incongruous elements, the use of impure rhymes, vernacular and colloquial expressions and foreign words. This planned technique of incongruity is indicative of an ironic stance which on the one hand may be employed to impart certain moral values and on the other hand may indicate the absence of a moral absolute (Noordhoorn 90-97, 120-130, 149-151). In this respect Busch's use of rhyme, particularly of rhymed couplets, plays the greatest role. It is dependent upon similarity or identity of sound and discrepancy of meaning (i.e., on a separation of form and content). Marxer points to the primacy of rhyme, its obtrusiveness and lack of mystery which is compounded by a rhythm corresponding largely to the alternating meter and the paratactic nature of the verses which match the linear progression of the action. Enjambment, split and broken rhymes, creation of new onomatopoetic words to suggest sounds or motion often lead to rhyme becoming mere sound and losing its inner substance. The rhyme's resulting hallowness and its disintegration into external and internal components (i.e., sound versus thought) lead to form and content going in opposite ways (71-105). Therefore image and word are often deceptive in not being what they purport to be but may point in contrary directions. Thus the supposedly solid, upright and honorable pillars of society depicted by Busch may turn out in fact to be hypocritical, egotistic and self-serving beings and the moral standards of the society that they claim to uphold may merely be the means of protecting the power and maintaining the status quo of a group which in its limited sphere of influence will brook no opposition.

It is precisely this combination and interplay of visual and verbal components that create the unique artistic style, oft imitated but never equaled, which Wilhelm Busch achieves so seemingly effortlessly in his picture books. Although each component is a distinct entity, Arndt views the "subtler, and essential function of either" as being "one of a pair of live wires between which comic-grotesque discharges occur. Picture and verse exist in mutual tension, they contrapuntally confront and mock, rather than complement one another" (10).

The "children's epic" *Max und Moritz* is framed by a cautionary preface showing a cheerful picture of the "bad children," and a summarizing conclusion without an illustration (1: 343, 389). The entire work is written in emphatically trochaic rhymed couplets with four stresses to a line, an irregular alternation of masculine and feminine endings, and a frequent use of enjambment. There is no symmetric division of text and pictures; many pictures are accompanied by one couplet, some by a longer series of verses and the final illustration, showing the behinds of ducks who have devoured the remnants of Max and Moritz, is telling enough to need no verse commentary.

The work was apparently taken at face value, in the tradition of the Struwwelpeter books, as a warning to children to desist from being bad.[5] Yet the apparent innocence and straightforwardness of the cautionary tale reveal an irony of expression and intent which indicates an attitude critical of the petit bourgeois values it professes to uphold. Thus our tale of seeming innocence — where crime is punished and good triumphs over evil — may because of the distortion of word and picture be read simultaneously as a tale of disillusionment, of mundane experience. The sanctity of property, the respect for adults, and above all the observance of social custom, law and order which the work seems to affirm are placed into question when this society has to resort to extreme means of suppression to cope with its mischief makers.

The movement at both levels is apparent from the very beginning, the preface, which programmatically contains the tale's development in a nutshell. The morally indignant tone combined with the false bathos of the anticipated end of our heroes:

---

[5]Walter Lampe, "Wilhelm Busch und das Recht," *Jahrbuch*, 1956, 44-59 sees Busch as the spokesman for the forces of deterrence. Lotze speaks about how Busch was misunderstood, 47; Gert Ueding, *Wilhelm Busch: Das 19. Jahrhundert en miniature* (Frankfurt am Main: Insel, 1977) talks about the traditional formulas in preface and conclusion which Busch meant ironically, 75-76.

Aber wehe, wehe, wehe!	But woe, woe, woe!
Wenn ich auf das Ende sehe!! (1,343)	When I foresee the end!!

are contrasted with the disappointing list of so called "evil deeds" and the picture of the cheerfully smiling faces of the youngsters — perhaps intent on doing mischief — and so indicate the author's ironic intent. It seems likely that the two exclamation marks anticipate the gruesome end of our dynamic duo.

The seven pranks are paratactically arranged. Each is clearly labeled by ordinal numbers with the seventh prank being identified as the "Last Prank." Each features a short introduction and — but for the final one — ends with the same refrain, indicating its end and pointing to the next one:

Dieses war der erste Streich,	And was this the last trick? Wrong!
Doch der zweite folgt sogleich. (1,349)	For the second won't be long. (Arndt 26)

Each prank shows a linear development which traces the confrontation of the evildoers and their victims. The entire tale — as is common in the larger picture tales — depicts episodes from the life of its heroes which often ends, as it does here, with a violent and bizarre demise.

The preface moves from a general to a specific introduction of "wicked children," before listing their misdeeds, ranging from mocking (their elders') wise teachings, teasing people, and torturing animals to stealing fruit in preference to being good and sitting still in church or school. Their coming to a bad end is anticipated and serves as the justification for depicting their crimes in picture and verse. The amusing illustrations coupled with the droll verse all hammering home the moral that evil tricks, disrespect for one's elders and betters, and failure to conform can only lead to a bad end was patently obvious.

The first four of the seven pranks — 1. The tricking of widow Bolte's three hens and rooster into hanging themselves, 2. the theft of the fried birds, 3. the taunting of tailor Böck (i.e., Billygoat) by imitating a goat's bleating and causing him to fall into the water by sawing the plank across it, and 4. the explosion of teacher Lämpel's (i.e., Little Light) pipe when he lights it — show the boys in a dominantly aggressive position. The tide, however, begins to turn from the fifth adventure on with the placing of the June bugs in Uncle Fritz's bed; these are unceremoniously and brutally dispatched by him, enabling him to sleep in peace. The sixth prank where the boys are caught trying to steal pretzels, are encased in dough, baked in the oven, yet miraculously escape, leads to the last prank where they are caught cutting holes into grain sacks, unceremoniously bagged, dumped into the feeder slot and ground into feed for the miller's ducks.[6] The conclusion expresses the villagers' glee and self-righteousness in sarcastic tones by listing all victims' (and intended victims') reactions and ends the tale with the moral:

Kurz, im ganzen Dorf herum
Ging ein freudiges Gebrumm:
"Gott sei Dank! Nun ists' vorbei
Mit der Übeltäterei!!" (1,389)

That entire place, in short,
Buzzed with joy at the report
And they offered heartfelt thanks
For deliverance from pranks!

(Arndt 35)

This schematic and stereotypical outline is characteristic of Busch, and according to Bonati depicts interchangeable figures which move at a level of common drives, needs, and wishes indicative of a pre-individual state. Bonati sees the pictures as the primary expressive means, therefore they must clearly stress the action and thus are dominated by bodies and the suffering that befalls them or they inflict upon each other. Dialog is reduced to terse commands, emotionally charged outcries, assertive and entreating formulas, allowing no communication between the parties and thus less significant than the action of the illustrations. The generalizing introductions indicate the course of the plot which illustrates a concrete example and confirms the generally valid principle set forth there ("Schema," 50-51).

Throughout the entire struggle between the rascals and the representatives of the rural bourgeois society whose property and values are under attack, Busch makes us aware of certain discrepancies and disparities, not only in the inappropriate severity of punishment meted out to the boys and its matter-of-fact acceptance by the community, but above all in what the boys and the solid citizens seem to stand for. In reference to the former's "wickedness," Busch's letters to Maria Anderson, dealing with the nature of man, are constantly referred to. In them Busch speaks about the good and evil daemons in man of which the latter is the stronger and equated with the "urge to live." Busch states that "natural, unspoiled(?) man, thus particularly the child, must predominantly be wicked," in or-

[6] *Gesamtausgabe,* 1, 343-89. For a diagrammatic progression of the pranks see Yves Gilli, " 'Max und Moritz' de Busch: Contribution à une étude de texte." *Recherches en linguistique étrangère* (=*Annales littéraires de l'Université de Besançon*) 147 (1973): 95-116.

der to survive (*Briefe* 1:157). He relates this to Schopenhauer's "will to power" which he views as the primary, strong and wicked element in man's nature (*Ibid.*, 1:144). Ueding provides the most insightful account of the unacculturated child by tracing the development of the European conception of the child from Rousseau's innocent in *Emile* to the wicked savage of the Protestant Prussian era. In his reading, the troublemaker's vitality threatens the precarious order of a society based on dubiousness, sociopolitical docility, sexual repression and orderliness of thought and manner. Those factors and the subconscious envy of the rebellious spirit may explain the viciousness with which the troublemaker is squashed and the calm smugness with which his demise is accepted (25-95). It also seems to Ueding that *Max und Moritz* became so popular precisely because it opposed the vision of a nearly perfect children's world with its own specific view of a world which bore no similarity to the uniform and boring harmony imposed upon the former by adults striving for discipline and order. The theme of all Busch's picture books is characterized as the successful or unsuccessful social taming (*Dressur*) of children or animals. Life is seen as a circus with occupational accidents, reduced as if viewed through an inversed telescope to bearable and cheerful dimensions. *Max und Moritz* is the most famous instance of a failed attempt at socialization and chronicles the evil consequences that arise when the unruly oppose domestication. The tale, however, does have a cathartic effect on both author and reader for the suffering of life is reduced to a puppet play and brings about that releasing laughter with which one distances oneself from a devastating reality (*Ibid.*, 13-17).

The depiction of the boys is straightforwardly simple, shows no sentimentality or yearning for a childhood past, and stresses only the relentlessness with which Max and Moritz execute their pranks, striking out at the greatest weaknesses of the adults: their property, comfort and self-satisfaction. Huder, believing that dualism is a central principle of occidental art, sees this also embodied in Busch's being and work. For the interpretation of reality an assumption of duality is required since life is always a movement of two principles, e.g., light and dark, matter and spirit, etc. The embodiment of this principle is seen in the great number of pairs, be they lovers, friends or siblings appearing in literature, with the pronounced tendency for one member of the pair to dominate. To literature's unequal male pairs, Busch added a perfectly equal villainous pair of unshakable solidarity, a fact emphasized by the alliteration of their names. Although not natural twins they are twins of stout-hearted malice, unified in thought and action, convinced of the rightness of their ideas, characterized by a total lack of bad conscience, and acting only out of a pre-moral orthodoxy to wage a class-struggle of the haves against the have-nots on the village level.[7] The portrayal of the other characters shows Busch's irony at work. None of these figures is appealing, either physically or by virtue of the characteristics ascribed to them. The "mild and tender" widow Bolte who raises hens for their eggs, meat and feathers expresses her agony upon seeing them strung up as follows:

"Fließet aus dem Aug', ihr Tränen!	"Flow, my tears, then, scoring, burning,
All mein Hoffen, all mein Sehnen,	All my comfort, hope, and yearning,
Meines Lebens schönster Traum	All I dreamt might come to be
Hängt an diesem Apfelbaum!!" (1,348)	Dangles from this apple tree!"
	(Arndt 26)

The variance between the bathetic and elevated tone of expression and the reality of the situation is further stressed when the widow decides to ingest the "young . . . departed" — silently and honorably — "nicely fried" (*Ibid.*, 27).

Tailor Böck, whose "purpose in life" and value to the community depends on making clothes and darning them, can put up with everything but being mocked, and chases the boys, yardstick in hand, only to fall into the water, to be pulled out by geese and to have his ensuing stomach cramps alleviated by his wife's hot iron. His final comment upon hearing of the boys' fate is that "Malice is not life's goal" (1,355,389).

The town's teacher whose very name Lämpel (little light) shows his limitations, who smugly supervises the children's learning of reading, writing, arithmetic and "wisdom's teachings" and to whom life's greatest joy resides in obtaining satisfaction — in his case — smoking a pipe, is rudely shaken when the pipe explodes. His "[h]ere we have one more example" echoes the banality of tailor Böck's final observation at the tale's end (1,389).

"Good" uncle Fritz, after whose comfort relatives are supposed to look, is attacked precisely in this area. His ruthlessness in despatching the June bugs who

[7] Walter Huder, "Max und Moritz oder die boshafte Heiterkeit," *Jahrbuch*, 1964/65, 32-38 see esp. 32-34. For Busch's view on the similarity between children and the lower classes' political views see Ueding, 94-95.

interrupted his sleep is underscored in his unfeeling and ungrammatical final commentary:

"Das kommt von dumme Witze!" (1,389) "That's the result of them silly jokes!"[8]

The tale's "pious" baker who gleefully makes loaves of the boys and puts them in the oven, only to be disappointed at their escape, provides a grotesque commentary upon hearing that they have been devoured by ducks:

"Warum ist der Mensch so lecker?!" (1,389) "Why is man so tasty?!"

His unfeeling nature is matched by that of farmer Mecke and the miller who with great mirth execute the boys and grind them into poultry feed. The "worthy" farmer shrugs off all responsibility in Low German dialect:

"Wat geiht meck dat an?!" (1,389) "Ain't no business of mine!" (Arndt 35)

Thus even the pillars of the community are shown to be filled with malice when their possessions and comforts are besieged, and they strike back ruthlessly or at least condone the evildoers' execution. This "Brueghelesque vision of the beast in bourgeois man" is "the more insidious for being couched in terms of bland mock-approval, and the more acute for venting the self-hatred of the accomplice, the native son" (*Ibid.,* 3). Lotze assumes that the amazing success of *Max und Moritz* over several generations is based on "general misunderstanding or the readers' unwillingness to face the truth," but Fleming, citing parental attempts to keep the work from children out of fear that it might lead to imitation, and bureaucratic efforts to forbid its sale to minors, suggests the other possibility, that people understood it too well.[9] Huder suggests that the popularity of the book may to some extent be due to the inferred references to Biblical and Classical sources which therefore grant it an aura of familiarity. He mentions the number seven as a traditionally unlucky one, and further cites the archetypal images of the widow, the bridge, the geese and the mill. Widows were already protected by law in the Old Testament and occupy a venerable place in German society as well. In widow Bolte's case, the boys attached her greedy self-indulgence by stealing her most prized possessions, in retaliation for which she chastised her dog whom Huder sees as her husband's reincarnation. The bridge, symbol of friendship and

[8]This is Lotze's rendering of the line, 46.

[9]Lotze, 47; Gerald Fleming, "Max und Moritz — Ein Kinderbuch?," *Jahrbuch,* 1975, 23-28, see esp. 24; Ueding, 92-93; Ulrich Beer, "Elternschreck und Kinderfreund," *Jahrbuch,* 1979/80, 49-64.

in tailor Böck's case a sign of self-satisfaction with his good name, is sawn in half and Böck, challenged by the boys' bleating, rushes outside to take revenge only to fall into the water. But the geese who saved the Capitol also come to his rescue. The boys overextend themselves in trying to steal the Easter pretzels, the pastry of the Resurrection, and the chair's breaking foreshadows their doom (again two exclamation marks accompany the crashing sound "Kracks!!"). They escape for the last time after having been baked in the oven, just as the three men survived Nebuchadnezzar's fiery furnace (Daniel 3:1-30). Ueding mentions that such baking practices for the ill were still done in some areas at the beginning of this century where these rites signified renewal, in this case it constitutes a final attempt at turning the naughty boys into good children. Alas, this attempt fails and when the boys violate the very foundation of life by slicing open the grain sacks, they are done for. The mill, symbol of completion and divine retribution, grinds them into feed for the miller's ducks.[10]

The final issue to be raised is how seriously the disparity between crime and punishment and the bizarre ending are to be taken. The last illustrations show the boys' remnants ground into grist in still recognizable form being devoured by ducks thereby underlining the final irony that the mills of justice grind finely and that in the dog-eat-dog world they who consumed widow Bolte's hens are in turn consumed by the miller's ducks. I prefer to see the conclusion as the last whimsical link in a series where causality and reality are imaginatively suspended; consequently it would fit in with the hanging of the fowl, Böck's rescue by geese and his wife's ironing his stomach, the boys' being baked in the oven, and ultimately coming to a bloodless end. I agree with Fleming who views Busch's trivializing of death as pointing to the absurdity of life as a whole.[11] Thus the "dread mixed with laughter" (i.e., the ridiculing of the daemonic [*Briefe* 1:157]), removes the final sting from the work without invalidating the criticism leveled at the German bourgeoisie and without providing the answer to a question that can probably not be resolved of where to draw "the boundaries between freedom and anarchic vio-

---

[10]Huder, 32-37; Ueding, 78.

[11]Fleming, 28. Walther Lampe, "Wilhelm Busch und der Tod," *Jahrbuch,* 1957/58, 50-56 sees death as punishment or atonement. An article that summarizes Busch's portrayal of death is Bernhard Adamy's, "Todesvorstellungen bei Wilhelm Busch," *Jahrbuch,* 1981, 12-25. On the portrayal of evil see Peter Bonati, *Die Darstellung des Bösen im Werk Wilhelm Buschs* (Bern: Francke, 1973).

lence and between social cohesion and reactionary bourgeois stuffiness" (Arndt 3). It is impossible to accept the view of Busch as spokesman of the forces of deterrence (Lampe 44-59) since that ignores the entire ironic mode of portrayal, and one may have some reservations about psychological interpretations such as Beer's who sees the aggressions, arising from a lack of love and Busch's underdeveloped Id, being transferred to the children's figures of his fiction.[12]

As a cultural phenomenon, the diverse interpretations of and the various issues raised by what is after all "merely" a children's picture book are unique. So is the immense popularity this work has enjoyed for over a century. Perhaps a reason for this can be found in the fact that *Max und Moritz* may represent a peculiarly German ambiguity of values: overtly, a pronounced veneration of law and order, neatness and an almost obsessive observance of the social niceties, and less manifestly so — as a glance at Germany's cultural heritage, history and literature show — a dark and destructive tendency of — what used to be called — the Teutonic soul. Although this is not the place to investigate this aspect of German culture and identity in depth, a brief look at two German idiomatic expressions that are especially suited to the context of this discussion and bring out this particular ambivalence may support this contention. The first expression describes the bourgeois values that Max and Moritz decidedly lack. In complimenting German parents on their children's behavior, one says that the children have enjoyed a "gute Kinderstube" (literally, a good nursery) in reference to the child's succesful social upbringing and acculturation. On the other hand, an expression for which there is again no appropriate translation in English is the specifically German concept of "Schadenfreude" or the malicious pleasure one takes in the misfortune of others. At a very basic level, *Max und Moritz* lets one have one's cake and eat it too in affording one a taste of both these contradictory qualities: on the one hand, an affirmation of the accepted middle-class values which ties one to one's fellow men, and on the other, a mischievous pleasure of at least vicariously breaking the rules of what constitutes acceptable social behavior. Thus perhaps the very fact that *Max und Moritz* satisfies these simultaneous conflicting feelings, that it may

[12]Ulrich Beer, " . . . Gottlos und beneidenswert": *Wilhelm Busch und seine Psychologie.* (Munich: Ehrenwirth, 1982) 37. See also Frank Pietzcker, *Wilhelm Busch: Schuld und Strafe in Werk und Leben* (Munich: Minerva, 1984).

be read at various levels, as a tale of innocence[13] as well as one of experience, and in so doing provides pleasure to young and old alike has made it such a unique work. One that still speaks to German sensibilities and therefore has managed to retain its hold on the public imagination and to remain a truly living German classic.

WORKS CITED

Adamy, Bernhard. "Todesvorstellungen bei Wilhelm Busch." *Wilhelm-Busch-Jahrbuch* (1981): 12-25.

Arndt, Walter. Ed. and tr. *The Genius of Wilhelm Busch: Comedy of Frustration.* Berkeley: U of California P, 1982.

Baumgärtner, Alfred Clemens. "Der Bilderbogen für Kinder in Deutschland." *Das Bilderbuch.* Ed. Klaus Doderer and Helmut Müller. Weinheim and Basel: Beltz 1973. 67-98.

Beer, Ulrich. "Elternschreck und Kinderfreund." *Wilhelm-Busch-Jahrbuch* (1979/80): 49-64.

——. ". . . Gottlos und beneidenswert": *Wilhelm Busch und seine Psychologie.* Munich: Ehrenwirth, 1982.

Bonati, Peter. *Die Darstellung des Bösen im Werk Wilhelm Buschs.* Bern: Francke, 1973.

——. "Schema, Spiel und Fülle." *Wilhelm-Busch-Jahrbuch* (1983): 46-61.

Busch, Wilhelm. *Gesamtausgabe.* Ed. Friedrich Bohne. 4 vols. Wiesbaden: Emil Vollmer, 1968.

——. *Max and Maurice: The Story of Two Rascals in Seven Pranks.* Tr. Walter Roome. Montreal: Mansfield Book Mart, 1961.

——. *Max und Moritz Eine Bubengeschichte in sieben Streichen.* 22nd ed. Munich: Braun & Schneider, 188?

——. *Sämtliche Briefe.* Ed. Friedrich Bohne et al. 2 vols. Hannover: Wilhelm-Busch-Gesellschaft, 1968.

——. *Sämtliche Werke.* Ed. Otte Noldeke. 8 vols. Munich: Braun & Schneider, 1943.

Doderer, Klaus. "Das bürgerliche Bilderbuch im 19. Jahrhundert." Das Bilderbuch. Ed. Klaus Doderer and Helmut Möller. Weinheim and Basel: Beltz, 1973. 183-224.

——. "Das Poetische Bilderbuch im 19. Jahrhundert." *Das Bilderbuch.* Ed. Klaus Doderer and Helmut Müller. Weinheim and Basel: Beltz, 1973. 99-139.

Fleming, Gerald. "Max und Moritz — Ein Kinderbuch?" *Wilhelm-Busch-Jahrbuch* (1975): 23-28.

Gilli, Yves. " 'Max und Moritz' de Busch: Contribution à une étude de texte." *Recherches en linguistique étrangère* (=*Annales littéraires de l'Université de Besançon*) 147 (1973): 95-116.

---

[13]Hemmo Möller-Suur, "Max und Moritz unmoralisch?," *Jahrbuch*, 1949, 36-41 finds that *Max und Moritz* belongs to the fairy tale age for children and no relation between it and reality are established, 38.

Glockner, Hermann. *Wilhelm Busch: Der Mensch. Der Zeichner. Der Humorist.* Tübingen: Mohr, 1932.

Görlach, Manfred. "Bibliographie aller Wilhelm Busch gewidmeten Beiträge in den Mitteilungen und Jahrbüchern der Wilhelm-Busch-Gesellschaft (seit 1931)." *Wilhelm-Busch-Jahrbuch* (1981): 41-69.

——. "Bibliographie der Max-und-Moritz-Übersetzungen (Stand: November 1981)." *Wilhelm-Busch-Jahrbuch* (1981): 28-40.

——. "Literatur zu Wilhelm Busch." *Wilhelm-Busch-Jahrbuch* (1985): 68-75.

Heine, Thomas Theodor. "Th. Th. Heine über Wilhelm Busch." *Wilhelm-Busch-Jahrbuch* (1961-62): 34-37.

Huder, Walter. "Max und Moritz oder die boshafte Heiterkeit." *Wilhelm-Busch-Jahrbuch* (1964-65): 32-38.

Kayser, Wolfgang. *Das Groteske in Malerei und Dichtung.* Munich: Rowohlt, 1960.

——. *Wilhelm Buschs grotesker Humor.* Göttingen: Vandenhoech & Ruprecht, 1958.

Korff, H.A. *Geist der Goethezeit.* 7th ed. 4 vols. vol. 4. Leipzig: Koehler & Amelang, 1966.

Lampe, Walter. "Wilhelm Busch und das Recht." *Wilhelm-Busch-Jahrbuch* (1956): 44-59.

Liebert, Ute. "120 Jahre Max und Moritz." *Wilhelm-Busch-Jahrbuch* (1985): 19-26.

Lotze, Dieter P. *Wilhelm Busch.* Boston: Twayne, 1979.

Marxer, Peter. *Wilhelm Busch als Dichter.* Zürich: Juris, 1967.

Müller, Helmut. "Struwwelpeter und Struwwelpetriaden." *Das Bilderbuch.* Ed. Klaus Doderer and Helmut Müller. Weinheim and Basel: Beltz, 1973. 141-182.

Müller-Suur, Hemmo. "Max und Moritz unmoralisch?" *Wilhelm-Busch-Jahrbuch* (1949): 36-41.

Noordhoorn, Max E. "The Element of Shock in Heinrich Heine's Lyric Cycles." Diss. The University of Michigan, 1971. Ann Arbor: UMI, 1972. 72-14, 259.

Novotny, Fritz. *Wilhelm Busch als Zeichner und Maler.* Vienna: Anton Schrall & Co., 1949.

Pape, Walter. *Wilhelm Busch.* Stuttgart: Metzler, 1977.

Pietzcker, Frank. *Wilhelm Busch - Schuld und Strafe in Werk und Leben.* Munich: Minerva, 1984.

Ueding, Gert. *Wilhelm Busch: Das 19. Jahrhundert en miniature.* Frankfurt am Main: Insel, 1977.

URSULA E. BEITTER

Identity Crisis in Fairy-Tale Land: the Grimm Fairy Tales and their Uses by Modern-Day Imitators

There is something truly astonishing about the amount of attention that the Grimm Fairy tales have been accorded in the past decade from both scholars and from the popular sector. All disciplines within academia, so it seems, have something to contribute to the understanding of tales: the folklorists trace common themes and elements in the fairy tale genres of many different peoples. Jungian psychologists maintain that the tales are but collapsed myths, whereas Freudian psychologists insist that tales contain, in symbolic form, solutions to many of the sexual, parental, and ego problems that children have while growing up. It is claimed that fairy tales can help children come to terms with childhood and adolescent conflicts.[1]

Other psychologists are less convinced of the tales' beneficence and claim that children ought not to read them or read them only in purified form on account of the cruelties that abound in the tales. According to these psychologists and educators, no other form of literature indulges in such noxious and terrible acts as tales: people are gobbled up, devoured, burned, decimated, turned into stone or into animals, or simply made into an entree. Other psychologists point out that children seem to show little interest in the bowdlerized versions and, when given a chance, will seek out the archaic and gruesome versions. From the Marxist camp we hear the accusation that tales pass on nothing but negative "repressive

---

[1]For further reading on interpretational approaches please see: Roger Sale, *Fairy Tales and After: From Snow White to E. B. White* (Harvard UP, 1978); Linda Degh, "Fairy Tales as Ways of Knowing: Essays on Märchen," *Psychology, Society and Literature*, ed. M. M. Metzger and K. Mommsen (Bern: P. Lang, 1981); Bruno Bettelheim, *The Uses of Enchantment: The Meaning and Importance of Fairy Tales* (New York: Vintage Press, 1977); A. Nitschke, "Aschenputtel aus der Sicht der historischen Verhaltensforschung," *Und wenn sie nicht gestorben sind . . . Perspektiven auf das Märchen*, ed. H. Brackert (Frankfurt: Suhrkamp, 1980); D. R. Thelander, "Mother Goose and her Goslings: the France of Louis XIV as Seen Through the Fairy Tale," *Journal of Modern History 54* (Sept. 1982); Marcia Liebermann, "Some Day my Prince will come: Female Acculturation through the Fairy Tale," *College English* 35 (1972-73).

bourgeois" values, such as obedience and subservience, which are meant to assure the continued existence of the bourgeois class (Zipes *passim*).

Vehement criticism of fairy tales comes from feminists who maintain that fairy tales reinforce stereotypical perceptions of woman, as well as stereotypical behavior in women. Feminists believe that tales teach women and girls to be passive and subservient, to pay attention only to their looks, and to wait around for the right prince to solve all their problems. According to Wälti-Walters, "nobody in her right mind could want to be a fairy tale princess. After all, what do they do except play dead across the path of some young man who has been led to believe that he rules the world" (180). It is argued that tales ought to be rewritten to bring them in line with the aspirations and duties of twentieth-century woman.

There are so many possible ways of interpreting and rewriting tales, that it is easy to lose sight of the fact that tales have an intrinsic value in themselves. They are not only important because they are versatile and adaptable; they have had a profound influence on generations of readers in the western world and they do transmit something of Germany's cultural identity to other peoples. The work of the Grimms, in particular their collecting and rewriting material from an oral tradition, has had a decisive influence on German language and culture. It is even argued that some of the tale's impact on the German language is second only to Martin Luther's translation of the Bible into German. The tales are widely read and much of what people in other countries know about Germany comes from tales. Dark forests and romantic towns are as much a part of people's conception of Germany as are messages inherent in tales: don't lie, don't steal, be honorable, and honor your parents. And, there are also the tales which seem to be overly didactic and use harsh measures to enforce their moral — all of this is transmitted in the tales. As a rule, German fairy tales have a serious message and the tales that are humorous are scant. Be they good or bad, benign and romantic, or realistic and cruel, the tales have become identified with the nineteenth-century Romantic movement in Germany in specific, and with German cultural identity in general. As is shown in this paper, bowdlerizing fairy tales, rewriting them in accordance with the tenets of currently fashionable ideals, and making them into situation comedies not only deprives them of whatever intrinsic values they had, but also destroys the value they had as a transmitter of another people's culture and identity.

While there seems to be much clamoring in academia about the importance and significance of the tales, the reality does look different. We should ask ourselves who, aside from academics and educators, really reads fairy tales, either for their own edification or to their children? Do children really hurl themselves at the family bookshelves looking for Perrault, Grimm or Andersen? Or do children resort to the T.V.? We should ask how many parents, busy with their careers, really have time to gather the children in a cozy nook and read them tales. How many grandmothers are left to sit down to tell tales? Simply put, the traditions, such as reading and story telling, are dying, and it is not surprising that their place has been taken by the television. The decline in reading, the prevalence of the bowdlerized Disney versions, both in print and in movie form, have overshadowed the tales. Television, movies, video games, amusement parks and videos have replaced parents and grandparents as providers of information and entertainment. And the biggest threat to the traditional fairy tale comes from the made-for-T.V. video-tales, produced by Shelley duVal's Fairy Tale Theatre, to which I would like to devote the rest of my discussion.[2]

What, precisely, has Shelley duVal done? In an introduction to one of her productions, she claims that she has taken the legends and tales to heart and that she brings this valuable material to children of all ages. Indeed, she has brought something to children, but it has little to do with fairy tales. To start, she has taken a three or five page tale, which takes 10 minutes to read, and turned it into a one-hour T.V. show. To turn the compact, economic structure of a fairy tale into a one-hour show required new characters, new plots and sub-plots. She provided elaborate explanations for a process known, in short, as padding. Where before we had simply, "a girl," "a boy," or "a king and queen," or "a serf," we now have Michael York, Steve Bridges, Vanessa Redgrave, Robin Williams, Bernadette Peters and Liza Minelli, just to name a few of the stars, in cameo roles.

To my knowledge, Fairy Tale Theatre has produced at least ten of the best-known fairy tales, such as Cinderella, Red Riding Hood, Rapunzel, Snow White, Rumpelstiltskin, Sleeping Beauty, the Frog Prince and the Princess and the Pea. It won't be feasible to discuss all tales in detail and I shall limit myself to an analysis of the Frog Prince and discuss three other popular tales in capsule form.

---

[2]*Fairy Tale Theatre Productions* were seen regularly on PBS. They are now very popular rental items in video rental stores.

The Frog Prince is an elaborate and clever production, written and directed by Eric Idle who was, and still is, one of the guiding spirits of Monty Python's Flying Circus. First we find out how the prince came to be a frog. It seems that the childless royal couple had to seek the advice of a witch who, after working at her cauldron, concocts a brew that brings about the much-desired heir. The king and queen had to promise the witch Griselda to let her be the godmother of the child and invite her to the christening. The queen forgets the promise and, in an act of revenge, Griselda turns the boy into a frog. (20 minutes have elapsed.)

Next we meet the other royal couple, whose vain and beautiful daughter, the princess is preening so that she can look her best when she meets Hal, the frog prince's younger brother, at a tea party arranged by their parents so the children can meet and get to like each other. The princess, played by Teri Carr, is very reluctant to meet Hal, to whom she refers as a "macho meat-face" whose sole passion is "murdering large fire breathing scaly animals." The princess assesses Hal's cerebral capacity to be that of a shrimp, but a lady-in-waiting whispers in her ear that, while that may be the case, Hal does have a "nice body." With much ado, the princess manages to tear herself away from her mirrors and gets herself to the tea party an hour late, only to find out that Hal is not there. The princess intimates that he "prefers the company of boys and they are out slaughtering dragons." The princess lets the assembled parents know that she finds this reprehensible, as dragons are quickly becoming extinct.

To make amends for his absence, Hal sends her a huge golden sphere that has the magic property of being able to float. The princess goes to amuse herself with it at the well. It is here that frog meets girl. Robin Williams, dressed in a frog suit, sits at the well catching his lunch. He tells the princess to please be quiet, because her singing and playing scare away the flies. An altercation ensues — insults are hurled — during which we find out that R. Williams is not a toad, but a frog — and "fiercely proud of it" and that, in addition, he is an amphibian and bi-elemental to boot. During the argument the ball falls into the well and the princess offers him anything he wants to fetch the toy. He rejects her offer of receiving a diamond ring which he "could certainly wear around his neck, together with a sign, advertising himself as snake food." Bargaining follows, but the frog rejects all material goods. He wants to be her friend, have dinner at the palace, and sleep with her. The princess replies: "What - shack up with a frog?" and the frog hastily assures her that what he really meant was to sleep near her, on a silken pillow. An arrangement is made, they agree and, after a laborious climb up the well walls, the frog emerges to the music of Zarathustra, to have the ball snatched from him and the princess disappear (35 minutes have elapsed).

The frog reappears at a dinner banquet but, before meeting the court, he is kidnapped by the French cook who wants to turn him into a frog's legs entree (5 minute digression). After escaping the garlic and the hatchet, he does a song/dance/comedy act routine on the banquet table in front of the king and queen. The king is impressed. He explains to his daughter why she must keep her promises. His reasoning is that in their particular society, the little people have to see that the royal folks are reliable and can be trusted. If the "little" folk find out that royalty is untrustworthy and dispensable, "off comes the head" (45 minutes are gone). The frog, after some banter and bargaining in the princess' bedroom, winds up sleeping on her silken pillow, but he remains unkissed. During the night, a scorpion is about to attack the princess and (while dramatic music is playing in the background) the frog, armed with a needle kills the scorpion. Now he is kissed and turns into a prince. The king enters the room and seeing his daughter with a scantily clad man, thinks the imaginable. He has the prince arrested and thrown into a dungeon, and the princess is sent to a strict boarding school, where she has to learn Latin. The king now turns to drink, and the kingdom falls into disrepair. The bleakness is relieved when the witch appears to the king in the floating, golden sphere and explains everything to him. The video ends with the wedding portrait being taken. As the camera pulls back, we see a happily smiling R. Williams furtively snatching at passing flies.

Red Riding Hood follows a similar pattern. An elaborate prologue establishes a family history and provides Riding Hood with a boyfriend. The wolf has seen better days. His joints are aching; he has gray whiskers on his face and a suspiciously red nose. Before he can take a chomp out of Red, he has to put in his false teeth. Grandma is a feisty old lady and, in the end, they are all rescued by Red Riding Hood's romantic interest. In Rapunzel, 20 minutes and elaborate special effects are devoted to the woman's obsession with radishes who pursue her in her dreams. In general, the tale focuses on the possessive mother instead of on the daughter. In Sleeping Beauty, Steve Reeves plays the handsome but dim-witted prince who, by the way, travels in the disguise of a footman to escape the vengeance of women whose attentions he ignored. In Snow White, Vanessa Redgrave plays the wicked stepmother, Vincent Price the mundane mirror. The tale is no longer about Snow but about the destructive narcissism of her mother who, on the way to the dwarfs' house, encounters a lute playing prince and proceeds — not very successfully — to seduce him.

The Princess on the Pea, as it is called in English, stars Liza Minelli who drops in on the prince after she has suffered an accident on the road. The doltish prince is dominated by his mother who has decided to find a wife for him. The prince came to the conclusion that he needed a wife because the court jester found him moping about the castle and asked what he wanted. The prince makes various gestures which seem to imply that he wants something small, cuddly and soft. No, it is not a hamster nor a kitten, but a wife (30 minutes have elapsed!). The mother is domineering, and the prospective wife is rude, arrogant and snobbish. She informs the prince that she does not care for him, that he is merely an object to be stepped on her way to the royal top. In this version, the prince is a complete whimp, whereas in the original he was the one who went out into the world to find a bride. Of course, Minnelli can't sleep on her 20 mattresses because of the pea, thereby proving that she is a princess. But before prince gets princess, Minnelli walks out on him because she is very upset at having been tested and having her word doubted.

These brief summaries must suffice to give an idea of what has been perpetrated upon Grimm fairy tales.[3] Fairy Tale Theatre has systematically deprived the old tales of all their magic and incongruities, something with which children have little trouble. Adults, however, want a logical framework and world, requisites that do not stop at entertainment. As a result, the tales are bereft of magic and poetry; we are left with clever special effects, not much else.

Next, we turn our attention to the structure of the tales. Here, the dramatic narrative has been padded by providing genealogies that did not exist, motivations that had hitherto remained obscured. Digressions have been added, subplots provided, and extra characters proliferate. Also, in many tales, the emphasis has been shifted away from the trials of the protagonist in the title to another character,

---

[3]For English versions of the tales: Jack Zipes, *The Complete Fairy Tales of the Brothers Grimm* (Bantam, 1987).

usually the domineering mother or step mother. The tale that had focused on one character, usually a child about to find his/her way into the world, now has a multitude of characters and interests. We are not able to really empathize with one character. Second, the best videos are humorous and clever, the original tales are not. The video, with its one-liners and clever asides, its song-and-dance routine by R. Williams, is indeed funny. But if the videos are not funny, they are terribly boring. We have to ask ourselves whether a child would sit through 20 minutes of exposition that dealt with radishes. What child could catch the double entendres? What child would smirk at the slightly off-color sexual innuendoes? What child is willing to sit through 45 minutes of unrelieved boredom?

The answer to these questions is: probably very few, and I have come to the conclusion that Fairy Tale Theatre is really entertainment that is intended for adults. We are no longer dealing with fairy magic tales, but with situation comedies based on a common denominator, the tales. We are really dealing with a new genre of T.V. entertainment: the fairy tale situation comedy, whose quick-fire repartee has nothing to do with Grimm, Perrault or any other fairy tale we know of. Fairy Tale Theatre has produced travesties of an older genre; the old tales have been gutted and the resulting void has been filled with famous stars and actors, all of whom have a jolly good time parading as frogs, dwarfs and mirrors. We are no longer dealing with literature for children, but with childish literature for adults.

So far I have addressed myself mainly to the structure, and now I would like to touch the question of content. It is agreed amongst main stream psychologists that the traditional fairy tales have a salutary effect on children's psyches by helping them to resolve conflicts that are going on within them in relation to their parents, environment, and their sexuality. The new tales prevent any identification with any character, they explain everything in logical terms and dissolve any possible conflict into laughter. Instead of letting the child intuit solutions, the child is presented with a prefabricated, standard, and socially acceptable solution. Shallow, superficial, and merely of visual interest, the modern video tales do not have the many faceted riches of Grimm or Perrault tales. It is also accepted that tales do teach children values or did, when people still told stories and read and, depending on whose camp one is in, these messages are either good or detrimental. What, we should ask, do video fairy tales teach? Perhaps that everything in life can be solved with a one-liner?

And what of the other issue, that of the tale as a transmitter of another people's values, or as a poetic record of how a certain people felt about themselves at a certain point in their national development? The present video tales are devoid of values and they also lack any information about the foreign societies in which they originated, or where formed. Or are we to gather from the tales that they reflect our present-day American values and beliefs? That is, that we live in a spectacular society, full of glitter and superficiality, but without substance and value?

It is my opinion that the future of the older tales is rather dim. Of course, it will always be alive within academia and special interest groups, such as parents who value reading. But, in general, it appears that reading is diminishing. Ultimately, it is not only the children who will suffer, but also the tales whose very existence depends of either an oral tradition or on developing a reading habit. The more video and computer games and T.V. are in the ascendancy, the less people will read; thus, the future for the Grimm and Perrault tales appears to be rather "grim."

WORKS CITED

Wälti-Walters, Jennifer. "On Princesses: Fairy Tales, Sex Roles and Loss of Self." *International Journal of Women's Studies* 2 (1979) 180-88.

Zipes, Jack. *Fairy Tales and the Art of Subversion.* New York: Wildman, 1983.

ANTONIO OLLIZ-BOYD & GABRIEL ASOANAB ABUDU

Afro Iberian Identity in the Early Literature of Spain: Precursor to the Afro Hispanic Identity

The awareness of blacks as part of the national culture of Spain has been lost in the confusion of ethnic and racial identification. While it is accepted, however, that the presence of Arabs and Moors are a vital part of Spain's national fiber, an acknowledgment that both groups had identifiable black men and women is not so readily admitted. Yet the creative literature that attests to the Arab and Moorish experiences in Spain leaves no doubt about the racial description of the individuals that comprised both groups.

The same confusion of ethnic and racial identification confronts those who are interested in the Afro Hispanic person as a concept of racial reality in Latin America. Again, while some acknowledge that African slavery did become a reality in the demography of Latin America, others dismiss the impact that this fact has had on the genotype of the population. For many, the perception of race, in terms of a black Spanish-speaking native, is a mute question. This group usually takes refuge in the "Cosmic Race" theory proposed by Jose Vasconcelos in 1925. His thesis decreed that Latin Americans would one day be considered a homogeneous synthesis of disparate genotypical elements: African, Indian, European. Of course the phenotype would tend more toward European traits and produce a new race: the Latin American or Hispanic race (Vasconcelos 32-33).

In spite of denials, the image of identifiable African descendants has appeared consistently in Hispanic letters, on a continuum. From the early literature written in Spain in Arabic, to that written in Spanish as a recognizable national language, and more contemporarily to the protest literature of present day Spanish-speaking America, one finds a black presence. Typical of the latter is the short story by Ana Lydia Vega entitled "Encancaranublado." Her approach relies on racial identity to highlight protest issues of the Caribbean. Thus we see Haitians, Dominicans, Cubans and Puerto Ricans as equal blacks, in a metaphorical sea of economic misery, and as national prototypes (Vega 13-20). On the other hand, for much earlier examples, it is not difficult to learn from the Spanish conquerors facts that confirm that there were Afro Iberians actively participating in the social life of the Spain of that period. Thus, in the accounts of the "conquistadores" we find that a certain black man, Juan Garrido, came directly from Spain, and not from Africa, to participate in the conquest of the Americas. It was he who introduced wheat into Mexico, in the sixteenth century (MacLachlan and Rodríguez O. 217).

The input of blacks, like Juan Garrido, in the New World conquest is not the only appearance of an Afro Iberian presence. In the vibrant Spanish literary movement of the Golden Age of Spanish letters, (approximately 1500 A.D. to 1650 A.D.), the characterization of black men and women was part of the standard literary stock. Both transplanted Africans and native born blacks were used by some of the most outstanding writers of that period, such as Lope de Rueda (b. circa 1510 A.D.), Lope de Vega (b. 1562 A.D.), and Cervantes (b. 1547 A.D.). Prior to this, in the writings of the thirteenth, fourteenth and fifteenth centuries, there is some doubt as to the true national identity of the black men and women that one finds in the Spanish letters of that era. Historical facts however, lead one to ascertain that in spite of the politics of the day, there were Afro Iberians in the major towns and cities of Spain before their major appearance in the Golden Age literature of the sixteenth to seventeenth centuries.

What historical facts do make clear, however, is that there was unusual confusion as to ethnic identification. Moor and black were often used interchangeably. A strong Christian backlash equated race with religion and acceptability. Nonetheless, racial amalgamation amongst blacks, Arabs and Europeans was an undisputable actuality. As C. Baranda Leturio points out in her monograph on black speech patterns in early Spanish literature, it was not the least bit unusual to find both Arab terms and Portuguese sound patterns as an integral part of the linguistic systems of black characterization in the national literature of fourteenth and fifteenth century Spain. The Moorish hegemony had fallen to become the cursed lot of black invaders. Negative imagery of blacks (i.e., Moors) by Christian writers became the vogue. More than anything else, from individual references to self identity and the literary intent of Spanish authors, one learns that Ghana, Senegal and other African countries had undeniable roles in the Moorish conquest of Spain. In this respect, also, it is of particular interest to re-

read the twelfth-century work of *The Cid* (ca. 1140) for its ethnic content. Known as the oldest extant example of Spanish used as a literary tongue, *The Cid* becomes a key factor in determining the reaction of non-African Spaniards towards native Islamic blacks during the eighth to the thirteenth centuries.

Written some 430 years after the Moslem invasion of Spain, one finds in *The Cid* a mention of Christians and Moors only as ethnic groups. The term Moors, in this long epic poem, had become a color code to denote a class or warrior caste whose ethnicity was defined by the region from which they proceeded, namely Mauritania, in Western Africa. Race, in this context became identified with religious hegemony.

Literary Context and Color Codes

It is not unusual to rely on texts, such as *The Cid*, to determine the social content and/or social context of a given geographical space or time period. Most texts carry an inherent semiotic relationship with the environment in which they were created. To illustrate this point, and to show the thematic range of the early Afro Iberian identity that led up to the time period of the Cid, we have considered some of the poetry that was produced in Arabic, in southern Spain, during the eighth to the thirteenth centuries. The color codes for racial identification offer an unrefutable indication that the interplay between black and white phenotypes had become an established social norm. There were both covert and overt symbols for rejection or acceptance based on color. A short poem found in most anthologies of Hispano-Arabic poetry, "The Black Swimmer," written by Ibn Khafacha of Valencia (1058-1138) illustrates this attempt. Our translation of this poem into English is based on a Spanish version by Emilio García Gómez:

> A black man was swimming in a pool
> whose waters did not hide the pebbles at the bottom.
> The pool was like the blue pupil of an eye in
> which the black man was the iris.
>
> (*Poemas arábigoandaluces* 133)

The historical background during which this poem was written supplies the context. The context in turn adds a dimension of meaning for the reader toward understanding the range of the black man as a code.

Ibn Khafacha was a native of Alcira, Spain, and is said to have lived there all his life. It was during this period that a fundamental Islamic brotherhood called the Almoravids (Al-Murabitun) banded together as a group in the upper Senegal.

Their influence began to spread from the Western Sudan to the North African coast, including Mauritania and Algeria. Led by a warrior chief named Yusuf, the Almoravid forces swept over into Spain (Al-Andalus) in 1086. They defeated the Christian forces of King Alfonso VI, and reduced the native Andalusian Spanish civilization to a provincial status within an African empire (Imamuddin 258-80). What is of primary interest, at this juncture, is the poetic metaphor observed in "The Black Swimmer" as a code to convey the definitive concept of a social dynamic. Although it became obvious that the semantic process of the poem had suffered cultural changes because of various translations: Arabic to Spanish to English, nonetheless, the three versions do share in both a dimensional concern, and a social perspective with the black man used as a code to give ethnic meaning to an inferred hegemony within a social construct.

First, there is seen in the poem a *locus in quo* for the action: a body of water which becomes the eye. Second, there is the figure of the black swimmer who becomes not only the essence of the spatial parameter but an object to whom identity is assigned as a controlling factor of social intent. The Arabic version juxtaposes the terms "lujjatin" and "aswad" (a "body of water" and a "black man" respectively). The Spanish translator opts to use the terms "alberca" and "negro." The English translation based on the Spanish version is required to employ *pool* and *black person*. The Arabic term "lujjatin" does have a relationship to the Spanish "alberca" but is nonetheless connotatively different and suggests a large wave, a vast expanse of water. Spanish "alberca" has its etymological origin in the Arabic word "al-birkt," often used to indicate a pool. While denotatively the Spanish translator may have understood the concept, the underlying connotative atmosphere suggests a wider expanse of water.

One must consider, in this respect the wordplay based on an understanding of the function of language within a social context. Pool as an embedded homonym for a wide expanse of water, e.g., the straits of Gibraltar, was an integral part of Andalusian linguistic ideology during the tenth to the thirteenth centuries, not only for Arabic poets but Spanish Hebrew poets as well (Blumenthal 113). Within the social context of "The Black Swimmer" there is formulated content: The black man is herein seen as the pivotal figure in the poet's metaphorically constructed society. The overall semantic process shows both integration of the figure and its positive acceptance into the society as the focal point of leadership.

Consequently, the black swimmer has become, for this twelfth-century Spanish Moslem poet, more than a metaphor. He is a symbol. His swimmer takes form as an overt sign or code of cultural communication, perceived undoubtedly by a twelfth-century reading audience as a semiotic reality.

From our vantage point, the metaphoric language of Ibn Khafacha the author of "The Black Swimmer," suggests to us a strong relationship between "a wide expanse of water" (the Mediterranean which the Almoravids had crossed?) and the sociopolitical leadership of the non-Caucasoid Moor. We have considered the fact that in the original version the term black which the poet used in Arabic "aswad" is void of the usual qualifier "abdun" (slave), so often used in Arabic poetry to imply social caste. The poet consequently establishes a context wherein the black man is not seen as a slave but as part of a higher hierarchy. "The Black Swimmer" thus alludes to Iberian blacks in a positive light.

We should not, though, conclude from this one entry by a Spanish poet who is noted for his delicate and sensitive treatment of the Valencian landscape, to the point of influencing other poets of his era (*Poemas arábigoandaluces* 38), that all blacks in early Spanish society were seen with positive signs of color acceptance. There was indeed evidence of overt racism such as one finds displayed in the poem of Ibn Hamdin, also of twelfth-century Spain. We have translated an excerpt as follows:

> I saw perched on a lily a raven whose presence
> announced a year of misfortune.
> What an honor for the ebony brush that
> applies the ointment.
> Yet what vilification for the delicate ivory
> receptacle of the ointment.
>
> (*Libro de las banderas* 177)

The context for the above verse is as enlightening toward an understanding of twelfth-century racial aesthetics in Spain as the actual verse, which delicately portrays a pornographic image of a black man in sexual contact with a white woman.

The manuscript from which the verse was taken states that a black slave (Abdun Aswad), in order to file a complaint against his white wife, appeared before the twelfth-century Spanish jurisprudent Ibn Hamid. Cultural *lacunae* obscure the dimensions of implied racism, since it is not pointed out that the "white wife" was also a slave. However, we have researched the fact that southern Spain, at this historical moment, ruled by the Almoravids (Moors), was under the jurisprudence of Malikite Islamic law, which decreed that a slave man could only marry a slave woman.[1] Within the social context, the jurist feels that "the ebony brush is honored" while "the ivory receptacle is vilified." With the not too subtle appeal to ethnicity, his meaning is all too apparent.

We should not overlook the fact that meaning, within the social context, facilitates understanding the social system. In this sense aesthetically both entries, ("The Black Swimmer" and "The Raven and the Lily"), substantiate the fact that blacks were an absolute part of the social context of Moorish/Islamic Spain. Furthermore the imagery in each entry displays the implied hierarchy of blacks within the social system. Further investigation confirms that even in spite of a caste system and miscegenation, there was social negativism attached to the black phenotype. While black skin and social negativism were not all inclusive, negative race relations have influenced investigators of the period. In this respect, Henri Peres who claims to have carefully researched the ethnicity of Spain during the Moorish occupation declares that the influence of the blacks on the Spanish as a race was inconsequential (*Esplendor de Al-Andalus* 267). Not only does Peres allege that to be black was an abomination, but that even mulattos were "mal vistos," that is, scorned (268). Yet the literature offers contradictory imagery as to

---

[1] We have worked from the following sources found in García Gómez's publication of the *Libro de las banderas de los campeones*, which, as he has indicated, is based on an anthology compiled in 1243 by Ibn Sa'id al-Magribi. The classical Arabic text which García Gómez studies has been transliterated by Ibrahim Mohamed Zien, Ph.D. of the Department of Religion of Temple University:

Wa aswada yasbahu fi *lujjatin*
La T'kun al-Hsba' *ghdranuha*
Ka' nnaha fi shakliha muqlatin
Zrqa' wa al-aswada insanuha. (p. 87).

García Gómez translated the Arabic text into Spanish as:

Un negro nadaba en una alberca cuya agua
no ocultaba los guijarros del fondo.
La alberca tenía la figura de una pupila azul,
donde el negro era la niña. (p. 256).

Our translation into English is cited in the body of this study. There are other English translations available (Arberry, Cope, Morland); however, their renditions did not capture the aesthetics we found inherent in Garíca Gómez's Spanish version. For example, his use of Spanish "alberca" to translate the Arabic "lujjatin" incorporates the denotative meaning of "al-birkt" as a body of water. The translation by the authors relied on the original Arabic text. This concept was first brought to our attention by Dr. Ibrahim Mohamed Zein who assisted in the Arabic translations and offered invaluable aesthetic insight from a Moslem's scholar's point of view.

the influence of blacks in early Spanish society. This contradiction is perhaps best illustrated with the anecdote of Abu Muhammad Ibn Hud al-Yudami who wandered from court to court in the north of Spain until he finally settled in Portugal. There he was made governor of Lisbon because of his sharp intelligence. To Ibn Hud al-Yudami is attributed the following poetic fragment which he dedicated to his parents who had rejected him because of his color:

> I am not inferior to the sun; it is only that the thick clouds (of my black skin) overcast me and impede me from shining and showing the force of my light . . . (Peres 268. Tr. Olliz-Boyd).

Peres's research fails to mention that Ibn Hud al-Yudami, although black and a member of the Hud tribe, belonged to one of the power base families who ruled Saragossa between 1010 and 1118 (Imamuddin 377).

History in addition to literature shows that contradictions where racialism is concerned are not uncommon. An example from historical accounts is "Ziryab," the popular musician and trend setter in the court of Abderrahman II, one of the famous Ummayad rulers of Cordoba (821-852). "Ziryab" who was born Abu'l Hasan 'Ali ibn Nafi, in Baghdad in 789, came to Spain at the invitation of Abderrahman II. His name became linked with illustrious Spanish Moslem men of science, poets, the military, civil ministers and princes of his period. Ziryab set the pace for dress, manners, customs and music in ninth-century Spain. Learned and refined, he was a figure to be copied. His contributions to Spanish society ran a curious gamut: not only is he credited with introducing into Al-Andalus, (southern Spain) the five-stringed lute, but it is also said that because of him short hair styles became popular (Read 64-65). Why was this figure called "Ziryab"? "Ziryab," it is said, was the name of a black-plumed bird found in the east that had a prodigious memory (Read 64). Nonetheless, for the legendary Ziryab, an accepted court figure, the color question was always a delicate matter. It is recorded that at least on one occasion he was reprimanded and banished from court for singing about a ruler who had "a mother who was as black as a crow" (Imamuddin 95).

This allusion to black ancestors in the creative literature of Spain during the reign of the Arabs and the Moors (eighth to fifteenth centuries) seems to have been a constant. Research shows that ethnically derived color codes were part of the sociolinguistic coding orientation of the prose and poetry of the period, and were used to control meaning where race was concerned. In spite of this, interaction between blacks and Caucasoid Spanish phenotypes was also a normal occurrence, since there were Spaniards who stayed behind in the areas that were conquered by the Arab/Moorish invasion. Some Spaniards remained Christian or converted to Islam. Even Spanish Jews, who had been in Spain before the Arab/Moorish invasions remained Jewish, converted to Christianity, or adopted Islam. It is said that "in a society that comprised at least six distinct ethnic-religious communities [Jews, Arabs, Berbers, Muwalladun (native Iberian converts to Islam), Musta 'ribun (Arabicized Christians) and Saqaliba (European slave soldiers)] the apprehension if not the reality of cultural ambiguity was widespread" (Blumenthal 105). Race becomes an issue of cultural confusion. This cultural ambiguity certainly must have confused the concept of Moor and black. Blumenthal's observation that focuses on ethnicity and obscures race is typical of those statements that have been used as a distraction from the reality of an Afro Spanish identity in Islamic Spain. Where are the blacks in this hodgepodge of ethnic acculturation? Given the political moment and the hierarchy of Islamic society it is an indisputable fact that they were integral factors to be considered in the cultural, political, religious and literary environment of the period.

Throughout this study, we have looked at the text in relationship to the environment in which it (the historical or creative text) was written and have focused particularly on the language that is operational in a context of situation. This method has enabled us to confirm not only the presence of blacks in early Spain, but also their importance in the composition of a national identity.

The importance of Moors, who came from a region in Africa where there are blacks, and who are a part of Spain's national identity, is often diffused amongst considerations of race. The question, for some researchers, is whether Arabs (black and brown) are part of a Caucasoid race. If we focus on a tenth-century Hispano-Arabic epic poem to illustrate our references to the relation of language to its environment, (what is said or written), and the nonverbal or situational environment which determines word choice and semantic focus, it will be seen how race can be diffused. The concept we use, based on Halliday's *Language as Social Semiotic* (113), illustrates clearly how race as a codified construct works. The following example taken from Ibn 'Abd Rabbihi (Cordoba, 860-940) serves as a model:

> Verse 68: [He campaigned] . . . against the person . . . who had disobeyed the law and done mischief, whose origin may be traced back to a certain black *Sawada* if he should boast of his origin.
>
> Verse 95: After it came the campaign of the fifth year against the descendants of *Sawada*, the *ally* of misfortune. (Monroe 82, 86)

In both verses, the poet focuses on the symbol "Sawada," an Arabic term for black person. "Sawada" has become an active part of the poet's lexico-grammatical system, in the form of a discrete option, controlled by meaning. Meaning is approached through the historical background of this long epic poem written originally in Arabic. The poet used as origin the battle campaign of 'Abd al-Rahman III (912-961) against Omar Ibn Hafsun who was from the northeastern part of Malaga, Spain. For the poet Rabbihi, Ibn Hafsun is a *Sawada* (black descendent) whose ancestors would identify him racially "if he should boast of his origin," as the verse says.

For historical background, we referred to two sources. Condé in his 1820 study of the history of Arabs in Spain declares that Omar Ibn Hafsun, later known as Ibn Hafsun Ibn Giafar Ibn Arius, was of obscure, perhaps totally *unknown* origin (Foster 302). Yet Dozy, in his account of Islamic Spain, also written in the nineteenth century traces Ibn Hafsun's genealogy as having descended from a good family and that Ibn Hafsun was fifth in descent from a Visigothic count Alfonso (Dozy 316). If the latter account is true, Ibn Hafsun could claim as ancestors the Teutonic tribe that invaded the Roman Empire in the fifth century to set up a kingdom in Spain which lasted until the Moslem invasion. Thus he could claim only white forebears. Are we to accept posterior historical accounts about Ibn Hafsun? Or should we accept the *in situ* poet who alleges that Ibn Hafsun became Samuel the Christian renegade after abandoning Islam and "disobeying the law [of his Moslem faith]"? Whatever his true racial background happened to have been, Ibn Hafsun's contemporary, the poet Ibn Rabbihi opted to refer to him by using the term *Sawada* ("descendent of a black"), and perhaps expose him through the epithet.

The semantics of early Spanish literature written in Arabic, or perhaps better defined as Arabic literature written in Spain during the eighth to the fifteenth centuries, in no uncertain terms attest to an Afro Iberian identity within the process of cultural transmission. Consequently the terms *Sawada, Aswad* and *Abdun Aswad* appear consistently as racial references in the literature. The fact that not all Afro Iberians were Moslem and that some converted to Christianity is also accepted in the early creative literature of Spain. As a matter of fact, pictorial representations confirm the social context we have found in the poetry of this period. The *Cantigas de Santa Maria* or "Songs in Praise of St. Mary" composed by Alfonso X of Castille, circa 1255, is an example. Perhaps the most interesting feature of the collection are the 1,262 miniatures done by various Spanish artists. They are a mirror of daily life in thirteenth-century Spain. Some of the miniatures have been reproduced in a study by R. I. Burns, entitled *Islam Under The Crusaders* (cf. pp. 318-19). There are black Moslems (Cantigas 63, 95, 99) shown as Moorish warriors; there are black Mudéjars (Moslems who lived in areas recaptured by Christians), and in Cantiga 192 there is an extremely realistic series of black Moslems in various stages of conversion to Christianity. It is at this point, seemingly, in the thirteenth century, that historians and researchers begin to confuse or rather manipulate the term "Moor." Are the Moors white, black, brown, or an amalgam of races analogous to the "Cosmic race" theory suggested at the beginning of this study?

The miniatures opposite page 319 of Burns' study are typical of the confusion where color code and context elude the observer. Burns refers to the caption under the illustration as "Negro gentlemen at Chess." There are four men who are visibly black and one who seems to be white. However, Burns rejects the notion that the blacks are a typical representation of Moors and suggests they could be "Christian Negroes" [sic]. It seems that by the thirteenth century, the term "Moor" had lost its ethnic denotation to assume a religio-cultural connotation to include all those who had fought under the banners of Islam.

The African Connection to the Moors in Spain

Most historians agree that as a group the Moors came from Africa. Perhaps the confusion arises from the fact that Arabs who were phenotypically black, and dark brown to light-skinned had settled in Western Africa by the eighth century. The religion that the Arabs brought, Islam, plays an important part in determining who was to be called a Moor; and the name "Almoravid" becomes exceptionally important. Some writers say that they descend from barbarian Africans or Berbers whose chief ambition was to destroy the "noble Arabs." Others say that the Almoravids, including their leader Yusuf Ibn Tashfin, were pure Arabs. The Almoravids as tribe were based on an island in the Senegal river and had been introduced to Islamic culture by a teacher from Andalusia, (southern Spain), Abdulla Ibn Yasin al Juzulli.

Abu Bekr, an Almoravid chief, took control of Ghana around 1076 and imposed Islam on the people. Ghana eventually became an Islamized kingdom (Sékéné-Mody 29-30). Consequently, under the religious tenets of Islam, non-Arab Ghanaian people were also obliged to go into Spain, with all the other troops, and fight to maintain the religious hegemony of Islam under the concept of "Jihad" or Moslem Crusade.

Ghana was a kingdom inside the territorial limits of the region then known as the Sudan, which included parts of Nigeria, Niger, Mali, Mauritania, today's Senegal and stretched further east to what is present day Sudan.[2] The Sudan as such became a popular source of manpower for the Almoravids. Some of these Africans and Arabized Africans were sent to Spain as enforced labor. Others were shaped into an elite troop of black warriors, supplied with the finest horses, and had their social status raised before being sent to fight the Christians in Spain, (Condé II, 218).

Another dimension of the Almoravids emerges when we consider that ethnicity and race often overlap in the historical perspective. It has been said that the Almoravids might possibly be Berbers. The Berbers were themselves a mixed group, and were given this name because they did not speak either Latin or Greek. The term included a composite of western Asiatic tribes, southwestern Europeans, Numidians and Mauritanians. These groups stretched out over a vast geographical area. The Numidians and the Mauritanians have historically been classified as black. It has also been determined that the Almoravids were a mixed group with black kings. This was the ethnic group that advanced northward out of Mauritania through Morocco and Algeria into Spain. Mauritania on the other hand, as a geographical point, becomes crucial in the identification of that group of warriors who came to be known later as Moors. As a matter of fact, the name Mauritania itself refers to racial blackness. Early Greek explorers, prior to Christianity, raided the northern and western coasts of Africa. They located a region in Western Africa whose inhabitants they called "Mauros" due to their black color. That re-

[2]It must be pointed out that this entire region was previously considered to be the Sudan. The ancient kingdom of Ghana, Mali and Songhai formed the Sudanese kingdoms.

gion later became known as Mauritania and at the time included more territory than present day Mauritania (Fernández de Palencia P. cdxviii).

Ultimately, the racial ties with Africa become subterfuged. What one finds is the confusion between Arab as Moor and Moor as Arab, in the conquest of Spain. Subsequent usage of the terms as an ethnic code void of racial indications but replete with religious connotations diminishes the contribution of phenotypically black men and women to the culture and genealogy of Spain from the eighth to the thirteenth centuries. It cannot be denied that it is historically correct that the arrival of Arabized Africans reinforced the introduction of Arab culture into Spain. Likewise, because of the presence of the Moors, and other Arab groups who were identified as black (for example, the musician Ziryab), an Afro Iberian identity was unquestionably established as part of the ethnic image of early Spain. One can conclude that the geographical point of reference as a mother land for the progeny of these groups was unquestionably Spain.

In spite of later denials of the African contribution, as the Christian reconquest became more vigorously pursued, it appears that the generic term Moor connotated not only a direct relationship with Islam, but that Africa came into play as the site of Islam's ethnic origin. The Afro Iberian identity began to lose ground. For example, the anonymous author of the *Poema de Fernán González,* a work which appeared in the thirteenth century, illustrates this concept with direct references:

> When their weapons were broken and burned
> The news was sent to *Morocco;*
> the *Africans* were soon rounded up
> at the port they soon arrived . . . .
> All these *pagans* to Africa were sent, . . . (71, 73a).

Islam for Christians was tantamount to paganism. In this sense, as the poem progresses, the term Moor seems to include Turks, Arabs and Almohads, those Arabized Africans from Mauritania (see verses 77c, 78b, 81b, 383a, 384a for example). We must recall from the examples cited at the beginning of this study that Moslems, on the other hand, saw the residents of their Iberian world as white, black, brown, etc.

The image of the Afro Iberian as seen by Moslem and Christian writers differs according to the relationships of roles and status. Although the black image was seen in the texts of Ibn Khafacha as positive and in Ibn Hamdin as negative, neither made specific reference to Africans in generic terms, more than likely due to the indicated factor of role relationships. However, with the onrush of the reconquest of Spain by Spanish Christians there seems to be more of a focus on the exoticism of blacks, and blacks as an image alien to the Iberian identity. Consequently, in the *Libro de Alexandre,* a thirteenth-century work of disputed authorship, an appeal to the bizarre, where blacks are concerned, takes precedent over visible reality. One finds, in the text, a black man who measured some thirty arm lengths from his "feet to his neck" (1364b, c, d) as a concept of realism. Unusual physical qualities, for the black person, becomes the norm. Yet, none is pictured as native Iberian.

There is no doubt that from the thirteenth century on, with the rising hegemony of Christian control, the image of blacks with an Iberian identity became less and less acceptable. In *El Conde Lucanor* and the *Poema de Yusuf* both of the fourteenth century, there are black characters endowed with both wit and limited social responsibility, but they are slaves and no reference is made to their nationality. A perusal of the literature of that period has enabled us to conclude that a work such as *El Cavallero Cifar* or *Cifar the Knight* (fourteenth century) can be taken as an example of the consensus for the period. There are no identifiable black characters in this book, but Africa is referred to with biblical allusions as being the land of black people. Cifar, the protagonist, is East Indian. Oriental Indians are dark, according to the author, due to India's contiguous borders with Africa. What we find revealing in the shift from an Afro Iberian image to blacks with non-Christian imagery, however, are the author's aesthetics where Africans are concerned:

> God keeps them [the Indians] from becoming like them [the blacks], from acquiring their crudeness, and gave them [the Indians] wisdom and kindness in manner and thought more than to many whites. (56)

At first glance there would be a tendency to say that negative racial attitudes had become concretized under Christian rule in Spain. However, the authors of this study have concluded that the racialist features of this text are predicated more on a Christian antipathy toward Africans *qua* Moors (Almoravids, Almohads, etc.). We have considered that during the thirteenth-century period in which *El Cavallero Cifar* was written, Spanish Christians did not have ready access to the African continent; it was geographically unfamiliar. Islamic Moors still controlled southern Spain and the Mediterranean, and those Moors that did remain behind in territories recaptured by the Christians lived usually in religious ghettos called "morerías." Furthermore, by placing India, the land of Cifar, contiguous with Africa, as we have seen, the author of the book confirms his geographical ignorance. Consequently, we feel that "Africa as land of the blacks" had begun to be seen, for some authors of this period, as the code for a religious backlash, a form of interaction.

It can also be concluded that social interaction controls the semantics of the writer's imagery. Again, in the *Poema de Fernán González,* the same construct of ethnicity and religion is very clearly expressed in stanza 385:

> There is an onrush of people without rhyme or reason,
> not from the same place, nor of the same language
> but they were uglier than Satan and all of his cohorts
> when he came up from hell, dirty and black as soot.

There is no expressed Afro Iberian identity. However, the negative qualities of being hideous and black become associated with being the Moor or Moslem invader.

While we are considering the African dimension of the Moor, we should also remember that not all of the Moors were expelled from Spain in 1492, the year of the "great expulsion of Moslem and Jews." Some remained as nominal Christians and were controlled by The Inquisition (1492) who also directed religious thought and social customs. There *were* Afro Iberians in Spain during the thirteenth to the sixteenth centuries; these are basically the years between the downfall of the Spanish Moslems and the discovery and peopling of Hispanic America. Afro Iberians accompanied Columbus and other conquerors of the New World, not as not as slaves, but as crew and helpers according to first hand accounts.[3] Vincente Graullera Sanz gives an interesting account of the non-Caucasoid population of the Spain of this period. He refers in particular to the wide range of phenotypes that one finds due to miscegenation: "the constant mixture of the races that has taken place all throughout our history" (126). The fact that slaves were both black

---

[3]Early Spanish diaries written during the conquest of the New World give the names and occupations of some of the black Spanish (Iberian) men who were among the crew of the fifteenth-century Spanish conquerors.

and white and a variety of skin tones in between establishes a racial context for the literature of early Spain.

Afro Iberian Cultural Assimilation

The image of the Afro Iberian as an entity in creative literature seems to acquire a more definitive form as a national figure, towards the middle of the sixteenth century, if we use *Lazarillo de Tormes,* (circa 1550), as an example. Lazarillo and his mother, victims of economic adversity, accept Zaide, a black man, into their home. Not only do they begin to eat well, but Lazarillo's mother also has a son for Zaide, described by Lazarillo as "un negrito muy bonito," that is, "a very beautiful little black child" (64). Race is also used as an element of social protest. In *Lazarillo de Tormes,* Lazarillo's half-brother, the son of Zaide, finds his father's black color to be intimidating and prefers the phenotype of Lazarillo and his mother who are white: "How many people must there be in the world who flee from others because they don't look at themselves," is Lazarillo's philosophical comment (65). As a code construct, Zaide has a multidimensional ideational range. Through him the author advises us of the reality of the Afro Iberian experience of that period (sixteenth century): some are free, work for a living, have interracial relationships, and function with some degree of normalcy within the society.

It is obvious, nonetheless, with the characterization of Zaide in *Lazarillo de Tormes* that Afro Iberians had at least become an integral part of Spain's popular society. The reference that Lazarillo makes about his half brother, "a beautiful little black child" and his half brother's refusal to accept his black-related phenotype could suggest one of the reasons why the Spanish prototype finds it inadmissable to accept black ancestry as part of the national genotype. Yet, there has been a verifiable Afro Iberian Identity in Spanish literature, from the time of the Arab and Moorish invasions, up to the point of a recognizable cultural and racial assimilation in the sixteenth and seventeenth centuries. However, for some scholars of Spanish literature, admission of this fact has the tendency to become clouded in specious arguments of doubt, based on false premises of the absence of blacks in the Arab and Moorish conquest of Spain, and a subsequent black citizenry as part of the national demography.

Likewise, some writers until recently, rejected the notion of an identifiable

Afro Hispanic corpus in Latin American literature, or viewed the black presence as incidental. Recent and ongoing research has changed this perspective (Jackson, Lewis *et. al.*). In this respect, a black identity in Spain and Spanish literature has yet to be researched with an equal amount of serious endeavor. Nonetheless, when accomplished, we are certain that the realities of this triadic movement from Africa to Spain to Hispanic America will add another dimension to the African identity and contribution to creative literature in both Spain and Hispanic America.

There are many approaches to an investigation of racial identity in national literatures. The authors of this study suggest creative literature because of its social orientation as a premise of direction in ethnicity and aesthetics. While other methods of literary criticism are perhaps just as valid, we have focused on research that used a semiotic approach to aesthetics.

WORKS CITED

Arberry, Arthur J. *Moorish Poetry. A Translation of the Pennants by Ibn Sa'id.* Cambridge: CUP, n. d.

Baranda Leturio. "Las hablas de negros. Orígenes de un personaje literario." *Revista de Filologia Española.* LXIX, 1989. 311-33.

Blumenthal, David R., ed. *Approaches to Judaism in Medieval Times.* Vol. III. Atlanta, Georgia: Scholar's Press, 1988.

Burns, Robert I. *Islam under the Crusaders.* Princeton: Princeton UP, 1973.

El Caballero Cifar. Ed. Martín de Riquer. 2 vols. Barcelona: Selecciones Bibliófilas, 1951.

Condé, J. A. *History of the Dominion of the Arabs in Spain.* Trans. Mrs. Jonathan Foster. 3 vols. London: George Bell and Sons, 1909-1913.

Cope, Joan Penelope, trans. *Arabic-Andalusian Casidas.* Kent England: The Pound Press, 1953.

Dozy, Reinhart. *Spanish Islam: A History of the Moslems in Spain.* Trans. Francis Griffin Stokes. 3 vols. London: Chatto and Windus, 1913.

Fernández de Palencia, Alfonso. *Universal vocabulario en latín y en romance.* 2 vols. Madrid: Comisión Permanente de la Asociación de Academias de la Lengua Española, 1967.

Fiore, Robert L. *Lazarillo de Tormes.* Boston: Twayne, 1984.

——. *El libro de las banderas de los campeones de Ibn Said al-Magribi.* Barcelona: Seix Barral, 1978.

——. *Poemas arábigoandaluces.* Madrid: Espasa-Calpe, 1959.

Graullera Sanz, Vicente. *La esclavitud en Valencia en los siglos XVI Y XVII.* Valencia: Consejo Superior de Investigaciones Científicas, 1978.

Halliday, M. A. K. *Language as Social Semiotic: The Social Interpretation of Language and Meaning.* London: Edward Arnold, 1979.

Imamuddin, S. M. *A Political History of Muslim Spain*. Pakistan: Najmah Sons, 1969.

Jackson, Richard L. *Black Literatures and Humanism*. Athens, Georgia: U of Georgia P, 1988.

Juan Manuel, Don. *El Conde Lucanor*. Ed. José Manuel Blecua. Madrid: Cátedra, 1982.

Lewis, Marvin A. *Afro-Hispanic Poetry: 1940-1980. From Slavery to "Negritude" in South American Verse*. Columbia: U of Missouri P, 1983.

Libro de Alexandre. Ed. Jesús Cañas Murillo. Madrid: Editora Nacional, 1983.

Monroe, James J. *Hispano-Arabic Poetry: A Student Anthology*. Berkeley: U of California P, 1974.

Morland, Harold. Trans. *Arabic Andalusian Casidas*. London: Phoenix Press, 1959.

Norris, N. J. *The Berbers in Arabic Literature*. Lebanon: Librairie du Liban, 1982.

Peres, Henri. *Esplendor de al-Andalus*. Trans. Mercedes García-Arenal. Madrid: Hisperión, 1953.

——. *La poésie andalouse en arabe classique au XIe siecle*. Paris: Adrien-Maisonneuve, 1953.

Poema de Fernán González. Barcelona: Vosgos, 1975.

"Poema de Yúsuf." *Poesía española medieval*. Ed. Manuel Alvar. Barcelona: Planeta, 1969. 338-48.

Read, Ian. *The Moors in Spain and Portugal*. London: Faber and Faber, 1974.

Sékéné-Mody, Cissoko. *Histoire de l'Afrique Occidentale. Moyen Age et Temps Modernes*. Vol. I. Paris: Présence Africaine, 1966.

Vasconcelos, José. *La raza cósmica: missión de la raza iberoamericana*. Buenos Aires: Espasa-Calpe Argentina, 1948.

Vega, Ana Lydia. *Encancaranublado y otros cuentos de naufragio*. Río Piedras, Puerto Rico: Editorial Antillana, 1983.

PATRICIA HART

Catalan Culture and Identity Through Popular Forms: The Collaborative Efforts of the Ofèlia Dracs Group in *Negra i consentida* (*Hardboiled and Spoiled*)

Unsuspecting readers who pick up a volume signed by Ofèlia Dracs and start to leaf through it may quickly begin to wonder why they have never heard of this fairly prolific woman before. The book in hand will give no clue to her identity, but before long, hopefully someone will let the readers in on the joke, and they will discover that Ofèlia Dracs is a pseudonym for ten Catalan writers who have published four collective books to date. Friends of the same generation who began publishing at roughly the same time, the collective members one day decided at a party that publishing things in common might be an effective means of promoting the Catalan language and cultural identity through popular forms.

The idea of writing collective works is not a new one, and in fact has a long tradition that ranges from the glorious to the notorious. An example of the latter in our century is the erotic collaboration in Paris and then New York in the 1930s of the group that included Henry Miller and Anaïs Nin, writers with great stylistic differences but at least one ideological bond — a desire to praise the liberty of natural man and woman, to exalt sexuality, to escape middle-class morality, and along the way, to shock the bourgeoisie. Eventually, of course, both Nin and Miller published their erotica separately, under their own names, destroying the illusion of collectivity, and returning to the post-romantic convention of insistently identifying a work with one individual, highly individualistic author. Another set of models for Ofèlia Dracs could be the Victorian poets and painters of the Pre-Raphaelite school who wanted to return to what they felt was a happy innocence of style in Italian visual art before Raphael, before the materialism of industrialized England. Together they published a periodical called *The Germ* that included collective works, and put forward romantic ideas into the somewhat hostile environment of Victorian England. Another example would be the Tory writers of Queen Anne's time, a century earlier in England — Pope, Swift, Gay,

Parnell, Congreve, Dr. Arbuthnot, Bishop Atterbury, and Lord Oxford — who opposed Whig politics favoring the merchants and arms makers who were getting rich from the War of Spanish Succession. Together these Tory writers of classical bent formed the Scriblerus Club around 1713, and even published together a book of the purported "memoirs" of one Martinus Scriblerus, "designed to ridicule all the false tastes in learning under the character of a man of capacity enough that had dipped into every art and science, but injudiciously in each."

Both the Pre-Raphaelites and the members of the Scriblerus Club had a central set of practical goals, both were drawn together to oppose a larger external political reality as well as aesthetic trends they did not like, both groups collaborated on some works, read each other's manuscripts, corresponded, and suggested things to be written by one member or another to fill in perceived gaps.

The collaborative efforts of the Ofèlia Dracs group has elements in common with these and other forerunners. Like the Nin/Miller group, Ofèlia Dracs produced a collection of erotica, but their works are not limited to the erotic. Like the Pre-Raphaelites and the Tories, Ofèlia Dracs has a central purpose they are intent on promoting through their fiction — doing everything possible to ensure the continued existence of Catalan language and literature, and encouraging each other to produce works with both popular and aesthetic appeal. As a region of Spain with a new separate language, literary tradition, and culture, Catalonia suffered greatly under the dictatorship of Francisco Franco, who tried to impose a cultural uniformity on the entire country. During this period Catalonia was subject to a series of oppressive laws restricting the use of the Catalan language in written and spoken form, and a whole generation of Catalans was denied schooling in their native tongue. Thus, post-dictatorship Catalan authors struggle to make publishing in Catalan viable and to encourage the new generation to read in their native tongue. Part of this process includes producing works of fiction in popular as well as "high" literary forms.

One of the members of the group, Maria-Antònia Oliver, explained to me the birth and procedure of the collective:

> One of us invented the pseudonym of Ofèlia Dracs, and we began to write genre fiction together. It started with a book of erotic stories, and then I think we wrote a group of horror stories, one of science fiction, a collection of detective tales, and finally a cookbook. Every time we each write one story. First we have a planning meeting, we divide up the themes, then

> we write the stories, then we meet and critique them mercilessly, and when we finally reach a minimum accord as to quality, then we publish it with our pseudonym, that is, the stories are not individually signed. We have the convention that it's a secret, and it's fun for people to try to guess who wrote each one. (Personal Interview)[1]

As with other collaborative groups like those cited above, ultimately the Ofèlia Dracs collective provided an incentive, a meeting ground of stimulation, and a starting point from which various members have gone on to or continued with more important individual contributions.

In this article I would like to discuss the role one of these collections, *Negra i consentida* (*Hardboiled and Spoiled*), played in the overall development of the *novel.la negra* (*roman noir,* dark detective novel) as written by the collective's best-known authors, singling out Jaume Fuster, Maria-Antònia Oliver, Joaquim Carbó, and Antoni Serra. As one of the most popular types of genre fictions in Spain, hardboiled detective fiction has long been translated into Spanish and read in Catalonia, so to the Ofèlia Dracs group it seemed the ideal form to use in order to recruit a broad base of new readers in Catalan.

The highest profile of the group belongs to Jaume Fuster, whose interest in Catalan detective fiction predates the Ofèlia Dracs collective by more than a decade. In 1972, Fuster translated into Castilian Manuel de Pedrolo's crime masterpiece, *Joc brut* (*Dirty Pool*), and the same year published his own first novelistic attempt on the genre, with *De mica en mica s'omple la pica* (*Little By Little the Basin Fills*), in which he introduced his recurring protagonist, Enric Vidal. Like Philip Marlowe and Sam Spade, to whom the book is in part dedicated, Enric is a loner, and like them, he reflects the injustice of existing social situations. But he has other influences on him as well, and we remember that the novel's dedication also recognizes Rafael Tasis and Manuel de Pedrolo, "who had the nerve to write detective novels and then publish them in Catalan."

On the surface, Enric Vidal is a fairly typical product of postwar cynicism and the force of economic despair. At the beginning of the novel, Enric has been expelled from Pharmacy studies in the University for misdeeds explained in full in the short story, "Ofèlia a les tres" ("Ofèlia at Three") Fuster's contribution to *Hardboiled and Spoiled.* Enric is an expert at taking advantage of women. Not

---

[1]This and all of the other translations of titles and quotations from Catalan into English have been done by me.

above cadging money from his sister, Enric then scrounges work from the married man who is keeping her, smuggling money across several borders. From there, he moves to blackmail and a variety of other legal infractions large and small, but as he gradually realizes who pulls the strings in this puppet show, Enric reveals eventually that he does have a conscience, albeit a deeply buried one. The death of his sister, combined with his encounters with Pere, a coveraled labor organizer who reminds Enric of his father, practically convinces him that he can stand alone against a corrupt system, side with the downtrodden laborer, and come out ahead. Now it is significant to remember that a key explanation to this side of Enric's personality is provided precisely in the story that forms part of the collective work. In "Ofèlia a les tres," when searching for a convenient explanation for his expulsion from the university, Enric pretended that he had been kicked out for participating in a student demonstration. At the climax of *Little By Little*, it is as if Enric tries to convert these lies and fantasies into reality. We read:

> The memory of my father, of the words of my father, came alive in my head. I could help them and I would! Of course I would! (142)

At this point Enric has visions of riding to the rescue of the workers, a knight in shining armor, but the illusion soon tarnishes, and Enric realizes once more that if every man has his price, his own is embarrassingly low.

In his subsequent novels in which Enric reappears — *Tarda sessió contínua* (*Continuous Afternoon Session,* 1976) and *La corona valenciana* (*The Valencian Crown,* 1982) — Fuster continues to exploit the notion that a lone hero (ethical or otherwise) can never succeed in solving collective problems. He told me in a 1983 interview:

> Enric Vidal wants to solve the problem of the working man all by himself. Marlon Brando wants the same. Brando succeeds, and Enric Vidal doesn't Why not? Because I believe that individuals have never resolved labor problems. It has always been collective effort that has done that. (Hart, *The Spanish Sleuth,* 82)[2]

How appropriate it is, in view of this belief, that a collective work like *Hard-boiled and Spoiled* should shed light on Enric Vidal's ideology on the subject of group effort! Fuster himself pointed out:

> The difference in treatment, then, is a difference between North America and Europe. The American is basically an individualist, and nevertheless he succeeds. But that is false! What really happened is that the workers

---

[2]This interview was originally conducted in Spanish, and the translation is mine.

> got together, went on strike, lost most battles but won a few. Enric Vidal sells out, and Bogart in *Afternoon Session* sells out in the end too because the individual always sells out. (Hart, 82-3)

Collectivity is also a key ingredient in Fuster's short puzzle pieces first published in a continuing column in the magazine, *El Món* (*The World*), and then collected in a book, both under the title, *Les claus de vidre* (*The Glass Keys*). Each of the stories presents a short mystery resolved by Barcelonan detective Lluis Arquer (a tribute to Ross MacDonald's Lew Archer, just as the title of the series is a tribute to Dashiell Hammett). At the end of the book is a brief explanation of the way Arquer arrived at his brilliant conclusions in each case, but before turning to it, the reader has a chance to match wits with the detective and suggest his own explanation. Thus the reader must collaborate with Fuster to make the stories function fully. These delightful stories work perfectly well as mysteries and effortless escape reading, but at the same time give a run-down on Barcelonan society from top to bottom, collect Catalan sayings, comment on local foibles, and even provide linguistic insight into the differences between Catalan accented from provincial Cerdanya versus metropolitan Barcelona. His ten page, "El rapte de les sabines" ("The Rape of the Sabines") shows a decidedly more clever use of the allusion than García Pavón made in an entire novel; "Assegurança de vida" ("Life Insurance") rings with double meaning, from the tribute to James M. Cain's *Double Indemnity* in the title; "Fiat lux," ("Let There Be Light") "Març, marçot, mata la vella i la jove si pot," (From a a silly yet sinister children's poem that literally translates, "March, big old March, kill the old woman, and the young one if you can!") and "No dispareu contra el burgés," ("Don't Shoot the Bourgeois Man" — a takeoff on Truffaut's film title, "Don't Shoot the Piano Player") — are all as much fun as their titles imply. Once more, Fuster proves that although a spark of inspiration may come from a foreign source, he knows how to synthesize inspiration with experience to make the whole decidedly Catalan and definitely his own. Once more, collective experience is the key.

Fuster continues this collective experiment in a second collection of "Glass Key" mysteries, *Vida de gos* (*Dog's Life*, 1989). This time the adventures stray further from the Barcelonan home beat of Arquer, when the detective travels to Paris over a puzzling last will, to Cerdanya for a session of high fashion photography, to Menorca for the filming of a movie, and back again to post-modern

Barcelona, always solving the mysteries with the participation and help of the reader.

Another member of the collective whose hardboiled tales predate Ofèlia Dracs is Joaquim Carbó, whose *Solucions provisionals* (*Provisional Solutions*) won the Premi Víctor Català in 1964, and who followed it with *L'escapada* (*The Escape*) in 1967. Carbó's contribution to *Hardboiled and Spoiled* is the first tale in the book, a story with a frame that shows us a glimpse of the "author," a poor writer and avid reader whose book collection is being carried off by a philistine used book buyer who has the nerve to measure the sale by shelf meter. The man rudely carries off the writer's most prized possessions, including the yellow-backed series from the original *Cua de Palla,* directed by Manuel de Pedrolo.[3] With this sordid beginning, Carbó then launches into a grim tale of old accounts settled, full of references to *El Camp de la Bota* (an outlying area of Barcelona where mass shootings of political prisoners took place after the Spanish Civil War). The politically produced rancor that has accompanied the protagonist since childhood is the main theme, and Carbó uses the popular form to clarify this important issue to Catalan culture and identity. This story, which opens the collection, sets the tone for the entire book, which will focus on the dark underside of Barcelona, a world peopled by characters like la Tanguista (The Tango Dancer), el Tirabuzones (Corkscrew Curls), Police Commissioner D'Olivier, and a Barcelona that consists of a dirty port, the *barri xinés* (Red Light District), poor neighborhoods, and lingering postwar resentments. By opening the book with Carbó's framed tale, the group makes a point about their collective belief in the oppression of Barcelona and by extension Catalonia under Franco, something their united efforts seek to expose and prevent from recurring. Carbó's self-conscious, circular story also lets the reader know from the start that although the genre may be popular, the writers involved have not taken that to mean the opposite of art.

Unlike Carbó and Fuster, Mallorcans Maria-Antònia Oliver and Antoni Serra

---

[3]The original *Cua de Palla* series was an initiative of Max Cahner and Jaume Casajoana, who proposed that Manuel Pedrolo direct the series, which he did from 1963 to 1970. The series, which gets its name from an old Catalan saying ("if you have a straw tail, it may catch on fire"), published detective novels in translations done by some of the best-known writers in Catalunya, including Pedrolo himself, Rafael Tasis, Josep Vallverdú, Maria-Aurèlia Capmany, and Joan Oliver. Authors translated included Chandler, Hammett, Cain, Burnett, Ross MacDonald, Himes, Hadley Chase, Simenon, Pierre Véry, and a long list of others. In the eighties the series was recommenced.

had not brushed with the crime genre directly before Ofèlia Dracs, but have since published several detective volumes each. As Maria-Antònia Oliver told me:

> It is thanks to Ofèlia Dracs that Lònia Guiu exists, because even though I live with a writer [husband Jaume Fuster] who knows a lot about detective fiction, it was enough that he was my companion for me to not want to do anything to copy him. By contrast, when urged on by the collective I decided to take a stab at it. (Interview)

Oliver's entry, "On ets, Mònica?" ("Where Are You, Mònica?") saw the birth of her tough, liberated heroine, Lònia Guiu, in a case involving the disappearance of a Barcelonan woman from the upper class. In the story we see in embryo most of the major themes that emerged in the two subsequent Lònia novels (*Estudi en lila,* (*Study in Lilac,* 1987), and *Antípodes,* (*Antipodes,* 1988), the most important being that men and women rarely manage better than an uneasy coexistence spiced by sex, and close behind this the notion that the monied class is actually much more dangerous than the so-called criminal one. Thus, the uniqueness of Mallorcan culture and language are accompanied by universal feminist beliefs which have made the novels popular sellers in the U.S. Although Oliver claims to have read practically nothing in the detective genre before writing the story for Ofèlia Dracs, and insists on total unfamiliarity with Agatha Christie, the "surprise" at the ending involves one of the grande dame of English potboilers' most oft-used and least believable tricks — a woman passing for another closeup in the daylight with nothing more than the aid of higher heels, wigs, make-up, and a voice disguised thanks to fortuitous "acting ability."[4] In spite of this, however, the story is entertaining and did motivate Oliver to write two further adventures of Lònia to date.[5]

There is also a positive side to Oliver's unfamiliarity with many detective conventions. In the hard-boiled detective tale, even more clearly than elsewhere in the mystery story since its inception, there are traditionally very few roles for women characters: *femme fatale,* hankie-wringing damsel in distress, loyal secretary, witness, or victim, and most of these appearances register on just two moral

---

[4]For example, in *Witness for the Prosecution,* and in a host of other novels and stories.

[5]I do not doubt that a wig and a clothes change could fool someone who only caught a glimpse of someone they did not know, but in general, body shape, size, the way of moving, voice, and so on are harder to disguise than Christie would have us believe. Here, where the detective speaks to the disguised person at length face to face, I found the device impossible to swallow, as the culprit is attempting not only to disguise herself from someone who knows her, but also at the same time to pass for someone else in particular.

extremes: active and evil, or good and helpless. Oliver's relative ignorance of the genre and its conventions was probably all to the good in helping her break away from these phallocentric strictures. Moreover, the virtue in these stories comes more from contradicting traditional Catalan culture and the female sense of identity it imposes than from reinforcing them.

Oliver's protagonist, Lònia Guiu, is a Mallorcan native who has forged a private detective business for herself in Post-Franquist Barcelona assisted by her male sidekick, Quim. Through Lònia, Oliver shows us brilliantly that the problem of creating feminist fiction in Catalonia or anywhere else is nowhere near as easy as just plugging women into the starring roles, for all of the subordinate relationships between detective and bad guy, detective and corrupt businessman, detective and female victim, detective and loyal secretary, involve different sexual politics and even physical risks when the detective is a woman. In *Study in Lilac,* Oliver charts the difficulty women themselves have in abandoning the role of victim — specifically with regard to rape. It is to her credit that she suggests no easy answers, and instead points out where the extremes lead — the young woman who cannot manage to fight back against societal responses to rape is eventually destroyed, while the woman who does fight becomes a vicious destroyer herself. Lònia is left alone at the end of the novel to ponder whether there may be a middle ground between these extremes.

In *Antipodes*, the plot centers on the prostitution of women, both the traditional sexual brand, as well as the kind also known as "domestic service." As the title suggests, the women in Oliver's novels are often islands, isolated from each other and men, and connected only by a sea of exploitation. Once more Lònia shows in the book that being female and a private eye is not a simple inversion of the male role, but actually involves additional dangers. Lònia must not only take physical blows from her opponents the way a Sam Spade or a Lew Archer might, but she takes them on a smaller, weaker frame that sustains permanent damage, as her injured ear shows. Moreover, she also faces the constant, humiliating threat of rape when she deals with the male thugs who are essential to a good crime story. Feminist crime fantasy, like Lourdes Ortiz's 1979 work in Spanish, *Picadura mortal* (*Mortal Coquetry*), has detective Bárbara Arenas disarm burly bodyguards and ruffians right and left with nothing more than a well-timed *culada,* (or what in football I believe is called a "butt block"), but Oliver chooses instead to be realistic, with the result being a story that is less exhilarating but more authentic.

The novel also shows pointed examples of women socialized to undermine other women in a way they might not undermine a man in the same role — once more showing why Lònia must work twice as hard at times as a male detective to succeed. Her relationships to young women victims in both novels are especially interesting inversions of hard-boiled conventions. In a male detective who helps out a young damsel in distress, his paternalistic concern often masks sexual interest, an interest that is not infrequently rewarded at the case's resolution, when it comes time for the former victim to express gratitude. By contrast, the relentlessly hetero Lònia has no physical attraction to Sebastiana, the rape victim in *Study*, or to Cristina, the young girl forced into prostitution in *Antipodes*. Her desire to help is more altruistic than in her traditional male counterpart. In one instance she fails completely to save the victim, and in the other discovers that she herself has been victimized by the person pity had moved her to help. Even when she tries the time-honored solution favored by male flatfeet (slugging some satisfaction out of her victimizer at the end of *Antipodes*), the gesture is less gratifying than she had hoped. All of these insights are ones Oliver might not have found a vehicle to express without the Ofèlia Dracs experience.

Fellow Mallorcan Antoni Serra's entry to the collection, "Localizació Four," ("Location Four") by contrast, does not star his Portuguese sleuth, Celso Mosqueiro, who has appeared in three novels subsequent to the publication of *Hardboiled and Spoiled*. Rather, his story is a puzzle piece, strongly reminiscent of Borges' "La muerte y la brújula," ("Death and the Compass") with elements of his "Hombre de la Esquina Rosada" ("Man from Rose-colored Corner") as well (or with elements of Agatha Christie's *The Death of Roger Ackroyd*, if you prefer, to which both Borges and Serra are indebted). This story is more in line with novels published by Serra before *Hardboiled and Spoiled* than with his later work, but with him as with Oliver, the collective experience provided impetus toward what he later continued in a different vein with the Mosqueiro adventures.

For Mosqueiro, as for Fuster's Enric Vidal, the world of investigations is a corrupt place where justice rarely prevails and the rich (like the old Nazis in *El blau pàl.lid de la rosa de paper* (The Pale Blue of the Paper Rose) or the financier Maldà in *Espurnes de sang — Drops of Blood*) routinely escape punishment, while lesser criminals tangle with an ineffectual police force. In this way, both

Fuster's and Serra's mysteries are classic examples of what Italian critic Stefano Tani baptizes, "innovative anti-detective fiction," in his ground-breaking study, *The Doomed Detective*. Tani defines "innovative anti-detective fiction" as fiction that renews and at the same time undermines the traditional detective novel by stressing social criticism, solutions in which justice does not prevail, and the detective's inability to maintain detachment.[6]

But while Serra's basic plot structures may be said to fit loosely within Tani's category of innovative anti-detective fiction, there is one way in which they are unique, even among the Catalan authors discussed in this study. This uniqueness lies in a very personal treatment of and attitude toward the language of the novels' composition. For many Catalans, it is language itself that defines their culture and identity. Language is the dividing line that separates them from the rest of Spain and makes them something different. Therefore, to hardcore Catalanists, Spanish-speakers who live among them and share their customs can never be identified as Catalans unless they are also willing to make Catalan their first language.

That detective novels have been written in Catalan at all attests to a desire to preserve and strengthen the tongue, as everyone from Tasis to Pedrolo to Fuster has freely admitted. But the approach of Toni Serra goes one step further, showing an endearing relationship to his native Mallorcan that is distinct from the others. To understand how this relationship works, I would like to draw a comparison between Mosqueiro and detective-spy James Bond.

Ian Fleming's James Bond was a man of impossible virtues — a photographic memory, technical expertise, and considerable prowess not only in love but also in language. Nothing was more common in the series than for Bond to be sent to an exotic locale where he immediately spoke the language (whatever it was) fluently enough to pass for a native. When his adventures were translated to the screen, English-speaking viewers saw this represented by the device of having dwellers of foreign lands speak to Bond in accented English. Indeed, a child who watched Bond represent Her Majesty's interests abroad might have concluded that the entire world spoke English, with simple variations of pronunciation. Since English was the tongue of the once-mighty British Empire, and of the U.S. of the Cold War where the films earned the most money, the device was considered ac-

---

[6]Tani cites as examples of innovative anti-detective fiction *A ciascuno il suo*, by Leonardo Sciascia, *The Sunlight Dialogues*, by John Gardner, and *Il nome della rosa*, by Umberto Eco.

ceptable, and rarely questioned or even mentioned by English-speaking critics.

What Toni Serra does in his three Celso Mosqueiro novels is to turn this device upside down for the purpose of parody. In *Pale Blue* (1985), we are introduced to detective Celso Mosqueiro, who is presented to us as a Portuguese native policeman who is called in to help the Mallorcan police solve a murder with international implications. Serra makes no attempt at all to explain Mosqueiro's fluency in the language of the island, rather simply presents him directly meeting his Mallorcan counterpart with a cordial, "molt de gust. Som Celso Mosqueiro" ("Pleased to meet you. I'm Celso Mosqueiro" 10). A wealth of information is conveyed in the phrase. Not only does the author show by this that he considers it absolutely natural for the language of the island to be spoken by all and sundry (just as Cubby Broccoli's various avatars of Bond find English natural), moreover, he shows Mosqueiro speaking in Mallorcan, not Catalan standardized in the Principat, by having him say *som* instead of *sóc* (a Mallorcan variation for "I am"). Throughout the novels, Mosqueiro's speech is consistently in Mallorcan — he calls girls "al.lotes," stops to "xerrar" with witnesses, and conjugates all verbs in Mallorcan ("supós" instead of "suposo," for the first person singular of "I suppose," for example), and this refusal to write in what Barcelonans may consider "standard" Catalan reinforces Serra's thesis that Mallorcan is a language to be used with no apologies and no explanations.

The relation between Mallorcan and other languages is also interesting. Some reviewers have commented, thinking to point out a flaw, that when Serra inserts words in English or German, they are almost invariably misspelled and that the names of Germanic places and people are highly improbable. After reading the three books, I am convinced that Serra did this deliberately to prove a point about attitudes of cultural superiority in German and English tourists who frequent the island, and also about foreign writers who use it as a backdrop with little attempt at accuracy or insight.[7]

For example, George Sand's *A Winter on Majorca* collects a great number of sweeping generalizations about Mallorcan culture, some accurate and many more that could be argued, yet few critics have bothered to take her to task on the point.

[7]As evidence of this, consider that Serra's treatment of French, Italian, and Spanish names and words is completely different, always scrupulously accurate.

Likewise, in detective criticism one rarely reads of people scornfully dismissing Agatha Christie's *Hercule Poirot's Christmas* on the basis of her ridiculous characterization of young Pilar or the gross oversimplifications about the Spanish Civil War. Why, then, is it apparently acceptable to be careless in the treatment of certain languages and cultures, but not others? Through Mosqueiro, Serra brilliantly challenges this assumption.

His portrayal of German characters as all decadent (if not outright practicing Nazis) or of the English as criminals, sexual deviants, or fools, is less xenophobia than it is a deliberate, aggressive challenge, a provocation to rethink old stereotypes, a Brechtian use of initial alienation to force the reader to think.

By misspelling *Leipzig* (As *Liepzig, Blue,* 142), *Händel* (as *Haëndel, Blue,* 93), *Gutenberg* (as *Guttemberg, Drops,* 26), Thomas Mann's *Der Zauberer* (as *Zubenberg, Blue,* 41), or Munich's *Hoffbräuhaus* (as *Holfbraühus, The Archeologist,* 61), he issues a belligerent challenge to the reader to re-evaluate passive submission to cultural imperialism from without.

Like James Bond, Mosqueiro moves through a novelistic world where everyone speaks to him on his terms, in his tongue, and where other languages must fend for themselves. In sex, too, Mosqueiro resembles Bond. Just as Bond routinely beds treacherous foreign agents (frequently communists), Mosqueiro triumphs sexually over the German and English women in his path who are his ideological enemies. Like the "chicas Bond," the "al.lotes Mosqueiro" tend to be either dangerous or empty-headed, but all come equipped with "pits bellugadissos" ("jiggling tits"). And if Sabeth Peeperkon, Marlen Distracken, Qwerdeen Crack, Moira Peecpack, or Konstanz Koëring seem unlikely names, consider if they are any less likely or more offensive than Fleming's Kissy Suzuki, Pussy Galore, Bambi, Thumper . . . and so on. As if to reassure the reader in the end that the sexual politics of Mosqueiro are not his own, Serra pointedly gives his hero abrupt departures from Bond-like sexual prowess, cursing Mosqueiro with a gigantic, hideous abscess on his bottom that makes him look like a baboon in *Blue,* and a hernia in *The Archeologist.* In the second book, in one ironic scene, Mosqueiro kisses a young woman, and what she thinks is his "member of steel" turns out to be the metallic truss (constructed by sadistic German orthopedists) the detective is wearing in order to continue detecting while ruptured. With details like these, Serra reminds us not to take Mosqueiro and his attitudes too seriously.

Although in *The Archeologist* Serra actually added a few words of cursory explanation for Mosqueiro's fluency in Mallorcan (his mother was a *catalana* from the *barri de Gràcia* in Barcelona who required him as a small boy to read Mercè Rodoreda and Joanot Martorell — 31), still, the series manages to maintain its inversion of the stereotype of linguistic and cultural imperialism, deftly switching Mallorcan from the dominated to dominant (even within the Catalan-speaking world). Perhaps the best expression of this comes in *Drops of Blood,* when Moira Peecpack admits with a complete lack of embarrassment that she has no idea who Josep Pla was, or what "L'Empordà" might be. Mosqueiro's answer, "Tu t'ho perds, petita" ("Your loss, little one," 80), underscores Serra's point. Why should he be required to speak of German culture with hushed reverence (and careful orthography) if German visitors to his adoptive home show blithe unconcern toward things Catalan and Mallorcan? Part of the Mallorcan cultural identity that Serra is pushing for involves never needing to apologize or explain to people who should be educated enough to know better.

Serra's is a detective series conscious of its antecedents with ironic references not only to English and American masters (for example, Mosqueiro meets Georges (sic) Smiley in London), but also Spanish contemporaries as well (Mosqueiro is also acquainted with Barcelonan, Pepe Carvalho). Serra's spare style and imagistic *Blitzkrieg* descriptions (to make an allusion which Mosqueiro would doubtless understand, but stubbornly refuse to spell correctly), all attest to his journalistic training, and most importantly of all, his love for Mallorcan lore and tongue is something his native readers can take to heart as a healthy escape valve for accumulated stresses brought on by the beautiful Balearic Islands' economically solvent, but frequently uncouth Germanic visitors.

From the four examples cited in this paper, it is clear that the meeting of minds that the Ofèlia Dracs collective supposed, served as a forum for some commonly held beliefs and goals, as publication of entertaining tales that encourage reading in Catalan by consumers of many different backgrounds, and most importantly of all, as a catalyst for individual production by the group's members. As a tool for preserving the Catalan culture and defining that culture's identity, these stories in the popular detective format are invaluable, as I have demonstrated. So in the end, that is the solution to the mysterious question I posed at the beginning of who is Ofèlia Dracs and what did she do? Not a bad contribution from a woman who, it seems, never really existed at all.

WORKS CITED

Carbó, Joaquim. *Escapada*. Barcelona: Alfaguara, 1967.
——. *Solucions provisionals*. Barcelona: Selecta, 1964.
Fuster, Jaume. *Les cartes d'Hércules Poirot*. Barcelona: Edicions 62, 1983.
——. *Les claus de vidre*. Barcelona: Magrana, 1984.
——. *La corona valenciana*. Barcelona: Eliseu Climent, 1982.
——. *De mica en mica s'omple la pica*. Barcelona: Edicions 62, 1972.
——. *Vida de gos*. Barcelona: Magrana, 1989.
Hart, Patricia. *The Spanish Sleuth*. Cranbury, New Jersey: Fairleigh Dickinson UP, 1987.
Nin, Anaïs. Prologue, adapted from the story, "Marianne." *Little Birds*. New York: Harcourt Brace Jovanovich, 1979.
Oliver, Maria-Antònia. *Estudi en lila*. Barcelona: Magrana, 1987.
——. *Antípodes*. Barcelona: Magrana, 1988.
——. Personal interview, Biniali, Mallorca, 11 August 1988.
Pope, Alexander, et al. *The Scribleriad*. Los Angeles: UCLA, Clark Memorial Library, 1967.
Sand, George. *Un hiver á Majorque*. Barcelona: Luis Ripoll Arbós, 1988.
Serra, Antoni. *L'arqueóloga va somriure abans de morir*. Barcelona: Magrana, 1986.
——. *El blau pàl.lid de la rosa de paper*. Palma de Mallorca: Moll, 1985.
——. *Espurnes de sang*. Barcelona: Magrana, 1987.
Tani, Stefano. *The Doomed Detective*. Carbondale and Edwardsville: Southern Illinois UP, 1984.

JAUME MARTI-OLIVELLA

Bachelardian Myth in Rodoreda's Construction of Identity

> Catalans were on the losing side in the Spanish Civil War, and immediately afterwards were forbidden to speak their language outside the home. For writers like Rodoreda, who did not reestablish her residence in Spain until 1979, the fate of Catalan was a matter of artistic survival. A writer's native language is normally his or her only medium of expression. If a language dies or is killed, then the writer also dies. Thus, as with many Catalan authors, her personal story is a kind of death followed by a recent and partial rebirth. (Rosenthal 8)

> *La plaça del Diamant* is a novel concerned with connections, with their frustration and reestablishment . . . . The collective unity that will be broken with the war and exile is enacted in the popular dance at the square, where colored paper strips linked by means of flour and water paste symbolize the fragility of popular happiness . . . . But language, as precarious as flour and water paste, can establish connections between past and present, can transmit the image and feeling of a life which was interrupted by a different, hostile temporality.
>
> (Resina 242-43)

What both Rosenthal and Resina underscore is the crucial role of language, of the Catalan language in Rodoreda's personal survival, in her struggle to preserve a cultural and national identity that was dramatically shattered by the outcome of the Spanish Civil War. That "death and partial rebirth," the archetypal journey to one's own hell, will be inscribed in Rodoreda's text through the myth of language: its capacity to reconnect past and present, loss and memory and, thus, to represent history and identity.

In 1980 Mercè Rodoreda was awarded the *Premi d'Honor de les Lletres Catalanes* (Award of Honor in Catalan Letters), the first woman writer to achieve Catalonia's most important literary award. She had just recently returned from her exile at Geneva where she had barely managed to survive during the long years of her retreat. Born in 1908 in Barcelona, Rodoreda never attended school because her family decided that "she could be harmed there since she learnt things too fast" (Casals 31), in fact her lack of formal schooling was due to the family's precarious financial situation. Rodoreda's precocious talent, however, was nourished by the magical world of her grandfather's stories. As she put it: "As a child my life was a constant wonder" (Rodoreda, 1981, 20). This childhood full of wonders soon became the nightmarish world of adulthood and violence. Her arranged marriage to her uncle Joan the day she turned twenty marked the beginning of a life-long conflict with the opposite sex that will occupy a prominent position in her fiction. Before 1936, the year of Franco's uprising against the legally established government of the Spanish Republic, Rodoreda had managed to publish five novels and numerous short stories in several Catalan periodicals of the time. During the Civil War she worked for the *Generalitat* (Generality), the Catalan government, in its *Comissariat de Propaganda* (Department of Propaganda). The end of the Civil War, therefore, brought about the collapse of her personal universe and the beginning of a dramatic exile that became a sort of permanent state, as Rodoreda herself vividly recounted in an interview:

> I was just coming out of one of those journeys "au bout de la nuit" during which writing seems the most frivolous thing to do . . . . The prewar world seemed unreal to me, and I still hadn't reconstructed it. And the time I spent! Everything burned inside, but imperceptibly it was becoming a little anachronistic. And perhaps this is what hurt most. I couldn't have written a novel if they'd beaten it out of me. I was too disconnected from everything, or maybe too terribly bound up with everything, though that might sound like a paradox. In general literature made me feel like vomiting. I could only stand the greats: Cervantes, Shakespeare, Dostoyevsky. I'm sure I've never been as lucid as I was then, possibly because I hardly ate anything. (Rodoreda in Rosenthal 6-7)

How did Rodoreda manage to emerge from her profound crisis? How could she reconnect with a reality that had turned unreal despite haunting her obsessively? Joan Triadú answers this question, outlining, at the same time, the essential characteristic that defines the best narrative of the Catalan postwar period:

> Once temporal and geographical distance from the facts allows critical perception to develop itself, the conditions are set for the creation of a new world, one that establishes a mythical relationship with reality . . . . Myth, while giving to the reality of the novel its autonomous meaning, allows the writer to go back to the origins in order to recover himself/herself while being "another." . . . Through the process of mythification, the writer deepens the knowledge of reality and is capable of creating her/his own reality instead of evading it. (Triadú 20-21; my tr.)

Like most Catalan writers in the postwar period, Rodoreda emerged from her crisis by means of a radical process of interiorization and mythical projection. *La plaça del Diamant [The Time of the Doves,* its American title, hereinafter *Doves*], is Rodoreda's best example. As Resina reminds us: "The maiming effect of the war on the original community has been followed by the experience of loss and separateness. Natàlia's discovery (and Rodoreda's statement) is, however, that unification can be reestablished in consciousness through the awareness of interiority" (Resina 245). It is precisely Rodoreda's almost magical awareness of interiority that leads us to analyze her creative gesture from the perspective of Bachelard's phenomenology of the artistic imagination and, especially, his subtle analysis of the symbolic spatial configurations of the human mind, always already constituted by the dialectics of large and small. As Bachelard has it:

> How hard it is to situate the values of being and non-being! And where is the root of silence? Is it a distinction of non-being or a domination of being? It is "deep." . . . Being myself a philosopher of adjectives, I am caught up in the perplexing dialectics of deep and large; of the infinitely diminished that deepens, or the large that extends beyond all limits. In Claudel's *L'Annonce faite à Marie* . . . the touch goes so deep that one would have to meditate at length upon a world that exists in depth by virtue of its sonority, a world the entire existence of which would be the existence of voices. This frail, ephemeral thing, a voice, can bear witness to the most forceful realities. (Bachelard 180)

It is that deep sonority of being that Rodoreda's textual voice transcribes. Like the depths of the sea contained in the seashell's whispers, the soft, frail, almost faltering voice in Rodoreda's text manages to encompass the profound drama of her historical time. Thus, Miquel Dolç, one of the first commentators of Rodoreda's *Doves*, already wrote: "Beneath the layer of an almost childish monologue that barely transcends the realm of a family circle, the whole tragedy of our time emerges" (Dolç 14). Rodoreda's *Doves* is both a poetic elaboration of the Bachelardian symbolic universe of primal images and an attempt to reconnect with a historical past through the recovery of a "childish" vision, a new and innocent gaze at the things that are life. Indeed, Natàlia, like most of Rodoreda's protagonists, is a woman-child who finds herself in an orphan-like situation, lost/exiled in a male, hostile world, longing for that ideal corner wherein to fulfill her "dream of inhabiting" (Bachelard 131). It is only through this mythical orphan that Rodoreda has been able to express herself and her "universal truth," as Michel Cournat has it:

> One feels that this little working woman in Barcelona has spoken on behalf of all the hope, all the freedom, and all the courage in the world. And that she has just uttered forth one of the books of most universal relevance that love, let us finally say the word, could have written.
>
> (Cournat in Rosenthal 11)

Doves is indeed a book about love. After having read it, one fully understands the opening epigraph, George Meredith's "My dear, these things are life" under the advocacy of which the entire novel is written. It is the things that are life that Natàlia so deeply and intimately loves and it is her innocent and dramatic recording that moves the reader. As Triadú points out:

> Natàlia explains herself with the realism of children . . . . She's always disturbed by the degradation of her illusory reality, a reality all too natural to her. She registers minutely and precisely all the tiny actions, the minor events, that erode the untouched reality, the deep innocence of things.
> (Triadú 111; my tr.)

Mercè Rodoreda's passage from reality to myth is expressed by this recreated childhood, by this childish look upon the "deep innocence of things." It is ultimately this childish account that convinces us, that turns the book into a true "epic" of our time. As Maria Aurèlia Campmany formulates it: "Rodoreda has mastered the difficult art of transforming the tragedy of existence into the dimensions of daily life" (Campmany 47; my tr.). Through Natàlia's unmediated selection of the things she tells us, Rodoreda is able to inscribe a historical reality without having to describe it. Again it is Resina's comment that clarifies this point: "Things are certainly time's harbingers, but not so much on account of their resistance to time as for the reason that they are marked by it . . . . Natàlia relates to things, humanizes them and is in turn given meaning by them, historicized by her attachment to their transitory character" (Resina 235). Which are some of these meaningful things? How do they help Natàlia's/Rodoreda's dream of inhabiting, her struggle to preserve a cultural identity threatened by the estrangement of those very things? Before attempting to address these questions in the text, it might be necessary to explain how the dove and the seashell, the "things" I have chosen to analyze here, emblematize the duality of presence and absence, the essential components of our desiring economy. As Bachelard puts it:

> A nest-house is never young. Indeed, . . . we might say that it is the natural habitat of the function of inhabiting. For not only do we *come back* to it, but we dream of coming back to it, the way a bird comes back to its nest . . . . This sign of *return* marks an infinite number of daydreams, for the reason that human returning takes place in the great rhythm of human life, a rhythm that reaches back across the years and, through the dream, combats all absence. (Bachelard 99)

Rodoreda's extended daydream, her *Doves,* encompasses this transhistorical dimension of Bachelardian primordial dreaming while at the same time chronicling the emergence of woman as a speaking subject, the partial fulfilment of her historical dream of inhabiting. Again in Bachelard's words:

> The function of inhabiting constitutes the link between full and empty . . . . Here a man wants to live in a shell. He wants the walls that protect him to be as smoothly polished and as firm as if his sensitive flesh had to come in direct contact with them. The shell confers a daydream of purely physical intimacy. Bernard Polissy's daydream expresses the function of inhabiting in terms of touch. (Bachelard 131)

In Rodoreda's case, it is a woman who wants to inhabit the shell of language, who aspires to regress into the primary and archaic stages of language formation by means of a "purely physical intimacy" with the world, with life. That is the basis of her literary "illusion" of an oral language. As Francis Wyers has it:

> Rodoreda creates the illusion of speech . . . . Nowhere in Natàlia's account do we find references to writing or to print; there are no letters, books, newspapers, advertising street signs. It is as if, amidst the timeless objectifications of the printed word, we stepped once again into the realm of verbal flux . . . . The sense of an audible delivery, a story-telling in "viva-voce," seems to give us an echo, faint enough, of a communal life prior to civilization and its discontents, prior to literature . . . . The terrible experience of a woman's speechless imprisonment comes to us through the novel's implicit faith in the communal language. We put Natàlia's seashell up to our ear and hear the speech of a people. (Wyers 308)

To perceive the natural sound of the world is in the case of Rodoreda's seashell, an attempt to recover the hidden, submerged and repressed sounds of woman as speaking subject, it is to inscribe the obliterated traces of gender in history, or, as Kristeva has it: "to be able to name what has thus far never been an object of circulation in the community: the enigmas of the body, the dreams, secret joys, shames, hatreds of the second sex" (38). When, at the end of her journey of self-discovery, Natàlia, renamed *Colometa* (little dove) by Quimet and deprived of her own space in the house turned dovecote, manages to inscribe her name on the door, she is reasserting an identity of what is finally her own territory. A gesture that anticipates the feminist outcry emblematized by Hélène Cixous' "Sorties": "She has been forbidden the possibility of the proud "inscription above my door" marking the threshold of The Gay Science. She could never have exclaimed: The house I live in is my own, I never copied anyone . . . She has not been able to live in her "own" house, her very body" (Cixous 68).

Combining Bachelardian myth and historical inscription, Rodoreda's *Doves* proposes a double articulation of patriarchal chronology and female temporality that inaugurates, for Catalan letters, the writing of woman's history, the recovery of her suppressed identity. In what follows I will try to illustrate some of the strategies used by Rodoreda to achieve her purpose.

The narrative of *Doves* starts with Natàlia's work in a pastry shop. She is tired since she has been standing all day tying small packages for the customers. It is *Festa Major* (Major Town Festival) and everybody is celebrating. Almost unwillingly, she accepts Julieta's invitation to go together to the fair in the *plaça del Diamant* (Diamond Square). She describes herself in this way:

> I was dressed all in white, my dress and petticoats starched, my shoes like two drops of milk, my earrings, and a white purse Julieta said was made of vinyl with a snap shaped like a gold shellfish. (*Doves* 15)

The first symbolic nuances are clearly stated in these very few lines: Natàlia's description suggests her flower-like innocence and purity, the gold shellfish snap anticipates the symbolic seashell that will be Natàlia's refuge. Her constant dealing with ties and ribbons also anticipates the symbolic import of the linking elements, especially relevant because of Natàlia's own precarious situation in life:

> My father remarried and me without my mother whose only joy in life had been to fuss over me. And my father remarried and me a young woman all alone in the Plaça del Diamant . . . and before my eyes the flower-covered lights and the chains pasted on them and everybody happy. (*Doves* 16)

Natàlia, all in white, alone amidst the merry fair, is like those fragile decorative paper-flowers. Without the link to her mother she feels lost and alienated in the middle of that general merriment that estranges her:

> There were asparagus plants around the bandstand to keep the crowd away, and the plants were decorated with flowers tied together with tiny wires . . . . And my mother dead and me caught in my tracks and that waistband pinching, pinching like I was tied with a wire to a bunch of asparagus. (*Doves* 16-18)

Natàlia's isolation and entrapment, symbolized in her broken ties to her dead mother and in that oppressing waistband will be immediately expanded into an emblem of identity loss: her name will be taken away by Quimet. Just before that, as in passing, the waistband is associated with a "knife": "The waistband was like a knife in my skin" (*Doves* 18). This happens precisely when she is being addressed by Quimet, who has invited her to dance. Quimet, the man she will marry and from whom she will try to escape at the end of the chapter, not without having been previously and appropriately rebaptized as "Colometa," the bird of flight and return:

> He called me Colometa, his little dove. I looked at him very annoyed and said my name was Natàlia and when I said my name was Natàlia he kept laughing and said I could only have one name: Colometa. That was when I started running again like all the devils in hell were after me. (*Doves* 18-19)

This is Natàlia/Colometa's first flight from a reality she will never be entirely able to escape. It is, moreover, a poetic condensation and a narrative anticipation of all the evil to come. The "dove's" flight from "hell" sets the symbolic disposition of the whole text. Under the disguise of the endearing diminutive (Colometa/little dove), one can easily see the male gesture of appropriation and reification, Quimet's reaching out to Natàlia as that other that is going to reinforce his own self, as Cixous' critique of the dialectics of subject formation according to the Freudian model reminds us (Cixous 78-83). Natàlia's renaming literally reproduces that gesture. As a reflection of Quimet's "sortie," Natàlia is reduced to return always to the order of the one who renamed her. In case the reader might miss that point, Rodoreda gives us a clear example in the decision to baptize the newly born whose name will be determined between Quimet and Natàlia's father. As Kathleen McNerney has it: "Quimet is the one who bosses in the house . . . . Natàlia does not have any saying when it comes to deciding the name to be given to her own children. That will be established in a discussion between her father and Quimet" (299; my tr.). Natàlia's narrative obliteration, thus, betrays Rodoreda's own feeling of being ignored and marginalized. Indeed, Rodoreda had to pattern her life according to that model of flight and return. Her forced exile at the end of the war was followed by an even more radical form of exile: the rejection by her own compatriots. This happened during her stay at Roissy-en-Brie, where the French government had given political asylum to a group of Catalan intellectuals. There, Rodoreda's "illegitimate" love for Armand Obiols became the source of another crucial estrangement. As Anna Murià, another Catalan woman writer who shared those intense days with Rodoreda explains: "There was an awful scandal about the liaison between Mercè (Rodoreda) and Armand Obiols since Armand was married to Montserrat Trabal. Everybody in Trabal's family and all their friends became their enemies . . . . The split was so obvious and the coexistence so difficult that the French decided to send an entire group to Saint Cyr, another mansion lent to Central European refugees" (Murià 23). Rodoreda, who had left her mother and son behind, was now also bereft of communal support by her daring love. It comes as no surprise, therefore, that *Doves,* a book that is certainly about love, the most universal kind of love, was, as Rodoreda herself told us, conceived in hatred:

> I wanted it Kafkian; very Kafkian, absurd, indeed, with many doves; I wanted the doves to choke the protagonist from beginning to end . . . . And the novel that was intended to be a nightmare of doves became *La Plaça del Diamant,* with doves, yes, but in another way. (Rodoreda, 1983, 6-7, my tr.).

What Rodoreda wanted in the initial conception of the novel was to get rid of her own anger and frustration because of her desperate isolation and the fact of having recently sent the original of *Jardí vora el Mar* (Garden by the Sea) to an important literary prize with the result of a complete rejection from its male jurors. Rodoreda needed to take "revenge" upon a male world which so utterly obliterated her. She conceived her book, therefore, as a univocal symbolic destruction of the dove/male equation. As its basic theme, the male/female clash remained central in *Doves,* in this sense, as Francis Wyers puts it: "The novel portrays the relentless process of a woman's self-estrangement and her confinement in the prisonhouse of domesticity" (302). Rodoreda's novel, however, goes far beyond the restrictions of any symbolic univocity. It is, as I have already pointed out, a fairly subtle account of a woman's struggle to find means of expressing her suppressed identity. Rodoreda's textual seashell becomes a "witch's cauldron," (Bachelard 108) within which brews the universal experience of what Kristeva called "woman's time" (32-38). Once, asked about the passage of time in an interview, Rodoreda said these revealing words:

> Concerning the fear of aging, I think it is very human. Sooner or later everybody has it. A woman begins to feel it in her mid-thirties when she realizes how she moves slowly from fairy to witch. (Rodoreda in Porcel 75; my tr.)

Anticipating the claims of many feminist manifestos, Rodoreda's *Doves* convincingly depicts this universal passage, this poetic metamorphosis from fairy to witch. What Natàlia/Colometa learns in the refuge of her seashell as witch's cauldron is, more than anything else, the radical otherness of motherhood. An aspect of motherhood that Madelon Sprengnether persuasively argues in her insightful reading of Freud's "The Theme of the Three Caskets":

In the light of his idealization of the mother/son relationship, it is almost

> shocking, however, that Freud should reveal the hidden face of the mother as death . . . . Despite Freud's position as an agnostic Jew, his account of the vicissitudes of desire via the Oedipus and castration complexes parallels and reinforces the split encoded in Western Christianity between woman as asexual mother (Mary) and as erotic object (Eve). The third and most terrifying aspect of the preoedipal (m)other, the autonomy of her desire, perceived by the infant as the threat of death, is frequently marginalized and scapegoated in the figure of woman as witch.
>
> (Sprengnether 9-12)

Rodoreda's Natàlia is the first of a series of women/witches who bear witness to such a process of scapegoating and marginalization. In Natàlia's case, such a process may be exemplified by the fact that the height of her dispossession comes about when she is entirely devoted to the maternal function, the most blessed of all patriarchally imposed roles on women, as this passage clearly illustrates:

> We built the dovecote. The day Quimet had chosen to start work it rained cats and dogs . . . . He took everything I had out of the shed: my clothes basket, my chairs, my hamper for dirty clothes, my basket full of clothesline. "We're evicting Colometa." (*Doves* 67)

Such an incident might seem trivial, removed from its contextual significance, as it is, though, it represents one of the best illustrations of Rodoreda's technique of symbolic reversals. As we know, Quimet started his possessive and alienating process by renaming Natàlia as Colometa. Now, he offers her a dovecote. To build it, however, he has to empty out all of Colometa's belongings, he has to deprive her of "a room of her own." This is obviously what happens. Here, the dovecote is not a Bachelardian metaphor of the loving "house-nest" (Bachelard 93). It is rather a reductive metonymy for the whole house or, as the American title of the novel emphasizes, for the entire historical context. And yet, Rodoreda's use of ambivalence does not stop at that level of symbolic reversal. It is again necessary to go back to the Bachelardian world of primal images in order to see through the imaginative mechanisms at work in this novel. What the dovecote scene shows, from a Bachelardian perspective, is Natàlia's confrontation with her most obsessive imaginary nightmare, that of being emptied out:

> And I'd wake up in the middle of the night feeling like someone had tied a rope around my guts and was tugging on them, like I still had the cord on my belly button from when I was born and they were tugging all of me out through my belly button and as they tugged everything went out: my eyes and hands and nails and feet and my heart with that tube down the middle with a drop of black blood caught there and my toes still alive but feeling like they were dead . . . it was the same feeling. Everything sucked out into nothingness again through that little tube that had dried out after they

> knotted it. And all around that tugging which was taking me away there was a soft cloud of dove feathers so no one would see what was happening. (*Doves* 112-13)

It is only the reader who bears witness to Natàlia's nightmare, to her metonymic reduction into a dove-girl who is forced to tend to the house/dovecote in a transferential mockery of her motherly role. Natàlia's complete isolation, on the other hand, finds in the seashell image its most emblematic symbol since the hidden life cycle of that ancillary creature offers the best objective correlative to Natàlia's troubled consciousness. In this respect, Natàlia may be seen as an example of Bachelard's ideal "naïve observer":

> For here too, as with nests, enduring interest should begin with the original amazement of a naïve observer. Is it possible for a creature to remain alive inside stone, inside this piece of stone? Amazement of this kind is rarely felt twice. Life quickly wears it down. And besides, for one "living" shell, how many dead ones there are! For one inhabited shell, how many are empty. (Bachelard 107)

Rodoreda's own experience in the cruel years of her exile contains a historical referent to this fable of survival: she became a "living shell," specially in those days of her "paralysis": As she herself recalls it: "And I stopped writing stories . . . . Slowly, my right arm became paralyzed. I could sew, in fact that activity was the only source of my income; I could do all kinds of house work, everything, except writing" (Rodoreda in Porcel, 74, my tr.). Like Rodoreda, Natàlia's fable of survival will be thematized in the image of the inhabited shell, that "thing" that represents the dream of inhabiting herself in/and the world. Rodoreda's ironic portrayal of the contradictory aspects of the shell, on the other hand, prevents the reader from being ensnared by its hypnotic beauty. As in this peculiar scene:

> When summer came, the midwife said I needed lots of fresh air and swimming. So out came the motorcycle and off we went to the beach. We took everything we needed: food and clothing. We used a yellow-and-blue-and-black-stripped towel as curtain. Quimet held it stretched out full length so I could get undressed behind it. He laughed at me, because you could see I looked funny with a belly that wasn't mine. And I watched the waves come in and go out, always the same, always the same — all of them in a hurry to get there and in a hurry to get away — As I sat facing the sea, sometimes gray and sometimes green, most of all blue, all that living and moving and talking water carried my thoughts far away and left me empty. And when Quimet noticed I'd been quiet for a long time, he'd ask me, "Hey, how's it going?" . . . And once we met I-don't-remember-who and I felt so embarrassed I wished the earth would open up and swallow me because he said: "She's all filled up now." (*Doves* 58)

In this scene, Rodoreda uses the empty/full polarity to offer a miniaturized version of the male/female clash that plays with the simultaneous, double articulation of the two confronting imaginaries. What Quimet sees is a full stomach which is both object of scorn inasmuch as it shows a deformed sexual object and subject to possessive praise as it proves his own maleness. With his total inability to share in Natàlia's daydream, moreover, Quimet shows his spiritual emptiness, ironically sharpened by the contrastive possessive fullness of the male who, after having reduced the woman to an ornamental, silent, and empty seashell, is now boasting of her being filled up. On the other hand, Natàlia's daydream of the sea waters that empty her is again a figuration of life and death. In order to be an inhabited, a full shell, Natàlia, as a woman, has to be emptied out of her own self.

Before closing this analysis of the dove and the seashell as examples of Rodoreda's Bachelardian imagination, I would like to take the reader into the very center of communal life, that is, into the marketplace, in order to see one of the book's most beautiful epiphanies:

> My fish seller, laughing through her gold teeth, was weighing some fresh cod, and the light bulb hanging above her shone, so tiny you almost couldn't see it, from every fish scale. The mullet, the flying fish, the haddock, the groupers with their big heads, looking like they'd just been painted with their spines pressing against their backs like the thorns on a big flower, all the fish came from those waves that left me empty when I sat and watched them. They came out with their tails flapping and their eyes bulging. (*Doves* 70)

I must include here the Catalan original of this epiphanic scene since the English version has not captured entirely its musicality and some of its symbolic nuances:

> La meva peixatera, amb dents d'or i rient, pesava palangres i a cada escata hi havia, petita que gairebé no es veia, la bombeta que penjava damunt de la panera de peix. Les llisseres, les lluernes, els llobarros, les escórpores de cap gros, que semblaven acabades de pintar amb les espines a la ratlla de l'esquena com les punxes d'una gran flor . . . tot sortia d'aquelles onades que a mi em deixaven buida quan m'hi asseia al davant, a cops de cua i amb els ulls fora del cap. (*La Plaça* 90)

Anticipating the final poetic image of the book in which the sky is contained in a puddle of the park, here one may see how every single fish-scale contains the light of the bulb, the light which is life is contained in the smallest parts of the dismembered bodies of the dead fishes. Death turned into life, intensified by the alliterative beautiful succession of slippery, sparkling, *llísseres, lluernes, llobarros* (mullet, flying fish, haddock). We are no longer in front of a fish market stall but facing a colorful still-life painting full of big headed fishes with spines pressing against their backs like the thorns on a big flower, with their tales flapping and their eyes bulging! We are, in fact, inside Natàlia's unconscious imaginary since the "spiny fishes," the "flower girl," like the empty "seashell" are her recurrent, oneiric figurations of sex, of life and/or of death. Thus, subtly, almost in a subdued way, Rodoreda captures the ambiguities and contradictions inherent in the shell image as it encapsulates both life as a dream and as a nightmare. Using Quimet's and Natàlia's opposing views, Rodoreda offers simultaneously an objective correlative for the image of woman/mother and for that of woman/object.

There is still the third, repressed figure of the woman/witch or, as Sprengnether called it, the (m)other. As I have already mentioned, Rodoreda herself characterized the passage from woman to witch as a kind of culminating moment in the growing process of the female subject in her struggle to preserve her own identity. It is this passage into "woman's time," precisely, that Rodoreda expresses beautifully while projecting the seashell image into the utmost figuration of the Bachelardian dream of inhabiting: the dream of the mother-of-pearl. As Bachelard himself has it:

> And doesn't the finger that dreams as it strokes the intimate mother-of-pearl surface surpass our human, all too human dreams? (Bachelard 115)

The dream of the mother-of-pearl will be the dream of the impossible union, the dream of arrested Time, as Rodoreda's description of the mother-son dance dramatically illustrates:

> And when I danced with my son the soldier, pressing my palm with that whole span of wrinkled skin that goes from your wrist to your fingers against his palm, I felt like that bedpost made of wooden balls piled on top of each other was breaking and I dropped his hand and put my arm around his neck and squeezed it and he said, "What's up?" and I said, "I'm strangling you." And when the dance ended my cultured pearl necklace got caught on a button on his uniform and it broke and all the pearls spilled on the floor. (*Doves* 190)

Life and death, the sense of loss in Natàlia's life, leading us again to the primal seashell image:

> The seashell was in the middle of the console, and I felt like I could hear the sea stirring inside it . . . boom . . . boom . . . And I thought maybe it didn't make any noise when no one was listening and how no one would even know if there were waves inside a seashell when nobody's ear was at the hole. I took the pearls out of my purse and put them in a little box and kept one and threw it in the seashell so it could keep the sea company . . . and I sat there in the dark till the streetlights came on and a beam of pale light came in like the ghost of light and streaked the red tiles. I picked up

> the seashell and very carefully turned it first one way and then the other so I could hear the pearl rolling around inside. It was tan with white spots and little spires and the spire on the end was worn away and there was mother-of-pearl inside. (*Doves* 190-91)

It is difficult to imagine a better example of arrested Time than this symbolic epiphany in which an almost incestuous caress is blended with the painful memory of childbirth and the attempt to choke the kid as a means of stopping time, of preventing one's own emptying out. It is, moreover, Rodoreda's most beautiful figuration of the (m)other inasmuch as it shows the life/death relationship inherent in the mother-of-pearl dream of inhabiting: the pearl (son/daughter) inevitably falls from the woman/mother, thus inaugurating time, the (m)otherly time of mourning. The clashing between the soldier-child and the mother-of-pearl is, besides, Rodoreda's poetic culmination of the conflict between the male and female imaginaries. A conflict that can only be resolved in the caressing intimacy of the seashell dream, that is, in the intimate space of Rodoreda's magical gesture, the textual myth that informs *Doves*.

To conclude, I would like to emphasize again, with Joan Ramon Resina, the political dimensions of Rodoreda's effort to preserve her cultural identity:

> The political, hence collective, dimension of this novel stems, paradoxically, from the author's faithfulness to individual experience . . . . The endeavor to recapture the linguistic identity of objects involves nothing less than the attempt to reterritorialize language, to return to the community its power of speech. (Resina 228).

Deterritorialized in her triple exile as a Catalan intellectual deprived of her linguistical community, as an "adulterous lover" denied access to the blessings of the patriarchal family and as a historical expatriate bereft of a political project, Rodoreda's tremendous identity loss was transformed in a subtle literary myth: the myth of language as preserver. Her radical faith in the Catalan language kept it alive in the seashell of her imagination and allowed her to survive artistically, emotionally and politically. Her survival, that mythical story of death and rebirth alluded to by David Rosenthal in the beginning of this essay, was the survival of a whole nation.

WORKS CITED

Bachelard, Gaston. *The Poetics of Space*. Boston: Beacon, 1969.

Campmany, Maria Aurèlia. "Mercè Rodoreda o les coses de la vida." *Serra d'Or* (May 1968): 45-47.

Casals Couturier, Montserrat. "El 'Rosebud' de Mercè Rodoreda," in Jaume Martí-Olivella, ed. "Homage to Mercè Rodoreda." *Catalan Review* 2:2 (1987): 27-47.

Cixous, Hélène. "Sorties" in *The Newly Born Woman*. Trans. Betsy Wing. Minneapolis: U of Minnesota P, 1988: 63-132.

Cournat, Michel. "Trop blessée pour mourir." *Nouvel Observateur* 362. 18-24 October 1971: 11. Quoted and translated by David Rosenthal.

Dolç, Miquel. In Joan Sales, "Una mica d'història de *La plaça del Diamant* in Mercè Rodoreda, *La plaça del Diamant*. 26th ed. Barcelona: Club dels Novellistes, 1983:11-18.

Kristeva, Julia. "Woman's Time." *Feminist Theory: A Critique of Ideology*. Eds. Nannerl O. Keohane, et. al. Chicago: U of Chicago P, 1982. 31-54.

McNerney, Kathleen. "La Identitat a *La plaça del Diamant:* supressió i recerca." In Nathaniel B. Smith et. al., ed. *Actes del Quart Colloqui d'Estudis Catalans a Nord-Amèrica*. Barcelona: Publicacions de l'Abadia de Montserrat: 290-302.

Murià, Anna. "Entrevista," in Mercè Rodoreda, *Cartes a l'Anna Murià*. Barcelona: La Sal, Edicions de les Dones, 1985: 13-32.

Nichols, Geraldine C. "Exile, Gender, and Mercè Rodoreda." *Modern Languages Notes* 101 (1986): 405-17.

Porcel, Baltasar. "Mercè Rodoreda o la força lírica." *Serra d'Or* (March 1966): 72-74.

Resina, Joan Ramon. "The Link in Consciousness: Time and Community in Rodoreda's *La plaça del Diamant*." In Jaume Martí-Olivella, ed. "Homage to Mercè Rodoreda," *Catalan Review* 2:2 (1987): 225-46.

Rodoreda, Mercè. "Pròleg." *La Plaça del Diamant*. 27th ed. Barcelona: Club Editor, 1983. 6-8.

——. "Pròleg." *Quanta, quanta guerra*. Barcelona: Club Editor, 1981: 13-24.

——. *The Time of the Doves*. Trans. David Rosenthal. New York: Taplinger, 1980.

Rosenthal, David. "Translator's Note" in *The Time of the Doves*: 6-10.

Sprengnether, Madelon. "Some Revisions of the Fall in Fiction by Women Writers." Paper read at the Conference on "Feminism and Psychoanalysis." Normal: State U of Illinois, May, 1986: 9-12. (I thank the author for her authorization to work with the unpublished manuscript.)

Triadú, Joan. *La novel.la de postguerra*. Barcelona: Edicions 62, 1979.

Wyers, Francis. "A Woman's Voices: Mercè Rodoreda's *La Plaça del Diamant*." *Kentucky Romance Quarterly* 30 (1983): 301-09.

NANCY LOPEZ-ARANGUREN

Bums, Scoundrels and the Ideal Society in *Vidas sombrías* (*Somber Lives*) by Pío Baroja

The outcast as hero has been a familiar figure in Spanish Literature since the invention, in Spain, of the picaresque novel in the sixteenth century. Pío Baroja, one of the most widely known and read Spanish authors in the first half of the twentieth century, wrote several important novels around this kind of figure (Dos Passos, 86; 98). But in his earliest work, a collection of thirty-five short stories and prose pieces called *Vidas sombrías (Somber Lives),* Baroja distinguishes between the outcast as hero and the outcast as villain, using two identifiable Spanish cultural types — "vagos" (bums) and "golfos" (scoundrels) — as emblems of a universal ideal of moral excellence on the one hand and of a natural state of total depravity on the other.

Vidas sombrías is the first book published by Pío Baroja. It grew out of the stories, sketches and informal essays Baroja wrote and published in daily newspapers and in magazines during his earliest years as a writer. Valuable for what it reveals about the range of styles, tones and approaches characteristic of the early Baroja, it is also interesting because it is full of allusions to local customs, institutions and types, elements of popular culture that serve as a background for, and illustrations of, the views of mankind and morality that formed the basis for Baroja's early utopian ideals.

From the beginning, Baroja's hopes for an ideal society were faint ones, and, following the publication of *Vidas sombrías* in 1900, they faded away entirely. But, he acknowledges in his address to the Spanish Academy on the occasion of his induction, at the beginning of his career the influence of the non-violent, humanitarian anarchism of Tolstoy and the lesson in compassion learned from Schopenhauer and from Buddhism was a powerful one, and it yielded a distinctive vision of utopia in his first book ("Formacion" 436-437).

The vision comes in a parable titled "Piedad postrera" ("Latter-day Grace"). In this piece, Baroja evokes a world in which man's compassion outweighs his desire for material gain. Bloodshed is abolished from the universe, and every living thing identifies with every other living thing. The rhythms are Biblical; the scene is flooded with light; harmony reigns supreme:

> El Hombre ya no podía soportar el espectáculo del sufrimiento ajeno y se desvivía por los demás. El rico había comenzado por desprenderse de lo supérfluo y quería partir con sus semejantes lo necesario y el pobre se resistía a tomarlo, y ambos eran felices. (*Vidas* 70)[1]

Elsewhere in the collection, the vehicles Baroja chose to express his views on mankind and morality were of the more realistic, and less visionary, kind. They were sketches and stories about common, familiar figures from the subculture of Spanish society: the ragpickers, peddlers, vagabonds, grave-diggers, petty thieves, and assorted bums, cads, gigolos, bohemians and other hangers-on that he saw in the streets and on the roads around him. The kind of people that made good citizens shudder when they passed them, and made Baroja, who took delight in attacking middle-class complacency, revel in stowing away within them Schopenhauer's philosophical speculations on the cure for the essential ills of mankind.

Two of these figures stand out as particularly representative of the views peculiar to the early Baroja. They are "el vago" and "el golfo," each of whom embody contrasting attitudes toward life that sustain the vision of utopia in this book.

Who are "el vago" and "el golfo"?

The pages of *Vidas sombrías* are full of individually dramatized scoundrels and bums and their separate stories, but in "Patología del golfo" ("Pathology of the Scoundrel"), a serio-comic treatise on the syndrome of golfismo, and in "El vago" ("The Bum"), a mildly ironic character sketch, the dominant traits of each are isolated and defined.

"Patología" or pathology is the science treating of diseases, their essential nature, causes, and development, and the structural and functional changes produced by them. This is the framework Baroja uses to examine the phenomenon of the "golfo." After defining the phenomenon, he explores the causes of its development, isolates its major symptoms and varieties, makes a prognosis about its ef-

---

[1] "Man could no longer bear to see his fellow creatures suffer and was doing his utmost for others. The rich man had begun by giving up luxuries and by offering to share necessities with his fellow man and the poor man would refuse to accept them, and both felt blessed." All translations from Spanish to English have been done by the author, who is grateful to Philip Sutton, lecturer in English at the Universidad Autónoma de Madrid, for his help.

fect on society and prescribes treatment for its eradication. He even signs it Dr. Baroja. The effect is comic and the antecedent is literary. "Patología del golfo" is a parody of a then current best seller in Europe called *Degeneration*, by Max Nordau, in which turn-of-the-century sensibility and disillusionment — which manifested itself in art and literature as modernism — are treated as symptoms of disease (Mosse, Introduction xx-xxi).

Nowhere does Baroja state that "Patología del golfo" is a parody of Nordau's book. Yet the subtitles of his essay ("Concept of the Scoundrel," "Etiology," "Symptoms," "Prognostic Signs," "Therapeutics") neatly parallel those of Books I and V of *Degeneration* ("The Dusk of Nations," "The Symptoms," "Diagnosis," "Prognosis," "Therapeutics") and, for the well-read among Baroja's public, his mocking mimicry of Nordau's format gave the entire piece a humorous cast.

Baroja mocked because he was upset. Nordau's attack on authors and on artists he admired unsettled Baroja, and in a contemporary magazine article he vigorously protested Nordau's book, calling it one of the most insane and most disturbing that had ever been written ("Nietzsche" 853-56). Nonetheless, Baroja took "golfismo" seriously, and his description, for all the clinical fol-de-rol of its framework, captures in swift strokes an accurate visual image of the golfo:

> Muchos de ellos son esos tipos mixtos de chulo y de polizonte, que se ven a las altas horas de la noche en las tabernas, buñolerías, cafetines, chirlatas y garitos de toda clase. Visten a la última moda de los barrios bajos, el pantalón ceñido en los muslos, holgado en la pierna y con dobleces hacia el tobillo, la chaqueta corta, aunque no tanto como la de los toreros; el pañuelo de seda en el cuello, y en la cabeza un sombrero ancho los días de toros y un *huito* negro o de color de café, un tanto inclinado hacia la oreja, en los días ordinarios. (*Vidas* 194-195)[2]

In this passage, the image of the "golfo" is accurate but impressionistic. Unlike the nineteenth-century social satirist Larra, who goes into great detail in his description of a similar character-type in *Los calaveras* or *The Ne'er-do-wells*, Baroja is as content to suggest and to identify as to describe. We learn that the "golfo" is a rogue, a rascal, a scoundrel. More specifically he can be a scalper, a

[2]"Many of them are the sort of people who act like a cross between a vigilante and a swaggering bully and who, late at night, are seen haunting taverns, cheap eateries, small cafés, gambling dens, and gaming joints of all kinds. They are dressed in the latest poor neighborhood fashions: pants cut tight over the thigh, wide down the leg and cuffed at the ankle; the jacket short, although not as short as the kind bullfighters wear; a silk handkerchief around the neck, and on the head, a wide-brimmed hat worn on bullfight days and a black or coffee-colored cap, slightly tilted toward one ear, for every day use."

black marketeer, a fence, a loan shark, a pimp, bouncer, pickpocket or any other kind of minor gangster. For "golfos" changing occupations is like changing shirts, Baroja says, and the hours always are flexible ones.

In spite of all this, as Baroja hastens to point out, "golfismo" is not strictly a lower-class phenomenon, but a human one, and it can be found in the middle and upper classes too: the dissolute student, the blackmailing newspaper reporter, the swindling ambulance chaser, and the aristocratic "golfo" whose life's work consists of finding a rich woman to marry and silly friends to amuse.

Whatever his class of origin, the "golfo" devotes his whole existence to catering to the demands of his selfish desire, and since his energies arise out of his baser instincts, his characteristics are the kind that have no social redeeming value:

> En todas las clases el golfo tiene la misma filosofía: el egotismo, la filosfía del yo. Al perder la moral de su medio ambiente, al no tener utilidad para el los preceptos morales de su clase, desaparece de su espíritu toda relación de deber para con los demás . . . . Es partidarío de Nietzsche sin saberlo. (*Vidas* 192-193)[3]

Like Larra in *Los calaveras,* Baroja uses local color as a platform from which to launch critical ideas. In Larra's case, the target was hypocrisy, the act or practice of feigning to be what one is not. In Baroja's case, the target is appetite, the abstract force of selfish desire in each and every man.

In the character sketch devoted to the "vago," Dr. Baroja disappears. A completely different and more personal kind of subjectivity dominates this piece, and Baroja himself seems particularly close at hand. The narrative tone is confidential and conversational, and the frequent direct appeals to the reader tempt one to think that the narrator's voice is the author's own:

> Apoyado en una farola de la Puerta del Sol, mira entretenido pasar la gente.
>
> Es un hombre ní alto, ni bajo, ni delgado, ni grueso, ni rubio ni moreno; puede tener treinta años y puede tener cincuenta; no está bien vestido, pero tampoco es un desarrapado.
>
> ¿Qué hace? ¿Mira algo? ¿Espera algo? No, no espera nada. De vez en cuando sonríe; pero su sonrisa no es sarcástica, ni su mirada es oblicua. (*Vidas* 147)[4]

---

[3]"No matter what social class he belongs to, "el golfo" subscribes to the same philosophy: that of self-interest, the philosophy of me first. Set adrift from the ethical standards of his environment, having no use for the moral code of his class, he loses all sense of responsibility to his fellow man . . . . He is a follower of Nietzsche, without knowing it."

[4]"Leaning against a lamp post in the Puerta del Sol, he watches with amusement as the people

Physically, the "vago" is everyman, but morally, he belongs to that higher class of people who are capable of withdrawing from the society's rat race and ignoring the demands of their vital desires. He is resolutely unambitious: "Does he have a job? No. Any property? No. A business? Pst . . . ."; and uncompromisingly unsociable: "He greets no one. Probably has few friends. Maybe none. A sign of intelligence" (*Vidas* 147; 149). Cultivating the shadow of disillusion rather than the chimera of expectations and accepting the futility of improving his lot at the expense of others, he devotes his existence to observing the foibles and absurdities of mankind:

> . . . tiene la mirada profunda, la boca burlona, el ademán indolente.
> Mira como un hombre que no espera nada de nadie.
> Es un espectador de la vida; no es un actor.
> Es un intelectual. (*Vidas* 148)[5]

Three or four times in the course of this very brief sketch the "vago" is described as intelligent or intellectual. Baroja is not the first author to endow literary characters drawn from the subculture with noble attributes, but he may be the first to connect the popular figure of the "vago" — a bum, an idler, a loafer, a vagrant and a loner — with a capacity for the higher forms of knowledge or thought. The "vago's" knowledge is not derived from systemized learning nor does it yield scientific advancement for mankind. Instead it is a profound, spiritual knowledge based on an understanding of the truly arbitrary nature of the universe and of the ultimate absurdity of life. The "vago" is a modernist, not a positivist, and Baroja does not want us to dismiss him lightly:

> Un vago apoyado en un farol es un motivo de reflexión. El farol, la ciencia; la rigidez, la luz; el vago, la duda; la indecisión, la sombra.
> ¡Glorificad a los faroles! ¡No despreciéis a los vagos! (*Vidas* 148)[6]

What do the "vago" and the "golfo" represent?

It is not immediately obvious to the casual reader, but neither "Patología del

go by. / He is neither tall, nor short, nor thin, nor fat, nor dark, nor fair: he could be thirty years old and he could be fifty; he is not well dressed, but he is not a ragamuffin either. / What is he doing? Looking at something? Waiting for something? No. He is not waiting for anything. From time to time he smiles; but his smile is not sarcastic, nor is his gaze askance."

5" . . . his gaze is profound, his mouth mocking, his manner indolent. / He watches like a man who does not expect anything from anybody. / He is a spectator of life; he is not an actor. He is an intellectual."

6"A bum leaning against a lamp post is something to think about. The lamp post, science; rigidity, light; the bum, doubt; indecision, shadow. / Glory to the lamp posts! Do not scorn the bums!"

golfo" nor "El vago" could have been written without Schopenhauer. Baroja read Schopenhauer's *Parerga and Paralimpomena,* a collection of essays on various topics and themes, during his medical student days (*Desde* 319), and he was still deeply under the influence of Schopenhauer when he wrote *Vidas sombrías* (Fox, 351). Two ideas in particular shaped his views on morality and mankind and determined the configuration of the "golfo" and of the "vago." The first comes from the essay "Aphorisms on the Wisdom of Life" and the second comes from "On Ethics." They are:

> 1. Happiness depends on developing intelligence to the point at which it operates independently of the will and even contrary to its demands.
> (1: 311-497).
>
> 2. The ethical life depends on curbing the aggressiveness inherent in every will, and therefore morality is a function of compassion and asceticism.
> (2: 201-239).

For Schopenhauer, the original essence is a force he calls the eternal will and everything that exists is a manifestation of will. In its struggle to manifest itself, the will in one of its forms is constantly fighting for existence against the will in another of its forms. Life is therefore a continuous process of suffering as one blind striving clashes with the next. To make life bearable, Schopenhauer counsels the suppression of the will to the greatest degree possible. In his essay "Aphorisms on the Wisdom of Life," Schopenhauer illustrates his idea that intelligence can be developed to the point at which it operates independently of the will and contrary to its demands. In this essay, he creates the image of a man who is spared much suffering on the one hand and boredom on the other because his superior intelligence has released him from an enslavement to the demands imposed by the will. Untroubled by worldly desires, he serenely dedicates his life to the pursuit of philosophy and art. In contrast to this figure, Schopenhauer creates another one of an anxious dullard who is completely preoccupied with himself and with satisfying the insistent but often frivolous demands of the will (1: 338-345).

Baroja had this contrast in mind when he created the two character-types that appear in *Vidas sombrías* in "El vago," and in "Patología del golfo." Original with Baroja is the characterization of both the "vago" and the "golfo" as colorful characters that live on the margins of society, but the idea that intelligence predominates over will in one figure, and will over intelligence in the other has its genesis in the essays of Schopenhauer.

Parerga and Paralimpomena is so crucial to an understanding of Baroja's writing in *Vidas sombrías,* that parts of "El vago," for example, are incomprehensible if one has not read Schopenhauer's essays first. Toward the end of "El vago," the narrator makes the following connection between himself and the subject of his sketch:

> El vago del farol y yo nos conocemos, y nos hablamos.
>
> *Me protege*. Es un hombre que no saluda a nadie. Debe tener pocos amigos; quizá no tenga ninguno. Señal de inteligencia. El mayor número de amigos marca el grado maximo en el dinamómetro de la estupidez. Creo que es una frase. (*Vidas* 149; emphasis added)[7]

According to Schopenhauer, privation causes pain. Once privation is overcome, however, want continues. Security and affluence give rise to new demands for pleasures of the senses in a constant and often really desperate struggle against boredom:

> Nothing protects us so surely from this wrong turning [the craze for society, amusement, and luxury of every kind which lead many to extravagance and so to misery] as inner wealth, the wealth of the mind, for the more eminent it becomes the less room does it leave for boredom. (1:329)

In "El vago," the "He protects me" comes out of nowhere, and never is explained but, read in connection with Schopenhauer's essay, the message is clear. The "vago," and the inner-wealth of the mind he symbolizes, *protects* the narrator from the inevitable unhappiness brought on by an enslavement to the demands of the will.

Also in "Aphorisms on the Wisdom of Life," Schopenhauer says: "Accordingly we shall find on the whole that everyone is sociable to the extent that he is intellectually poor and generally common" (1:331). And in another part of the same essay he says:

> . . . a man's sociability is roughly in inverse ratio to his intellectual worth; and 'he is very unsociable' is tantamount to saying 'he is a man of great qualities.' (1:424)

In the passage from "El vago" quoted above, Baroja adopted this expression al-

[7]"The bum at the lamp post and I know each other, and we talk to each other. / *He protects me*. He greets no one. Probably has few friends; maybe none. A sure sign of intelligence. He who has the most friends scores highest on the dynamometer that measures stupidity. I think someone said that once."

most verbatim: "He who has the most friends scores highest on the dynamometer that measures stupidity." In this case, he had the delicacy to add the disclaimer: "I think someone said that once."

To further curb the aggressiveness inherent in every will, Schopenhauer recommends a morality founded on compassion and asceticism. Repeatedly throughout *Parerga and Paralimpomena* Baroja was able to find examples of Schopenhauer's thought in this respect. A typical example occurs in the essay "On Ethics." In it, Schopenhauer says:

> The readers of my *Ethics* know that with me the foundation of morality rests ultimately on the truth that has its expression in the *Veda* and *Vedanta* in the established mystical formula *tat twam asi* (This art thou) which is stated with reference to every living thing, whether man or animal, and is then called the *Mahavakya* or Great word. (2:219)

For Schopenhauer, this Hindu truth yields the purest morality because it is not based on duty or even on the promise of an eternal reward. Instead it is based on one individual's recognition of himself as identical with another individual even though each exists in complete separation from the other.

At the end of "Patología del golfo," under the heading "Therapeutics," Baroja prescribes the following treatment for eradicating "el golfo," who is a microbe that threatens the health of society:

> I can think of only two remedies indicated in the pathological case of the scoundrel. One is therapeutic: educate him. The other is hygienic: hang him. (*Vidas* 197)

In keeping with the more radical treatment, Baroja exterminates "golfismo" in several of his most contemptible characters in *Vidas sombrías*. In one story, a scoundrel is transformed from cruel villainess to compassionate heroine by a mystic kiss; another, a covetous miser, is regenerated on his deathbed. In others, morally corrupt characters are awakened to compassion by the suffering they see around them. In each case, moral regeneration is brought about by the recognition that one's own nature is absolutely identical with that of others, and that every being, apparently individual and unique, is in reality a fleeting manifestation of a common essence into which it will ultimately be reabsorbed.

On balance, in *Vidas sombrías* the "golfos," or rather what they stand for, prevail. No story in the collection parallels, on the realistic level, the ideal, harmonious society Baroja portrays in the visionary "Piedad postrera." The perfect society is never achieved. But throughout the somber lives portrayed here, there flashes the light of multiple compassionate acts, which are there to show the reader the way to achieving it.

Baroja later repudiated the ideals on which *Vidas sombrías* was based. "The strong dominate the weak; life is action" became his motto in place of "The strong dominate the weak; life is compassion" ("Formación" 437). In his maturity, he was also painfully aware of the extent to which he borrowed, pilfered, adopted, and adapted ideas and images during his earliest years as a writer, and he rarely had a kind word to say about this book (*Desde* 558).

Nevertheless the collection is a memorable one. Some of the stories in it are fine examples of Baroja's art, and others are remembered for characteristics of style, content and tone that reappear in Baroja's later works. "Patología del golfo" provided the inspiration for his trilogy *La lucha por la vida* or *The Struggle for Life*, in which the characters are "golfos" of all social classes and types (Sobejano 362). Among these, the "golfo" as hero is modeled on the type of the "golfo que filosofa" or philosopher-scoundrel. As described in "Patología del golfo," the philosopher-scoundrel is different in every respect from the egoistic, unprincipled "golfo" that we have been discussing up until now. More of an intellectual than a scoundrel, he is a spectator rather than a knower (*Vidas* 196).

In fact, the philosopher-scoundrel is none other than the "vago." Identical in everything but name, these two character types are free spirits. In contrast to the figure of the unprincipled scoundrel, emblematic of all that is morally corrupt, the bum and the philosopher-scoundrel are emblems of Schopenhauerian virtues of intelligence, ironic detachment, lack of ambition and indifference to worldly things. Perfectly suited to life in an ideal society but somewhat of a misfit everywhere else, the figure of the bum or philosopher-scoundrel is the forerunner of the typical Barojian hero, and a fascinating object for study in its melding of conventional Spanish popular types and cross currents of modern mysticism, pessimism, and humanitarian anarchism that were surging through Europe at the time of the turn of the century.

WORKS CITED

Baroja, Pío. *Desde la ultima vuelta del camino.* 1944. Rpt. as *Desde la ultima vuelta del camino: Memorias* Vol. l. Barcelona: Planeta, 1970.

——. "La formacion psicologica de un escritor" (Discurso de ingreso en la

Academia Espanola, 12 de mayo de 1935). Rpt. in *Baroja y su mundo*. Ed. Fernando Baeza. Vol. 2. Madrid: Arion, 1961. 417-52.

——. "Nietzsche y su filosofía." *Revista Nueva* February 15, 1899. Rpt in *Obras Completas*. Vol. 8. Madrid: Biblioteca Nueva, 1948. 853-56.

——. *Vidas sombrías*. 1900. Rpt. in *Vidas sombrías (Cuentos)*. Madrid: Caro Raggio, 1974. 9-198.

Dos Passos, John. *Rosinante to the Road Again*. New York: Doran, 1922. 80-100.

Fox, E. Inman. "Baroja and Schopenhauer: El árbol de la ciencia." *Revue de litterature comparée*. XXXVII July-September, 1963. 350-59.

Larra, Mariano Jose de. "Los calaveras" (articulos primero y segundo). 1835. Rpt. in *Articulos de costumbres*. Ed. Azorin. 10th ed. Madrid: Espasa-Calpe, 1969. 81-92.

Mosse, George L. Introduction. *Degeneration*. By Max Nordau. New York: Howard Fertig, 1968. xv-xxxiv.

Nordau, Max. *Degeneration*. New York: Howard Fertig, 1968. Translated from the Second Edition of the German Work.

Schopenhauer, Arthur. *Parerga and Paralimpomena: Short Philosophical Essays*. Trans. E. F. J. Payne. 2 vols. Oxford: Clarendon P, 1974. 1: 311-497; 2: 201-39.

Sobejano, Gonzalo. *Nietzsche en España*. Madrid: Gredos, 1967.

EDUARDO LOPEZ-ARANGUREN

The Image of the Basque Country and Basque Culture in the American Press[1]

Introduction

The fundamental objective of this paper is to identify and analyze, using well-known tools of sociological research, the image that exists in the United States of the Basque Country as a differentiated nation within the Spanish State, and of the Basque people as a people with their own collective identity quite distinct from that of Castilians, Catalans, Galicians, or Andalusians. More specifically, I am trying to ascertain the image that Americans have of Basque people and Basque culture, of Basque political, cultural, economic, and social institutions, and of Basque contemporary problems. That is, the paper centers on the analysis of existing perceptions and stereotypes but it will also attempt to answer the question of how Americans view the problems that the Basque Country is facing and the possible solutions to such problems.

The period of thirty-four years covered by the research project starts in 1953 — the year that marks the beginning of a close bilateral military, political, and economic relationship between the USA and the Spanish State — and ends in 1986. Thus, we should be able to discover the *changes* that have taken place in the perceptions, stereotypes, and problems of the Basque Country and the Basque people presented by the American press from the time of the military and economic agreements of 1953 until the present, taking into account the death of General Franco in 1975, the transition to a democratic regime, and especially the establishment of the Basque Autonomous Community following the approval of the Basque Statute of Autonomy — the *Estatuto de Gernika* — in 1979.

The fact that the United States is the indisputable leader of the Western world

---

[1]An earlier version of this paper was presented at the 18th Annual Meeting of the Popular Culture Association (New Orleans, March 23-26, 1988). This paper contains the first findings of a research project still in progress, undertaken in June of 1987 and financed with a grant from the University of Basque Country. This research project is, in turn, part of a wider project to study the image of Spain and Spaniards in the American daily press and periodicals.

and the most powerful country in the world both economically and militarily would justify by itself a research project on the image that Americans have formed about any nation or people. But in the Basque Country's case there are reasons of more weight that explain better the interest of such an undertaking.

Firstly, there is the well-known Basque migration to the United States starting in 1848 and their settlement in California and later in other Western states, especially in Nevada and Idaho. The impact produced by Basque immigrants in the field of cattle raising, and the preservation until the present of a Basque ethnic identity have induced the editors of the *Harvard Encyclopedia of American Ethnic Groups* to include the Basques as a differentiated ethnic group in the United States. In it we can read the following: "Today Basque Americans are among the most visible ethnic groups in the western United States." And a few lines below we find elements of an image of the Basques, the precise subject of this paper: "The Basques' propensity for hard work, honesty, and thrift is esteemed within the American value system" (178).

Secondly, there are the economic relations between the Basque Country and the United States. As far as commerce is concerned, figures indicate that the United States is the second client for Basque products, after France, (in 1986, 12.8 percent of all exports from the Basque Autonomous Community were sent to the U.S.) and the fourth provider to the Basque Autonomous Community — after France, West Germany, and the United Kingdom — (9.2 percent of all Basque import came from the U.S. in 1986).[2] American capital investment in the Basque Country is another very significant aspect of the economic ties between the Basque Country and the U.S. Although exact figures about the amount of American capital investment in the Basque economy, particularly in industry and services, are not available, we know that some companies are totally or almost totally owned by American corporations and that the percentage of American capital in other companies is indeed significant. We also know that the U.S. is the country that invested most heavily in the Basque Country during the period April 1985-February 1986. But it may be more revealing to underline the continued Basque interest in attracting American capital, as illustrated by the publication entitled *Investing in Bilbao*, edited wholly in English in 1983 by the Bilbao

[2]*Comercio Exterior Vasco 1986.*

Chamber of Commerce, Industry and Shipping.

Among the various strategies available to attempt to reach the objectives of this research project we have decided to investigate the image of the Basque Country and the Basque people in the United States using the methodological technique of analyzing the content of communications referring to anything Basque in the American mass media. The mass media whose content is analyzed in this research project belong to the categories of *daily* and *periodical press* and they fulfill three requirements: The publications chosen are of general interest, they are nationally distributed, and they have a large circulation (generally, above half a million copies).[3] Newspapers such as the *New York Times* and the *Los Angeles Times*, and magazines such as *Business Week, Life, National Geographic, Newsweek, Time,* or *Reader's Digest* are some of the publications that have been selected because they fulfill the above conditions.

It is both appropriate and legitimate to raise the issue of whether or not the image of the Basque Country presented by the American daily press and periodicals is indeed the image of that country that the American people have. In this article I will make the assumption — firmly anchored in the "cultural norms theory" (DeFleur 1970) — that the image held by the people is basically the image presented by the media, that is, the assumption that to the extent that Americans carry a picture of the Basques in their minds, such a picture has been acquired and is acquired through the mass media. The reasoning is essentially the following: The mass media is often our primary source of information about many parts of the world. In fact, one of the principal functions of the mass media is the provision of information, which generally we consider valid. The coverage of a phenomenon, event, or situation by the media provides by itself a certain type of validity or status to that event or situation. Therefore, the information that we receive through the media strongly influences our images of those parts of the world about which we cannot acquire first hand knowledge. Obviously, this last proposition has important implications: For example, if the mass media present an

[3]The analysis is limited to daily and periodical press for two reasons. To begin with, communications referring to the Basque Country and the Basque people are much more frequent, more complete, and more accessible in the press than on radio or on television. Secondly, an important part of this research project is the study of the changes that may have taken place in the images of the Basques that are presented by the media, and the analysis of the press allows more depth in the study of change than the analysis of other forms of media.

incomplete, distorted, stereotyped, or biased picture of a country, event or situation, and if we are unable to examine by ourselves its accuracy and validity, then the image that we will form based on the informations provided by the media will be most likely an incomplete, distorted, stereotyped, or biased image.

The data

The nature and characteristics of a research like the present one imply the existence of four universes or populations, and therefore they require making four different kinds of decisions involving selection. The four universes are the following:

a) *Years* in the period 1953-1986: We had to decide which specific years of the above thirty-four years were going to be selected for study. Between 1953 and 1973 we selected the following ten years using the criterion of *historical significance*, that is, significant events in the history of Spain or in the history of the Basque Country that happened during the years 1953-54, 1957-58, 1962-63, 1965-66, 1969-70. From 1973 until the present we have included every year in the analysis.

b) *Titles* of the daily and periodical publications that satisfy the three conditions mentioned earlier: We had to decide which daily newspapers and which magazines we were going to examine. Only two newspapers have been selected, one from the East Coast and one from the West Coast" the *New York Times* (*NYT*) and the *Los Angeles Times* (*LAT*). Both are, however, large circulation dailies that provide news services, often with penetrating comment and reportage, to dozens of smaller newspapers throughout the United States. The periodical publications whose content is analyzed, in the years in which they are available, are: *Atlantic, Business Week, Esquire, Forbes, Harper's, Holiday, Life, Look, National Geographic, New York Times Magazine, New Yorker, Newsweek, People, Reader's Digest, Saturday Evening Post, Saturday Review, Smithsonian, Time*, and *US News & World Report.*

c) *Issues* (dates) of the selected dailies and magazines that were published during the selected years. We had to make a decision about which issues or numbers to concentrate on. In the case of the two newspapers, the only issues or dates that have been included in the sample are the Sunday issue of every week of the selected years, the justification being that the Sunday circulation of both newspapers is significantly higher than their daily circulation (around 600,000 more copies for the *New York Times* and around 300,000 more copies for the *Los Angeles Times*). In the case of the periodical publications, we made the decision to examine every issue published each selected year, regardless of the frequency of their publication.

d) *Content units,* that is, sections (news items, articles, editorials, etc.) that contain messages or communications about the Basque Country, the Basque people, or the Basque culture. This final decision concerned the selection of the content units to be analyzed. Here we decided to include in the analysis every unit (news item, article, commentary, or editorial) whose content referred in any way to the Basque country, the Basque people or the Basque culture.

We located the items of interest using the *New York Times Index,* the *Los Angeles Times Index* (unfortunately we found no *LAT* Index available before 1972), and the *Reader's Guide to Periodical Literature.* The key words used in this search were "Basques," "Basque Country" and all cross references, as well as "Spain," "Spanish people" and all cross references. Items located with the key words "Spain," "Spanish people" and cross references were read and included in the sample if they contained references to the Basque Country or the Basque culture. Following this procedure we ended up with a sample of 455 elements which included news items, signed and unsigned columns and articles, and editorials, whose origin was the following: 206 from the *New York Times,* 73 from the *Los Angeles Times,* and 176 from the nineteen periodical publications.

Analysis and results

A) The Fifties

The setting: Image of the Basque economy

In 1955, per capita income in Spain was $312, while that same year per capita income in the United States reached $1,881. But the Basque Country was one of the most developed regions in Spain and thus per capita income there was significantly higher than the Spanish average: $578 if Navarre is included, and $646 if we consider only the three provinces that today constitute the Basque Autonomous Community: Alava, Guipúzcoa and Vizcaya.[4]

[4]The nationalist discourse maintains that Navarre (Nafarroa in Euskera) is part of the Basque Country, along with the provinces of Alava (Araba), Guipúzcoa (Gipuzkoa), Vizcaya (Bizkaia), and even three territories at the other side of the Pyrenees, in southern France. The Autonomous

Other figures indicate that in 1955 the Basque Country was much more industrialized than most of the rest of Spain (see Table 1), although important differences existed between Guipúzcoa and Vizcaya on the one hand and Alava and Navarre on the other hand.

Table 1
Distribution of the Active population by economic sector in Spain and the Basque Country in 1955 (percentages)

	Industry	Agriculture	Services
Spain	26.9	37.8	35.3
Basque Country	44.7	17.4	37.9
Alava	34.5	24.1	41.4
Guipúzcoa	50.4	10.1	39.5
Vizcaya	53.1	9.0	37.9
Navarre	23.0	42.4	34.6

Source: Banco de Bilbao. *Renta nacional de España y su distribución provincial-1955*. Bilbao, no date.

However, the image of the Basque Country that is presented in this period does not always accurately reflect the above economic reality. The picture of the Basque Country that emerges from most of the writings about the area is that of a predominantly rural region, of a pristine bucolic scenery unspoiled by the ravages of industrialization, a region where the people make their living from agriculture and fishing, where industry is concentrated in one space — the city of Bilbao — and where social organization is based on the continued importance of traditional units — the rural family and the farmhouse (*el caserio*):

> The Spanish Basque provinces . . . form the sudden green corner of the dry peninsula, the country of short steep mountains . . . lush with the fall of rain. Rock and mountain come down precipitously into kind woods, vivid pasture and fast streams that turn silver when the light catches them (*Holiday* 1 Mar 58: 88).

> Once the Basques hunted the right whale (sic) . . . . Now tuna and sardines keep many Basque families from poverty . . . . The United States has lately passed

Community of the Basque Country, constituted following the approval in 1978 of the present Spanish Constitution, is formed by Alava, Guipúzcoa and Vizcaya, while Navarre has become another one of the 17 autonomous communities into which the Spanish state has been divided.

> special laws admitting sheepherders most of whom are Basques. Basques are noted for their skill as shepherds (*Nat. Geo. Mag.* Feb 54: 152, 159).
>
> This section around Pamplona, Navarre has rich agricultural resources that provide a solid basis for prosperity and development (*Nat. Geo. Mag* . Feb 54: 176).
>
> Basque social and family life is unique. Everything revolves around the ancestral House — a unit that may include the dwelling and other buildings, tilled land, meadows, heath, and mountain pastures (*Nat. Geo. Mag.* Feb 54: 159).

The city of Bilbao is the "steel producing city," the "iron-making city," the "large industrial city" of the Basque Country, but it also is "the Spanish Pittsburgh" and the site of the "dirty Nervión River industrial complex." Often, references to Bilbao are related to labor unrest in Franco's Spain:

> [Bilbao is] a modern city . . . with a wealthy trade with Cardiff, Manchester and London . . . (*Holiday* 1 Mar 58: 149)
>
> Bilbao, largest and most prosperous of all Basque centers, has built up a flourishing trade in iron and ore and has busy foundries and shipyards (*Nat. Geo. Mag.* Feb 54: 159).
>
> In the ever-restless industrial center of Bilbao, 2800 Basque workers at Spain's major shipyard began a sit down strike for more pay (*Time* 16 Sep 57: 4).

There is in our sample a long, exceptional article that provides a more balanced view of the Basque Country, a view more consonant with the brief statistical picture provided above. It is an article written by V.S. Prichett and published in *Holiday* on March 1, 1958. The image of the Basque Country presented there is made up by the following components:

a) The Basque Country is not an homogeneous region but rather a country characterized by significant differences between the French and the Spanish sides as well as important differences within South Euskadi:

> The only difference [between the French Basques and the Spanish Basques] are that . . . the French Basque is a peasant living on poor land, while the Spanish Basques are successful farmers, seamen, industrialists and businessmen (89). The traveler in the Basque provinces will find himself in a small green region of extraordinary local differences . . . . [The Basque] is poorer in Alava; he is well off in Vizcaya and Guipúzcoa (156).

b) Industrialization is not limited to the Bilbao area but has spread through much of the provinces of Guipúzcoa and Vizcaya:

> The narrow valleys of Guipúzcoa and Vizcaya on the Spanish side are dotted

> with small factories, mills, marble quarries, potteries. The wider valleys of the French side . . . are rural (89). . . . That province [Guipúzcoa], and Vizcaya . . . are losing their peasant character (90). . . . Electric power came here earlier than in the rest of the peninsula, and instead of the old crawling railroads of Spain, they have a network of fast narrow-gauge lines (152-3).

c) The industrialization that has taken place has attracted a flow of immigrants from other regions of Spain, a fact that has serious consequences:

> the purely Basque character has been adulterated by the Castilian . . . . Since the civil war large numbers of half-starved peasantry from poorer Spanish regions, especially Andalusia, have moved into the Basque provinces (90-l).

Basque Stereotype Traits

Most of the articles containing references to the Basques published in this period are characterized by a neutral tone but a few, primarily the longer ones, are clearly sympathetic. Therefore, we find in them few negative stereotype traits. From another perspective we can classify the traits found according to a different criterion: whether they refer to "physical & behavioral," to "personality," or to the "mind." The cross-classification yields the following picture:

Basque Stereotype Traits

	Physical/Behavioral	Personality	Mind
Positive	Brave Strong Physically skilled Masculinity (men): prefer company of fellow men Energetic	Proud Dignity, self-respect Honest, sincere Hardworking, industrious independence (of women) Serious minded Affectionate Friendly, hospitable Independence of spirit	Practical
Neutral	Unknown origin Big eaters Big drinkers Love to sing	Deeply religious Conservative Tradition loving Reserved (at first) Not gay or cheerful	Dryly humorous Ironic Phlegmatic Slyness
Negative	Wild A little brutal	Simple Suspicious	Not very imaginative

Physical/Behavioral	Personality	Mind
Sudden bursts of violence	Obstinate, Stubborn Uncompromising Determination to do things their own way	Not innovative

Image of the Basque Culture

The principal components of the image of the Basque culture that are presented by the printed media in the 1950s are the following: The Basque language, the game of *pelota*, the Basque folk dances, the Basques' fondness for food and wine, and the popular fiesta of San Fermin in Pamplona, Navarre.

a) The *Basque language* — Euskera — is generally described as a primitive, unique, incomprehensible language, unrelated to other European tongues, and thus extremely difficult to learn, so difficult indeed that "it baffled even the Devil":

> The Devil, it seems, decided to visit Euskal Herria to learn the language and tempt the devout Catholic Basques.
> After seven years of effort, he was forced to flee by way of the Bridge of the Holy Ghost. In his panic he fell against one of its corners. The blow knocked out of his head the only two words he had managed to learn — *bai* and *ez* (yes and no)! (*Nat. Geo. Mag*. Feb 54: 150).

Several explanations are provided for the difficulty that foreigners experience to learn Euskera: One is the already mentioned lack of affinity with other languages and another the existence of eight separate Basque dialects. But the crucial factor is that in order to master Euskera one has to think in Basque, and that "requires an entirely different attitude of mind" (*Nat. Geo. Mag*. Feb 54: 150).

The picture of the Basque language that we find in this period is completed with two negative traits: It has "very little literature" and it "is not a beautiful language":

> It is spoken loudly, in short manly sentences and in a clipped manner; it has the abrupt sound of a sack of coal being shot into a cellar. Sung in male choruses . . . it is richer and more melodious (*Holiday* 1 Mar 58: 89).

b) The game of *pelota* (also identified with the Basque term *jai alai*) is overwhelmingly perceived as the Basque sport *par excellence*, a cultural element as closely linked to Basque culture as basketball is to American culture. *Pelota* is described as "the fast and furious Basque game," the sport that "shows the physical skill and power of the Basques," the "national passion," the sport that every Basque learns to play because "every village has its pelota court."

Although there are several varieties of the game of *pelota* (it can be played with both hands, with a narrow flat wooden racket — a *pala* — or with a basket called *cesta* or *txistera*) little or no attention is paid to the first two forms in the items that we sampled. On the other hand, we find detailed descriptions of the game of cesta *punta*: The material used to make the *txistera*, the procedure to make it, and the way it is used by the player (the *pelotari*); the pelota, the court, the game itself — the way it is played; the *pelotari*, what makes a good player (speed, skill, agility, energy, endurance), what the player wears, what he makes (he is poor and ill-paid), his character (he is temperamental); the betting that takes place; and, finally, the relationship between players and fans:

> A sideshow is the betting, the bookies trafficking with the customers by throwing the betting slips up to the grandstand stuffed inside a rubber ball (*Sat. Rev*. 24 Oct 53: 45).

> Games bring out the character of a people very quickly. The audience is quick to ridicule a bad shot or to shout abuse at an unpopular player, and an interchange of obscene signs between players and audience is frequent (*Holiday* 1 Mar 58: 156).

c) *Folk dances* are viewed as another important element of Basque culture. Basques are presented as a people who love to dance, who consequently maintain their traditional dances, and who spend a lot of physical energy when they perform them:

> Physical energy is characteristic of Basques. They drink deeply and dance furiously, being most famous for their high leaping . . . At the end of a high-kicking dance called the Binokoo two dancers heave a third up in the air and hold him horizontally and stiff above their heads (*Holiday* 1 Mar 58: 155).

Among the many Basque folk dances ("there are dances in which men and women dance together and ritual dances performed only by men") there is one that is considered a particularly spectacular dance and that, therefore is described in detail — The Goblet Dance:

> First a circle was cleared in the heart of the crowd. Then the mayor stepped forth . . . carrying a heavy goblet half filled with wine, which he placed on the ground in the center of the space . . .
> The performance represented a struggle between Good and Evil . . . The show's star was the Horseman [or *Zamalzain*], who wore strapped about his waist a miniature hobbyhorse made of a framework draped with scarlet cloth and white lace flounce . . . . The climax came when the Horseman, though unable to see his own feet below his equipment, jumped onto the goblet. He stood on it with one foot, making the sign of the cross with the other, for two or three seconds. There was dead silence.
> Suddenly he made a wild leap that took him clear without upsetting the glass. A roar of applause greeted the feat. Had the dancer spilled a drop of wine, a Basque spectator later told me, he would have been jeered from the arena (*Nat. Geo. Mag*. Feb 54: 174).

d) References to the Basques do not fail to comment, sometimes extensively, about Basque *gastronomy* as a fundamental aspect of Basque culture — and particularly of Basque male culture. That means, firstly, that Basques love to eat.

> They eat and drink enormously . . . the Basque is a glutton with a strong stomach . . . toward two in the afternoon, after picking at oysters and prawns and filling up with *chacoli* [Basque green wine], the crowds fill the restaurants and eat enormous meals (*Holiday* 1 Mar 58: 89, 150, 151).

It also means that Basques love to eat *well* and that they value good cooking (the Basques "have the best cooking in Spain") — and thus the selection and the preparation of the food is a skill very much appreciated. But, from a cultural perspective, the most significant fact is that cooking and eating becomes a set of ritualistic social activities from which women are excluded when Basque men leave their wives and children to spend a day with their friends, immersed in the classless male world of the gastronomic society:

> All over the Basque provinces are these male *sociedades*. You'll see a doctor, a journalist, a shopkeeper, a fisherman carry food into his club. He gets a pan, chops his garlic or his parsley, makes his sauce, goes to the charcoal grill and cooks his supper. He carries it to a long table, gets knives, forks, bread, pepper, salt and a bottle of wine, and eats with his friends. And having done so, he takes his things to be washed up. There is only one woman in any club and she is not allowed to leave the sink (*Holiday* 1 Mar 58: 91).

e) *The Running of the Bulls* that takes place in the city of Pamplona every year, early in the morning between the seventh and the fourteenth day on the month of

July is to Americans the most unusual and spectacular of all Spanish popular festivals. The description of the event, and the degree of accuracy of that description, varies from publication to publication. It is accurate to write that:

> the huge, fierce beasts are not only fought in the arena, but are run through barricaded streets from the bullpens set up in the plaza to the bullring in another part of town (*Sat. Rev.* 2 Jan 54: 35).

> Boards protect some shop fronts, but many merchants merely trust that the mass of struggling humanity will make its own wall between charging bulls and store windows (*Nat. Geo. Mag.* Feb 54: 176).

But on the other hand, it is not accurate to say that the bulls are "turned loose" or "set free in the streets of Pamplona" nor that "even women may be knocked down and trampled," simply because in the fifties women were not allowed to run in front of the bulls.

The bulls that run in the morning are fought in the bullring in the afternoon in the well-known traditional way, but writings about this event tend to emphasize that Basques prefer the morning action to the afternoon action:

> The Basque notion of a bullfight is not the ritual ceremony of the bullring in the south (*Reader's Digest* Aug 54: 115).

> Bullfighting is not their passion. The Basques favor sport and do not care for art, ritual or pageant (*Holiday* 1 Mar 58: 150).

Thus, the image of the Basque people that is presented is far from one of a refined, elegant, fashionable, or civilized people. Rather, it is one in which the following attributes stand out: daring, wild, uncultivated, rough.

> [The Fiesta of San Fermin] is an orgy of wine drinking, danger and excitement. The women's eyes brighten with ferocious pleasure when they talk of it, and the men are eager for the hullabaloo (*Holiday* 1 Mar 58: 155).

To sum up: Writings and references to the Basque Country and the Basque people appearing in the fifties in the American press tend to present a picture in which the Basques are depicted as a rural, unsophisticated, wild and primitive people, a people who enjoy simple pleasures like eating and drinking, singing and dancing, playing *pelota* and risking their lives running in front of fighting bulls. The language that Basque speak is characterized as a primitive language, and their religion is likewise described as "plain, prosaic and domestic," a religion of "ordinary moralists," quite different from the "fanatical, mystical, decorative, theatrical and passionate" Catholicism that is found in much of the rest of Spain (*Holiday* 1 Mar 58: 90-91).

B) The Eighties

The setting: Image of the Basque economy

In 1983, per capita income in Spain had risen to $3,583, while that same year per capita income in the United States reached $11,675. Per capita income in both the Autonomous Community of the Basque Country and Navarre was still higher than the national average — $4,084 and $3,931 respectively — but their advantage relative to the national average was not as significant as in the fifties. In per capita income terms, the Basque Country was fourth and Navarre was sixth among the 17 autonomous communities. The data show (see Table 2) that the Basque Country, including Navarre, was more industrialized than most of Spain — although the differences were not as high as in the fifties — and that agriculture had more weight in Navarre than in the provinces of Alava, Guipúzcoa and Vizcaya.

But in 1983 the Spanish economy was in the middle of an economic crisis, and the Basque economy was particularly affected because the recession was having a serious impact on traditional Basque industry. At the end of 1983, unemployment in Spain, practically non-existent in the fifties, reached 18.4 percent and was still increasing. In the Basque Country, unemployment was higher than the Spanish average (20.2 percent) while in the more agricultural Navarre it was lower: 15.5 percent.[5]

Table 2.
Distribution of the active population by economic sector in the Basque Country and Spain in 1983 (percentages)

	Industry	Agriculture & Fishing	Commerce & Services
Spain	36.6	16.6	46.9
Alava	47.8	8.9	43.2
Guipúzcoa	50.3	7.7	42.0
Vizcaya	47.8	4.7	47.5
Navarre	42.5	14.8	42.7
Basque Country	47.5	7.8	44.7

Source: Banco de Bilbao. *Renta nacional de España 1983 y su distribución provincial.* Bilbao, 1986.

[5]Instituto Nacional de Estadística. *Encuesta Población Activa*, 4th quarter, 1983.

How is the Basque Country viewed by American journalists in the 1980s? The image that emerges from the items in our sample is a rather complex one, made up by the following components:

1) The Basque Country is a beautiful, picture-card pretty region, except the industrial valleys, and particularly the Nervion river valley (that is, the Bilbao area) which are contaminated with filth, smoke, fumes, yellow sulphur haze, and pollution:

> [It is] a region rich with natural beauty (*US News & WR* 17 Mar 80: 56).
>
> Bilbao and the surrounding industrial belt . . . is one of the most densely populated and dirtiest cities in Europe (*NYT Mag*. 4 May 80: 95).

2) During the 1950s and 1960s the Basque provinces experienced spectacular economic development. Already leading Spain in heavy industry, the Basque economy attracted foreign capital, expanded, created jobs that pulled immigrants from poorer regions, and strengthened their position as one of the most prosperous areas in the peninsula:

> For years, Basque provinces led Spain in shipbuilding and the production of steel, machine tools, wire and cable . . . (*US News & WR* 17 Mar 80: 56).
>
> the Basque country became fertile ground for multinationals, such as Westinghouse, Firestone and General Electric, who came in search of cheap labor and easy profits.
> In their wake came the immigrants: agricultural workers from Andalusia and Estremadura, Spain's poorer regions . . . . They came in such numbers . . . that today more than a quarter of the population was born outside the Basque country (*NYT. Mag*. 4 May 80: 94).

3) Today, however, the Basque economy is facing grave problems. Old industries are obsolete, unproductive and uncompetitive. Many firms have gone out of business and this has created a persistent problem of unemployment. In addition, terrorist violence and the so-called "revolutionary tax" that the revolutionary terrorist organization ETA levies on local firms to finance insurgency operations compounds an already difficult situation:

> Recession has gripped Spain for three years, plunging Basque firms into bankruptcy, throwing thousands out of jobs and rendering the robust economy one of Spain's most depressed. Steel and shipbuilding facilities have become obsolete, unable to match world competition in the fact of rising energy costs . . . .
> In economic terms alone, terrorism has been costly. Businessmen blame the vi-

olence for drying up outside investment and for sparking a sustained flight of investment capital . . . (*US NEWS & WR* 17 Mar 80: 59).

Many Basque businessmen have fled the area for the relative safety of Madrid. Good bye, job creators (*Forbes* 7 July 80: 132).

Apparently adding to [ETA] attraction to many youths is a 22 percent official Basque unemployment rate, 2 points above the national average, as the region's old industries like steel and shipbuilding decline (*NYT* 24 Aug 86: 12).

4) There is no easy nor quick solution to an economic problem that is linked to a political problem:

Economic revival, experts say, will require a shift from heavy industry to new, more sophisticated enterprises. But recovery is far more complicated than that. If the Basque country ever is to retrieve economic vitality, many experts maintain it must achieve political stability (*US News & WR* 17 Mar 80: 59).

Basque Stereotype Traits

Compared to the earlier period, in the eighties there are many fewer references to Basque stereotype traits. There are also fewer positive traits mentioned, while there are relatively more traits in the neutral category. Some traits in the eighties' list already appeared in the fifties' list, and thus we might consider those characteristics (identified below with an asterisk) as the hard-core of the Basque stereotype.

Basque Stereotype Traits

	Physical/Behavioral	Personality	Mind
Positive	Energetic* Strong* Able to resist invasions	Tough Proud* Serious* Sharp sense of identity	
Neutral	Unknown origin* Ethnically distinct A race apart Good drinkers*	Reserved* Individualistic Conservative* Tradition loving* Devoutly Catholic* Inclined to action Deep sense of cultural separateness	
Negative	Clannish Never forgive insults	Stubborn*	No aesthetic sense

Image of the Basque Culture

The Basques must appear to Americans as a people short on *heroes,* since only two are mentioned in all the material that we have reviewed: Juan Sebastián Elcano (born in Guetaria, Guipúzcoa) who, taking over command when Magellan was killed in the Philippines, became the first man to circumnavigate the globe (in 1522), and the saint Ignatius de Loyola (born in Azpeitia, Guipúzcoa), the founder of the Society of Jesus (in 1534).

The number of popular Basque *symbols* that American journalists find is greater. The red, green and white Basque flag (or *ikurriña*), designed by Sabino Arana, the founder of the Basque Nationalist Party (in 1894) and Guernica (or Gernika) are the ones most often mentioned.

Guernica is a symbol of different things. Pablo Picasso's painting "Guernica" evoking the German air raid, at the request of rebel forces of General Franco, on the defenseless little Basque town is a symbol of protest against "the savagery of war," against "brutal inhumanity," and thus it is not a symbol exclusive of the Basques. But Guernica is also described as "the ancient seat of Basque self-rule" and as such it has become "the focal point of Basque nationalism" and the Basques' "spiritual center." The power of Guernica as a Basque symbol of political life and self-rule resides primarily on the Oak Tree of Gernica:

> Local assemblies representing the people gathered around the sacred oak of Guernica once every two years and took council with their elders (*NYT Mag.* 4 May 80: 88).

> The oak tree of Guernica, an ancient hollow tree stump some 15 feet high, sits inside a columned monument on a small bluff. On these warm spring days, busloads of children from all over the Basque region come to see it (*NYT* 6 May 84: 1).

The ancient laws and privileges called *fueros*, that is, "the laws by which Basques exchanged limited homage to the Spanish crown for the right to run their own affairs" (*NYT* 6 May 84: 1), represent the Basques' "most cherished dream," — self-rule, or, in other words, their tradition of political freedom, which they say is the oldest in Europe (*NYT Mag.* 4 May 80: 88). One indicator of the distinctiveness of the fueros as a symbol is that the motto of the dominant Basque Nationalist Party is "God and the old *fueros* " (*US News & WR* 17 Mar 80: 59).

There are other less significant Basque symbols that are identified — like

"Eusko Gudariak," the hymn of Basque defiance to central authority — but undoubtedly the element of Basque culture most written about by American journalists in this period is the Basque language, *Euskera.* The basic themes that we find in their writings are the following:

a) Euskera is the oldest tongue in Europe. "Many scholars are convinced that it is at least 4000 years old" (*NYT* 6 Jan 80: 27). It is a unique language of mysterious origin, unrelated to any other known language:

> Euskera [is] the oldest spoken non-Indo-European language in Europe. Euskera has no relation to any spoken European or Semitic language, and its origin are shrouded in the kind of thick mists that settle over the knobby green hills of Euskadi . . . . Legend traces Euskera back to the Tower of Babel . . . (*NYT* 6 Jan 80: 27).

> Euskera is remarkable for its peculiar grammar and archaic vocabulary. It still includes, for example, a large number of words for stone-cutting tools (*NYT Mag.* 4 May 80: 88).

b) Euskera is, therefore, an extremely difficult language to learn. The difficulty is compounded because it is more a collection of regional dialects than a common language, with so many dialects and sub-dialects that the academy of the Basque language is proceeding to unify the various strands. Today it is spoken by about 22 percent of the 2.5 million people in the region. Many Basques agree that the only way to master Euskera is to learn it young.

c) Euskera suffered sharp erosion in the last few centuries. And that decline was accentuated by the fact that during the 40-year Franco dictatorship the public teaching of the language was outlawed and its public use was forbidden. Children were slapped by their teachers when they spoke Basque in school, and adults were fined or even worse:

> It became largely the property of rural, uneducated folk and only recently developed a written literature . . . [It] has survived orally, from parents to children (*NYT* 6 Jan 80: 27).

> speaking Basque in public was forbidden — some women caught doing so had their heads shaved, and militants were treated far worse (*US News & WR* 25 Aug 86: 28).

d) Basques are proud of their language, and many of them study Euskera in night schools. Euskera is "at the heart of intense Basque nationalism" and even those Basques who are unable to speak it define themselves in terms of that unique language. Thus, as soon as conditions became more favorable, Basque intellectuals and publicists fostered literary campaigns, broadcasting radio programs in Euskera and publishing newspapers and magazines that print some, if not all, the news in Basque. Nevertheless, most of the weight for the long-term diffusion of Euskera rests on the *ikastolas,* the Basque schools where education is completely in Euskera in the first years and the curricula ease simultaneously into Castilian as students near secondary school:

> The ikastolas . . . are the cornerstone of a heroic, possibly quixotic, effort to revive and spread Basque . . . .
> Under Franco, the ikastola phenomenon was viewed with great suspicion; students studying in Euskera were perceived, with some validity, as using their education to make themselves Basques first and Spaniards a very distant second . . . .
> One of the gravest problem facing the expansion of the ikastola network — and education in Euskera generally — is the shortage of qualified teachers (*NYT* 6 Jan 80: 27).

There is, finally, one other element of Basque popular culture that continues to fascinate the media: *the running of the bulls* in the city of Pamplona, which has become for many the highlight of the San Fermin Festival, "a week long fiesta of bullfighting, wine drinking and general merrymaking in honor of the city's patron saint":

> The festival has two ingredients, wine and bulls. The Basques are good drinkers, which is a mercy in such an alcoholic event. Women seem to move around without much danger of being pinched or menaced. The rhythm for the day is set by early rising, or no sleeping, because of the 8 a.m. running of the bulls. After this event, many younger people flop in the city's gardens and sleep until lunch . . . (*NYT* 24 Nov 85: 15).

> Although the runs are restricted to males, several women have reportedly disguised themselves as men, donning the traditional white pants and shirt with red scarves and sashes (*LAT* 8 Jul 84: 9).

Some of the writings report on the controversy over whether or not the event, popularized in Ernest Hemingway's novel *The Sun also Rises,* is losing its Basque character with the influx of visitors:

> [Hemingway] came to regret in some measure the success with which he had spread the raucous sanfermines . . . . For a while, many natives concurred. "There is a debate over whether or not Hemingway was positive for the identity of the sanfermines," acknowledged Julian Balduz, the city's mayor. "What happened is

> that Hemingway put the sanfermines at the disposition of the whole world, and the whole world doesn't fit into Pamplona." Yet the fact is that the number of foreign tourists . . . has dropped off in recent years (*NYT* 24 Nov 85: 15).

Basque violence and political culture

This section about the current image of the Basque Country in the American media would be incomplete if it did not deal with the subject matter that first comes to mind when the Basques are mentioned: the subject of terrorist violence and the still unsolved political problems that underlies it.

This paper and this book are not the most appropriate media for the analysis of such complex political and sociological problems like Basque nationalism and ETA violence. Nevertheless, there are two questions that I would like to address, even if briefly: 1) How important is the theme of violence in the overall picture of the Basque Country in the American printed media? 2) What are the basic elements of Basque political culture in the eighties that are presented by the media?

The evidence shows that the answer to the first question is very clear indeed. The motif of violence in relation to the Basque Country appears in one way or another in most of the 143 items that constitute the 1980s sample of printed matter. Another indicator of emphasis is to look at certain key words within headlines (readers often read only headlines), that is, at words connoting violence, like murder, kill, shoot, bomb, burn, terror, and the like, excluding non-political violence like accidents and natural disasters. Here we have found that in the period 1980-86, words connoting violence show up in 62 of the 143 items. That means 43 percent, a proportion that is maintained throughout the period.

Earlier we saw that violence is perceived as having negative effects on the Basque economy. On the other hand, there are in our sample very few comments emphasizing harmful social consequences or indicating possible negative effects of the violence upon the Basque social structure or social institutions.

The second question deals with the content of the present political culture in the Basque Country, that is with the set of values, attitudes, beliefs and norms that guide the Basque political system and that are established jointly by the history of the system and the experiences of its members. The picture of the political culture that is presented by the media is too elaborate to report here in detail, but it has three aspects that in my opinion should be pointed out because they help to understand the complexity of the political problem in that region.

The first has to do with values, and more specifically, with the basic political goal or objective that the Basque people seek: Is this autonomy of the Basque Country, self-rule within the Spanish state, or is it, rather, separation and independence? The view that emerges from the material reviewed is that although "the Basques have always resented government from afar, a tradition that goes as far back as the eighth century," the majority of them consider separation and independence a "wildly unrealistic goal" (*Time* 10 Aug 81: 42) endorsed only by about 20 percent of the population. Miguel Castells, a leader of the Herri Batasuna Party is quoted as saying:

> We are working for minimum of democratic liberties . . . . Once we get there, we'll work for independence and socialism. We can't use the words in our program, but that's what most of us want (*NYT* 6 May 84: 18).

But what journalists and commentators write is that "self-rule" or "a modern version of the *fueros*" is the region's most cherished dream and what most Basques hope for (*US News & WR* 17 Mar 80: 59). And the support for that view is found, for example, in the words of Xabier Arzallus, the head of the Basque Nationalist Party:

> If we could be independent, we would, because we are up to our noses with Madrid. But independence isn't practical, so what we fundamentally want is more autonomy at a political level. Not independence. Autonomy (*NYT* 21 Sep 86: 3).

The second aspect is the Basques' attitude toward the terrorist organization ETA. What the American media report in this respect is a profound ambivalence on the part of the Basque population. ETA was born in 1959, and developed in the sixties, as the primary fighting resistance to the Franco dictatorship, and as such it enjoyed enormous popular support in the Basque Country. But with the establishment of a formally democratic regime, and the increasing resort to terrorist activities, the argument goes, popular support for ETA decreased progressively. Thus, we read that "there are some signs that ETA is losing its almost mystical hold on Basque consciousness" (*NYT* 6 May 84: 18) and that ETA "has become increasingly isolated from the mainstream Basque public opinion" (*NYT* 15 Feb 81: 18). But the picture painted is not all that sharp. It becomes muddled when we see references to a positive attitude towards ETA like the following:

> Yet the heavily Roman Catholic Basques still remain sympathetic to ETA demands (*US News & WR* 17 Mar 80: 59).

> But in calling for an end to the "military occupation" of the Basque country and for a fairer distribution of the region's wealth, the ETA has struck a deep and responsive chord . . . . They have deep roots among the people (*NYT Mag* 4 May 80: 93).

> One Madrid journalist estimates that, while there are probably fewer than 200 active ETA commandos in all of Spain, "each one can knock on a million Basque doors for shelter" (*US News and WR* 25 Aug 86: 28).

An attempt to clarify the picture is to link popular support for ETA to elements of Basque consciousness that transcend politics. In this view, ETA is not primarily a political symbol but rather a symbol of what it means to be Basque and, as such, it will lose significance in Basque life much more slowly:

> There is a historical dimension to their battle with Madrid over autonomy, . . . continuing stories of torture in police stations, a romance about rebellion and a deep sense of culture if not racial separateness — all of which makes for a base of popular support for ETA that is perhaps dwindling but only slowly (*NYT* 15 Apr 84: 3).

Finally, the third element of Basque political culture that in my opinion should be emphasized is the popular attitude towards the Guardia Civil and the national police (there is also a Basque police force of recent creation controlled by the Basque government), an attitude that is obviously related to the earlier one towards ETA. Here, the image presented by the U.S. press is unambiguous and conclusive: Most Basques, whatever their feelings about ETA and their political preferences, consider them an alien anti-Basque force always ready to hurt, torture and kill; they resent their presence in region, reject outright the possibility of collaborating with them in their fight against terrorism, and feel unable to regret their losses in their gun battles with ETA members or when victims of assassinations. If ETA enjoyed popular support in the past for its fight against dictatorship, the police and the Guardia Civil, in a parallel way, were — and are — always looked upon with hostility and suspicion as the brutal guardians of the dictator's political order:

> If there is one force that still unites the Basques, it is a hatred of the Guardia Civil, a paramilitary group, and the national police, who are still regarded as members of an occupying army. Indeed, not a single member of the police force in the region speaks the Basque language.
> Stories of torture and casual brutality by police in the Basque country are endless (*Time* 10 Aug 81: 43).

> The police and their families have a life apart . . . . Subject to taunts and abuse from the Basques, who regard them as representatives of an alien, occupying force, they are often refused service by bartenders and shopkeepers. When a policeman dies, his death is greeted not with sympathy but with the cry: "Uno menos [one less]" (*NYT Mag.* 4 May 80: 86).

> Ramón Jáuregui, Madrid's representative in the Basque region acknowledges that the Government's Civil Guard campaign against ETA is hindered because many Basques resent the Guard as Franco's old enforcers (*NYT* 24 Aug 86:12).

Conclusion

Although the ordinary newspaper or magazine reader may not subject the material that he reads to a sophisticated analysis, there is one question that probably comes to his mind every so often: Is this a valid picture? In other words, is this image of the Basque country and the Basque culture that is presented by the American printed media a complete and accurate image?

On the question of completeness, there are some gaps that are so glaring that they ought to be pointed out. Firstly, there is practically nothing written about the Basque province of Alava, the southern section of which is part of the famous wine-producing region of Rioja, or about its capital Vitoria (or Gasteiz) — a prosperous city that recently became the seat of the Basque government. Secondly, leaving the game of pelota (or jai *alai*) aside, and in spite of the fact that the Basque love of sports is mentioned in several items, we have found no references to any of the following very popular sports in Basque Country: Rowing, or the rural sports among the particular Basque traditional sports; soccer or cycling among the modern sport activities. *Rowing* has spread from the traditional *trainera* rowing at sea (*stropadak*), derived from the ancient Basque fishing of the whale, to other forms of the sport not linked to the fishing activity. The various rural *sports* (stone lifting, log chopping and sawing, tug of war, stone dragging and others) are very much alive and competitions and exhibitions draw good crowds. Often, exhibitions by professionals are organized for the benefit of foreign visitors. *Soccer* is played by many Basques, the boys starting to play very young in local teams. Three of twenty teams in the first division of the national league are from the Basque area — Bilbao, San Sebastián have adopted the local-talent-promoting policy of only hiring players born in the Basque region, thus rejecting the opportunity to compete against other clubs for other Spanish players, as well as the chance to employ foreign players. *Cycling* is another very popular sport, practised by the young and the not-so-young.

On the issue of accuracy the answer cannot be as straightforward as on the question of completeness. As far as specific statements about the Basque Country or about Basque culture are concerned, one finds here and there descriptions or assertions that, in my opinion, do not reflect reality,[6] but most of the writing has a degree of validity that is sufficiently high for it to be accepted, I believe, by a majority of the Basques. However one must distinguish between the validity of specific statements and the validity of the general or overall impression that the published items as a whole convey. And this general impression has changed from the 1950s to the 1980s. If in the fifties items the Basques were primarily depicted, as noted above, as a rural, unsophisticated and rather primitive people, the Basques of the eighties are presented as modern, urban and industrial people who, nevertheless maintain some idiosyncrasies (some examples would be: a non-functional language impossible to learn, nationalist violence and the popular support for it, and the practice of running in front of the bulls).

Primitiveness and exoticism have their charm, and when they go, so does the magic. This is what, in my judgment, has happened to the image of the Basques that the American printed media present today. We find in that image no enthusiasm about the Basque Country, no admiration of the Basque people. It is remarkable, for example, the absence of positive stereotype traits — like intelligent, innovative, artistic, efficient, imaginative, progressive, or scientifically minded — applied to the Basque mind. Not a word about beautiful women in the Basque Country (a common remark about Andalusian women, for example).

Americans are intrigued by the Basque people, by their idiosyncrasies, by their distinctive cultural traits, but they do not understand them. In the material reviewed we have not run across any big or small "theories" trying to explain this or that behavior, this or that personality trait. The writers do not seem to know the Basque Country well, and, in contrast to other cities or regions — like Andalusia, Madrid, Barcelona, or Costa del Sol — they show little desire to visit it or to rec-

---

[6]For example: "Traditionally, the Basques have been fishermen and hill farmers and *they continue in these pursuits, farming corn, sugar beets, grapes and apples, though many now are also miners* (*NYT Mag.* 4 May 80: 88)." [Emphasis added.]

ommend a visit to it, except perhaps, like Hemingway, to the Sanfermines of Pamplona.

WORKS CITED

Banco de Bilbao. *Renta nacional de España y su distribución provincial,* 1955. Bilbao: Banco de Bilbao, no date.

Banco de Bilbao. *Renta nacional de España 1983 y su distribución provincial.* Bilbao, 1986.

Comercio Exterior Vasco. Bilbao: Cámaras de Comercio de Alava, Bilbao y Guipúzcoa, 1987.

DeFleur, Melvin L. *Theories of Mass Communication.* New York: David McKay, 1970.

Harvard Encyclopedia of American Ethnic Groups. Cambridge: Harvard UP, 1980.

Instituto Nacional de Estadistica. *Encuesta Población Activa.* 4th quarter. Madrid, 1983.

Investing in Bilbao. Bilbao: Cámara de Comercio, Industria y Navegación, 1983.

Notes on Contributors

Vicki Adams (Ph.D. Comparative Literature, Indiana University) teaches French and English at Kent State University and the University of Akron. Her research interest is in the concept of the reader in French and American literary theory.

Margaret Kent Bass is an assistant professor of English at Vanderbilt University in Nashville, Tennessee.

Ursula E. Beitter is associate professor of German at Loyola College in Baltimore. Her research interests are nineteenth-century German Literature and foreign language pedagogy.

Jorge Febles is professor of Spanish at Western Michigan University, Kalamazoo. He has published extensively on contemporary Latin American and Cuban American literature.

David William Foster is Regents' Professor of Spanish and Director, Spanish Graduate Studies at Arizona State University. He has published widely on Latin American literature and culture.

Renate Gerulaitis is professor of German and Chair, Department of Modern Languages and Literatures, Oakland University, Rochester, Michigan, and publishes on eighteenth-century German literature and German popular culture.

Patricia Hart is the author of one novel, *Little Sins* (Tower Books, 1980), and two critical books, *Narrative Magic in the Fiction of Isabel Allende* (1989) and *The Spanish Sleuth* (1987), a history of detective fiction in Spain (both published by Fairleigh Dickinson UP). She is an associate professor and chair of Spanish and Portuguese at Purdue University.

David M. Jordan completed a doctorate in Comparative Literature at the University of Toronto in 1991, and teaches at the University of British Columbia. He is currently editing a collection of essays on new approaches to regionalism.

Renu Juneja is a professor of English at Valparaiso University. She has published in such journals as *Philological Quarterly* and *Comparative Drama*. Realigning her scholarship with her inner history as post-colonial subject, she has shifted her focus to post-colonial literatures. She is presently working on a book entitled *Fictions of Identity: Becoming a People in West Indian Literature.*

Raymond J. Lewis is an associate professor of Social Science and Anthropology at Eastern Kentucky University. A 1962 Fulbright scholar to India, his most recent publication is "Hispanic Folk Medicine in the United States" in the *Mid-Atlantic Almanack* (October 1992).

Eduardo López-Aranguren obtained a Ph.D. in Sociology at the university of Wisconsin-Madison and is currently a professor of Sociology at the Universidad Carlos III of Madrid.

Nancy López-Aranguren has a Ph.D. in Spanish from the University of Wisconsin-Madison. She has taught at UW-Oshkosh and Mankato State University. Currently, she teaches English at the Universidad Autónoma de Madrid.

Jaume Martí-Olivella teaches Spanish and Humanities at Reed College. He is a founding member of NACS (North American Catalan Association). His recent work includes "Mercè Rodoreda i el dialogisme poètic" and "Dona i nació a la narrativa de Manuel de Pedrolo", both forthcoming in *Edicions 62* (Barcelona).

Frederic W. Murray is professor of Spanish and Chair of the department of Foreign Languages and Literatures, Northern Illinois University. He is the author of *The Aesthetics of Contemporary Spanish American Social Protest Poetry* (Edwin Mellen P).

Ashton Nichols is assistant professor of English at Dickinson College. He is the author of *The Poetics of Epiphany: Nineteenth-Century Origins of the Modern Literary Moment* (1987) and recent essays on Achebe, Browning, and African exploration narratives.

Max E. Noordhoorn was born in Indonesia, spent his youth in the Netherlands and came to the United States at age 18. His Ph.D. is from the University of Michigan and he has been teaching German at Albion College since 1968.

Rafael Ocasio is an assistant professor of Spanish, and acting advisor of the Latin American studies program at Agnes Scott College in Decatur, Georgia. His principal research interests are in African Cuban literature, *santería* and Reynaldo Arenas. His interview with Judith Ortiz Cofer was published in *The Kenyon Review* (1992).

Tejumola Olaniyan is an assistant professor of English at the University of Virginia, Charlottesville.

Antonio Olliz-Boyd (Ph.D. Stanford) is associate professor of Spanish and Portuguese languages and literature at Temple University, and director of the University's Portuguese program. ***Gabriel Asoanab Abudu*** (Ph.D. Temple) is assistant professor of Spanish, York College, York, Pennsylvania, and has special interest in the poetry of contemporary Afro-Cuban writers.

Reynaldo Ruiz is professor of Spanish, Chicano, and Latin American literature. He is also the author of a novel, *Encuentro con Estanislao Eckermann.*

Helen Ryan-Ranson is acting head of the Department of Modern Languages at the University of Akron and area chair of Continental, Caribbean and Latin American Culture and Literature of the Popular Culture Association.

Matthew Stewart lives in Quito, Ecuador, where he works as an independent scholar and writer. He is the author of one dozen essays and reviews about war literature.

Chezia Thompson-Cager is a native of St. Louis and a graduate of Washington University and Carnegie-Mellon University, who has studied in Jamaica, Nigeria and Haiti. A poet and dramatist, her writing seeks to connect the lives of people of African descent throughout the diaspora.

Elizabeth A. Wheeler is a Comparative Literature doctoral candidate at the University of California, Berkeley. Her work has appeared most recently in *Postmodern Culture* and *Black Music Research Journal.*

Lauren Yoder is professor of French at Davidson College, where he teaches African and Caribbean literature. His interest in the Caribbean grew out of his experiences in Africa, where he lived and taught for several years.

www.ingramcontent.com/pod-product-compliance
Lightning Source LLC
Chambersburg PA
CBHW031931110726
47902CB00001B/126

* 9 7 8 0 8 7 9 7 2 5 8 1 5 *